UNLOCKING
THE TORAH TEXT
AN IN-DEPTH JOURNEY
INTO THE WEEKLY PARSHA

BAMIDBAR

SHMUEL GOLDIN

Copyright © Shmuel Goldin
Jerusalem 2013/5773

All rights reserved. No part of this publication may be translated, reproduced,
stored in a retrieval system or transmitted, in any form or by any means,
electronic, mechanical, photocopying, recording or otherwise,
without express written permission from the publishers.

Cover Design Concept: S. Kim Glassman
Cover Layout: Leah Ben Avraham / Noonim Graphics
Typesetting: Irit Nachum

ISBN: 978-965-229-525-5

3 5 7 9 8 6 4 2

Gefen Publishing House Ltd.
6 Hatzvi Street
Jerusalem 94386, Israel
972-2-538-0247
orders@gefenpublishing.com

Gefen Books
11 Edison Place
Springfield, NJ 07081
516-593-1234
orders@gefenpublishing.com

www.gefenpublishing.com

Printed in Israel

*Dedicated to the memory of two extraordinary women
who left us this year:*

My mother, Pnina (Pearl) Goldin, *a"h*

During a life of unending discovery, she never stopped learning and never stopped teaching. The worlds of hundreds of students were enriched by her genuine warmth, enthusiasm and personal care. Each of her countless friends considered her "my best friend." Her children and grandchildren were unalterably shaped by her boundless love, sparkling eyes, brilliant smile, heartfelt devotion, deep spirituality and unending excitement in all that surrounded her. Her passing leaves a void in our lives, but her legacy remains with us forever.

My mother-in-law, Tillie Leifer, *a"h*

She was her family's anchor. From the moment you entered her home, before she even said a word, you felt nurtured and protected in her presence. With innate wisdom, she bestowed her precious gift of unconditional love freely and equally upon each member of her family. Somehow you knew that she would do anything to ensure your happiness. The sense of peace that she projected during her lifetime will be forever cherished by those she loved.

They will be deeply missed.

This set, *Unlocking the Torah Text*,
is lovingly dedicated to the memory of

my parents
Naftali and Lola Goldman
נפתלי בן יוסף הכהן
לאה בת חנניא יום טוב ליפא הלוי

who exemplified love of
תורה, ארץ ישראל ועם ישראל

and my grandparents, aunts and uncles, and great-grandparents
who perished in the Shoah

Josef (Yussel) and Bayla Goldman
Avrum, Ascher and Gittel

Leopold (Lipa) and Rose Weinfeld
Ascher Weinfeld

Yosef and Bina Korn

Shiya and Miriam Weinfeld

and to the memory of
David (Dudek) Fink
אריה דוד בן משה מאיר הכהן
stepfather and *bompa* extraordinaire

JOSEPH (YOSSI) AND GAIL GOLDMAN
NEIL, DANIEL AND MICHAEL

Contents

Acknowledgments xv

Introduction xvii

BAMIDBAR PARSHA SUMMARY 1

Bamidbar 1
A Calendar Coincidence and a Strange Book 3
    Context 3
    Questions 3
    Approaches 4

Bamidbar 2
Tribe by Tribe, Rally 'Round the Mishkan 7
    Context 7
    Questions 7
    Approaches 7
    Points to Ponder 14

Bamidbar 2a
Forward March? 16
    Context 16
    Questions 16
    Approaches 17

Bamidbar 3
Disappearing Descendents 19
    Context 19
    Questions 19
    Approaches 20
    Points to Ponder 26

NASO PARSHA SUMMARY 29

Naso 1
Tying Things Together 31
    Context 31
    Questions 31
    Approaches 31

Naso 2
A Tragic, Troubling Trial 35
    Context 35
    Questions 35
    Approaches 36
    Points to Ponder 44

Naso 3
Sinner or Saint? 46
    Context 46
    Questions 46
    Approaches 47
    Points to Ponder 53

Naso 4
A Superfluous Role? 55
    Context 55
    Questions 55
    Approaches 56
    Points to Ponder 62
        I. Conveying and Creating Blessing 62
        II. A New/Old Application 63

Naso 5
You Said That Already! (Understanding a Midrash) 65
    Narrative 65
    Questions 65
    Approaches 65

BEHA'ALOTCHA PARSHA SUMMARY 69

Beha'alotcha 1
Second Chances 71
    Context 71
    Questions 71

Approaches	72
Points to Ponder	81

Beha'alotcha 2
Fellow Travelers 82
Narrative 82
Questions 83
Approaches 83
Points to Ponder 85

Beha'alotcha 3
Of Booths and Clouds: A Retrospective 86

Beha'alotcha 4
Blow Your Horn 91
Context 91
Questions 91
Approaches 92
Points to Ponder 96
    I. *Chatzotzrot*: Awakening 96
    II. The Clarion Call of the Shofar 97

Beha'alotcha 5
Interpreting an Interruption 99
Context 99
Questions 100
Approaches 101

Beha'alotcha 6
The Turning Point 103
Context 103
Questions 104
Approaches 105
Points to Ponder 108

Beha'alotcha 7
A Divine Misfire? 109
Context 109
Questions 110
Approaches 110

Beha'alotcha 7a
A Prophetic Postscript 113
  Context 113
  Questions 113
  Approaches 114

SHELACH PARSHA SUMMARY 117

Shelach 1
Chet Hameraglim *1: Unfair Blame?* 119
  Context 119
  Questions 119
  Approaches 120
  Points to Ponder 123
  I. Making the Leap 123
  II. Facts or Opinions? 124

Shelach 2
Chet Hameraglim *2: Please, God, Forgive Someone Else* 125
  Context 125
  Questions 125
  Approaches 125
  Points to Ponder 128

Shelach 3
Chet Hameraglim *3: A Tale of Two Sins* 129
  Context 129
  Questions 129
  Approaches 130
  Points to Ponder 134

Shelach 4
Fringe Element 135
  Context 135
  Questions 135
  Approaches 136

KORACH PARSHA SUMMARY 143

Korach 1
Korach's Rebellion 1: Dramatic Devastation 145
  Context 145
  Questions 145

  Approaches... 145
  Points to Ponder.. 152
  I. Direction in the Darkness...................................... 152
  II. It's Not about Us... 153

Korach 2
Korach's Rebellion 2: Give and Take........................... **155**
  Context.. 155
  Questions.. 155
  Approaches... 155
  Points to Ponder... 158

Korach 3
Korach's Rebellion 3: Pushing God's Hand................. **160**
  Context.. 160
  Questions.. 161
  Approaches... 161

Korach 4
Korach's Rebellion 4: Making Sense of the Incense..... **164**
  Context.. 164
  Questions.. 164
  Approaches... 165

Korach 5
Korach's Rebellion 5: A Misunderstanding?................ **169**
  Context.. 169
  Questions.. 169
  Approaches... 170
  Points to Ponder... 173

Korach 6
Is this Miracle Really Necessary?................................ **175**
  Context.. 175
  Questions.. 175
  Approaches... 176
  Points to Ponder... 177

CHUKAT PARSHA SUMMARY............................... 179

Chukat 1
An Abundance of Mystery... **181**
  Context.. 181

    Questions 181
    Approaches 182
    Points to Ponder 188

Chukat 2
My, How Time Flies… 190
    Context 190
    Questions 190
    Approaches 191
    Points to Ponder 192

Chukat 3
Punishment Fitting the Crime? 194
    Context 194
    Questions 195
    Approaches 195

Chukat 4
The Nature of Natural Events 203
    Context 203
    Questions 203
    Approaches 204
    Points to Ponder 214

BALAK PARSHA SUMMARY 217

Balak 1
Look Who's a Prophet Now! 219
    Context 219
    Questions 219
    Approaches 219
    Points to Ponder 226

Balak 2
Why Bother? 228
    Context 228
    Questions 228
    Approaches 229

Balak 3
If I Could Talk to the Animals 234
    Context 234

Questions 235
Approaches 236
Points to Ponder 241

Balak 4
Does the Leopard Change Its Spots? 244
Context 244
Questions 244
Approaches 244
Points to Ponder 248

Balak 5
A Devastating Epilogue 250
Context 250
Questions 250
Approaches 251

PINCHAS PARSHA SUMMARY 253

Pinchas 1
Yes and No 255
Context 255
Questions 255
Approaches 255

Pinchas 2
Righteous Reward 259
Context 259
Questions 259
Approaches 260

Pinchas 3
Keeping Things Complicated 264
Context 264
Questions 266
Approaches 267

Pinchas 4
Teaching Moshe 269
Context 269
Questions 269
Approaches 269
Points to Ponder 272

MATOT-MASEI PARSHA SUMMARY 275

Matot-Masei 1
Changing World, Unchanging Law 277
    Context 277
    Questions 277
    Approaches 278
    Points to Ponder 284

Matot-Masei 2
Jewish Jihad? 290
    Context 290
    Questions 290
    Approaches 291
    Points to Ponder 302

Matot-Masei 3
Falling Short 305
    Context 305
    Questions 306
    Approaches 307
    Points to Ponder 314

Matot-Masei 4
In Retrospect: A Troubling Travelogue 319
    Context 319
    Questions 319
    Approaches 319

Sources 325

Index 349

Acknowledgments

I continue to believe that my association with Gefen Publishing House was *bashert* (divinely ordained) from the start. I could not have asked for a better match. Ilan Greenfield and Michael Fischberger, Gefen's publishers, are masters of their craft, dedicated, responsive, creative and always ready to help in any way. This series would not be possible without their unfailing support and commitment.

My editor, Kezia Raffel Pride, is an absolute joy to work with. Not only does she catch, with unerring accuracy, each and every textual inconsistency, but she is unafraid to challenge me on the rare occasions when we philosophically disagree. Her contributions to each volume are immeasurable.

Lynn Douek, Gefen's project coordinator, is a wonderful addition to the team. Her technical expertise and gentle prodding kept even a procrastinator like me moving in timely fashion towards the finish line.

Our partnership with OU Press greatly expands our reach and remains a source of great pride. I am deeply grateful to my esteemed colleagues Rabbi Menachem Genack and Rabbi Simon Posner for their confidence in me and in this project.

Thanks to Raphael and Linda Benaroya, Bruce and Hannah-Jean Brafman, Danny and Thalia Federbush, Jeremy and Gail Fingerman, Kenneth and Susan Greif, Jonathan and Mindy Kolatch, Lee and Cheryl Lasher, Solomon and Sharon Merkin, Drew and Careena Parker, Dina Perry and her family, for their generous sponsorship of this volume. Thanks even more for their warm friendship and unfailing support. It means the world to me.

Eileen Gorlyn, my administrative assistant, capably juggles a wide array of responsibilities as she keeps my professional life on track. This project, like so many others, is made possible through her diligent, professional, steady management.

My associate rabbi, Chaim Poupko, has become a cherished partner in all aspects of my rabbinate. My ability to rely on his expert assistance has enabled me to expand my own horizons substantially.

With each passing year, I appreciate my synagogue community, Congregation Ahavath Torah in Englewood, New Jersey, more and more. My shul has provided me with professional and personal experiences that have deeply enriched my life. Few communities can boast of the human resources, intellectual wealth, generous spirit and genuine warmth that can be found within its walls. As with the earlier volumes of this series, many of the lessons found within this book stem from my shared learning with my community. Reflected as well are countless hours of study, discussion and debate with my students at Yeshiva University, the Eve Flechner Institute, the Isaac Perry Beit Medrash and various other venues. I am grateful for our shared exploration.

My world has broadened considerably over the past four years, as I have been honored to serve in the capacity of vice president and then president of the Rabbinical Council of America, the largest body of Orthodox rabbis in the world. That tenure has enabled me to interact with a wide variety of extraordinary Jewish leaders in America, Israel and across the globe. I have learned much from all. In particular, I thank the RCA officers with whom I have served. Their wise perspective on Jewish life has certainly made its way onto the pages of this volume, in ways that even I can scarcely realize.

Thank God, our family continues to grow. Our children, Avi and Rena, Yossi and Shifra, Yehuda and Noa, Donny and Tamara, and Rivka, are a constant source of joy. We watch with pride as each of our children successfully maps out his/her own life path, and we feel a deep sense of gratitude to the Almighty as we witness their commitment to the traditions of our people. Our grandchildren, Isaac, Benjamin, Temima, Jacob, Chaim, Racheyl, Mordechai, Julia and Yehudit, fill our lives with excitement, as each develops into the unique person that he/she is destined to be. In them, we see the future of all that we hold dear. Special thanks again to Yossi for so expertly serving as in-house editor of this series.

On a sad note, this is the last volume of our series that will benefit from my dear mother's loving, painstaking editing. As indicated in the dedication, her passing has left us bereft in so many ways. As with all else, I will miss the opportunity to share her pride in this volume's publication.

Finally and most significantly, my deepest thanks are reserved for my true partner in all aspects of my life, my wife, Barbara. Only I know the truth. Without Barbara's constant encouragement, advice, support and sacrifice, none of this would have been possible.

Introduction

I have long felt that the book of Bamidbar can justifiably complain of "middle child syndrome." Although this volume is technically not the Torah's "middle child" (that distinction is, of course, claimed by the book of Vayikra), it is, nonetheless, a text that is sorely underappreciated and misunderstood.

The problem lies, first and foremost, with the book's apparent lack of focus. While the scope of each of the other volumes of the Torah is easily defined – the epic sweep of Bereishit, the nation's birth in Shmot, the balance of ritual and ethic in Vayikra, the poignant passion of Moshe's farewell addresses in Devarim – Bamidbar is much harder to "peg." What are the global messages of this text? The volume's overall narrative often seems strung together with no clear cohesive pattern. Even the internal structure of some of its parshiot is difficult to comprehend, as one theme abruptly follows another with no evident connection.

The temporal issues surrounding much of the text only serve to compound the problem. Forty years of wilderness wandering disappear in Bamidbar without a trace. The exact placement of pivotal events, such as the rebellion of Korach, becomes the subject of debate among the commentaries.

Finally, as we will note in this volume's initial study, Bamidbar seems at first glance to be the least directly practical of all five books of the Torah, the events therein rooted in the past with little apparent application to our lives.

And yet, as we have so often seen in our previous studies, relevance is found in the Torah text where it is least expected. For I believe that, properly understood, the book of Bamidbar conveys some of the most important lessons of the entire Torah. As the narrative unfolds, two pivotal, contrasting turning points become the fulcrums upon which the entire volume turns. The first of these, the departure from Sinai, is fraught with promise and challenge, as God weans the newborn Israelite nation from the site of its birth and launches its march across the pages of history. The second, the sin of the spies, is marked by devastating despair, as it becomes evident that this generation's journey must be aborted. From these events, as well as from all the steps leading to and following them, we will learn much about our heritage, our people and ourselves.

And so, I again invite those of you who have been traveling with us to continue – and those who are beginning now to join – our shared journey through the text. Together, we will begin with the preparations at the foot of Mount Sinai, share in our ancestors' momentous departure from that site, experience the challenges and failures of a doomed generation, witness the blossoming of hope with a new generation forged in the wilderness, and arrive finally at the border of the promised land of Canaan. All along the way, we will explore the age-old lessons of a text that continues to speak to us with uncanny timeliness.

To set the stage for this journey, I repeat a brief review of the parameters of our search. (This review is reprinted, with minor changes, from the introductions to volumes 2 and 3. A fuller discussion of these principles can be found in the introduction to volume 1.)

1. While traditional Torah study is based on a fundamental belief in the divine authorship of the text, questioning and challenging the text itself is not only allowed but encouraged. Unless we struggle with the narrative, God's word and God's intent remain distant and unclear and the Torah remains a closed book.

2. The treasures of the Torah can only be uncovered when the narrative itself is seen as the truth, comprised of real events that happened to real people. The heroes of the Bible were human beings, not gods, and the stories of their lives are not fables.

3. No part of the text or its contents will be off-limits to our search. We will explore the motives and actions of the personalities who populate its pages. We will probe God's desires for us reflected in His unfolding law, and we will attempt to discern what the Torah reveals about His divine will. We will seek to understand why events took place as they did and how the narrative might inform our lives. And we will explore the deep philosophical currents coursing through the laws and events described to us.

4. Two distinct approaches to the Torah text are reflected in rabbinic literature: *pshat* and *drash*.

Pshat refers to the straightforward explanation of the text. When we operate within the realm of *pshat*, we search for the literal, concrete sense of the narrative before us. *Proper understanding of pshat reveals deep, unexpected meaning within the text itself.*

Drash refers to rabbinic commentary serving as a vehicle for the transmission of lessons and ideas beyond the literal narrative. Many authorities maintain that Midrashic commentary is not meant to be taken literally, nor is it meant to be seen as an attempt to explain the factual meaning of a specific Torah passage. The key question in the realm of *drash* is: *What are the rabbis trying to teach us?*

When, as unfortunately often happens, we confuse these two approaches to text – when we ignore the *pshat* and instead offer *drash* as the literal interpretation of the text – we end up understanding neither of these interpretive realms. In our studies, therefore, we will make every attempt to distinguish between *pshat* and *drash* and to present each approach appropriately.

5. Each of our studies on the parshiot of Bamidbar will raise a series of questions designed to strike to the core of a particular passage of the text.

Our search for answers to the questions raised will take us on a journey through traditional commentary and original thought. In each study, a sampling of rabbinic opinion on the issues will be reviewed and original approaches will be offered as we humbly continue our own struggle with the text.

Finally, many studies will include a "Points to Ponder" section in which connections are made between the Torah passage and relevant concerns that touch our lives. This section is specifically designed to encourage ongoing thought and debate.

I close, as I have in the past, with the hope that our continuing journey will be, for each of us, a passionate one, inspiring continuing exploration and thought, sparking conversation, dialogue and debate each week in homes, synagogues, schools and beyond, as together we unlock the treasures of the Torah text.

Bamidbar

CHAPTER 1:1–4:20

במדבר

פרק א:א–ד:כ

Parsha Summary

Taking stock and setting the stage…

As the book of Bamidbar opens, preparations for the nation's departure from Mount Sinai begin on the first day of the second month of the second year after the Exodus, with the following steps.

God commands Moshe to count the male Israelites above the age of twenty, "to their families; to the homes of their fathers…" A representative from each tribe is divinely chosen to assist in this census, and the results of the count are recorded, tribe by tribe. The tribe of Levi, appointed to the service of the Sanctuary, is excluded from this general census.

The structure of the Israelite encampment is divinely delineated, as God divides the tribes into four formations of three tribes each, surrounding the Mishkan. Each formation is to be headed by one specific tribe and marked by a separate banner.

The children of Aharon are enumerated and marked as the Kohanim (priests). A separate census of the Levi'im is conducted and they are designated, in place of the firstborn, for the Temple service.

The first of the three Levite families, the family of Kehat, is assigned to its specific tasks.

1 A Calendar Coincidence and a Strange Book

Context

Two seemingly disparate phenomena, one technical and one philosophical, converge as we open the book of Bamidbar. Considered together, they provide powerful insight into the significance of this book of the Torah.

First, as a result of an apparent calendar coincidence, the reading of the book of Bamidbar begins each year in the synagogue on the Sabbaths *directly before* the festival of Shavuot.

Second, the book of Bamidbar is unique among the five books of the Torah as it is almost entirely limited to the description of the historical events and temporal commandments that mark the Israelites' sojourn in the wilderness. Very few lasting mitzvot are recorded in this volume.

Questions

The calendar-created relationship between the opening of the book of Bamidbar and the festival of Shavuot is puzzling.

The book of Bamidbar opens with God's detailed instructions to the Israelites preparatory to their *departure* from Sinai. Shavuot, on the other hand, marks the nation's *arrival* at Sinai and the onset of Revelation, all of which occurs two years earlier.

Why do we read, each year, of our *leaving* Sinai specifically on the Sabbaths before we *arrive*?

Must we accept this reverse highlighting of the endpoints of the Sinaitic experience as a simple twist of calendar fate? If not, what possible lessons can be gleaned from this phenomenon?

More broadly, with the opening of the book of Bamidbar, the question could well be raised: What place does this book occupy within the eternal

Torah text? Why are the time-bound details of Bamidbar significant enough to record for posterity? In what way is this text relevant for later generations?

Approaches

A

The seemingly coincidental calendar connection between Parshat Bamidbar and the festival of Shavuot may not be coincidental at all, but, instead, a clear reminder of a fundamental truth: *the most important moment of Revelation is the moment the Israelites leave.*

The instant of the nation's departure from Sinai determines the quality of all that has come before. If the Israelites leave the site of Revelation changed by the experience, *carrying the Torah with them and within them*, then the dramatic events of Sinai will have achieved their purpose. If, however, upon leaving the site of Revelation, the people *leave Sinai behind*, then those miraculous proceedings will have been little more than a divinely orchestrated "sound and light show," impressing the observers in transient fashion.

As we open the book of Bamidbar each year on the Sabbaths before Shavuot, as we read of our departure before we arrive, we proclaim our understanding that *the years spent at Sinai achieve their significance in retrospect*.

B

What, however, is the verdict regarding the lasting impact of Revelation upon the people? Are the Israelites ultimately successful in their transition from Sinai?

The parshiot unfolding before us will reveal a mixed verdict concerning these questions.

On the one hand, the specific generation that witnesses Revelation fails its ultimate test. "Like a child running away from school,"[1] the Israelites leave Sinai with alacrity, anxious to rid themselves of the obligations thrust upon them by divine law. Their immediate rebellion launches a series of cascading calamities culminating in the sin of the spies, the transgression

---

1. Yalkut Shimoni, Bamidbar 729; Ramban, Bamidbar 10:35.

that ultimately seals their fate in the wilderness. On a temporal level, the departure from Sinai clearly leads to failure.

On the other hand, in spite of the failure of the generation of the Exodus, Revelation does successfully launch the majestic story of the Jewish people. Transcending the tragedies of the moment, a nation is forged at the foot of Sinai: a people that will be bound, across time and place, by the commandments and values of Torah law. In a timeless, eternal dimension, the departure from Sinai leads to success.

C

The Torah's interplay between the transitory and the eternal, so evident at the moment of the nation's departure from Sinai, is the key to understanding the book of Bamidbar.

As noted above, this book appears to be the least directly practical of all five books of the Torah, outlining, as it does, events rooted in the past with little apparent application to our lives. The detailed preparations for the departure from Sinai, the departure itself, the ensuing rebellions and their tragic aftermath, the forty years of wandering in the wilderness, all seem specific to a long-gone time and place. Few lasting mitzvot emerge from the text, and the stories therein do not possess the timeless character of many of the classic tales found in the other four books of the Torah.

The Ramban describes the uniqueness of Bamidbar's character in his introduction to the book:

> This book [concerns itself] completely with the temporal commandments that were transmitted to them [the Israelites] during their sojourn in the wilderness and with the miracles that were afforded to them…. There are within this book few lasting mitzvot….[2]

D

And yet, when we move beyond the time-bound specificity of the narrative, eternal lessons begin to emerge.

Properly understood, the journey from Sinai represents not only the passage of those present at that historic moment, but the launching of our national journey across the ages. God's instructions to the nation prior to

---
2. Ramban, introduction to the book of Bamidbar.

their departure from Sinai reveal the human elements He considers critical not only to the success of that generation's mission but to the success of the entire Jewish enterprise. Even the tragic shortcomings of our ancestors are powerfully relevant, revealing inherent flaws that threaten our own personal and communal achievements, as well. Finally, the Israelites' forty years of wilderness wandering emerge as a critically formative period, cementing the relationship between God and His people and effecting essential changes in the developing nation's psyche.

With the departure from Sinai serving as the turning point, the momentous event towards which the first half of the book of Bamidbar leads and from which the second half descends, this book of the Torah emerges as a blueprint for our journey across time. The ancient passage of our ancestors – *bamidbar*, in the wilderness – yields surprising lessons that continue to shape our lives.

2 Tribe by Tribe, Rally 'Round the Mishkan

Context

The book of Bamidbar opens with a myriad of technical details.

God commands Moshe to count the male Israelites from the age of twenty and above, "to their families; to the homes of their fathers…" The results of the census are then recorded in the text, tribe by tribe. Only the tribe of Levi is excluded from the count.

The Torah then outlines the structure of the Israelites' wilderness encampment. God commands the people to surround the Sanctuary on all sides, in four groups of three tribes each; each group in a specified location, delineated by that group's banner. The tribal clusters are to bear the names of the leading tribe in each section: Yehuda, Reuven, Ephraim and Dan.[1]

Questions

Why is all this detailed technical information included in the eternal Torah text?

While the data might satisfy the curiosity of historians, it would seem to be of little lasting significance to the Jewish people across the ages.

Approaches

A

Before we can begin to address the Torah's inclusion of this historical material, we must first attempt to understand the described phenomena themselves.

---

1. Bamidbar 1:1–2:34.

The rabbis wrestle with perplexing issues concerning both the divinely ordained census and the details of the Israelite encampment described as the book of Bamidbar opens.

What, they ask, is the purpose of the national census?

Given that the Israelites were already counted through the donation of half shekels only a short time before,[2] why does God command that they be counted again?

Even if a reason can be deduced for this second counting, why does this census differ so radically from the first? The census conducted before the building of the Sanctuary simply arrived at a total number for the entire nation. Now, however, God commands a separate tally for each individual tribe.

Concerning the Israelite encampment, why does God involve Himself in the details? Why not allow the people to determine the physical plan that works best for them? What hidden lessons might be embedded in the divinely ordained structure of the wilderness camp?

As the rabbis struggle to answer these and other questions, a variety of perspectives concerning these phenomena begins to emerge.

B

Ever the rationalist in matters of textual interpretation, the Rashbam suggests a simple, straightforward reason for God's commandment to count the Israelites at this time. The journey from Sinai toward the Land of Israel is about to commence. The people must, therefore, ready themselves for the battles that they will face during the conquest of the land. To determine the strength of the nation's "fighting force," God thus commands that all males of military age be counted.[3]

Building on the Rashbam's approach, we can suggest that at this pivotal historical moment, as the nation prepares to leave the site of Revelation, God conveys a powerful message: *Do not misunderstand. The extraordinary phenomena that were essential to your national birth will not continue. The miracles of the Exodus and Revelation cannot characterize our continuing relationship across time. As you begin this national journey, recognize that I will, as a rule, allow your story to unfold through natural*

---

2. Shmot 38:26.
3. Rashbam, Bamidbar 1:2.

means. You will be called upon to play an active role in our continuing partnership. The challenge begins now. Prepare for battle. I will be by your side, but you must defeat the enemy.

Centuries later, the rabbis will capture this ongoing truth concerning the man-God relationship with the simple declaration: *Ein somchin al haneis*, "One must not rely on miracles."[4]

— C —

After first emphatically stating, "I have not understood the reason for this [divine] commandment,"[5] the Ramban offers a series of possible reasons for the census, from the rational to the mystical. Many of these explanations are noted by later commentaries, including the Abravanel:[6]

1. The military motivation mentioned by the Rashbam (to determine the strength of the nation's fighting force).

2. To demonstrate the kindness bestowed by God upon the nation: the Israelites have been transformed from the family of seventy who descended to Egypt into a people "as numerous as the sands of the sea."

3. To reassure the people that their cherished relationship with God remains intact even after the tragic sin of the golden calf: "He increases the nations,"[7] "He wounds and He makes whole."[8]

4. To grant each Israelite the spiritual benefit of a direct encounter with Moshe and Aharon: these great leaders will automatically pray on behalf of the individuals who, one by one, pass before them.

5. To bestow upon every Israelite the personal respect due to him: no shortcuts may be taken in the census procedure; instead of asking the head of each family to list the number of people in his household, Moshe and Aharon must count every individual directly.

6. To ensure proper division of the Land of Israel based upon accurate counts of each tribe and family: the expectation is, at this point, that the journey from Sinai will lead the nation directly into the land.[9]

---

4. Talmud Bavli Kiddushin 39b.
5. Ramban, Bamidbar 1:45.
6. Abravanel, Bamidbar 1:1.
7. Iyov 12:23.
8. Ibid., 5:18.
9. Ramban, Bamidbar 1:45.

D

Moving past the census to the second set of directives featured at the beginning of Parshat Bamidbar, the Ramban heads a group of commentaries that view the Israelites' wilderness encampment as a *divinely ordained re-creation of the scene of Sinaitic Revelation.*

The divine commandment of *hagbala*, central to the scene of Sinai, drew boundaries around the mountain during Revelation – boundaries to be respected by the nation, on pain of death (see *Shmot*: Yitro 2, 3). Similarly, says the Ramban, boundaries are now drawn as the nation surrounds the Sanctuary, regulating the approach of those who would draw near to the sanctified space at the center of the camp.

As a basis for his position, the Ramban correlates a series of passages rooted at Sinai with a parallel series found in God's instructions concerning the Sanctuary.[10]

	Mount Sinai	The Sanctuary
1.	"Set a boundary for the people roundabout, saying, 'Beware of ascending the mountain or touching its edge; whoever touches the mountain shall certainly die…'"[11]	"And the stranger who approaches shall die."[12]
2.	"Lest they break through to God to see, and many of them will fall…"[13]	"And they shall not approach to view as the holy items are wrapped lest they die."[14]
3.	"Even the Kohanim who approach the Lord shall be sanctified, lest the Lord break forth against them…and the Kohanim and the nation shall not break through to ascend to the Lord, lest He burst forth against them."[15]	"And they shall guard the charge of the Sanctuary and the charge of the Altar, and there will be no wrath again against the children of Israel."[16]

---

10. Ramban, introduction to the book of Bamidbar.
11. Shmot 19:12.
12. Bamidbar 1:51.
13. Shmot 19:21.
14. Bamidbar 4:20.
15. Shmot 19:22–24.
16. Bamidbar 18:5.

In similar fashion, Rabbi Shimshon Raphael Hirsch uses textual evidence at the close of the book of Shmot to correlate the investiture of God's presence on Mount Sinai during Revelation to the investiture of His presence in the Sanctuary upon that structure's completion.[17]

The German scholar Benno Jacob beautifully captures the approach of these scholars: "God moves His presence from the mountain to the Mishkan, from the location sanctified by His hands to the sanctified location built by the Israelites.... *The Sanctuary is the Sinai which travels in their midst, is the heavens and the vault of the heavens which has been uprooted and lowered to the earth* [my italics]."[18]

— E —

Other commentaries focus on the further spiritual imagery conveyed by the divinely designed camp.

Rabbeinu Bachya, for example, cites Midrashic sources that perceive an evocation of two parallel camps. The earthbound Israelite encampment, surrounding the Sanctuary on all four sides, is matched by a celestial camp comprised of twelve angelic tribes surrounding the Divine Presence in the heavens, again in groups of three tribes each.[19] This technique of mirror imaging between heaven and earth is often cited in rabbinic literature as a way of underscoring the unity between God and His creations.

With exquisite attention to detail, Rabbeinu Bachya notes another striking phenomenon. In the process of delineating the location of each tribe within the Israelite camp, the text notes the names of the leaders of the twelve tribes. Four, and only four, of these tribal princes possess names that contain the name of God (*E-l*): Netanel, Shlumiel, Gamliel and Pagiel. Each one of these four princes participates in the leadership of a different tribal cluster: Yehuda, Reuven, Ephraim and Dan, respectively. The presence of God is thus symbolically attached to every section of the Israelite encampment, woven into the very names of the leaders of the camp.[20]

---

17. Rabbi Shimshon Raphael Hirsch, Shmot 40:18.
18. Benno Jacob, *Der Pentateuch*, p. 155 (quoted in Leibowitz, *Iyunim Chadashim B'Sefer Bamidbar*).
19. Rabbeinu Bachya, Bamidbar 2:2 (citing Midrash Ma'aseh Merkava 6).
20. Ibid., Bamidbar 2:2–25.

Yet other scholars struggle to decipher the internal fabric of the wilderness camp. The Kli Yakar, for example, maintains that God deliberately groups the tribes so that each tribal cluster contains a combination of the four basic attributes critical to human success: wisdom, character, strength and wealth.[21] The Ramban, turning to Midrashic sources, delineates the characteristics of each tribe and correlates those characteristics to that tribe's location within the camp. One thing is clear, the Ramban concludes, "[the division of the tribes was designed] fully in wisdom, honor and glory for Israel, and the text therefore enumerates each detail [of this division]."[22]

—— F ——

Moving in a different direction and in line with the Rashbam's approach to the national census (see above), other scholars discern military significance in the details of the Israelites' wilderness encampment. The Ibn Ezra, for example, maintains that the physically powerful tribes of Yehuda and Dan are selected to command the most strategically significant sections of the camp: the front and rear lines, respectively.[23] The Abravanel points out that these sections of the camp are also the most heavily populated, adding another dimension to their military strength.[24]

These practical approaches to the camp's structure bring us full circle to the message conveyed, according to the Rashbam and others, by the earlier census: *God will be with you, but He will not fight your battles. Be prepared, therefore, to meet the enemy.*

—— G ——

We can now return to the questions raised at the beginning of our study concerning the inclusion of this technical material within the Torah text. Clearly some of the above approaches to both the census and the Israelite encampment justify that inclusion.

Coursing beneath the seemingly arcane historical data with which Parshat Bamidbar opens lie lessons of powerful eternal import, including

---

21. Kli Yakar, Bamidbar 2:2.
22. Ramban, Bamidbar 2:2.
23. Ibn Ezra, Bamidbar 1:19.
24. Abravanel, Bamidbar 2:1.

the challenge of national self-sufficiency, the image of the Mishkan as a traveling Mount Sinai, the concept of partnership forged by the tribal clusters and more. The first footfalls of the Jewish national journey are thus marked by ideas that will shape the people's experience across the centuries.

H

A final, unified approach to the passages before us can be suggested by building on the comments of the eighteenth-century German scholar Rabbi Shimshon Raphael Hirsch concerning the national census. Reflecting the opinions of a number of earlier scholars, including the Akeidat Yitzchak,[25] Hirsch maintains that *the census is designed to strike the critical balance between the unity essential to the nation's survival and the diversity that will enrich its character.*

On the one hand, at the onset of the count, God refers to the nation by the term *eida*, a term that Hirsch believes designates a people joined together for a common calling. On the other hand, the methodology of the census itself underscores the multiplicity of backgrounds within the nation. Each family, each tribe, is to be numbered separately. The people must learn to appreciate the value inherent in their natural diversity.[26]

I

With Hirsch's observations serving as a foundation, a global approach to the opening portions of the book of Bamidbar can be offered. Both the census and the divinely planned Israelite encampment are designed to counteract a potential danger arising out of the overpowering experience of Sinai.

A well-known Midrash maintains that a primary prerequisite of Revelation was unity of purpose on the part of the nation. The Torah testifies upon the Israelites' arrival at Sinai, *Va'yichan sham Yisrael neged hahar*, "And Israel there encamped opposite the mountain."[27] Based upon the text's use of the verb's singular form *va'yichan*, encamped, Rashi quotes the *Mechilta*, saying, "[This time the nation encamped] as one man

---

25. Akeidat Yitzchak, Bamidbar, sha'ar 72.
26. Rabbi Shimshon Raphael Hirsch, Bamidbar 1:2.
27. Shmot 19:2.

with one heart."²⁸ Apparently, only a fully united camp could merit God's miraculous revelation.

But what does "fully united" really mean? Too often, unity of purpose can be confused with uniformity of thought and idea.

God therefore addresses any possible misunderstanding through a series of clear mandates designed to counterbalance the Sinaitic experience. *If Revelation is marked by a heightened sense of national unity, the march from Sinai underscores the nation's diversity.* A national census is conducted, specifically "to their families; to the homes of their fathers…,"²⁹ and the results are recorded, tribe by tribe. The details of the Israelite encampment are further delineated through divine mandate, each tribe with its own specific place marked by the appropriate banner.

As their journey from Sinai begins, the Israelites learn that *unity does not connote sameness.* A rich variety of background, personality and idea will power the development of the Jewish people across the ages. This diverse nation, united in common cause, claims Rabbi Shimshon Raphael Hirsch, will serve as a "model for the whole human race."³⁰

Points to Ponder

The challenge arising out of our own national diversity confronts us today as never before. After thousands of years apart, we finally face each other… and the confrontation can be unsettling.

We have, after all, through the force of our exile history, become a widely disparate people, a nation reared in a multitude of worlds; our attitudes, outlooks, beliefs and personalities refined in developmental settings as different from each other as day is from night. In theory, this diversity of idea and background should be welcome, potentially enriching our national experience in manifold ways. In practice, however, things can be much more difficult, as we struggle to understand each other on the most basic of levels.

Nowhere is the challenge more keenly felt than in the Land of Israel, where survival increasingly depends upon an ability to create a working, cohesive state out of the often volatile mix of native Israelis and immigrants

---

28. Rashi, Shmot 19:2.
29. Bamidbar 1:2.
30. Rabbi Shimshon Raphael Hirsch, Bamidbar 1:2.

from Russia, America, Ethiopia, Europe, India, Iran, Arab lands and other countries across the globe. *For centuries we prayed for the ingathering of the exiles. Now that this miraculous process has apparently begun we are faced with the very human challenge of making it work.*

Add to the mix the growing fractures between the various religious and political communities in Israeli society, and the task of nation building becomes daunting, indeed.

Outside the Land of Israel, denominational distinctions largely shape the face of the unity/diversity debate. Here, as well, the questions are real. Can we work with – even learn from – other Jews, from other denominations, with whom we differ fundamentally in both philosophy and practice? What are the boundaries of possible dialogue and cooperation? What are the risks? How do these risks compare to the cost of our separation from each other?

At the core of these issues lies a basic question: Is it possible to value each other without validating each other's beliefs?

These concerns acquire crisis proportions when we consider the overwhelming potential tragedy in which we, through inaction, are arguably complicit: the fast-disappearing population of unaffiliated Jews outside our borders, who care little about our debates and whose connection with Judaism might be strengthened through shared, positive, creative efforts on our part.

The balance struck at the dawn of our national history between unity of purpose and diversity of idea comes under increasing strain during our days. Time will tell whether we, both in Israel and in the diaspora, will rise to the challenges before us. More than we may realize hangs in the balance.

2a Forward March?

Context

In stark contrast to the detailed textual description of the Israelites' stationary desert encampment, only vague references to the nation's traveling formation are found in the Torah. Responding to this omission, the Jerusalem Talmud quotes a dispute between the Tannaitic sages Rabbi Chama bar Chanina and Rabbi Hoshaya but leaves their respective positions anonymous.

Basing his position on the biblical phrase "as they encamped thus did they travel,"[1] one of these scholars insists that the structure of the Israelite camp did not change at all during their journeys. *Just as the people encamped around the Sanctuary in a "box-like" formation, so did they travel.*

The second scholar, quoting a different biblical passage that refers to the tribe of Dan as the "gatherer of all the camps,"[2] adamantly disagrees. In order to serve as a gatherer, this sage argues, one tribe must travel behind all the others. The text thus indicates that when the Israelites broke camp to travel, *the tribes lined up in single file and traveled in a "beam-like" formation*, with the tribe of Dan at the rear.[3]

Questions

Given the great detail devoted in the text to the stationary Israelite camp (see previous study), why is the Torah strangely silent concerning the nation's marching formation?

Are Rabbi Chama bar Chanina and Rabbi Hoshaya simply arguing a point of historical curiosity or is there deeper significance to their discussion? Can lessons similar to those reflected in the details of the

---

1. Bamidbar 2:17.
2. Ibid., 10:28.
3. Talmud Yerushalmi Eruvin 5:1.

nation's standing camp (again, see previous study) be derived from the Talmudic debate concerning their traveling formation?

Approaches

—— A ——

Given the general proposition that the Israelites' journey from Sinai serves as the paradigm of the Jewish nation's passage through history (see Bamidbar 1, *Approaches* D), a symbolic approach to the debate between Rabbi Chama and Rabbi Hoshaya can be suggested.

Perhaps the Torah omits a clear, one-dimensional description of the nation's marching formation specifically because the structure of our nation's historical journey is multidimensional. This reality is reflected in the pictures painted by Rabbi Chama and Rabbi Hoshaya.

—— B ——

On the one hand, the notion that the Jewish nation marches in linear fashion across the face of history is clearly integral to Jewish belief. *We travel in "beam-like" formation, from a fixed starting point to a fixed goal.*

No less a luminary than Rabbi Joseph Soloveitchik maintains that the Patriarchic Covenant introduced a new concept into history.

> While universal (non-Jewish) history is governed by *causality*, by what preceded, covenantal (Jewish) history is shaped by *destiny*, by a goal set in the future.
>
> Universal history is of an etiological nature; every event is brought about by a preceding cause.... Covenantal Jewish history, by contrast, is teleological, not etiological. This means that it is propelled by a purpose.
>
> What happens to Jews emanates from a Divine promise foretold about the future, rather than by events impelling from the past. Jewish history is pulled, as by a magnet, towards a glorious destiny; it is not pushed by antecedent causes. This is the meaning of the Patriarchic Covenant; it is a goal projected, a purpose pursued, a destination to be reached.[4]

---

4. Abraham R. Besdin, *Reflections of the Rav*, vol. 2, *Man of Faith in the Modern World* (Hoboken, NJ: Ktav Publishing House, 1989), p. 70.

Through the introduction of the concept of a Messiah and a messianic era, Judaism brings a new way of looking at history to the world. *We march across the world stage "beam-like," in a straight line; not only pushed by a rich past, but pulled by a glorious future.*

C

At the same time, however, the journey of the Jewish nation unfolds on a second dimension as well. *In each generation, we encamp and create community, constructing the "box" that defines our people's character and delineates our philosophical boundaries.*

Pulling inward, at the center of the camp, lies the Torah, with its strong call of tradition and stability. Pulling outward, beyond the camp's boundaries, the siren call of an external society beckons. At the edges of the communal "box," at the interface between our camp and the outside world, powerful ferment develops as we struggle for self-definition: *What's in and what's out?* we ask ourselves, *What are the limits of the "acceptable" in our camp, in our time?*

Critical issues of deep philosophical principle and wrenching personal challenge hang in this struggle's balance. Jewish identity, religious outlook, gender roles, sexual orientation, political positions, secular culture and scientific exploration are just some of the swirling forces that collide at the camp's boundaries. The manner in which we reconcile these forces shapes the face of the Judaism we live in our day and the Judaism that we hand down to our children. They, building upon our efforts, will then define the boundaries of their own camp, as will the next generation and the generation after that, continuing until the end of days.

D

As is always the case in rabbinic disputes, both points of view are, on some level, correct. Rabbi Chama and Rabbi Hoshaya remind us of the multifaceted, complex path upon which we march toward our national destiny.

3 Disappearing Descendents

Context
After instructing Moshe concerning the national census and the structure of the Israelite camp, God commands a separate census of the Levi'im and appoints them to their specific tasks.

Immediately before this second census is recorded in the text, however, a five-sentence passage is inserted:

> And these are the descendents of Aharon and Moshe, on the day that God spoke to Moshe at Mount Sinai.
>
> And these are the names of the sons of Aharon: the firstborn, Nadav, and Avihu, Elazar and Itamar. These are the names of the sons of Aharon, the anointed Kohanim, whom he inaugurated to minister.
>
> Nadav and Avihu died before the Lord when they offered foreign fire before the Lord in the wilderness of Sinai, and they had no children; and Elazar and Itamar ministered on the face of Aharon, their father.[1]

Questions
The textual problems with this passage are glaring….

Why does the Torah enumerate the children of Aharon yet remain silent concerning Moshe's descendents? Furthermore, if for some reason the text intends to list only the children of Aharon, why open the passage with the misleading statement "and these are the descendents of *Aharon and Moshe*"? Why does the Torah open a subject it does not intend to complete?

---

1. Bamidbar 3:1–4.

What is the meaning of the phrase "on the day that God spoke to Moshe at Mount Sinai"? Are these the descendents of Moshe and Aharon only on that day?

Why, after enumerating the names of Aharon's sons, does the text again repeat, "These are the names of the sons of Aharon, the anointed Kohanim, whom he inaugurated to minister"?

What is the meaning of the Torah's strange declaration that Elazar and Itamar "ministered *on the face of* Aharon, their father"?

Finally, given that all this information is already known to us, what is the purpose of this entire passage and why is it placed immediately before the census of the Levi'im?

Approaches

A

Numerous commentaries, confronted with the apparent omission of Moshe's progeny from the text, view the passage before us in conjunction with the Levite census that immediately follows. The Rashbam, Ramban and the Da'at Zekeinim Miba'alei Hatosafot, for example, explain that God, having numbered the Israelites, now turns His attention to the counting of the Kohanim and Levi'im.

These new censuses begin with a listing of Aharon's descendents, who, while a subset of the tribe of Levi, are designated separately as Kohanim by divine command. The descendents of Moshe, on the other hand, are not listed separately but are, instead, anonymously included in the general counting of the Levi'im.[2]

As evidence of this approach, which he refers to as *pshat*, the Ramban cites a parallel proof text from Divrei Hayamim (Chronicles): "The children of Amram were Aharon and Moshe; and Aharon was separated that he should be sanctified as most holy, he and his sons, forever.... And as for Moshe, the man of God, his children were named among the Tribe of Levi."[3]

---

2. Rashbam, Da'at Zekeinim Miba'alei Hatosafot, Ramban, Bamidbar 3:1.
3. Divrei Hayamim I 23:13–14.

B

Moving on in the text, these and other commentaries debate the significance of the second half of the sentence: "And these are the descendents of Aharon and Moshe, *on the day that God spoke to Moshe at Mount Sinai*." The Rashbam and the Da'at Zekeinim Miba'alei Hatosafot, remaining faithful to the approach of *pshat*, explain that the Torah is simply outlining the tragic transformation that has taken place in the composition of Aharon's family. Before the erection of the Mishkan, "on the day that God spoke," Aharon had four sons. The tragic death of Nadav and Avihu, simultaneous with the inauguration of the Temple service, however, leaves this great leader with only two sons.[4]

The Rashbam, in fact, quotes this sentence as the source for a general rule which he postulates in his introductory comments to the book of Bamidbar: Whenever a discussion or event is introduced in the text as taking place "at Mount Sinai," that discussion or event occurs during the first year of the Israelites' two-year sojourn at Sinai. In contrast, events or discussions occurring during the second year, after the erection of the Mishkan, are uniformly introduced by the phrase "in the wilderness of Sinai, in the tent of meeting."[5]

While the Ramban accepts the approach of the Rashbam and Tosafists to this passage, he adds another interpretive layer. He suggests that the carefully worded text also reflects the chronology governing the separate appointments of the Kohanim and Levi'im to their eternal roles. The Kohanim are appointed at the beginning of the Sinaitic Revelation and are, therefore, associated by the Torah with the "day that God spoke to Moshe at Mount Sinai." The Levi'im, however, who are not appointed to their functions until this point in time, are not connected to that prior moment.[6]

The Ba'al Haturim quotes an approach that stretches the chronological timeline even further.[7] The phrase "the day that God spoke to Moshe at Mount Sinai," this scholar suggests, references a dramatic moment

---

4. Rashbam, Da'at Zekeinim Miba'alei Hatosafot, Bamidbar 3:1.
5. Rashbam, Bamidbar 1:1.
6. Ramban, Bamidbar 3:1.
7. Quoted in Yehuda Nachshoni, *Hagot B'parshiot HaTorah* (Tel Aviv: Zohar Publishing, 1979), Vol. 2, p. 562.

earlier in time that may well mark the true birth of the *kehuna*. During the first encounter between God and Moshe at the burning bush, on the summit of Mount Sinai, God responds to Moshe's repeated objections by appointing Aharon as Moshe's partner.[8] This sudden mention of Aharon, suggests one position in the Talmud, actually reflects Aharon's election to the *kehuna*, at Moshe's expense[9] (see *Shmot*: Tetzave 2, *Approaches* A).

C

Addressing the next textual puzzle, Rabbeinu Bachya explains that the Torah repeats "These are the names of the sons of Aharon, the anointed Kohanim…" immediately after the naming of Aharon's sons, in order to underscore the uniformity of God's justice. Even though Nadav and Avihu are "anointed priests," God punishes them immediately upon their transgression. No favoritism is shown.[10]

For his part, the Sforno views this same sentence as reflecting a one-time historical anomaly. From this point on, the priesthood will be inherited without ceremony. Only Kohanim Gedolim, High Priests, will require anointment. The sons of Aharon, however, were all born before their father assumed his priestly role. Nadav, Avihu, Elazar and Itamar, therefore, cannot simply inherit the priesthood as a birthright. For them, the ritual of anointment is required even to assume the position of simple priests.[11]

The Ibn Ezra, however, demurs and maintains that the sons of Aharon are referred to as "anointed priests" because each eventually assumes the role of Kohen Gadol.[12]

D

Diametrically opposed opinions are cited in Midrash and reflected in the commentaries concerning the Torah's declaration that Elazar and Itamar "ministered *in the face of* Aharon, their father."

---

8. Shmot 4:14.
9. Rabbi Shimon bar Yochai, Talmud Bavli Zevachim 102.
10. Rabbeinu Bachya, Bamidbar 3:1.
11. Sforno, Bamidbar 3:3.
12. Ibn Ezra, Bamidbar 3:3.

The Midrash relates that Rabbi Yitzchak interprets this phrase to mean that Elazar and Itamar served *during their father's lifetime*. If Aharon contracted ritual impurity, Elazar served as Kohen Gadol in his stead, and if Elazar subsequently became ritually impure, Itamar assumed the mantle of the High Priesthood. As proof of Rabbi Yitzchak's position, the Midrash quotes the passage in Bereishit stating that Avraham's brother Haran "died *on the face of* [during the lifetime of] his father, Terach."[13]

Rabbi Chiya, on the other hand, interprets the statement concerning Aharon's sons to mean that they served *after their father's death*. When Aharon died, Elazar became the High Priest, and when Elazar expired, Itamar assumed that role. To bolster Rabbi Chiya's position, the Midrash cites the passage "and Avraham rose up from *on the face of* his dead,"[14] referring to Avraham's actions after Sara's death.

Rashi, following the position of Rabbi Yitzchak, explains that the Torah's statement "and Elazar and Itamar ministered *on the face of* Aharon, their father" indicates that Aharon's sons served as High Priests during their father's lifetime. The Chizkuni, on the other hand, interprets the same passage to mean that Aharon's sons served in that capacity upon their father's death (in line with the position of Rabbi Chiya).[15]

A powerfully poignant alternative is suggested by the Chatam Sofer, who maintains that Elazar and Itamar served *against their father's will*.[16] Deeply frightened by the fate of his older sons, Nadav and Avihu (see *Vayikra*: Shmini 1), Aharon did not want to expose his younger children to the dangers associated with the priesthood. Nevertheless, Elazar and Itamar, recognizing their responsibilities, insist upon assuming the *kehuna*. The Torah's statement that Elazar and Itamar "ministered *on the face* of Aharon," the Chatam Sofer explains, is similar to the phrase "and the tribute passed *on his face*,"[17] describing the gifts sent by the patriarch Yaakov to his brother Esav. There, Rashi explains that Yaakov was angered by the need to appease his brother this way.[18]

---

13. Bereishit 11:28.
14. Ibid., 23:3.
15. Rashi, Bamidbar 3:4.
16. Torat Moshe, Parshat Naso.
17. Bereishit 32:22.
18. Rashi, Bereishit 32:22; see Siftei Chachamim there.

E

Finally we return to the problem with which we began: the apparent disappearance of Moshe's children from the text. In contrast to the commentaries cited above, Rashi approaches the textual omission midrashically by citing a well-known Talmudic explanation: "Anyone who teaches the son of his friend Torah is considered by the text to have fathered him."

Thus the Torah states, "and these are the descendents of Moshe and Aharon," but continues by naming only the children of Aharon. Moshe is listed as his nephews' father because, serving as their mentor, he shapes their lives.[19]

While the Talmudic message is beautiful, underscoring the elemental relationship between student and teacher, significant questions remain. Moshe, after all, taught the entire nation Torah. Why, then, does the Torah list him as the "father" only of Aharon's children? Based on the Talmudic formula, Moshe should be considered the "father" of every Israelite. Even more troubling: Didn't Moshe teach his own children, Gershon and Eliezer? Why, then, are they completely omitted from the text?

F

The Maharal of Prague explains the identification of Aharon's sons as Moshe's students, to the exclusion of the rest of the nation. Moshe's teaching of the people as a whole, he maintains, was not a volitional act, but was, instead, an essential component of the Revelation process at Sinai. Moshe's personal decision to teach his nephews in further depth, however, gives rise to their unique parent-child relationship.[20]

The most troubling question, however, remains, a question that neither the Talmud nor the above commentaries seem to address.

What of Moshe's children? If we accept the Talmudic approach that the Torah references the actual children of Aharon, why are Moshe's children conspicuously absent?

---

19. Talmud Bavli Sanhedrin 19:2, quoted in Rashi, Bamidbar 3:1.
20. Gur Aryeh, Bamidbar 3:1.

G

Once this question is raised, we are forced to confront an uncomfortable truth. After references at the time of each of their births and another mention when they are reunited with their father in the Wilderness of Sinai, Moshe's children do not openly appear again in the Torah text.

The Midrash does suggest that the older brother, Gershom, anonymously resurfaces for a brief moment as "the lad" who rushes to protect Moshe's honor later in the book of Bamidbar. Brief references to Moshe's progeny are also found in Divrei Hayamim, where we learn that Shevuel, the son of Gershom, is appointed as the chief officer over the treasury,[21] and that Eliezer's descendents are very numerous.[22]

Aside from these cryptic citations, however, Moshe's children, Gershom and Eliezer, disappear into the mists of history.

Compounding the mystery is a frighteningly disturbing reference rooted, centuries later, in the book of Judges. There, the text refers to an idolater by the name of "Yehonatan the son of Gershom the son of Menashe."[23] The letter *nun*, however, in the name Menashe is suspended in small print above the line of text. The rabbis explain that the evil Yehonatan is actually a descendent of Moshe. In order to protect Moshe's honor, the letter *nun* is inserted in Moshe's name, changing it to Menashe. This insertion is clearly marked (through the unusually written *nun*), however, so that the truth concerning Yehonatan's ancestry will be everlastingly, if obliquely, preserved.

Not only do Moshe's progeny vanish from the historical record, but, even more troublingly, a possible textual reference to his descendents indicates that at least one of them becomes a notorious idolater.

H

Can it be, then, that we have come full circle; is the glaring absence of Moshe's children in the passage before us to be taken at face value?

Through the omission of Gershom and Eliezer from the text, the Torah underscores a harsh reality.

---

21. Divrei Hayamim I 26:24.
22. Ibid., 23:15–17.
23. Shoftim 18:30.

In stark contrast to the descendents of Aharon (the Kohanim, whose identity is known to this day), Moshe's children simply disappear. They play no major role in the unfolding saga of their people and are, therefore, deliberately omitted from the Torah text.

Points to Ponder

The disappearance of Moshe's progeny from our nation's historical record conveys messages that are at once encouraging and discouraging.

On the positive side of the ledger, the Torah teaches us that greatness within Jewish tradition is not automatically inherited. While certain roles, such as the *kehuna*, are the product of birthright, other leadership positions must be earned (see *Vayikra*: Tzav 2). Gershom and Eliezer are judged by the verdict of history as individuals in their own right and not as the sons of Moshe. They have no greater lock on achievement than anyone else. The opportunity for greatness is open to all.

At the same time, the mysteries surrounding Moshe's descendents raise cautionary concerns that certainly reverberate within our own lives.

Can it be that for all his overwhelming success, Moshe somehow fails with his own progeny? Rabbinic sources reflect a willingness to consider this disquieting prospect. The Midrash describes Moshe as disturbed by his own children's inability to rise to leadership.[24] The source quoted above, identifying the idolater Yehonatan as a descendent of Moshe, raises the frightening specter of deep failure in Moshe's line.

An even more disturbing possibility, however, must be considered. Can it be that Gershom and Eliezer recede from public notice not in spite of, *but specifically because of* Moshe's greatness? How often do children of great leaders struggle in the shadow of their parents' achievements? How many fail to achieve because the bar for success is automatically set too high? How many fall below the radar because their parents are too busy to notice?

The Midrash comments that, under the burdens of leadership, Moshe regularly fails to return to his home. He journeys, first from Sinai and later from the Sanctuary, directly to the nation, without stopping to care for his own personal needs.[25] The Chatam Sofer, based on a passage in the book

---

24. Sifrei, Devarim 305.
25. Mechilta, Shmot 19:14.

of Shmot,[26] goes so far as to maintain that Moshe teaches only those who come to him of their own volition. Tragically, the Chatam Sofer continues, Moshe's own children never come.[27]

Perhaps Aharon and Moshe, two vastly different leaders (see *Shmot*: Shmot 5, *Approaches* D; Mishpatim 4, *Approaches* B3; Tetzave 2, *Approaches* E), are also vastly different fathers. Aharon, warm and accessible, manages to transmit teachings to his children in a way that his brother, distant and reserved, simply cannot.

While we can wonder about these issues, we cannot assume. We have no way of truly knowing whether our troubling suggestions are accurate or whether we are simply reading too much into the absence of information concerning Moshe's progeny.

The Torah's very silence, however, challenges us with possibilities. At the very least, the disappearance of Moshe's descendents from the historical record reminds us to be vigilant. There are no guarantees in the area of childrearing, even if you are a Moshe.

---

26. Shmot 33:7.
27. Quoted in Nachshoni, *Hagot B'parshiot HaTorah*, Vol. 2, p. 563.

Naso

CHAPTER 4:21–7:89

Parsha Summary

Preparations continue, from one thing to the next....

The curtain rises on the longest parsha in the Torah and one of the most varied, as preparations for the departure from Sinai continue.

The Levite families of Gershon and Merari are counted and assigned to their specific tasks relating to the Mishkan.

God instructs Moshe concerning the following topics: the temporary exile of individuals afflicted with specific forms of tuma (ritual impurity) from various sections of the camp; laws regarding theft and the subsequent denial of responsibility; laws governing a Sota, a married woman whose behavior raises suspicion of adultery; the laws of a Nazir, an individual who vows to take upon himself increased religious obligation; and the rules of Birkat Kohanim, the Priestly Blessing.

The parsha closes with a repeated enumeration of the identical offerings brought by each of the twelve tribal leaders on the occasion of the sanctification of the Sanctuary, the Altar, and the utensils.

1 Tying Things Together

Context
Parshat Naso, the largest single parsha in the Torah, is also one of the most fragmented.

Central to the parsha is a section consisting of disparate legal themes, including:

1. The temporary exile of individuals afflicted with specific forms of *tuma* from various sections of the camp
2. Laws concerning theft and false denial of financial obligation
3. The regulations governing a Sota, a married woman suspected of adultery
4. The laws of a Nazir, an individual who vows to undertake more rigorous religious observance
5. The rules of Birkat Kohanim, the priestly blessing

Questions
What, if any, unifying thread connects the seemingly disparate laws found in Parshat Naso? Why are these regulations specifically commanded now, as the Israelites prepare for their monumental departure from Mount Sinai?

Approaches

—— A ——

While, at first glance, a global theme uniting all of Parshat Naso's laws remains elusive, connections between specific sections of the text are suggested by traditional sources.

The Talmud, for example, notes that the laws concerning theft close with an admonition to respect the legal rights of the Kohanim. Immediately thereafter the text records the regulations governing a Sota. Interpreting this textual flow midrashically in "cause and effect" fashion, the rabbis proclaim that anyone who holds back the portions meant for a Kohen will be punished with family strife and will ultimately require the services of a Kohen at the ritual trial of his suspected wife.[1]

The Talmud likewise explains the positioning of the laws of *nezirut* immediately following the regulations governing a Sota. The irresponsible, licentious behavior that can be caused by intoxication is starkly highlighted by the spectacle of the Sota. "Anyone who personally witnesses the degradation experienced by a Sota," the rabbis maintain, "will be moved to separate himself [like a Nazir] from wine."[2]

Numerous commentaries address the potential link between the textual section concerning *nezirut* and the section immediately following, delineating the laws of Birkat Kohanim. The Ibn Ezra simply states that after discussing the Nazir, an individual of sanctified status, the Torah turns its attention to another sanctified group, the Kohanim.[3] The Abravanel and, centuries later, the Alshich, maintain that the textual message strikes deeper. The path towards sanctity need not be inherited, as in the case of the *kehuna*, but can be earned, as in the case of *nezirut*[4] (see *Vayikra*: Tzav 2).

Adding our voice to the mix, a tantalizing additional approach can be suggested to explain the flow between the regulations of *nezirut* and the laws of Birkat Kohanim. Perhaps the Torah means to highlight the critical overall similarities and distinctions between the categories of *nezirut* and *kehuna*.

On the one hand, both the Nazir and the Kohen are bound by strikingly similar rules. Each, to a varying extent, is commanded to refrain from contact with death, and each, again to a varying extent, is governed by regulations concerning the consumption of wine (see *Vayikra*: Shmini 2 for an analysis of the textual passage restricting the Kohen's consumption of intoxicating beverages[5]).

On the other hand, these two spiritual categories rise from contrasting origins.

---

1. Talmud Bavli Brachot 63a.
2. Ibid.
3. Ibn Ezra, Bamidbar 6:23.
4. Abravanel, Bamidbar 6:1; Torat Moshe, Bamidbar 6:1–4.
5. Vayikra 10:9–11.

The Nazir is motivated by a desire to separate, to move away from the surrounding society (see Naso 3 for a fuller discussion of *nezirut*). His religious search is *inherently isolating*.

The Kohen, in contrast, gains his spiritual power specifically from *connection* to the community. One cannot, after all, be a priest without constituents, without those who are dependent upon his services as a representative before God. *There can be no kehuna in isolation.*

More than any other ritual associated with the *kehuna*, the Priestly Blessing underscores this fundamental connection between priest and community. By commanding the Kohen to bless the nation on God's behalf multiple times daily, the Torah literally forces each priest to regularly and directly confront the true source of his own sanctity: the people themselves. The Kohen's *kedusha* emanates out of his role as a representative of the nation before God. Absent the people, there would simply be no need for the Kohen.

Not by coincidence, therefore, the Torah places the laws of Birkat Kohanim directly after the regulations governing *nezirut*. In sharp contrast to what many see as the flawed, isolating religious attitude of the Nazir, the Kohen must always recognize that his role rests upon his connection to – and his need for – the people.

B

Numerous other commentaries struggle to discern additional thematic and even linguistic associations between the various legal passages of Parshat Naso.

As instructive as these and other links may be, however, they fail to answer the two global questions raised at the beginning of our study.

On the level of *pshat*, is there one unifying thread that somehow connects all of the laws of this section of Parshat Naso? Will the discovery of this unifying thread help us understand why these laws are commanded specifically at this pivotal moment in time, as the preparations for the nation's momentous journey from Sinai near their end?

C

An approach to these issues can perhaps be suggested by reflecting on the overall placement of Parshat Naso itself in the text.

Until this point, the narrative of Sefer Bamidbar has focused mainly upon the physical structure of the Israelite encampment in the desert and upon the place of each family and tribe within that camp. Now, however, the Torah turns its attention to the *harmony* meant to reign within the camp's boundaries.

Through a series of sharp legal strokes, the text addresses potential sources of spiritual and social disruption, outlining the response to each. While each of the examples cited by the Torah is case specific, they are meant to serve as paradigms as well. The text thus purposely addresses, as the nation's journey is about to begin, a series of life arenas within which peace and harmony must be continually and assiduously cultivated:

1. *Spiritual disruption* will be addressed through the temporary expulsion of individuals afflicted with specific forms of *tuma* from various sections of the camp. Only once these individuals have regained the status of *tahara* can they return to full functioning within Israelite society (see *Vayikra*: Tazria-Metzora 1–3 for discussions concerning the concepts of *tuma* and *tahara*, ritual impurity and purity).

2. The *social fabric* of the camp will be preserved through adherence to the laws prohibiting theft and dishonesty.

3. The *structure of the family* – critical yet at times fragile – will be addressed through the laws of Sota (see Naso 2 for a discussion as to how these laws are designed to help salvage a family in extremis, suffering from the devastating forces of suspicion and jealousy).

4. The potentially divisive desires of those wishing to *move beyond the religious norm* will be addressed and controlled through the laws of *nezirut*.[6]

5. Finally, this entire section of text concludes with the *laws of Birkat Kohanim*, a blessing that culminates in the prayer for God's most precious gift of *shalom*, peace.

Through the interplay of law and prayer, the Torah thus communicates that true peace within the Israelite encampment will be dependent both upon the nation's conscious efforts and upon God's continuing blessings.

---

6. In his commentary on the text, the Ralbag (Shmot 5:1–6:27) takes this overall approach one step further by noting that the Torah's prescription for peace moves ever inward: from societal harmony (the laws of *tuma* and *tahara* and the laws of theft) to familial harmony (the laws of Sota) to internal personal harmony (the laws of *nezirut*).

2 A Tragic, Troubling Trial

Context
In a powerful departure from the normative process of Jewish law and jurisprudence, the Torah outlines the ritual trial to be conducted in the case of a Sota, a married woman suspected by her husband of adultery.

In the courtyard of the Sanctuary (and later, the Temple), under the direction of a Kohen, the Sota is to participate in a series of humiliating public rituals. These rites culminate in the consumption of a potion consisting of water from the Sanctuary's laver, earth from the floor of the Sanctuary and a dissolved parchment upon which has been written the section of the Torah text delineating the potential fate of the Sota herself.

The Sota's guilt, the Torah continues, will be determined by her reaction to the ingestion of the potion. If she is innocent of her husband's charges, she will emerge unscathed. If, however, she is indeed guilty, drinking the potion will cause her to suffer fatal injury.[1]

Questions
Few if any other passages in the Torah are as troubling as the passage concerning a Sota. The issues raised, intellectually and emotionally, seem to defy resolution.

How can the Torah suddenly undermine the very foundations of Jewish law by introducing what seems to be a "trial by ordeal"? Nowhere else in the ongoing process of Jewish jurisprudence is truth determined by God's miraculous intervention. The very idea, in fact, runs counter to the fundamental principles upon which the law rests. From Sinai onward,

---
1. Bamidbar 5:11–31.

divine law is placed in the hands of man. Prophecy, signs and miracles have no place in the Jewish courtroom.

Furthermore, the treatment of the Sota seems, at first glance, to be inexplicably harsh. In the absence of proof, how can mere suspicion of guilt on the husband's part result in his wife's public humiliation and potentially much worse? One does not have to be an ardent feminist to deeply question the way in which the Torah approaches this entire event.

Approaches

A

As with all mysterious sections of Torah text, our study of the case of Sota must begin with a disclaimer.

Judging eternal Torah law is a dangerous enterprise, hampered by our own limited vision. Our fundamental inability to comprehend God's ways is compounded by the transient nature of our own societal perspective. What we view as fair and just is colored by our own experience and by the outlook of the times in which we live. Social mores change over time; the Torah perspective is eternal.

Nonetheless, the timeless Torah is meant to be meaningful in each generation. We have the right, therefore, if not the obligation, to struggle with each section of the text in an effort to glean lessons relevant to our lives and times. We do not have the luxury of viewing any part of the Torah as anachronistic. Every passage of the text has something to say to us today.

Here, then, the challenge in a nutshell: to walk a fine line. To plumb the depths of even the most difficult passages of the Torah, but to recognize that the conclusions we reach may well be incomplete, if not inherently flawed.

The reward, however, lies in the process, which is as timeless as the Torah itself. Our serious encounter with the text will place us squarely within the ranks of those who have never taken any portion of the Torah for granted but have studied the text comprehensively across the ages for a glimpse of God's will.

We will find, as have those who toiled before us, that this very search is its own reward, bringing God into our lives and perpetuating His word across the ages.

B

Our journey into the ritual of Sota begins, by necessity, with a review of a basic question: What are the prerequisites for the ritual? Under what conditions does a woman become a Sota?

At first glance, the Torah's answer to this seemingly simple question is contradictory and confusing. The text states:

> Any man whose wife shall go astray and commit treachery against him, and a man lie with her carnally, and it be hidden from the eyes of her husband, and she was secluded and defiled – but there is no witness against her – and she was not forced.
>
> And the spirit of jealousy passed over him and he warned his wife and she became defiled; or a spirit of jealousy passed over him and he warned his wife and she did not become defiled.[2]

On the one hand, the Torah refers to the events with an attitude of certainty: "whose wife shall go astray and commit treachery against him," "and a man lie with her carnally," "and she became defiled"…

On the other hand, the Torah seems to indicate that the facts are far from clear: "and it be hidden from the eyes of her husband," "but there is no witness against her," "and she did not become defiled"…

Rising to the challenge created by these apparent textual contradictions, the rabbis explain the case before us. A woman becomes a Sota, they maintain, only if her prior behavior has created real grounds for suspicion on her husband's part. According to the law, in fact, the ritual of Sota can only take place after the following concrete prerequisite steps first unfold:

1. A husband is seized by a "spirit of jealousy," suspecting his wife of infidelity, based upon her actions in connection with another man.

2. Confronting his wife in the presence of two reliable witnesses, the husband objects to the relationship in question. He demands, in clear terms, that his wife not seclude herself in the future with this particular man.

3. Two reliable witnesses appear, testifying that, subsequent to her husband's warning, the wife secluded herself with the individual in question such that an adulterous act could have been possible. The

---

2. Ibid., 5:12–14.

witnesses, however, are unable to testify as to whether or not such an act actually occurred.[3]

C

This sequence of steps, outlined by the rabbis, explains the Torah's initially confusing language. The text speaks with an air of certainty because, while a Sota's adulterous relationship cannot be proven, she has certainly committed some wrongs.[4] A woman does not become a Sota in a vacuum, simply as a result of baseless suspicion. The case before us speaks of a situation where, in spite of her husband's clearly (and legally) expressed misgivings, a woman continues to actively perpetuate doubt as to her intentions. The festering sore created by her behavior threatens the integrity of her marital bond and must, somehow, be addressed.

D

Before we go any further, a word must be said at this point concerning the apparent inequity highlighted by the ritual of Sota. Why is only a woman subject to these laws? According to the Torah, isn't adultery committed by a man a capital offense, as well?

The answer to this question may not sit well with all readers but must be proffered, nonetheless.

From a Torah perspective, the marital obligations incumbent upon a man and a woman, respectively, are not the same.

After marriage, a woman is forbidden to engage in sexual relationships with any man other than her husband, on pain of death. Hers is to be a solely monogamous relationship. A man, however, is biblically permitted to marry more than one wife. Even extramarital relationships on his part with unmarried women are not technically prohibited in the Torah. By Torah definition, a man commits adultery only when he has physical relations with a woman who is married to someone else.

---

3. Rambam, *Mishneh Torah*, Hilchot Sota 1:1–2.
4. The Talmud Bavli (Sota 4a) explains, for example, the phrase "and she was secluded and defiled" (Bamidbar 5:13) to mean that she secluded herself long enough to become defiled, while the Talmud Yerushalmi (Sota 1:2) explains the phrase to mean that since she secluded herself the Torah considers her "defiled."

Not until the Middle Ages does the great Ashkenazic rabbinic authority Rabbeinu Gershom issue a ban on polygamy. Some Sephardic communities continue the practice of polygamy until modern times.

Why does the Torah mandate different marital requirements for men and women, respectively?

The answer is not clear.

Perhaps the Torah views men's and women's emotional and physical needs within marriage as different (a view certainly maintained by many in modern times, although not necessarily leading to the same conclusion as the Torah concerning marital fidelity). Perhaps a woman's central role within the home gives rise to a greater demand for faithfulness on her part. Perhaps Torah law reflects the attitudes of the society into which it is born, while allowing for halachic adjustment through rabbinic mandate as societal mores change (see *Shmot*: Mishpatim 1, *Points to Ponder* for a discussion of the relationship between the eternal and the temporal in the Torah text; see also *Shmot*: Yitro 5, *Approaches* C for a discussion of the role of *takanot*, rabbinic edicts, in the ongoing development of Jewish law).

Whatever the reasons for these stringencies, the Torah's expectations concerning a woman's marital fidelity are reflected in the laws of Sota.

Nonetheless, a number of Midrashic and halachic observations seem to level the playing field somewhat.

In the *Sifrei*, the rabbis comment on the last sentence of the passage concerning the Sota: "And the man shall be innocent of iniquity, but that woman shall bear her iniquity."[5] Among the interpretations offered is the startling suggestion that the waters administered to the Sota are only effective if her husband is "innocent of iniquity." If, however, the husband has acted immorally, the waters will not affect his wife, even if she is guilty.[6]

Even more telling, perhaps, is the Mishnaic contention that "just as the waters examine her, so they examine him."[7] The Talmud interprets this to mean that the miraculous Sota waters affect not only a woman guilty of adultery but her male partner in the adulterous act, as well. When a guilty

---

5. Bamidbar 5:31.
6. Sifrei, Bamidbar 5:31.
7. Mishna Sota 5:1.

woman ingests the potion and suffers fatal injury, her "partner in crime" experiences a similar fate, wherever he may be.[8]

These observations, which are not theoretical but codified as halacha by the Rambam,[9] clearly reflect rabbinic unwillingness to understand the laws of Sota in a totally one-sided fashion.

Additionally, in a number of Midrashic and Talmudic sources, the rabbis recognize the potential role that a husband can play in the disintegration of family harmony.[10] In this vein, the Chizkuni suggests that the offering brought in conjunction with the Sota ritual[11] actually serves as atonement for the husband's part in the unfolding events. Even when his wife is the adulterer, the husband bears a measure of blame. Had he approached his wife earlier, when the problems first began, perhaps the issues between them could have been resolved and this tragic point would never have been reached.[12]

E

Continued rabbinic explanation of the text yields a series of important laws that further shape our vision of the case of the Sota. Among the laws codified by the Rambam, based upon earlier Talmudic discussion, are the following:

1. *A husband who warns his wife in the presence of witnesses may recant* his warning at any time, as long as his wife has not yet secluded herself again with the man in question. Such recantation effectively nullifies the warning entirely and releases the woman from the possibility of becoming a Sota, unless a new warning is given. If the wife secludes herself with the man in question after her husband warns her, however, the effect of the initial warning may no longer be rescinded.[13]

2. *A woman cannot be forced to drink* the waters of the Sota ceremony. If the parchment containing the Torah passage has not yet been dissolved in the water (see above), she can refuse to continue with the ritual and still proclaim her innocence. The marriage, however, cannot continue

---

8. Talmud Bavli Sota 27b–28a.
9. Rambam, *Mishneh Torah*, Hilchot Sota 2:8; 3:17.
10. Talmud Bavli Gittin 6b, 90a–b.
11. Bamidbar 5:15.
12. Chizkuni, Bamidbar 5:15.
13. Rambam, *Mishneh Torah*, Hilchot Sota 1:7.

without resolution of the overwhelming doubts her actions have caused. The law, therefore, mandates that she be divorced without benefit of the *ketuba* payment that she would normally receive.[14] Once the parchment has been dissolved, the woman can still refuse to drink the potion. At this point, however, she must admit her guilt.[15] In this case she is, once again, divorced without benefit of the *ketuba* payment.

3. *A husband may relent at the last moment* of the process and insist that his wife not drink the waters of the Sota ritual. Once again, however, doubt makes the continuation of the marriage untenable. In this case, because the husband prevented the administration of the Sota ritual, he must divorce his wife but pay her the *ketuba* payment.[16]

As we consider these and other laws concerning the case of Sota, a different picture than we first imagined begins to emerge. This is not a trial by ordeal, where a hapless victim is forced to undergo an impossible physical test to prove his innocence. Such a travesty of justice, too often used in the historical persecution of the Jews, among others, clearly has no place in Torah law.

Instead, the Sota ritual and the steps that lead to it emerge as an action plan designed to discourage questionable behavior and, failing that, to deal with the corrosive doubt created by such behavior. No one is forced along the "Sota path." *Each step of the way choices are offered*. Even at the last moment either the husband or the wife can stop the process in its tracks by refusing to allow the ritual to continue. True, by then, the choices have become more difficult and their ramifications more serious. This growing difficulty, however, is the product of the actions of the participants themselves. The Torah implicitly begs those involved to somehow prevent the unfolding tragedy before it is too late. In the final analysis, however, the participants must bear the consequences of their own decisions and actions.

— F —

A central problem, however, yet remains…. What exactly is the true nature of the Sota ritual? Is the trial of a Sota the overwhelming departure from

---

14. Ibid., 2:1.
15. Mishna Sota 3:3.
16. Rambam, *Mishneh Torah*, Hilchot Sota 2:1.

the norm that it seems to be? Is this the one time when God overrules His own guiding principle, "the law is no longer in heaven,"[17] the one time in the ongoing application of Jewish law when a verdict is determined not through legal analysis but rather through divine, miraculous intervention?

To the overwhelming preponderance of rabbinic thought the answer is a resounding yes. No other reading of the biblical text, the majority of scholars maintain, is possible.

Representing this position, the Ramban states: "And behold there is no other instance of all the laws of the Torah where the verdict is dependent upon a miracle, aside from this case."[18]

The circumstances of Sota are extraordinary, explains the Ramban, because God, in His righteousness, desires to ensure the purity of his people, that they be worthy of receiving His Divine Presence. He therefore institutes this exceptional "legal miracle" as a fearsome deterrent, designed to prevent the women of Israel from adopting the immoral ways of surrounding nations.

The Ramban concludes by quoting the Talmudic assertion that God's intervention in the case of the Sota is dependent upon the nation's merit. Historically, when immorality became rampant within the nation, "the waters of Sota ceased."[19]

G

Swimming against the tide, a handful of scholars propose an alternative approach to the Sota ritual. At work here, they claim, is not divine intervention at all, but psychological suggestion.

In contrast to his acceptance of the miraculous nature of the Sota ritual in the *Mishneh Torah*, the Rambam hints at this second approach in his *Guide to the Perplexed* (*Moreh Nevuchim*). There, he emphasizes the public humiliation heaped upon the Sota, rather than the effect of the Sota waters themselves:

> Laws concerning a Sota are therefore prescribed to ensure that all married women will guard themselves intensely to avoid creating

---

17. Devarim 30:12; Talmud Bavli Bava Metzia 59b.
18. Ramban, Bamidbar 5:22.
19. Ibid.; Talmud Bavli Sota 47a.

suspicion in their husbands' hearts…for even death would be better than that public disgrace of uncovering the head, undoing the hair, rending the garments and exposing the heart, and being led around the Sanctuary in the presence of all…and *because of this fear great threats to the stability of countless homes are avoided.*[20]

The very risk of being forced to experience this humiliating ritual, suggests the Rambam, serves as sufficient deterrent to immoral behavior within the community.

Even more revolutionary are the suggestions of others, such as the eighteenth-century Talmudist Rabbi Moshe Chafetz, in his work *Melechet Machshevet*. Basing his position on the strange, twice-repeated biblical phrase "and then the waters that cause curse shall come into her for bitterness,"[21] this scholar maintains that the Sota's fear of death causes her to view the administered waters as bitter, to powerful effect:

> An individual's mind and imagination can have great effect upon his physical being…often something can be imagined that is not so with such strength and effectiveness *that the imagined phenomenon actually becomes real to the individual.…*
>
> And this is the intent of the text, that the Kohen should inspire fear within the woman's heart in order that she confess.… He therefore tells her that the potion is bitter, as if she is about to consume poison, and she imagines it to be so in her mind – to the point that when she ingests the potion she finds it to be so, as if they [the waters] are bitter in truth…*and the potion becomes for her bitter waters in truth and in fact.*[22]

Unwilling to accept the possibility of God's intervention in the legal process, this scholar instead perceives in the Sota ritual the power of suggestion inspired by overwhelming dread and fear. So terrifying is the entire Sota ritual that the very intimation of punishment causes the guilty to perish as they starkly confront their own culpability.

---

20. Rambam, *Moreh Nevuchim* 3:49.
21. Bamidbar 5:24, 27.
22. Rabbi Moshe Chaifetz, *Melechet Machshevet*, Bamidbar, Naso.

Points to Ponder

What could possibly cause God to break His own rules?

Whether we accept, as do most authorities, that the trial of a Sota reflects God's exceptional miraculous intervention in the judicial process, or whether we adopt the revolutionary notion that the trial works through psychological suggestion, one thing is clear: The point with which our study opened has been affirmed. The trial of the Sota represents a departure from the normative, sober, methodical administration of Jewish law.

What phenomenon powers this departure? What could possibly cause God to break His own rules?

The answer lies in the concept of *shalom bayit*, peace within the home, a concept recognized in rabbinic thought as overwhelmingly important,[23] yet too often treated popularly as a quaint notion.

At the center of the case of Sota lies a family in profound distress, a family that has lost the single most essential component in any human relationship: the component of trust.

In the face of this devastating development, everything is set aside. So pivotal is the family unit, so central to Jewish thought and practice, that the wheels of justice grind to a halt. All eyes focus on this one family, until the corrosive doubt within has been addressed.

Whatever the result of this one trial, the suspension of the legal norm will hopefully not have been in vain. Other families, witnessing the tragic spectacle, will take note and wonder: *What could possibly bring a family to such a point? What small steps, unnoticed as they occurred, were the first steps leading down the path of discord? How can we avoid making the same mistakes?*

And perhaps those witnessing will go one step further. Perhaps they will commit themselves to the active cultivation of trust within their own relationships; to the patience, understanding and hard work necessary to sustain the fragile equilibrium of *shalom bayit* within their homes.

Centuries later, while the ritual itself is long gone, the message of Sota continues to reverberate....

---

23. Note: In a number of sources, in fact, the rabbis use the example of God's willingness to allow His name to be erased in the Sota waters (through the dissolving of the parchment containing the Torah passage of Sota) as proof of the overwhelming importance of *shalom bayit* (see, for example, Talmud Yerushalmi Sota 1:4).

A well-known rabbinic maxim notes that the Hebrew words *ish*, man, and *isha*, woman, differ from each other through a one-letter variation: the *yud* in the word *ish* and the *heh* in the word *isha*. Taken together, the letters *yud* and *heh* represent the name of God. Absent those letters, the words *ish* and *isha* are each transformed into the word *eish*, fire.

When God is present in the male-female relationship, when there is continued striving for understanding, mutual acceptance and shared journey, the relationship remains healthy. When, however, such effort is absent, all that eventually remains is "fire."[24] The union between a man and a woman, the rabbis maintain, is tenuous by nature and must be nurtured continuously.

As one who has unfortunately experienced the sad dissolution of a number of marriages in my community and beyond, I have personally witnessed the "fire" that too often envelops a family in the throes of divorce. The line between love and hate turns surprisingly thin and the very depth of emotion that pulled two people together now turns them against each other, ripping them apart.

The Torah narrative serves as a stark reminder of the paths that we cannot afford to take, whether through action or neglect. The strength of a marriage can never be taken for granted and our most important relationships are too important to "set on autopilot." *Shalom bayit*, after all, is never fully *attained*, but rather, through effort and hard work, must be continuously *sustained*.

No life lesson, it would seem, is more critical. After all, God wouldn't break His own rules unless it were really important....

---

24. Mesechtot Ketanot Kalla Rabbati 1:7.

3 Sinner or Saint?

Context

Conflicting signals mark the Torah's attitude towards a man or a woman who vows to become a Nazir[1] and thus accepts the personal obligation to refrain from

1. Consumption of wine, grapes and any grape product
2. Haircuts
3. Any defiling contact with a human corpse[2]

On the one hand, the Torah emphatically states, "All the days of his *nezirut, sanctified* is he to God."[3]

On the other hand, if the Nazir comes into inadvertent, unavoidable contact with death, the Torah maintains that he must "atone" for his sin.[4] In addition, upon completion of the term of his vow, every Nazir is commanded to bring, among other *korbanot*, a *sin offering*.[5]

Questions

How does Jewish thought view a Nazir? Is the adoption of additional stringencies in the quest for holiness considered praiseworthy or not?

Why must a Nazir atone for circumstances beyond his control, in the case of unavoidable, inadvertent contact with death? Even further, why

---

1. Note: The etymology of the root *l'hazir* is defined differently by different commentaries. The majority opinion (e.g., Rashi, Bereishit 49:26) is that the term means "to separate from," while other commentaries (e.g., Rashbam, Bereishit 49:26) relate the term to the concept of majesty. Yet others combine the two approaches (e.g., Ibn Ezra, Bamidbar 6:6, 6:7).
2. Bamidbar 6:1–7.
3. Ibid., 6:8.
4. Ibid., 6:9–12.
5. Ibid., 6:14.

must every Nazir bring a sin offering upon completion of the term of his vow? Is this offering an indication of the Torah's disapproval of the original vow of *nezirut*?

If *nezirut* is less than optimal, why is it offered as an option in the Torah? If, on the other hand, *nezirut* is praiseworthy, why isn't this status mandatory for all?

Approaches

A

The textual hints of attitudinal ambivalence towards the Nazir emerge as full-blown debate in rabbinic literature. At the core of the argument lies the broader question: How does Jewish thought, in general, view the ascetic, someone who voluntarily abstains from that which God permits?

In a philosophical battle that rages across the ages, the sages map out widely divergent positions concerning the search for sanctity in a physical world. What follows is a representative – albeit far from exhaustive – sampling of their opinions.

B

A foundational Tannaitic dispute, quoted in the Talmud, sets the stage for the multigenerational discussion.

Rabbi Elazar Hakapar maintains that the Torah refers to a Nazir as having sinned because the individual unnecessarily deprives himself of the pleasure of drinking wine. "If an individual who deprives himself of wine is a sinner," this sage concludes, "how much more so is someone who deprives himself of all pleasures? We therefore learn that an individual who voluntarily fasts is considered a sinner."[6]

Rabbi Elazar (ben Shammua, not to be confused with Rabbi Elazar Hakapar) draws the opposite conclusion. The Torah clearly describes the Nazir as sanctified. "If someone who deprives himself of wine is considered holy," this sage argues, "how much more so is someone who deprives himself of all pleasures? We therefore learn that an individual who voluntarily fasts is considered holy."[7]

---

6. Talmud Bavli Ta'anit 11a.
7. Ibid.

The Talmud goes on to explain, however, that even Rabbi Elazar limits his encouragement of abstinence to those who can bear the burden without undue suffering.[8]

Other Talmudic sages weigh in on both sides of the debate.

─ C ───

As seen by the conclusions they draw, Rabbi Elazar Hakapar and Rabbi Elazar do not confine their debate to the case of *nezirut*. At issue is the overall question of asceticism within Jewish tradition. How does Judaism, they ask, a religion that generally embraces the physical world (see *Shmot*: Shmot 3, *Approaches* D, E; Yitro 2, *Approaches* C, D; Mishpatim 5, *Approaches* D; *Vayikra*: Shmini 3), view those who wish to retreat from it? Can such retreat result in the attainment of greater spiritual heights or is abstinence a fundamentally aberrant path? Furthermore, are the answers to these questions consistent across the board or dependent on the makeup of each individual?

Centuries later, in his halachic magnum opus, the *Mishneh Torah*, the Rambam clearly adopts the position of Rabbi Elazar Hakapar on this fundamental issue:

> A person should not say, "Behold: envy, desire, honor and the like are evil paths…; I will separate myself from them completely," to the point where he will not eat meat or drink wine, will not marry, will not live in a beautiful dwelling, will not wear nice garments; but instead wears sackcloth, rough wool and the like, as do the priests of the nations.
>
> This, as well, is an evil path upon which it is forbidden to travel; and one who travels this path is considered a sinner, for the text states: "And he [the Kohen] shall provide him [the Nazir] atonement for having sinned concerning the soul," and the rabbis further maintain: "If a Nazir, who only separates himself from wine, requires atonement, how much more so does someone who abstains from many things [require atonement]?"
>
> *Therefore, the rabbis instruct that an individual should not abstain except from those things prohibited to him by Torah law* [my italics]….

---

8. Ibid., 11a–b.

And concerning these issues Shlomo [King Solomon] proclaimed: "Do not be overly righteous nor overly wise; why should you destroy yourself?" (Kohelet 7:16).[9]

Nonetheless, in spite of this clearly stated position in opposition to asceticism as a lifestyle, the Rambam does defend the institution of *nezirut* in his *Guide to the Perplexed*:

> The purpose of *nezirut* is obvious: it provides for abstention from wine, a substance that has ruined lives in both ancient and modern times….
>
> For he who abstains from wine is considered holy and is placed on the level of a Kohen Gadol in terms of sanctity, to the point where he may not defile himself, even [upon the death] of his mother or father. This is the honor granted to him because he abstains from wine.[10]

The Rambam fails to clarify, however, how he considers the Nazir to be, at once, both a sinner (as he notes in the *Mishneh Torah*) and a sanctified individual (as he notes in the *Guide to the Perplexed*).

D

In stark contrast to those who consider the Nazir "sinful" for having restricted himself from that which is normally allowed, the Ramban adopts the position that *nezirut* is a totally laudatory state.

The sin offering brought by the Nazir at the end of his period of abstinence, the Ramban explains, is far from a negative comment on the state of *nezirut*. It is, in fact, exactly the opposite – a reflection of this state's loftiness:

> This individual sins to his soul on the day of the completion of his period of *nezirut*, for he now is a Nazir in his sanctity and in the service of God, and it would have been appropriate for him to separate forever and remain all his days a Nazir and sanctified to his God.…

---

9. Rambam, *Mishneh Torah*, Hilchot De'ot 3:1.
10. Rambam, *Moreh Nevuchim* 3:48.

And behold he now requires atonement upon his return to the defilement of earthly temptations.[11]

In a bold move, the Ramban thus redefines the entire thrust of the sin offering at the end of the Nazir's term. A Nazir requires atonement, this sage maintains, not for entering the state of *nezirut*, but for leaving its sanctified confines.

E

Numerous other commentaries offer their own solutions to the apparent contradiction between the Torah's identification of the Nazir as both "sanctified" and "sinful."

Rabbi Moshe Isserles (the Rema), for example, views the experience of *nezirut* as a spiritually curative process, in line with the Rambam's general prescription for positive behavior modification.

The Rambam maintains that in order to arrive at a healthy behavioral middle road, there are times when individuals must temporarily go to extremes. Someone who has a tendency towards haughtiness and pride, for example, should debase himself for a period of time. Through this exercise, all haughtiness will be driven from his system and he will be able to return to the desired middle road.[12]

In this vein, says the Rema, the Torah prescribes *nezirut* for someone who recognizes in himself the tendency to succumb to earthly pleasures. By temporarily adopting the extreme path of abstinence, this individual will train himself to eventually attain proper life balance.

The Torah's description of the Nazir as sanctified, the Rema explains, refers to his condition *after* the period of *nezirut* is concluded. Through the vows of *nezirut*, the Nazir enters a temporary period of extremes (and all extremes are inherently "sinful") in order to ultimately reach a "sanctified" equilibrium.[13]

Agreeing with the Rema's vision of *nezirut* as an exercise in positive behavioral modification, Rabbi Meier Simcha HaCohen of Dvinsk explains a strange choice of wording in the Torah's description of the end of the

---

11. Ramban, Bamidbar 6:14.
12. Rambam, *Mishneh Torah*, Hilchot De'ot 2:1–2.
13. Rabbi Moshe Isserles, *Torat Ha'olah* 3:71.

nezirut period. The text states: "And this is the law of the Nazir, when the days of his *nezirut* are fulfilled, *he shall bring himself* to the entrance of the Tent of Meeting."[14]

Why does the Torah make use of the cumbersome construction "he shall bring himself"? Why not simply state, "he shall come"?

Rabbi Meier Simcha explains that the fundamental purpose of *nezirut* is to cure an individual of his tendency towards lust, pride and excess. The Torah, therefore, mandates no specific length to the *nezirut* period. Each individual must determine for himself how long he must remain in this "corrective" period of *nezirut* in order to achieve the desired goals. The Nazir thus "brings himself"; he alone determines exactly when he should come to the doors of the Tent of Meeting.[15]

Concerning the sin offering brought at the end of the Nazir's tenure, Rabbi Meier Simcha offers an intriguing theory. The adoption of *nezirut* is not a sin, he suggests, but does create, by necessity, other ancillary sins of omission. During the time of his *nezirut*, the Nazir was proscribed from performing specific mitzvot such as the mitzva of honoring his dead (due to the *nezirut* restrictions concerning contact with death) and the mitzvot of Kiddush and Havdala over wine (due to the prohibitions concerning consumption of grape products). Although the acceptance of his *nezirut* may well have been positive, the Nazir still must atone for the mitzvot that he consequently missed.[16]

The Netziv maintains that God Himself will sometimes "weigh in" concerning the judgment to be passed on a particular Nazir. As proof, this sage focuses on the atonement required of a Nazir upon inadvertent contact with death. Why, asks the Netziv, should a Nazir be culpable for an unavoidable situation that arises, in the Torah's words, with "quick suddenness"? The Netziv therefore argues that, in reality, the Nazir atones, not for the contact with death that was beyond his control, but for his original decision to become a Nazir and deprive himself of wine. Such abstinence can be commendable, but only for the select few who are worthy of attaining a higher level of sanctity. By placing this particular Nazir in a situation of unavoidable contact with death, God sends a divine

---

14. Bamidbar 6:13.
15. Meshech Chochma, Bamidbar 6:13.
16. Ibid., 6:14.

sign that this individual is unworthy of being a Nazir. The individual must therefore atone for unnecessary self-denial in what has been a flawed attempt to attain a status beyond his reach.[17]

Finally, the Kli Yakar, in one of a number of approaches, views the Nazir's sin from a societal perspective. Quoting the Talmudic statement "Anyone who vows is considered to have built a personal altar [a practice forbidden by Jewish law],"[18] this scholar chastises the Nazir for separating himself from the community. By denying himself that which others are allowed, the Nazir embarks upon a search that is inherently isolating.[19] As we have noted before, from the perspective of Jewish thought, connection to and involvement with the surrounding community is essential. Any religious path that breeds isolation is, as a rule, fundamentally flawed.

— F

Yet other commentaries maintain that the mindset of the Nazir is the ultimate determinant of the value of his vow.

The Ohr Hachaim, for example, views the text itself as distinguishing between two different types of *nezirut*:

1. *Nazir*: Someone who accepts *nezirut* out of a personal predilection for an ascetic lifestyle.

2. *Nazir La'Hashem* (to God): Someone who accepts *nezirut* for the appropriate purpose of drawing near to God.[20]

In a similar vein, The Chatam Sofer differentiates between the Nazir who, mistakenly, views asceticism as a goal unto itself and the Nazir who, appropriately, views *nezirut* as a means to an end.[21]

To these and other like-minded scholars the message conveyed by the textual ambivalence towards the Nazir is clear: "It depends." An individual who embarks upon the path of *nezirut* for the appropriate reasons is "sanctified," while an individual whose motivation is faulty is "a sinner."

---

17. *Ha'amek Davar* 6:11.
18. Talmud Bavli Nedarim 59a.
19. Kli Yakar, Bamidbar 6:2.
20. Ohr Hachaim 6:2.
21. Torat Moshe, Parshat Naso.

G

When all is said and done, the most basic questions concerning *nezirut* still remain largely unanswered: Given the controversy surrounding these laws, why does the Torah offer *nezirut* as an option in the first place? Why not simply insist that all individuals find meaning and significance within the complex decrees that are already commanded to all Jews?

The answer to these questions reveals the brilliance of Torah law as it continues to strike a delicate balance between man's initiative and God's will.

On the one hand, *nezirut* reflects God's recognition of the need for "safety valves" within the structure of ritual worship. There will always be those, the Torah acknowledges, for whom the norm will not be sufficient – individuals who will aspire to a different, perhaps loftier path. And while, as we have seen, such aspirations are of questionable merit, *nezirut* provides the necessary structure within which these individuals can pursue their personal objectives.

There is, however, a catch….

For if *nezirut* provides a channel for individual religious expression, this very same phenomenon also clearly limits such expression. *Counterintuitively, the Torah denies the Nazir the right of self-determination in his religious search.*

In effect, God declares to the would-be Nazir: *You desire to move beyond the law, to be the exception governed by standards all your own? I will allow you to do so. If I attempt to stifle your initiative, if I deny you an avenue within the system, your need to be different may well find expression in other, less productive ways.*

Just one point, however. As you leave the box that governs the behavior of those around you, here is the new box into which you must move; here are the new laws that you must now observe. For, within the world of My Torah, even those who would travel beyond the law will be governed by the law.

Ultimately you must remember that I, not you, make the rules….

Points to Ponder

As our discussion has shown, the jury is still out concerning *nezirut*. Unlike other faith traditions that view asceticism as a goal, Judaism views the path of abstinence with caution. Under certain circumstances, for specific individuals and with the right motivation, temporary self-denial and social seclusion can sometimes lead to a heightened state of sanctity. As a rule, however, on a day-to-day basis, sanctity is to be found through connection to the community and within the context of the physical world.

Jewish tradition's ambivalence towards *nezirut* and the lifestyle that it represents should give us pause as we consider the nature of our own communal religious posture. Two areas of query can provide the framework for our brief self-analysis:

1. Is the adoption of greater ritual stringency necessarily always synonymous with deeper religiosity?

2. Given the clear value placed by our tradition upon belonging to the whole, shouldn't the search for communal harmony factor into our halachic decisions, as well?

These questions acquire greater urgency against the backdrop of growing conflict between the increasingly strident Charedi and the increasingly alienated secular communities in Israel. With growing frequency, as these societies drift further apart, Jews perceive other Jews as opponents rather than as allies, as problems rather than as partners. The voices of moderation and pride-filled cooperation, once so strongly represented by the National Religious camp, seem strangely weak and silent.

Can a halachically true model of religious observance be attained in Israel that engenders harmony rather than hostility? Can a measure of respect for that observance still be regained among those who feel so deeply disenfranchised?

The answers to these questions will determine, in great measure, the future viability of the State of Israel.

4 A Superfluous Role?

Context
The legal passages at the center of Parshat Naso draw to a close as God commands Moshe to instruct Aharon and his sons concerning Birkat Kohanim, the Priestly Blessing. This threefold blessing, to be pronounced daily over the nation,[1] reads as follows:

> May God bless you and safeguard you.
> May God cause His countenance to shine upon you and be gracious unto you.
> May God lift His countenance towards you and grant you peace.[2]

The passage concerning Birkat Kohanim concludes as God declares: "And they shall place My name upon the children of Israel, and *I will bless them.*"[3]

Questions
The last words of the passage concerning Birkat Kohanim, "and I [God] will bless them," bring a fundamental problem into clear focus.

What exactly is the role of the Kohanim in this ritual?

If, as God indicates, all blessings ultimately emanate from God, why are the Kohanim involved at all? God should simply bless the people when and how He sees fit.

As Rabbi Isaac Arama asks in his *Akeidat Yitzchak*: "What is the purpose of this mitzva…? The Exalted One is the source of blessing, and

---

1. Rambam, *Sefer Hamitzvot*, positive commandment 26.
2. Bamidbar 6:22–26.
3. Ibid., 6:27.

what will it add or detract if the Kohanim bless the nation, or not? [Does God] need their help?"[4]

Once these questions are raised, of course, we find ourselves confronting the global issue of interpersonal *brachot* (blessings bestowed by man) within Jewish tradition (see also *Bereishit*: Toldot 3).

What, exactly, are the source and nature of man's power to bless? What strength do the blessings that we recite on behalf of others, such as prayers for those who are ill, really have?

If God remains the ultimate arbiter of blessing, what is man's role in the process?

Approaches

A

Rabbinic interpretation of the closing statement of the Priestly Blessing, "And I will bless them," is not uniform, as evidenced by a Tannaitic dispute quoted in the Talmud and referenced in Rashi. Rabbi Yishmael maintains that the phrase "and I will bless them" refers not to the Israelites but to the Kohanim themselves. During Birkat Kohanim, this sage believes, "the Kohanim bless 'Israel,' and the Holy One, Blessed Be He, blesses the Kohanim."

Rabbi Akiva, on the other hand, explains the phrase at face value as referring to the Israelites. During Birkat Kohanim, he believes, "the Kohanim bless 'Israel,' and the Holy One, Blessed Be He, agrees [with their blessing]."[5]

By interpreting the phrase "and I will bless them" as referring to a *bracha* given by God to the Kohanim, Rabbi Yishmael alleviates the textual problem. From his perspective, there is no redundancy of roles. Two separate blessings occur simultaneously. As the priests bless the people, God blesses the priests.

Nonetheless, even according to Rabbi Yishmael, the basic issues remain. What is the nature of the power given to the priests through the ritual of Birkat Kohanim? Why does God, the ultimate arbiter of blessings, need the involvement of the Kohanim?

---

4. Akeidat Yitzchak, Bamidbar, sha'ar 74.
5. Talmud Bavli Chulin 49a.

— **B** —

As we have noted before (see *Bereishit*: Toldot 3, *Approaches* A), the overall concept of interpersonal blessing is so fundamental to Jewish thought that it emerges at the dawn of Jewish history, included as a divine gift in the very first instructions given to the first Hebrew. As God commands the patriarch Avraham to leave his homeland and embark upon his career, God states, "And you will be a blessing."[6]

The rabbis, in the Midrash, interpret this phrase as follows: "Blessings are given to your hand. Until now they were in My hand. I blessed Adam and Noach. From this time on you will bless whom you wish."[7]

By granting man the power to bless, God withdraws and deliberately limits His own range of action. As part of His divine partnership agreement with humanity, God will respect the words spoken by man and reckon with them when He makes His decisions. Man, thus, acquires the power of blessing and prayer.

God Himself grants effectiveness to our *tefillot*, prayers, both on our own behalf and for the welfare of others. So great is the power of heartfelt supplication that our words can even bend God's will.

— **C** —

The specific role played by the Kohanim during the ritual of Birkat Kohanim, however, remains the subject of debate among the scholars.

The Rashbam, for example, explains that the mitzva of Birkat Kohanim is actually a mitzva of *prayer* rather than a mitzva of *blessing*. In contrast to other biblical figures, such as the patriarchs, who actually bless the people before them, the Kohanim instead pray for the bestowal of God's blessings upon the nation. The threefold priestly blessing, therefore, begins with the words "May *God bless* you…"

This approach, continues the Rashbam, enables us to understand the enigmatic final sentence of the passage concerning Birkat Kohanim:

> "And they shall place My name on the children of Israel" – when the Kohanim bless the people in My name and not in their own name…

---

6. Bereishit 12:2.
7. Midrash Rabba Bereishit 39:11.

> "…I will bless them" – I will bless the people in response to the priestly prayer, "May God bless you…."[8]

The Abravanel goes a step further, maintaining that all interpersonal blessings are actually a form of prayer. This sage details three general categories of blessings in Jewish thought:

1. Blessings bestowed by God upon His creations, in the form of actual kindnesses granted to them

2. Blessings bestowed by man upon God, in the form of praise and expressions of gratitude

3. Blessings bestowed by man upon man

This third, man to man category, argues the Abravanel, differs from the other two categories of *bracha* in that nothing is actually "bestowed" by the individual delivering the blessing. Man has no power to actually "bless" another human being; that power is reserved for God alone. Instead, an interpersonal blessing is a prayer to God that He bestow of His kindness upon the recipient of the blessing.[9]

D

A sharp objection to this approach, however, is raised by Rabbi Moshe Alshich. If Birkat Kohanim is simply a prayer to God that He bless the nation, the Alshich argues, the text should be directed towards God rather than towards the people. The *bracha* should read "*God, please bless them and guard them*," rather than "*May God bless you and guard you.*" Instead, suggests the Alshich, the Priestly Blessing is neither, in and of itself, a blessing nor a prayer. The ritual, instead, serves as a practical vehicle through which the Kohanim prepare the people to receive God's blessing.

In order for a divine blessing to take hold, the Alshich argues, those on earth must ready themselves for the phenomenon. They must turn their hearts and minds heavenward, reaching out to God as He reaches out to them. By "placing God's name" upon the nation, the priests effectively turn the nation's attention towards God, readying them to receive God's *bracha*.[10]

---

8. Rashbam, Bamidbar 6:23.
9. Abravanel, Bamidbar 6:22–27.
10. Torat Moshe, Bamidbar 6:22–27.

The Alshich's contention that, according to God's plan, heavenly action requires partnership and participation from below is supported by a number of texts. Nehama Leibowitz cites two examples:[11]

1. "And you shall remove the barrier from your hearts…"[12] – "And God shall remove the barrier from your heart…"[13]

2. "And you shall make for yourselves a new heart and a new spirit…"[14] – "And I [God] shall provide for you a new heart and a new spirit…"[15]

To these examples, we add a third:

3. "You have distinguished the Lord today to be a God for you…"[16] – "And the Lord has distinguished you today to be for Him a treasured people…"[17]

Rabbi Shimshon Raphael Hirsch goes one step further, perceiving the Kohanim reciting the Priestly Blessing as "passive instruments in" – rather than independent contributors to – a pivotal section of the *avoda* (Sanctuary service). "The blessing of the priests does not flow from their well-wishing, their benevolence," he maintains, "but it is part and parcel of their service to the Sanctuary."[18] The exact role of the priests in the blessing, Hirsch maintains, is reflected in a series of rules that apply even today, centuries after the destruction of the Temple:

1. Any priest who does not begin to approach the platform while the reader recites the prayer relating to the *avoda* may not participate in the blessing.[19] This rule underscores the conceptual connection between the Priestly Blessing and the complete service that took place in the Sanctuary.

2. The priests cannot design their own blessing but must adhere to the text recorded in the Torah.[20]

---

11. Nehama Leibowitz, *Iyunim Chadashim B'Sefer Bamidbar* (Jerusalem: Joint Authority for Jewish Zionist Education, 1996), pp. 79–80.
12. Devarim 10:16.
13. Ibid., 30:6.
14. Yechezkel 18:31.
15. Ibid., 36:26.
16. Bamidbar 26:17.
17. Ibid., 26:18.
18. Rabbi Shimshon Raphael Hirsch, Bamidbar 6:23.
19. *Shulchan Aruch*, Orach Chaim 128:8.
20. Ibid., 128:27.

3. If two or more Kohanim are present, a representative of the congregation must publicly invite them to pronounce the blessing.[21]

4. Each word of the blessing is first dictated by the congregational representative and then repeated by the Kohanim (according to some traditions, the first word of the blessing is recited by the Kohanim alone).[22]

These details, Hirsch explains, reflect a process by which the *congregation literally blesses itself with the blessing commanded by God, through the agency of the Kohanim.*[23] The priests have no independent role in this or any other Temple ritual. They simply serve as representatives of the community.

E

At the opposite end of the spectrum, a number of scholars envision a more central role for the Kohanim in the securing of the nation's blessing. Representing this position, the Ba'al Hachinuch declares:

> At the root of this mitzva lies God's desire, in His great goodness, to bless His people via His servants [the Kohanim] who dwell constantly in the House of the Lord and whose thoughts are directed entirely towards His service and whose souls are bound continuously to His worship, *and in their merit [the merit of the Kohanim], the blessing will rest upon them [the nation] and all of their dealings will be blessed....*
>
> And lest you object: If God truly desires [that the nation] be blessed, let Him deliver the blessing directly without need for the Priestly Blessing.... I have stated often that *blessings will rest upon us through the power of the works of our hands*; for His hand is open to all who are prepared and ready to receive His goodness.[24]

The Ba'al Hachinuch goes on to identify, therefore, two pivotal factors at work simultaneously during the ritual of Birkat Kohanim:

1. The nation must be prepared, through refinement of thought and action, to receive God's blessing.

---

21. Ibid., 128:10, 18.
22. Ibid., 128:13 and the Rema there.
23. Rabbi Shimshon Raphael Hirsch, Bamidbar 6:23.
24. *Sefer Hachinuch*, mitzva 367.

2. The blessing must be delivered specifically by the Kohanim, whose righteousness and purity will help ensure that the blessing will rest upon the people.

The position expressed by the Ba'al Hachinuch is certainly in line with the general attitude of many authorities who maintain that, while the gates of prayer are open to all, the words of the righteous possess special power.

In a slightly different vein, a beautiful interpretation was shared with me by my son, Yossi, building upon an observation made by one of his teachers. This scholar maintains that the Kohanim, through their observance of special laws and rules, reflect an ideal of *kedusha*, sanctity, meant to serve as a model for the entire nation. Perhaps, adds Yossi, it is specifically in their capacity as role models that the Kohanim are able to "bless" the community. When the people learn to emulate the sanctified actions of the priests, they increasingly merit the divine gifts reflected in the words of the Priestly Blessing.

F

Finally, another layer to the concept of interpersonal blessings as a whole may be hinted at through a fascinating phenomenon uniquely associated with the mitzva of Birkat Kohanim (see also *Bereishit*: Toldot, *Points to Ponder* 2).

In general, the rabbis mandate that the execution of many positive mitzvot (whether from the Torah or of rabbinic origin) should be introduced by the recitation of a *birkat hamitzva*, a blessing preparatory to the performance of a mitzva. The Kohanim, therefore, upon ascending the podium in the synagogue to bless the community, recite the following preliminary *bracha*: "Blessed art Thou, Lord our God, Who has sanctified us in the sanctity of Aharon [the first High Priest] and commanded us to bless Your people Israel, *with love*."

While this blessing follows the general format of other mitzva blessings, its last two words are unique. No other blessing over a mitzva concludes with the words "with love." We do not say, for example, "to kindle the Sabbath candles, with love," or "to sound the shofar, with love."

This phenomenon can be understood if we view man not only as the *conveyor* of interpersonal blessing but as the *creator* of such blessing. The true role of the Kohanim is then reflected in both the Priestly Blessing and the preliminary blessing before it.

The Priestly Blessing culminates with the summoning of the greatest gift God can bestow upon man: *shalom* (peace). Peace may be a divine gift, but it is created in this world, as part of the God-man partnership, through our mortal efforts.

When the Kohanim bless the congregation "with love," therefore, they are not only bestowing God's blessing but *creating* it. The harmony inherent in their actions concretizes God's gift of peace and roots it in our reality.

So, too, every time we recite an interpersonal blessing, underscoring the love and connection between ourselves and those around us, *we play a role in bringing the blessing of peace, God's greatest blessing, to this world.*

Points to Ponder
I. Conveying and Creating Blessing
Too often, I believe, we lose sight of our partnership role with God in the creation of blessing, with devastating results. As a case in point, I cite a personal experience from the early years of my rabbinic career.

The synagogue in which I then served as rabbi determined that the congregation possessed enough funds to buy *either* tables *or* chairs to be used at communal Shabbat meals. *We simply did not have the funds to purchase both tables and chairs.*

A meeting was called to discuss the problem. When I showed up a little late, I was shocked to find that those present had divided themselves into two vociferous groups: the "chair faction" and the "table faction."

Heated debate quickly developed, and it soon became personal....

One individual who had originally belonged to one faction was even publicly branded a "traitor" for having, upon reflection, switched sides.

While I cannot remember the final outcome of the meeting, I do clearly remember reaching two personal conclusions by the end of the proceedings (actually, one hope and one realization):

1. I hoped that God has a sense of humor, for we are certainly a strange people.

2. I realized how easy it is for us to go off track in our pursuit of positive goals.

In the years that have followed, I have witnessed more examples of this phenomenon than I can count: reasonable people becoming unreasonable in the pursuit of valid, often laudable, goals. In settings such as synagogues, schools and other communal institutions, we often seem to feel that our good intentions and lofty objectives grant us license to treat others poorly. In discussions and debates concerning Israel, religious practice or a myriad of other Jewish concerns, we believe so strongly in our convictions that we are often dismissive of and downright insulting towards those who have the temerity to disagree with us.

The model of Birkat Kohanim serves as a clear reminder that the quality of our shared journey on this planet is determined not only by what we do but by how we do it; not only by what we believe, but by how those beliefs – deeply held as they may be – are expressed.

If we wait for God to bless us, we may well be missing the point. Our behavior towards each other can be the vehicle through which God's greatest blessings find their way to our world.

II. A New/Old Application

The words of the Priestly Blessing have, over time, found another home, quoted in the customary blessing recited by a father over each of his children every Friday night.

The use, however, of this age-old Temple blessing to mark a special moment of connection between parent and child seems a bit strange. Would it not have been more appropriate and meaningful to tailor a special *bracha* for the occasion? Why is the Friday night parental blessing an appropriate setting for the Birkat Kohanim, a blessing originally designed for a very different relationship, under very different circumstances?

If the authorities cited in our study were to visit our homes on Friday night, they might well defend our practice based on their interpretations of the Birkat Kohanim. The Rashbam and the Abravanel, for example, would argue (as they do concerning this "blessing" in its original setting) that the Priestly Blessing is not to be viewed as a blessing at all, but as a prayer. Moved by the warmth of the moment, a father lovingly intones a heartfelt prayer that God should bestow upon his children all the divine gifts enumerated in the words of the Birkat Kohanim. The Alshich would see things differently, suggesting that the father, with his words, turns the hearts of his children towards God, preparing them to receive God's blessings....

The most significant possibility might, however, emerge from the suggestion of my own son, Yossi, who points out that *the brachot are given by those who serve as role models for the ones they bless.* Just as the Kohanim are meant to set a sanctified behavioral standard for the community, a parent is meant to be a role model for his child. The greatest *bracha* that a parent can grant to a child is to model the behaviors towards which that child should aspire, behaviors which, in turn, will enable the child to receive the wonderful blessings that the parent wishes to bestow.

By channeling the words of the Kohanim during our blessings each Friday night, we challenge ourselves to face a significant truth. More than discussions, lectures, heart-to-heart talks or reprimands, the daily practical example we set for our children through our actions educates them. *They learn more from what they see than from what we say.* If, for example, we send our children to Jewish schools but do not engage in Torah study ourselves, our children will learn that "learning Torah" is important – for children, not for adults. If our children see us cheating on taxes and cutting ethical corners in our dealings with others, they will learn to advance their own interests in unethical ways. And if our children observe us demeaning those around us, they will be insensitive to the feelings of those with whom they interact throughout their lives.

In short, if we learn to "bless" our children through the people that we are, chances are, they will grow to make us proud.

5 You Said That Already! (Understanding a Midrash)

Narrative

Parshat Naso closes with a lengthy section describing the *korbanot nesi'im*, the offerings brought by the twelve tribal leaders, on the occasion of the sanctification of the Sanctuary, the Altar and the utensils.

The text enumerates each leader's offerings individually, even though all the offerings are identical.[25]

Questions

Why does the usually terse Torah text repeat itself, apparently unnecessarily?

Why not simply list the offerings once and then inform us that each tribal leader brought the same, identical *korbanot*?

Approaches

— A —

A fascinating Midrashic tradition suggests that although the offerings brought by the leaders were all the same, each leader, representing his tribe, arrived at these *korbanot* through a different path. The Midrash then continues by painstakingly relating the details of the offerings to the character and experience of each specific tribe.[26]

— B —

As is always the case, the Midrash expresses its ideas in an easily remembered, story-like manner. This deceptively simple Midrashic style, however, should never blind us to the powerful lessons the rabbis intend

---

25. Bamidbar 7:1–89.
26. Midrash Rabba Bamidbar 13–14.

to convey. While we may not always get it right, the struggle to uncover the meaning of a Midrash is consistently worthwhile and can often yield surprising results.

C

Confronted with a stark example of uniform ritual, the rabbis inject individuality into the repetitive rite. By doing so, they create a paradigm of religious observance that speaks to us clearly across the ages.

Judaism is built upon the model of detailed universal ritual. While minor differences have certainly developed over distance and time, all observant Jews basically do the same things. I, for example, put on the same tefillin as do my sons and my neighbors, as did my father and grandfathers, and as will, please God, future generations. My family observes the same Shabbat as have families across the globe since the dawn of our national history.

This constancy of ritual is vital to the preservation of our people, to the uniting of Jews throughout the world, to the transmission of pivotal ideas and concepts from generation to generation and to the creation of an ongoing connection between daily life and the Divine (see *Vayikra: Shmini, Points to Ponder*).

Constancy of ritual, however, need not and should not be marked by total uniformity of idea. While there certainly are unvarying concepts meant to be conveyed by each specific mitzva, there is great room for personal exploration within the rituals, as well.

In an oft-quoted passage, the Rambam places a powerful premium upon the process of individual intellectual inquiry into the mitzvot: "It is appropriate for an individual to contemplate the statutes of the Holy Torah and to come to know their essence according to his ability; and that for which he finds no reason…should not become unimportant in his eyes."[27]

We are challenged to make the mitzvot our own through study, analysis and thought-filled practice, and to find personal significance and meaning within each observance. While I put on the same tefillin as do my sons, the meaning of that mitzva is somewhat different for each of us, colored by our own individual personalities, environment and experience.

---

27. Rambam, *Mishneh Torah*, Hilchot Me'ila 8:8.

While my family observes the same Shabbat as countless other Jewish families, our Shabbat is also different from theirs, shaped by our unique, personal worlds.

— **D** —

Through the eyes of the Midrash, the repetitive section that closes Parshat Naso serves as an ongoing imperative. Just as each tribal leader found individual meaning within the same rituals performed by all, so too, we are challenged to create personal connections with the uniform, age-old practices of our people. We may do the same things, but they should mean slightly different things to each of us. If we make the traditions of our people our own, the full significance of those traditions will truly enter our lives.

Beha'alotcha   בהעלותך

CHAPTER 8:1–12:14   פרק ח:א–יב:יד

Parsha Summary

Final preparations, a journey begins, cascading tragedy…

The final instructions prior to the Israelites' departure from Sinai are delivered as God commands Moshe concerning the kindling of the menora, the consecration of the Levi'im, the laws of Pesach Sheini (a second Passover observance for those unable to participate in the first Korban Pesach due to being in a state of tuma or too far from the Sanctuary), the miraculous role of the Clouds of Glory in guiding the nation's wilderness travels, and the construction and use of the silver trumpets.

Finally, the moment of the nation's departure from Sinai arrives, as the Cloud of Glory rises from the Sanctuary, signaling the movement of the camp.

Moshe attempts to convince his father-in-law, Yitro, to join the nation on its journey. Although Yitro initially demurs, the final result of the conversation remains unclear.

The Torah interrupts the flow of the narrative with a two-sentence interjection, set off from the rest of the text by two inverted Hebrew letter nuns.

Immediately upon leaving Sinai, the nation begins to complain. God responds with a devastating heavenly fire that is lifted only as a result of Moshe's prayers.

An even more serious rebellion develops, as "mischief makers" within the camp convince the nation to demand food other than the miraculous manna. Moshe turns in despair to God, bemoaning the difficulty of caring for the people, his inability to lead the nation alone and the impossibility of providing the Israelites with the meat that they desire.

God responds to Moshe's pleas by instructing him to select seventy elders who will be divinely enabled to assist in the leadership of the nation. He also *commands Moshe to inform the people that their demands for meat will be answered – to their everlasting regret.*

Complying with God's instructions, Moshe assembles seventy elders to assist in the leadership of the nation. God allows these elders to share in some of the Holy Spirit resting upon Moshe. Two individuals, Eldad and Medad, who are not among those assembled, also receive some of this Holy Spirit, causing them to prophesy within the camp.

A heaven-sent wind brings an influx of quail into the camp, providing the nation with the meat they so desperately desire. As the Israelites consume these provisions, however, God strikes "a mighty blow against the people," causing many of the nation to die. In response to this tragedy, the location of the rebellion is named Kivrot Hata'ava, "The Graves of Desire."

The parsha ends as Miriam and Aharon, Moshe's sister and brother, publicly criticize Moshe. After reaffirming Moshe's unique relationship with the Divine, God afflicts Miriam with leprosy. When Moshe prays on her behalf, God insists that Miriam observe a seven-day quarantine outside the camp. The nation waits…resuming its journey only upon Miriam's return.

1 Second Chances

Context

As the first anniversary of the Exodus approaches, God commands Moshe to instruct the nation concerning the rituals of the Korban Pesach.

The people comply, offering the *korban* on the afternoon of the fourteenth day of Nissan.

A number of individuals, however, approach Moshe with a problem: "We are *tamei*, ritually impure [and are thus unable to offer the Korban Pesach]…*lama nigara*, why should we be diminished by not offering the Lord's *korban* in its appointed time in the midst of the children of Israel?"[1]

When Moshe turns to God for direction, God responds by introducing the concept of Pesach Sheini, a second Pesach: "If any man becomes contaminated through contact with a human corpse or is on a distant road, he shall make a Korban Pesach for the Lord. In the second month, on the fourteenth day, in the afternoon, shall they make it; with matzot and bitter herbs shall they consume it."[2]

While the full observances of the festival of Pesach are not repeated on Pesach Sheini, the occasion provides a "second chance" for those who were unable to offer the Paschal Lamb on Pesach itself to do so a month later.[3]

Questions

Why does God create a second chance in conjunction with – and only in conjunction with – the holiday of Pesach? The law does not provide, for example, a Yom Kippur Sheini for those unable to fast on Yom Kippur.

---

1. Bamidbar 9:7.
2. Ibid., 9:10–11.
3. Ibid., 9:1–14.

Nor is a Succot Sheini mandated for those who cannot sit in the *succa* on the holiday of Succot. What dimension unique to the festival of Pesach warrants the creation of an official makeup date?

Furthermore, if Pesach Sheini is warranted, why is it not included in the halachic code from the outset? Why doesn't God instruct the nation concerning the laws of Pesach Sheini when He first introduces the Korban Pesach on the eve of the Exodus? Why wait until those who cannot participate on Pesach object?

Finally, exactly who is allowed to participate in Pesach Sheini? While legitimate inability to offer the Korban Pesach at the appointed time is the apparent criteria, the Torah's definition of such inability is a puzzlingly restrictive. *Why limit the observance of Pesach Sheini only to those who are ritually impure or who are at a distance from the Sanctuary at the time of the offering of the Korban Pesach?* What of those individuals who are constrained from taking part in the Korban Pesach for other legitimate reasons? Is someone too ill to participate on Pesach, for example, included in the opportunities offered by Pesach Sheini? If not, why not? If so, why doesn't the Torah say so?

Approaches

A

Our analysis of Pesach Sheini begins with the most basic of the questions presented. What is the rationale behind this phenomenon? Why in the case of Pesach, and only in the case of Pesach, is a second chance for at least partial observance offered within the halachic code?

An answer to this question is potentially derived from an unexpected source that can help reframe and deepen our understanding of the Pesach festival itself.

Consider the approach mandated by Jewish law towards an individual who wishes to convert to Judaism (see *Shmot*: Vayakhel-Pekudei 4). Hesitation, caution and discouragement are the order of the day. Armed with the belief that those outside our faith tradition are not required to be like us, we confront the candidate with a sobering truth and an obvious question: *It is hard to be a Jew. Why, if you are under no obligation to do so, would you want to take this difficult step?*

Not so well known, however, is the exact form that this initial caution is meant to take. Contrary to expectations, we do not plunge immediately into a discussion of the mitzvot; we do not emphasize the difficult responsibilities and monumental life changes that the potential convert proposes to accept.

Instead, the Talmud lays out a vastly different introductory path for the would-be Jew:

> The rabbis taught: [if a prospective] proselyte comes to convert in the present era, we say to him: "What did you perceive that prompted you to come? Do you not know that Israel [i.e., the Jewish people] is, in this day, afflicted, oppressed, downtrodden and harassed – and that hardships are frequently visited upon them?" If the individual responds: "I know, and I am not even worthy [to share in their hardships]," we accept him immediately [as a potential convert worthy of education].[4]

Only after this interchange has taken place, continues the Talmud, do we begin to teach the candidate about the enormous responsibilities inherent in the halachic code.[5]

Why must the potential convert's formal journey towards Judaism open with a discussion of the historical persecution of the Jewish nation? Why not strike to the core issue facing the candidate immediately: his central challenge of *kabbalat ol mitzvot*, an understanding and acceptance of the yoke (the obligations carried by) the commandments?

Apparently the rabbis intuited a prerequisite to the acceptance of mitzvot. *The first step towards Jewishness is the step of "belonging."* Only someone who is willing to be part of the historical saga of the Jewish nation, who commits to share in that nation's challenges, to mourn its losses and celebrate its triumphs – only that person can begin to accept the Jewish faith as his or her own. In short, potential candidates must be willing to throw their lot in with the Jewish people, whatever trials that choice might produce, whatever difficulties might ensue.

---

4. Talmud Bavli Yevamot 47a.
5. Ibid.

---- B ----

What, however, is the basis of this rabbinic position? What source can Talmud scholars cite to support their confident claim that conversion to Judaism must begin with the choice to "belong"?

The answer, it would seem, is powerfully simple. The rabbis believe that the initial journey of an individual who wishes to join the Jewish nation must mirror the initial journey of the nation itself.

As we have noted before (see *Shmot*: Vayakhel-Pekudei 4), the birth of the Jewish nation unfolds in two formative stages: the Exodus and Revelation.

Before our ancestors could arrive at Sinai, they had to be willing to leave Egypt, to throw their lot in with a fledgling people traveling towards an unknown future, under the guidance of a relative stranger. Only those willing to take a chance on the Jewish people are privileged to stand in God's presence at Sinai when the Jewish nation is born.

A potential convert to Judaism, apparently, must undergo the two-step transformative process that defined the birth of the nation he wishes to join. The rituals of the conversion process itself are derived from the experiences of the Israelites immediately prior to and during the Revelation at Sinai (see *Bereishit*: Vayeishev 4, *Approaches* B; *Shmot*: Yitro 1, *Points to Ponder*; *Shmot*: Vayakhel-Pekudei 4).[6] *The first step towards those rituals, however, like the first step of our national journey, is rooted in the Exodus.*

Before a potential convert can "arrive at Sinai," before he can begin to encounter God's law, he must first "leave Egypt." He must consciously separate himself from the world he has known and affiliate with the Jewish nation. This act of affiliation, mirroring the Israelites' Exodus experience, launches his journey towards Judaism.

---- C ----

We can now begin to understand the rationale for the creation of Pesach Sheini. So elemental is the Korban Pesach, so fundamental to our Jewish identity and experience, that God provides a second chance for those who are initially unable to participate. Pesach is, after all, where we begin as a people. No one should miss out on the yearly renewal of our shared

---

6. Talmud Bavli Kritot 9a.

affiliation. No one should be excluded as we re-create our first steps together.

The journey towards Jewishness opens with the step of belonging. Each year, as that journey is reaffirmed, every member of the community must be given the opportunity to join.

D

Our analysis of the basis for Pesach Sheini may well shed light on a series of perplexing laws concerning this festival of second chances.

As noted above, the Torah seems to limit participation in Pesach Sheini to those who are ritually impure or at a distance from the Sanctuary on Pesach. The rabbis, however, interpret the biblical mandate much more extensively. In two sentences in the Mishna, they increase the reach of this makeup festival:

> An individual who is ritually impure or at a distance and did not perform the first [Korban Pesach] shall perform the second [on Pesach Sheini].
>
> [An individual who otherwise] erred or was legitimately constrained from performing the first [Korban Pesach] shall perform the second [on Pesach Sheini].[7]

The legal verdict of the Mishna is clear. The laws of Pesach Sheini apply not only to those who are impure or at a distance, but to all those who are legitimately constrained from participating in the Korban Pesach at its appointed time. This conclusion (and the Mishna's own construction), however, raises a much more difficult question. If Pesach Sheini applies to all those who are excluded from participation on Pesach, why does the Torah specify the categories of *tuma* and distance? Why not simply apply the laws of Pesach Sheini in broad strokes from the outset, to anyone who legitimately missed the Korban Pesach?

The Mishna itself answers this question with a terse response that is interpreted differently by different authorities.[8] The Rambam's formulation

---

7. Mishna Pesachim 9:1.
8. Ibid. Note Talmud Bavli Pesachim 92b and the comments of the Lechem Mishneh on the Rambam; *Mishneh Torah*, Hilchot Korban Pesach 5:2.

of the law, accepted by many, can be summarized as follows: All individuals who are legitimately constrained for any reason from participating in the Korban Pesach in its appointed time are obligated to offer a *korban* on Pesach Sheini. The Torah, however, distinguishes in the area of *punishment* between those who cannot participate on Pesach because of impurity or distance and those whose inability stems from other sources:

1. An individual whose legitimate failure to participate in the Korban Pesach arises out of a reason *other than impurity or distance* is liable to the punishment of *karet*, excision from the community, if he deliberately chooses not to take advantage of the second chance offered to him by Pesach Sheini.

2. An individual, however, who fails to participate in the Korban Pesach *because of impurity or distance* is not liable for the punishment of *karet* even if he deliberately fails to offer a *korban* on Pesach Sheini. Such an individual, the Rambam notes, "has already been exempted from the punishment of *karet* on Pesach itself."[9]

At face value, this halachic verdict seems totally counterintuitive. While Pesach Sheini applies to all who are unable to partake in the Korban Pesach at its appointed time, *the law is most lenient concerning the two categories that are specifically mentioned in the Torah: ritual impurity and distance.* Individuals who fall into these categories are exempt from punishment even if they deliberately ignore the opportunities presented by Pesach Sheini. All others, however, who legitimately miss participation on Pesach are liable for punishment if they deliberately fail to observe Pesach Sheini.

Wouldn't we expect the opposite to be true? Shouldn't the law show greatest severity towards those whose obligation in Pesach Sheini derives directly from the text?

So puzzling is the Rambam's codification of the law that the Ra'avad immediately objects: "Now [the Rambam] contradicts himself! What difference is there between impure or distant individuals who deliberately ignore the obligations of Pesach Sheini and others who deliberately ignore those same obligations?"[10]

---

9. Rambam, *Mishneh Torah*, Hilchot Korban Pesach 5:2.
10. Ra'avad commenting on the Rambam, *Mishneh Torah*, Hilchot Korban Pesach 5:2.

E

Our above-outlined discussion concerning the origins of Pesach Sheini, however, provides an approach towards the Rambam's halachic formulation based on the following assumptions:

1. The obligation to participate in the Korban Pesach derives from the root concept of affiliation with the community. All individuals "affiliated" with the Jewish community at the time of the Pesach Sacrifice automatically become fully obligated to share in the ritual.

2. An individual who, at the time of the first Korban Pesach, is fully affiliated with the community but who, for tangential reasons, cannot participate in the Korban Pesach at its appointed time (e.g., someone who is ill) nonetheless remains obligated in the ritual. This obligation derives from his connection to the community on Pesach itself. For such an individual, participation in Pesach Sheini becomes a full obligation, providing a second chance to fulfill a responsibility already incurred at the time of the first Korban Pesach.

3. In response to the objections of the group that approaches Moshe, however, God defines two categories of individuals who are essentially excluded from participation in the Korban Pesach. *Their exclusion is not tangential but rises out of a fundamental separation from the community at the time of Pesach.* These individuals – the ritually impure, who are spiritually separate, and the distant, who are geographically detached – never became obligated in the Pesach sacrifice in the first place and are thus completely exempt from potential punishment regarding the Korban. Pesach Sheini emerges for these individuals, as a unique halachic construct: *an obligatory opportunity*.

As a result of the historic request outlined in the text, the law affords individuals who legitimately find themselves separated from the community on Pesach with the *opportunity to affiliate* at a later date. Once offered, this opportunity becomes obligatory as the Torah enjoins these individuals to take advantage of the second chance for affiliation that Pesach Sheini represents. There is, however, no punishment for failure. The exemption from punishment reflects the fact that Pesach Sheini initially originates as an *opportunity* rather than an *obligation* for these individuals.

F

Two other fascinating cases considered by the Talmud may well connect to our analysis of the Rambam's halachic codification. What is the law, the rabbis ask, concerning an individual who converts to Judaism or a child who reaches the age of halachic responsibility during the month between Pesach and Pesach Sheini? Are such individuals obligated to bring an offering on Pesach Sheini or are they exempt because they never incurred any obligation at all at the time of Pesach?

While differing opinions are offered in the Talmud,[11] the Rambam is once again emphatic: both the convert and the young adult are obligated in the rituals of Pesach Sheini.[12] Even individuals who were not practicing Jews at the time of Pesach are to be given the opportunity to affiliate with the community once such affiliation becomes possible.

If our analysis is correct, however, such individuals should be exempt from punishment if they fail, even deliberately, to observe Pesach Sheini. The festival should emerge for them, as it does for the impure and the distant, as an "obligatory opportunity." Unfortunately, however, the Rambam does not comment on the issue of punishment for the convert and the young adult. No proof can therefore be adduced either for or against our arguments.

G

Finally, we turn to our last remaining question concerning Pesach Sheini. Why aren't the laws of this festival of second chances included in the halachic code from the outset? Why does God delay the transmission of these edicts until objections are raised by those unable to participate on Pesach itself?

A fascinating, well-known answer to this question is suggested in the Midrash and quoted by Rashi. God deliberately delays the transmission of the laws of Pesach Sheini in order to reward the individuals who approach Moshe concerning the Korban Pesach. So great is the merit of these individuals that God allows a section of the halachic code to develop as a result of their efforts.[13]

---

11. Talmud Bavli Pesachim 93a.
12. Rambam, *Mishneh Torah*, Hilchot Korban Pesach 5:7.
13. Sifrei, Bamidbar 68.

The Midrash, however, fails to define the rationale for such overwhelming reward. Why do these individuals deserve to have a section of Torah text recorded in their honor?

---- H ----

Compounding the mystery is the appearance, later in the book of Bamidbar, of a strangely similar event that seems to give rise to the very same issues.

After God prepares the nation for entry into the Land of Israel by delineating the rules that will govern the division of the land, four women, the daughters of Tzelafchad, approach Moshe with an objection: "Our father died in the wilderness…and he had no sons. *Lama yigara*, why should the name of our father be diminished among his family because he had no son? Give us a possession among our father's brothers."[14]

Once again, Moshe turns to God for guidance and, once again, God responds by outlining a new set of halachic guidelines:

> If a man will die and he has no son, you shall cause his inheritance to pass to his daughter. If he has no daughter, you shall give his inheritance to his brothers. If he has no brothers you shall give his inheritance to the brothers of his father. If there are no brothers of his father, you shall give his inheritance to his relative who is closest to him of his family.[15]

Once again, the rabbis ask, why weren't these rules conveyed to the nation from the outset? Why wait until the daughters of Tzelafchad object?

And once again, Rashi quotes the rabbinic response: "The passages of inheritance should have been written through Moshe, our teacher, but [since] the daughters of Tzelafchad were meritorious, it was written through them."[16]

And once again, we ask: Wherein lies the great merit of the protagonists in this episode? Why does God deliberately delay the transmission of a pivotal set of laws in order to pay tribute to the daughters of Tzelafchad?

---

14. **Bamidbar** 27:1–4.
15. **Ibid.**, 27:5–11.
16. **Talmud** Bavli Sanhedrin 8a.

I

As is often the case, the Torah embeds its answer in the text.

An uncanny linguistic parallel marks the seemingly disparate narratives of Pesach Sheini and the daughters of Tzelafchad. The heroes of both stories employ strikingly similar language as they raise their problems to Moshe:

> *Lama nigara*, why should we be diminished by not offering the Lord's *korban* in its appointed time…[17]

> *Lama yigara*, why should the name of our father be diminished among his family…[18]

In each of these episodes the petitioners perceive participation in a communal mitzva to be an opportunity, missed only at great cost. *We will be personally diminished*, they maintain, through our inability to take part.

Therein lies their greatness….

Legitimately excused from responsibility for the Pesach ritual, the petitioners who approach Moshe will not rest easy. *Exemption*, they argue, *is not an option. Why should we be denied the gift of participation? Why should the enriching experience of the Korban Pesach be disallowed to us?*

Facing their nuclear family's exclusion from inheritance in the Land of Israel, the daughters of Tzelafchad refuse to remain silent. *Why should our family be denied a permanent legacy in the land of our people? Why should the name of our father be erased from the roster of his brothers?*

In each of these cases, the divine legal verdict is clear: God provides those who mourn the loss of religious opportunity with new opportunity for fulfillment.

Even further, however, through a delicate interweaving of thought and law, in both the narrative of Pesach Sheini and in the narrative of inheritance, a more pervasive message emerges: when you perceive participation with your people to be a cherished gift worth fighting for; when you feel diminished by an inability to take part in Torah ritual;

---

17. Bamidbar 9:7.
18. Ibid., 27:4.

when you view a mitzva as an opportunity and not as an obligation, you are worthy of a portion of the Torah inscribed in your name.

Points to Ponder

Our age of immediacy – in which time is measured in milliseconds, easier is automatically viewed as better and goals must be instantly attained – inexorably shapes our religious attitudes. We find ourselves seeking quicker prayer services, devising shortcuts in holiday preparations and engaging in rote, undemanding ritual observance. We mark Pesach with mass exoduses to ever more exotic vacation spots, hire others to build our *succot*, buy prepackaged Purim *mishloach manot*…anything to make our lives a little easier as we balance multiple obligations and, at the same time, struggle to fulfill the letter, if not the spirit, of Jewish law.

In the process, however, we miss the whole point.

For while these commandments are obligations, they are also *opportunities*: prayer an *opportunity* to talk to God, Shabbat an *opportunity* to regain perspective, the holidays *opportunities* for shared family experience. All mitzvot are *opportunities* to glimpse the world that lies beyond, to connect with God, to sanctify our existence.

With the investment of time and effort, the observance of the mitzvot can deeply enrich our personal and family lives.

When we learn to view mitzvot as *opportunities* and not as *burdens*, we too will merit inscription in the unfolding scroll of our nation's story.

2 Fellow Travelers

Narrative

As the moment of the nation's departure from Sinai fast approaches, the text describes the role to be played by Clouds of Glory in directing the nation's imminent wilderness journeys. These clouds, which surrounded the Sanctuary by day, ascended to announce impending travel and descended to indicate encampment.[1]

In a short paragraph marked by great detail, the Torah presents a number of possible travel-encampment permutations:

> When the cloud lingered upon the Sanctuary *for many days*, the children of Israel…would not journey.[2]
>
> And sometimes the cloud would be on the Sanctuary for *a number of days*…[3]
>
> And sometimes the cloud would remain *from evening till morning*, and the cloud would ascend in the morning and they would journey; or *for a day and a night*, and the cloud would ascend and they would journey.[4]
>
> Or *for two days, or a month, or a year* [according to Rashi], when the cloud would linger over the Sanctuary, resting upon it, the children of Israel would encamp and not journey, and when it ascended they would journey.[5]

In addition to these possible combinations, the paragraph is also marked by a thrice-repeated refrain (with a slight variation):

---

1. Bamidbar 9:15–17.
2. Ibid., 9:19.
3. Ibid., 9:20.
4. Ibid., 9:21.
5. Ibid., 9:22.

According to the word of the Lord would the children of Israel travel and according to the word of the Lord would they encamp....[6]

...According to the word of the Lord would they encamp and according to the word of the Lord would they travel.[7]

According to the word of the Lord would they encamp and according to the word of the Lord would they travel.[8]

Questions

Is all this text really necessary?

The second sentence of this paragraph clearly states: "And *according to the ascension of the cloud* from atop the Tent, afterwards the children of Israel would journey, and in *the place where the cloud rested* there the children of Israel would encamp."[9]

This declaration seems to provide all of the information needed: *The people traveled as indicated by the cloud. When it ascended, they journeyed; when it rested, they encamped.* What does the rest of the paragraph add? In place of a nine-sentence passage, the Torah could have gotten its message across with one simple statement.

What, in addition, is the purpose of the repeated refrain stating that the nation traveled and encamped "at the word of God"? This point is so self-evident from the rest of the paragraph that it did not have to be stated at all, much less three times.

Approaches

— A

Many commentaries, including the Ramban and the Sforno, struggle to explain each of the travel-encampment combinations recorded in the text. Common to their interpretations is the belief that every example listed in the Torah further demonstrates the nation's willingness to journey only at God's command, in spite of great difficulty and hardship. Even if, for

---

6. Ibid., 9:18.
7. Ibid., 9:20.
8. Ibid., 9:23.
9. Ibid., 9:17.

example, the people were required to "linger for many days"[10] in a desolate location, leave a fertile camping ground suddenly after "a number of days,"[11] or travel after a respite of only "a day and a night,"[12] the Israelites, nevertheless, obeyed God's will.[13]

The Ramban also emphasizes the great difficulty created by the uncertainty of the journey. The Israelites had no way of predicting how long they would remain in any one location. At times they might, for example, completely unload their burdens and set up camp in anticipation of an extended stay, only to have the cloud precipitously rise and their travels resume without warning.[14]

B

Still problematic, however, is the repeated refrain concerning the Israelites' travel and encampment *at the word of God*. Why is this seemingly superfluous statement recorded no fewer than three times in a nine-sentence paragraph?

C

Perhaps this repeated assertion actually serves as the key to a deeper understanding of the paragraph before us. As we have noted, the first steps of our national journey from Sinai create the prototype for our travels across the face of history. From this perspective, the Torah's threefold declaration that the Israelites traveled and encamped "at the word of God" establishes a powerful, ongoing reality.[15]

Our nation's early path is clearly directed by God via the Clouds of Glory. *While those clouds eventually disappear, however, the continuing imperative to travel "at the word of God" does not.*

---

10. Ibid., 9:19.
11. Ibid., 9:20.
12. Ibid., 9:21.
13. Ramban, Bamidbar 9:19–22; Sforno, Bamidbar 20–22.
14. Ramban, Bamidbar 9:19–22.
15. An argument can even be made that the threefold repetition of the declaration symbolically establishes a historical *chazaka* (status quo, or new reality). In Jewish law, when a phenomenon is repeated three times, a *chazaka* is established that must be reckoned with.

From pillar to post, from one land to another across the face of a long, turbulent history, the descendents of those early Israelites will be called upon to continue their journey "at the word of God." Their enduring loyalty to an ancient tradition will earn them the hatred of a cruel, inhospitable world. At times they will "linger for many days," temporarily gaining a degree of stability in one particular location. At other times, their stay will last only "a day and a night," as they are not permitted even the briefest respite from the hands of their persecutors.

And yet, they will stubbornly travel along their uncertain path, the faithful among them clinging to the belief that, while He may be hidden from view, God continues to guide their steps towards a glorious destiny; that, if they steadfastly travel "at the word of God," the day will come when, against all odds, their journey will lead them home.

Points to Ponder

With no Clouds of Glory to direct us, we must discern God's will on our own….

What does it mean to "travel at the word of God" in an era when return to our homeland is within our reach? Have those of us who continue to live in exiles of choice voluntarily forfeited our place in the monumental national journey that began at Sinai?

These difficult questions should, at the very least, be raised, individually and communally, by diaspora Jewry.

Perhaps an honest confrontation with the issues will lead some of us to take the obvious step along the path: to make aliya, or, at least, to encourage our children to do so. Perhaps others, unable or unwilling to take such dramatic steps, will be moved to strengthen their connection with and activism on behalf of the State of Israel.

One way or the other, the historic question must be faced. At a time when our nation's journey has once again brought us home, will we continue to be fellow travelers?

3 Of Booths and Clouds: A Retrospective

I still remember my disappointment when I learned as a child that the rabbis did not agree with my understanding of the mitzva of *succa*.[1]

This mitzva had always been one of my favorites. Not only because the building of our family *succa* provided me with an opportunity to spend time with my father, z"l, but also because I felt that, somehow, the *succa* enabled me to touch history. Here I was, building and living in a *succa*, just as the Israelites had built and lived in *succot* while wandering in the wilderness; just as Jews had built and lived in *succot* in countless eras, in countless settings, across the face of history.

But then I learned to my chagrin that things were not so simple. True, no less a sage than Rabbi Akiva agreed with my assessment of the symbolism of the *succa*, maintaining that our booths represent the *succot mamash*, the actual booths built by the Israelites in the desert. Rabbi Eliezer, however, disagreed, insisting instead that our *succot* symbolize the Ananei Hakavod, the miraculous Clouds of Glory that surrounded the Israelites during their wilderness travels.[2] Furthermore, I soon discovered that subsequent scholars, from Rashi to the Tur to the *Shulchan Aruch*, all agree with Rabbi Eliezer's assessment that our *succot* represent these Clouds of Glory and not the physical booths built by the Israelites.[3]

For years, I remained troubled by this rabbinic approach. Why, I wondered, do the majority of rabbis reject Rabbi Akiva's obvious, practical explanation for the mitzva of *succa* and instead opt for Rabbi Eliezer's more esoteric path? Why can't the booths we build on the holiday of Succot simply represent the physical booths built by our forefathers during their wilderness wandering?

---

1. The mitzva to dwell in "temporary" booths over the Succot festival.
2. Talmud Bavli Succa 11b.
3. Rashi, Vayikra 24:33; Arba Turim, Orach Chaim 645; *Shulchan Aruch*, Orach Chaim 645:1.

I did consider the clear possibility, suggested by many, that the rabbinic choice is textually motivated. In the book of Vayikra, God commands: "And you shall dwell in *succot* for seven days," *ki va'succot hoshavti et B'nei Yisrael b'hotzi'i otam mei'Eretz Mitzraim*, "because I caused the children of Israel to dwell in *succot* when I took them out of the land of Egypt."[4]

By stating that God "*caused* the children of Israel to dwell in *succot*," the text arguably alludes to a God-created phenomenon (such as the Clouds of Glory), rather than a man-created phenomenon (such as the booths of the Israelites) as the basis for the mitzva of *succa*.

This argument, however, never seemed completely compelling. Rabbi Akiva, after all, maintains his position in spite of the textual evidence. Perhaps one can argue that God "causes the Israelites" to dwell in booths simply by leading them into the wilderness, thereby denying them permanent habitation.

My questions remained with me until this year, when a startling conversation in the Jewish and secular media prompted me to reconsider my objections to Rabbi Eliezer's explanation for the mitzva of *succa*.

The conversation to which I refer was launched by a study in the September/October 2011 issue of *Moment* magazine. In this study, fourteen Jewish thinkers were asked to respond to the following query: "Only a third to half of American Jews today believe in an almighty deity. *Can there be Judaism without a belief in God*?"[5]

The answers were split.

Once raised, this question was further probed in various venues, including a *Washington Post* article entitled "Judaism without God? Yes, Say American Atheists."[6] This article featured quotes from various observers, including the following from one communally involved Jewish atheist: "Atheism and Judaism are not contradictory, so to have an atheist in a Jewish congregation isn't an issue or a challenge or a problem. It is par for the course. It is our tradition to question God from top to bottom." Also cited in the *Washington Post* article were the results of a study conducted by Robert Putnam and David Campbell, authors of the book *American*

---

4. Vayikra 24:33.
5. Daphna Berman, et al., "Can There Be Judaism without Belief in God?," *Moment*, September/October 2011.
6. Kimberly Winston, "Judaism without God? Yes, Say American Atheists," *Washington Post*, September 23, 2011.

Grace,[7] who found that fully one half of all American Jews doubt God's existence.

A provocative observation offered years earlier by the award-winning investigative journalist and committed Jew Stephen Fried, in his popular book *The New Rabbi*, aptly predicts these sentiments: "*In Judaism, belief in God is optional* [my italics], something you may wrestle with your entire life. But respect for and fascination with the Torah, the first record of men and women's struggles with belief in God, is not optional."[8]

The question could well be asked: *How has Judaism, the major source of monotheistic belief in the Western world, a religion clearly founded on the belief in one God, come to allow, in the popular mind, for a dismissal of that belief?* How have we arrived at the point where the question "Can Judaism exist without a belief in God" can even be raised? Note that the *Moment* magazine survey did not ask, "Can Jews be part of the Jewish community without believing in God?" Asked, instead, is whether or not *Judaism, as a faith tradition*, can exist without belief. Asked about any other religion, this question would seem absurd. Would anyone even consider asking whether or not Catholicism can exist absent a belief in God; whether or not Islam can exist absent a belief in God? Yet, somehow, when asked about Judaism, this question, strangely enough, apparently strikes a resonant chord.

The explanations for this phenomenon are manifold, complex and rooted in certain realities of our circumstance and faith.

Firstly, while one can certainly become a Jew by choice, Jewish identity is, in the main, biologically determined. An individual can be born and identify as a Jew, as a member of the Jewish people, without necessarily identifying with that people's historical belief system. Ethnicity, nationality and family tradition often play a greater role than religion in defining who is a Jew today.

Secondly, Jews are raised in a tradition that encourages intellectual search, critical thinking and constant questioning. Each letter of the Torah is subject to scrutiny, discussion and debate. In such an atmosphere, it is

---

7. Robert D. Putnam, David E. Campbell, *American Grace: How Religion Divides and Unites Us* (New York: Simon and Schuster, 2010).
8. Stephen Fried, *The New Rabbi: A Congregation Searches for Its Leader* (New York: Bantam Books, 2002), p. 93.

understandable that even a committed Jew's relationship to God is not a given, but, instead, the focus of constant personal struggle.

Finally, and most importantly, over these past decades a seismic shift has taken place in the education of the modern Jewish community without our conscious realization. Jewish parents, educators and clergy of all denominations, faced with the challenges emerging from increasingly secular surroundings, have fought back with the vast intellectual wealth embedded in Jewish tradition. Recognizing our progeny's or congregants' discomfort with the realm of spirituality (a discomfort that we, ourselves, often share), we have come to preach to the head rather than to the heart. Powerful messages are conveyed about ethics, morality and Torah law, but God Himself is rarely mentioned at home, in school or from the pulpit. As a result a child can, in our time, grow up in an affiliated Jewish home, attend a Jewish school, participate in synagogue services regularly, yet never engage in a serious discussion about belief or even about the existence of God. *In a real sense, God has been absent from our Jewish teaching.*

We can now begin to understand, perhaps, the rabbinic embrace of Rabbi Eliezer's position that the booths built for the Succot festival represent the Ananei Hakavod, the miraculous Clouds of Glory, rather than the *succot mamash*, the actual booths built by the Israelites themselves.

The holiday of Succot falls at a critical time in a Jew's annual spiritual journey: at the beginning of the year, as he leaves the rarefied atmosphere of the High Holy Days and reenters the "outside world." In this process of reentry, the *succa* serves as the prism through which that world is meant to be seen. Powerful messages are conveyed by this frail booth, concerning vulnerability, the inexorable passage of time, the temporary nature of our physical accomplishments, the permanence of the Jewish journey across the face of history and more.

One aspect of the *succa*, however, is most important to the rabbis. *The prism through which we view our world, they maintain, must be a "God-present" prism. The message of the* succa *must be clear: as we encounter and interact with the events that touch our lives, God must be factored into the equation.*

Our respective *succot* will differ. Some (and I have always envied these individuals) will see the world through the prism of *emuna temima*, an unquestioning and uncompromising belief in God's presence and in

His personal, guiding hand in their lives. Others, like me, will struggle each day with the overwhelming questions that arise from our efforts to correlate Judaism's basic belief in a just, ever-present Creator with the seemingly conflicting evidence that often emerges from a puzzling world.

Whatever the nature of our *succot*, however, they cannot be only *succot mamash*, man-made booths. We cannot afford to see the world solely as the product of human endeavor. Each year, the prism through which we view our lives, our challenges, our responsibilities, our surroundings, our children, the Land of Israel and more must be the Ananei Hakavod, the "God-present" prism through which our forefathers saw their world as our nation's journey began.

4 Blow Your Horn

Context
Finally, the nation stands poised to leave Sinai and begin its historic journey. One final set of divine directives, however, must yet be given.

God turns to Moshe and states: "Make for yourself two *chatzotzrot kesef*, trumpets of silver; of beaten work shall you make them; and they shall be for you for the summoning of the assembly and to cause the camps to journey."[1]

Sounded by the priests, these silver trumpets will be used to herald a journey, gather the nation, strengthen the people in the face of challenge and mark the commemoration of festivals and celebrations.[2]

Based upon the specific language "Make for yourself," the rabbis discern a striking distinction between the trumpets and all other utensils fashioned by Moshe in the wilderness. While other utensils were appropriate for use in future generations, Moshe's trumpets were his alone, to be used only during his lifetime. Each future generation would have to fashion its trumpets anew.[3]

Questions
One can't help but be a bit disappointed by the final laws given at Sinai....

Firstly, why do the trumpets merit mention in the Torah text at all?

The Altar, the Menora, the Table and other similar utensils described in the text are clearly unique, sanctified objects to be used in conjunction with the worship of God in the Sanctuary. Their inclusion in the Torah is certainly understandable.

---

1. Bamidbar 10:2.
2. Ibid., 10:1–10.
3. Midrash Tanchuma Beha'alotcha 10.

The trumpets, however, seem to be primarily utilitarian in nature: "And they shall be for you for the summoning of the assembly and to cause the camps to journey."[4] Other practical tools must have been fashioned by the Israelites over the course of their wilderness journeys. Why are only the trumpets mentioned?

Secondly, the *chatzotzrot* occupy a powerfully pivotal place in the text. The laws concerning their creation and use represent the last directives given by God before the Jewish national journey begins. One would expect the final edicts transmitted at Sinai to be particularly significant, culminating commandments, designed to set the nation on its way. Even if the instructions concerning the *chatzotzrot* do belong in the text, why are they placed here? Couldn't God have found a more significant mitzva with which to launch our nation's journey?

Finally, why are the *chatzotzrot* generation-specific? Why are we not permitted to pass them down, like all other sacred utensils, from one generation to the next?

Approaches

A

A close reading of the text reveals that there is much more to the function of the *chatzotzrot* than first meets the eye. While the initially recorded use of the trumpets does seem utilitarian, their later recorded role is much more complex:

> And when you go to wage war in your land against the adversary that oppresses you, then you shall sound an alarm with the trumpets, *and you shall be recalled before the Lord, your God, and you shall be saved from your foes.*
>
> And on the day of your gladness, and on your festivals, and on your new moons, you shall sound the trumpets over your burnt offerings and over your feast peace offerings; *and they shall be a remembrance for you before your God*; I am the Lord, your God.[5]

---

4. Bamidbar 10:2.
5. Ibid., 10:9–10.

The sounding of the trumpets described in these passages is far from ordinary. Here, the *chatzotzrot* are apparently used to communicate with God, their sounding a form of wordless prayer, designed to pierce the heavens.

B

As our understanding of the role of the *chatzotzrot* expands, a fascinating pattern begins to emerge.

The Torah identifies two distinct sounds created by the *chatzotzrot*:

1. The *tekia*: A long, unbroken sounding of the trumpet; associated in the text with congregational assembly, leadership assembly and communal celebration.

2. The *terua*: A broken sounding of the trumpet; associated with a call to travel and the advent of war.

Apparently, even the initially mentioned usage of the trumpets is not solely utilitarian. *The sounds of the chatzotzrot consistently mirror the mindset of the people at the moment of their sounding.* Times of comfort and stability – such as occasions of assembly and celebration – are marked by a *tekia*, an unbroken sound of certainty. Times of uncertainty, challenge and distress, on the other hand – such as occasions of journey and war – are associated primarily with the *terua*, a broken, uncertain sound.

C

The concept of connection between ritually created sounds and the mindset of those sounding and hearing them finds further support from another, more familiar halachic source, recognizable to most Jews.

The broken and unbroken blasts created by the *chatzotzrot* are the same sounds created by the blowing of the shofar on the yearly "Day of Judgment," the festival of Rosh Hashana, the "head" of the Jewish year. In Temple times, in fact, the sounding of the shofar was actually accompanied by the simultaneous sounding of the trumpets.[6]

While both the *tekia* and the *terua* are sounded on Rosh Hashana, however, only the latter is clearly connected to the festival in the Torah text. So central, in fact, is the association between the broken sound of the shofar and Rosh Hashanah that the Torah refers to this holy day as Yom

---

6. Rambam, *Mishneh Torah*, Hilchot Shofar 1:2.

Terua, a day of *terua*,⁷ and Zichron Terua, a remembrance of *terua*.⁸ The message is clear. The aura of Rosh Hashana, the yearly Day of Judgment, is captured by the *terua*, the broken, uncertain sound of the shofar.

The deep bond between Rosh Hashana and the *terua* sound underlies the rabbinic attempt in the Talmud to define the actual nature of this broken blast. Tellingly, the rabbis identify the *terua* either as a series of nine short, staccato blasts, symbolizing an individual in the act of *sobbing*, or as a series of three somewhat longer sounds (a series known to us as a *shevarim*), symbolizing an individual in the act of *sighing*.⁹ According to both positions, the broken sound of the shofar dramatically depicts the image of a "broken" individual, standing in spiritual and emotional distress before the Heavenly Court.¹⁰

Just as the notes of the *chatzotzrot* mirror the internal state of the Israelites at the time of the trumpets' sounding, so, too, the blasts of the shofar reflect the internal turmoil of each individual standing on Rosh Hashana, in judgment before God.

D

The message emerging from this imagery, however, strikes even deeper. Once we thematically connect the trumpet and shofar blasts, further consideration of the sounding of the shofar on Rosh Hashana can help us better understand the role of the *chatzotzrot*. The blasts of the shofar, after all, are not meant to simply mirror the internal struggle of an individual standing in judgment before God. *These sounds are instead designed to awaken, cultivate and develop that very struggle.*

The halachic verdict in a fascinating rabbinic debate mirrors this understanding of the mitzva. Some authorities maintain that the blessing to be recited before the sounding of the shofar should read, "Blessed art Thou, Lord our God, Who has sanctified us with His commandments and commanded us to *sound the shofar*."¹¹

---

7. Bamidbar 29:1.
8. Vayikra 23:24.
9. Talmud Bavli Rosh Hashana 33b.
10. On a practical level, the universal practice is to sound the terua, the *shevarim* and the *shevarim-terua*, a combination of the two. This practice, already cited in the Talmud, is performed in order to satisfy all positions. Ibid., 34a.
11. Rabbeinu Tam as quoted in the Rosh, Rosh Hashana 4:10 and others.

The Rambam and others, however, argue for the text "Blessed art Thou, Lord our God, Who has sanctified us with His commandments and commanded us to *hear* the sound of the shofar."[12] Furthermore, the Rambam explicitly and repeatedly states that the mitzva is to "*hear the sound of the shofar.*"[13]

In practice, the Rambam's position is adopted as law and the blessing is universally pronounced "to hear the sound of the shofar."[14]

Numerous authorities amplify this halachic decision. *Clearly, they maintain, the shofar blasts are not only a form of wordless prayer directed to the Almighty, but also sounds that we direct to ourselves.*

The Rambam himself proclaims: "Although the sounding of the shofar on Rosh Hashana is an unexplained edict of the text, a lesson is embedded within it: 'Awaken slumberers from your sleep…examine your ways… return to and remember your Creator.… Look into your souls, examine your ways and actions, and let each one of you abandon his evil path.'"[15]

Set at the beginning of the year, as our personal journeys begin again, the sounding of the shofar is designed to arouse the one element essential to all religious striving: our own human spirit, our heart and our soul. That awakening accomplished, the shofar sounds then reflect our spirit back to God in wordless, heartfelt prayer.

— E —

Here, then, is the key to the mitzva of the *chatzotzrot*. Like the shofar sounds, the blasts of the trumpets are designed to awaken and to reflect the one final component essential to the success of the Jewish journey: the indomitable human spirit lying in the heart of each Israelite.

As the people prepare to depart Sinai, God turns to Moshe and says: *I have given you all that I can. The laws, the symbols, the rituals and the legal process are all in place. Now, however, you must add the one ingredient that I cannot; the one essential element that must come from each of you, of your own free will.*

---

12. Rambam, *Mishneh Torah*, Hilchot Shofar 3:10.
13. Ibid., 1:1; *Sefer Hamitzvot*, positive commandment 170.
14. *Shulchan Aruch*, Orach Chaim 585:2.
15. Rambam, *Mishneh Torah*, Hilchot Tshuva 3:4.

Create for yourself chatzotzrot...sound them again and again...and let those trumpets awaken your spirit, in times of certainty or doubt, in times of celebration or conflict. Meet each of these vastly different circumstances with the same inner strength and devotion. Above all, remember that all that I have given you will be meaningless without the investment of your spirit and your soul....

And if you are successful, then the notes of those trumpets will themselves be transformed into wordless prayer, piercing the vaults of the heavens and reaching My Heavenly Throne. For those sounds will represent your spirit and soul as no words can.

--- F ---

There could be no more appropriate mitzva with which to leave Sinai than the mitzva of the *chatzotzrot*: trumpets designed to awaken the spirit of the Israelites as their historic journey begins; trumpets that will be forged anew, over and over again, as each generation rouses its own unique spirit to meet the challenges of the day.

Points to Ponder

Two areas of consideration can be suggested as we consider the mitzvot of the shofar and the *chatzotzrot*.

I. *Chatzotzrot*: Awakening

I recently attended a rabbinic meeting called to consider the national agenda of the American Orthodox Jewish community. The question posed to us, a small group of rabbis gathered from across the United States, seemed straightforward enough: "Out of the multitude of possible religious, social, communal and national concerns facing the Jewish people today, what are the principal issues that we should be addressing most directly? What are our priorities, our burning concerns?"

It didn't take long at all, however, for the discussion to take an unexpected, extraordinary turn. Almost to a one, those present suggested that we had missed a step. *Before we could discuss issues of concern, we felt, first we had to discuss how to cultivate concern in the first place.* We each described common experiences – a sense that, together with our congregants, we were going through the motions, absent the passion and spark.

The older among us reminisced about our experiences during the Soviet Jewry movement, when an energized global Jewish community rallied around a common cause. We bemoaned the fact that today, in spite of the myriad issues confronting the State of Israel, national organizations are reluctant to convene major rallies for fear of disappointing turnout.

We all spoke of the challenges we face in our attempts to arouse the passion of our respective communities around the experiences of Shabbat, Torah study and prayer. "I just wish that my congregants could become half as passionate about their spiritual search," said one participant, "as they are about their sports teams."

Perhaps we rabbis are partially at fault for failing to properly convey the excitement that should accompany searching for God's will in all aspects of our lives, entering the eternal Jewish discussion through the portal of textual study, reaching beyond ourselves in heartfelt prayer and so much more. Perhaps times are different and "taking to the streets" has yielded to more sophisticated approaches, such as lobbying on Capitol Hill. Perhaps in our intellectual communities, we automatically look askance at emotionalism and fervor within religious worship.

Nonetheless, God's final commandments to the Israelites as they prepare to depart Sinai speak to us all. Absent the spark, spirit and passion that has characterized our people's relationship with God across the ages, our own personal religious experience is sorely lacking.

When it comes to the awakening of our spirit, we can hand the task to no one else. Each of us is challenged to fashion and sound our own symbolic *chatzotzrot* in order to truly experience the adventure of Sinai in our day.

II. The Clarion Call of the Shofar

Why is the shofar of Rosh Hashana always sounded in sets of three? The pattern is uniform: a broken sound of the shofar (a *terua*, *shevarim* or a combination *shevarim-terua*) unfailingly encompassed by two unbroken *tekiot*.

According to one position in the Talmud, the answer lies in a fascinating linguistic anomaly associated with the sounding of the *chatzotzrot*.

As indicated in our study, wilderness journeys were marked by the sounding of a *terua* on the trumpets. In recording this instruction, however, the Torah does not use the verb derived from the term *terua*, but rather the verb derived from the term *tekia*.¹⁶ In addition, the verb appears in the text both before and after the mention of the *terua*.¹⁷ Based upon this textual phenomenon, the rabbis conclude that a broken sound of the shofar is never sounded alone. Each time a *terua* is sounded, whether on the *chatzotzrot* or on the shofar, it is always to be preceded and followed by an unbroken *tekia*.¹⁸

While neither the Torah nor the rabbis offer a rationale for the consistent enclosure of *teruot* within *tekiot*, two suggestions might be offered.

Firstly, and most obviously, this halachic detail mirrors the faith-based optimism that permeates our entire tradition. The broken sounds of the trumpets and the shofar never appear in isolation. No matter how difficult the times may be, no matter how overwhelming the challenge, we believe with a full heart in God's personal care for us and in His promises to our people. *Even though a* terua *may define our present experience, the* tekia *will eventually be heard*.

Secondly, the threefold sounding of the *chatzotzrot* and the shofar speaks to the way that Jews view time. To the outside world, only the present is certain. The past is a dim memory, the future hidden in mists of mystery. To the Jew, however, the opposite is true. The past is as certain as the clarion call of the shofar at Sinai; the future, as certain as the *tekia* that will herald the Mashiach. *The only thing that is uncertain is the here and now*. What role will I play in the unfolding drama of my people?

The threefold sounding of the shofar squarely presents the Jewish vision of past, present and future for our consideration on Rosh Hashana. We are reminded that the task of each individual Jew is to transform his own personal *terua* into an unbroken *tekia*, thus uniting the clarion call of the past to the clarion call of the future, which is certain to come.

---

16. Bamidbar 10:5–6.
17. Ibid. The text thus reads "*u'tekatem terua*" as opposed to "*v'hareiotem terua*" and "*terua titka'u*" as opposed to "*terua tari'u*."
18. Talmud Bavli Rosh Hashana 34a.

5 Interpreting an Interruption

Context
At last, the journey from Sinai begins in earnest, only to be interrupted in the text – twice, in increasingly bewildering ways.

First the Torah disrupts the narrative to record a brief conversation between Moshe and his father-in-law, Yitro.[1] An analysis of this conversation and an examination of Yitro's mysterious (re)appearance at Sinai are presented in an earlier study (see *Shmot*: Yitro 1).

Even more puzzling, however, is the second textual interruption found immediately after the journey from Sinai begins. Two sentences, familiar to many from their eventual inclusion in the synagogue liturgy, are set off from the rest of the Torah text and enclosed by two inverted Hebrew letter *nun*s.

The strangely delineated passage reads as follows:

> And when the Ark would journey, Moshe said, "Arise, O Lord, and let Your foes be scattered, and let those who hate You flee from before You."
>
> And when it rested, he would say, "Return, O Lord, among the myriad of thousands of Israel."[2]

Two towering figures of the Tannaitic period offer differing explanations for the mysterious separation of this passage from the remainder of the text.

1. Rabbi Shimon ben Gamliel maintains that these sentences actually belong in another location in the Torah. *They are, however, uprooted from their place and inserted here, to serve as a buffer*

---

1. Bamidbar 10:29–32.
2. Ibid., 10:35–36.

between two tragic events: the disastrous manner in which the Israelites leave Mount Sinai and the tragic rebellion of Taveira that immediately follows their departure (see parsha summary).

2. Rebbe (Rabbi Yehuda Hanasi) argues that *this passage is set apart because of its significance as a "book unto itself."* The separation of this passage from the rest of the text, therefore, transforms the five books of the Torah into seven books, with the book of Bamidbar divided into three sections (the section preceding this passage, the passage itself and the section following the passage).[3]

Questions

Questions abound as we consider this second bewildering interruption in the text, specifically at the pivotal moment of the Israelites' departure from Sinai.

According to Rabbi Shimon ben Gamliel's contention, this passage is uprooted from its original location and inserted here to create a separation between two tragic events. Why, however, must the Torah create a buffer between these two tragedies? Over the next few chapters the text records a cascading series of devastating episodes, one after the other, without any interruption at all.[4] Why is this case different?

Furthermore, even if a buffer must be created between these two events, why, specifically, are these two sentences chosen to serve as that buffer? Why not a different portion of the Torah? Is there some relationship between the selected sentences and their apparent role in the text?

And on the other hand, if we accept Rebbe's position that the two-sentence insertion constitutes a "book unto itself," what aspect of this passage raises it to the status of a separate book? Aren't other portions of the text more deserving of this classification (e.g., the Ten Declarations, the paragraphs of the Shma, the commandment "Love your fellow as yourself")?

---

3. Talmud Bavli Shabbat 115b–116a.
4. The rebellion of Taveira, the rebellion of Kivrot Hata'ava, Aharon and Miriam's slander against Moshe, the sin of the spies; Bamidbar 11–14.

Approaches

— A —

Our search for understanding begins at the source, with Rabbi Shimon ben Gamliel's identification of the Israelites' departure from Sinai as a "tragedy."

The Talmud is quick to explain that the problem lay not in the retreat from Sinai (which was, of course, essential to the nation's development) but in the *character of that retreat*. Commenting on the biblical phrase "and they traveled from the Mountain of the Lord," Rabbi Chiya bar Chanina proclaims: "They turned away from following the Lord."[5] The Midrash, going a step further, asserts that the people left Sinai with relief, "like a young child fleeing school."[6]

Clearly, to the rabbinic mind, the Israelites sin, not because they leave Mount Sinai, *but because they leave Mount Sinai behind*.

Overwhelmed by the monumental responsibilities thrust upon them during their confrontation with God, the people are only too happy to flee the scene of that confrontation. *By escaping Sinai, they hope to escape responsibility to God's law, as well*.

What, however, motivates the rabbis to interpret the Israelites' departure from Sinai so negatively? The scant textual evidence concerning the event hardly compels such a position.

The answer perhaps lies in a simple observation periodically applied in rabbinic thought: "*the end result of a phenomenon illuminates its origins*."[7] While the Torah does not testify outright to the nature of the Israelites' departure from Sinai, the text does tell us what occurs immediately thereafter. Three days out from the site of Revelation, the nation descends into rebellion for no apparent reason.[8] This revolt launches a cascading series of tragic uprisings which culminate in the devastating sin of the spies, the event that seals the fate of this generation.[9] These self-inflicted tragedies are proof enough to the rabbis of the mindset that must have

---

5. Talmud Bavli 116a.
6. Yalkut Shimoni, Beha'alotcha 247:729.
7. Talmud Bavli Nedarim 48a.
8. Bamidbar 11:1–3.
9. Ibid., 11:4–14:45.

marked the Israelites' departure from Sinai. Only a people determined to "leave Sinai behind" could sin so grievously, so soon after experiencing the power of Revelation.

We can now understand why the Torah specifically creates a buffer to distinguish the tragic departure from Sinai from the ensuing events, devastating as they may be. God wants us to understand that the Israelites' "flight" from the scene of Revelation is not just another tragedy. *It is, instead, the root cause of all tragedies that follow.* Had our ancestors truly understood the significance of Revelation, had they carried the imperative of Sinai with them upon their departure, they would not have descended into the immediately subsequent rebellions. The generation of the Exodus would have marched directly and triumphantly into the Land of Israel rather than perishing in the wilderness.

— **B** —

We can also now understand the Torah's choice of text to serve as the "buffer." With unerring precision, as the Jewish nation's journey begins, God inserts an eternal message that is simple, powerful and clear – a message designed to directly offset the Israelites' flight from Sinai: *To succeed as My chosen people you must carry Sinai with you each day.*

"And when the Ark would journey…" *The Torah must accompany your journeys through time and across the globe.*

"And when it would rest…" *In each of your resting places, in your communities, towns, villages and cities, My law must define the parameters of your daily lives and determine the character of your societies.*

So critical is the message of this passage to the moment of the Israelites' departure from Sinai, maintains Rabbi Shimon ben Gamliel, that the Torah uproots these sentences from their original location in order to place them here.

So significant is the eternal message conveyed by this passage, maintains Rabbi Yehuda Hanasi, that it is considered a book unto itself.

— **C** —

Far from an arbitrary interruption in the text, the two "inserted" sentences launch Jewish history with a lesson critical to the nation's success: *You cannot leave Sinai behind. You will succeed only if you carry the Torah with you each day.*

6 The Turning Point

Context

Shortly after their departure from Sinai, the Israelites rebel over their forced reliance upon the heaven-bestowed manna for sustenance: "Who will feed us meat? We remember the fish that we used to eat in Egypt for free, the cucumbers and the melons and the leeks and the onions and the garlic…"[1]

Reacting to this upheaval, Moshe turns to God in frustration:

Why have You done evil to Your servant and why have I not found favor in Your eyes, that You place the burden of this entire people upon me?

Did I conceive this entire people, did I give birth to it, that You say to me, "Carry them in your bosom, as a nurse carries the suckling child…"?

Where shall I find meat to give to this entire people when they cry to me, saying, "Give us meat that we may eat"?

I cannot alone carry this entire people, for it is too heavy for me!

And if this is how You deal with me, then kill me now, if I have found favor in Your eyes, and let me not see myself in an evil state!"[2]

God answers Moshe by instructing him to select seventy elders who will be divinely enabled to assist in the leadership of the nation. God also commands Moshe to inform the Israelites that their request for meat will be honored – ultimately, however, to their own lasting regret.

In short order, God's predictions are dramatically fulfilled. Seventy elders are elevated to leadership, miraculously sharing in

---

1. Bamidbar 11:4–5.
2. Ibid., 11:11–15.

Moshe's holy spirit. A heaven-sent wind brings an influx of quail into the camp, serving as provisions for the people. The nation's joy over this bountiful sustenance, however, soon turns to anguish, as, in punishment, God strikes down many of their number.

The location of the Israelite rebellion thus earns the tragic designation of Kivrot Hata'ava, "The Graves of Desire."[3]

Questions

This episode hardly represents the first time that Moshe has been confronted with the Israelites' obstinacy and rebelliousness. At no other point, however, does this great leader descend into such deep, devastating despair. When faced, for example, with the sin of the golden calf at the foot of Mount Sinai, Moshe stands firm, rising to the people's defense, arguing passionately with God for their forgiveness.[4] Suddenly, however, at Kivrot Hata'ava a strikingly different Moshe appears. Shaken to the core, resigned to the people's waywardness, this Moshe prefers death to the burdens of leadership.

Why is the nation's demand for material bounty at Kivrot Hata'ava more deeply troubling to Moshe than the sin of the golden calf or the sin of the spies (which yet looms on the horizon)? What aspect of the Israelites' rebellion triggers such despondency in the heart of their great leader?

Even more startling is God's apparent silence concerning the core source of Moshe's despair. While concrete solutions to Moshe's immediate practical problems are divinely provided – through the appointment of the elders and the delivery of provisions for the people – absent is any reassurance or even an acknowledgment of Moshe's deeper personal crisis. The leader who plaintively asks, "Did I conceive this entire people, did I give birth to it, that You say to me, 'Carry them in your bosom, as a nurse carries the suckling child…'?"[5] never truly receives an answer to his question.

---

3. Ibid., 11:17–35.
4. Shmot 32:11–13.
5. Bamidbar 11:12.

Approaches

— A

In a strikingly incisive analysis, Rabbi Joseph Soloveitchik maintains that the Israelites' rebellion at Kivrot Hata'ava is substantively different from all preceding failings on the part of the nation. Revealed for the first time is the hold that pagan culture has taken upon the nation, a vestige of their years under Egyptian sway.

Paganism, the Rav explains, is distinct from idolatry in that it involves a cultural system, a manner of living. Deeper, more dangerous and more enduring than idolatry, paganism advocates unrestrained devotion to the natural world:

> The pagan worships deities which represent forces in nature. These deities are themselves without moral norms, and they make no demand of man beyond specific acts of propitiation. *For man lustily to partake of nature is, therefore, an act of identifying with such gods. Man actually sees himself as coextensive to nature and therefore craves unlimited indulgence* [my italics].[6]

Support for the Rav's approach can be found in the *pshat* of the text. The true nature of the revolt at Kivrot Hata'ava is established from the outset, in the Torah's strange introduction to the event: "And the rabble that was among them aroused a craving; and the children of Israel also wept."[7]

As portrayed in the text, the uprising at Kivrot Hata'ava is hardly spontaneous. There is no urgent crisis facing the people.[8] The rebellion instead arises out of a planned campaign on the part of a few[9] to "arouse

---

6. Besdin, Abraham, *Reflections of the Rav*, vol. 1, *Lessons in Jewish Thought – Adapted from the Lectures of Rabbi Joseph B. Soloveitchik* (Jerusalem: Jewish Agency, Alpha Press, 1979), p. 153.
7. Bamidbar 11:4.
8. The Torah attests to this fact in a striking textual aside, describing how the nation can easily and comfortably thrive on the manna. Ibid., 11:7–9.
9. Many sources identify this subgroup as the *eirev rav*, the mixed multitude of Egyptians and members of other nationalities who accompany the Israelites upon their Exodus from Egypt (see Rashi, Bamidbar 11:4). The *eirev rav* are often blamed by the rabbis for inciting the Israelites to sin, a reflection of the desire on the part of the rabbis to mitigate the crimes of the Israelites themselves.

a craving" within the entire nation. When this "rabble" successfully taps into the pagan desires rooted in the people's hearts, successfully inciting the masses towards the path of wanton self-indulgence, Moshe despairs of ever leading the Israelites back from the precipice.

The rebellion at Kivrot Hata'ava thus runs much deeper than first meets the eye. Far from simple revolt over the lack of more substantial sustenance, the event emerges as an example of "desire gone berserk, craving without any restraint."[10]

This perspective is further underscored by numerous rabbinic observations. In the realm of *pshat*, for example, Rashi underscores the false note in the people's complaint, "Who will feed us meat?"[11] The nation, he maintains, had a more than adequate supply of meat, as evidenced by the Torah's testimony that the Israelites left Egypt with "sheep and cattle, livestock in great abundance."[12] Midrashic opinions quoted in the Talmud interpret both the Israelites' declaration "We remember the fish that we ate in Egypt…"[13] and the Torah's depiction of the Israelites "weeping to their families[14] as references to the nation's illicit sexual desires."[15]

—— **B** ——

The orgiastic revolt at Kivrot Hata'ava thus emerges as a total repudiation of the Torah law so recently received by the nation at Mount Sinai.

Paganism preaches unfettered self-indulgence; the Torah of Sinai speaks of mastery over oneself and one's desires. The pagan worships and partakes of the physical world without inhibition; the Torah-abiding Jew demonstrates a disciplined use of the material world bounded by the dictates of God's law.

Moshe's deep despair is thus a natural reaction to the depravity evidenced by the nation at Kivrot Hata'ava. *How*, he asks, *can I possibly*

---

10. Besdin, *Reflections of the Rav*, vol. 1, *Lessons in Jewish Thought*, p. 154.
11. Rashi, Bamidbar 11:4.
12. Shmot 12:38.
13. Bamidbar 11:4.
14. Ibid., 11:10.
15. Talmud Bavli Yoma 75a. Fish are often perceived in Jewish tradition as a symbol of fertility because of their great reproductive powers. In addition, the rabbis point to the Torah's prohibition of intra-family relations as the source of the Israelites' "weeping to their families."

turn an entire people so deeply rooted in pagan culture towards obedience to God's will?

According to Rabbi Soloveitchik, however, Moshe's deepest fears originate from an even more primal source: from a newly gained instinctive understanding of the true nature of his own leadership responsibility. Until this point, Moshe had accepted upon himself, albeit reluctantly, his divinely mandated role as a *rebbe*, a teacher of the people. Now, however, Moshe recognizes that being a teacher is not enough. No amount of intellectual persuasion will sway a morally nihilistic people, a people determined to pursue a life without restraints. To offset the lure of the physical world, Moshe must identify with the Israelites on the deepest emotional level – as a parent would with a child. He must become an *omein*, a "nursing father," a role to which he bitterly objects: "Did I conceive this entire people, did I give birth to it, that You say to me, 'Carry them in your bosom, as a nurse carries the suckling child…'?"[16]

For the first time, Moshe recognizes the full extent of the leadership that has been thrust upon him. Demands will be made of him that will be made of no other leader to follow. Guiding the nation in its infancy, Moshe will be required to set his own personal and family needs aside in order to become one with his people.[17] Only by assuming the position of an *omein*, only by exhibiting the patient, sympathetic understanding of a "nursing father," will Moshe successfully nurture the nation through its formative years.[18]

── C ──

God's silence in the face of Moshe's deep-seated fears can, perhaps, now be understood, as well.

As we have noted before (see *Shmot*: Shmot 6, *Approaches* D and Yitro 3, *Approaches* C), there are times when God wants Moshe to realize and assimilate an important lesson on his own. On such occasions, God allows the message to develop through the unfolding circumstances, rather than through open communication. In this case, God challenges Moshe to

---

16. Bamidbar 11:12.
17. Talmud Bavli Shabbat 97a.
18. Besdin, *Reflections of the Rav*, vol. 1, *Lessons in Jewish Thought*, pp. 150–158.

realize that his own understanding of the circumstances is profoundly on target: *There is no need for Me to respond; you already know the truth.*

Moshe's pain-filled assessment of his difficult newfound responsibilities is accurate. God's silence is profound evidence of that fact.

Points to Ponder

The nature of Jewish leadership has not changed substantively since Moshe's wrenching experience at Kivrot Hata'ava. For while no other Jewish leader has been or will be called upon to make the extreme sacrifices made by Moshe, selfless dedication to individual and communal welfare remains the single most important aspect of the Jewish leader's work.

What does it take to succeed as a Jewish leader? Above all, it takes patience, empathy, understanding and the willingness to identify with and care about those in physical or psychic need. There will be times when the issues raised will seem petty, when you will wish that the members of your community would "get over themselves" and stop taking themselves so seriously. You will find yourself, at times, aghast at our ability to create unnecessary pain in a world where enough unavoidable pain already exists.

What seems petty to one individual, however, is real to another, and what one person perceives as gratuitous is unavoidable in another's eyes. The ability to recognize these truths and to empathize with another's pain, even when the source of that pain seems trivial, can spell the difference between success and failure as a leader.

After over thirty years in the rabbinate, I sometimes wonder: What will remain? Will my congregants and students remember the lessons shared in hundreds of Shabbat sermons, the ideas conveyed in a myriad of classes, the thoughts expressed in countless articles and studies? I certainly hope so – but I really can't be certain.

They will certainly remember, however, the shared celebrations, the quiet hospital visits, the expressions of comfort and sympathy, the personal conferences and counseling sessions, the countless hours of one-on-one consultations and discussions.

They will remember that I cared….

7 A Divine Misfire?

Context

Folded into the dramatic story of Kivrot Hata'ava (see previous study) is a short narrative detailing one of the strangest events in the Torah.

Responding to Moshe's complaint that he can no longer bear the burden of leadership alone, God commands him to assemble seventy of the nation's elders outside the Sanctuary. When Moshe complies, God miraculously increases Moshe's *ruach hakodesh* (prophetic spirit), allowing it to be shared with the elders. The elders respond with an eruption of prophecy (see following study).

The rabbis view this event as the establishment of the first Sanhedrin, the high court of seventy-one (in this case, seventy elders plus Moshe) that will serve across history as the highest legal body in the world of Jewish jurisprudence.[1]

Suddenly, the unexpected occurs. Eldad and Medad, two individuals who are not among those gathered outside the Sanctuary, are strangely affected by these miraculous proceedings: "And the spirit rested on them; and they had been among the recorded ones, that they had not gone out to the tent, and they prophesied in the camp."[2]

When word of this phenomenon reaches the ears of Moshe and his protégé, Yehoshua, Moshe's student advises swift action against the "renegade prophets."[3] Moshe, however, responds with equanimity: "Are you jealous for my sake? Would that God would make His entire people prophets, that God would place His spirit upon them."[4]

---

1. Mishna Sanhedrin 1:1.
2. Bamidbar 11:26.
3. Ibid., 11:28.
4. Ibid., 11:29.

Questions

Who are Eldad and Medad? Why does the Torah describe them as being "among the recorded ones"?

God carefully orchestrates the inauguration of the seventy elders into leadership. He underscores the divine source of their new powers by insisting that they gather around the Sanctuary. He demonstrates that their leadership flows from and is subordinate to Moshe by increasing Moshe's own power so that it can be shared.

What, then, goes wrong? Why are Eldad and Medad granted a gift that should have been reserved only for participants in the inauguration ritual? Can it be that we are witnessing a "divine misfire," that somehow God's miraculous bounty is accidentally extended to individuals who should not receive it? Such an eventuality would seem clearly impossible when dealing with an all-powerful God, Who, by definition, cannot make mistakes. What is the intent of the Eldad and Medad narrative and what are we meant to learn from it? How, as well, does this story relate to the overall lessons learned at Kivrot Hata'ava?

Approaches

— A —

According to the Talmud, the key to the story of Eldad and Medad lies in the Torah's statement that they were "among the recorded."

The rabbis explain that Moshe faces a difficult political dilemma as he moves to obey God's instructions concerning the creation of the first Sanhedrin. Recognizing the importance of the step he is about to take, Moshe struggles to find a balanced leadership model that will satisfy all twelve Israelite tribes.

What shall I do? If I choose six elders from each of the twelve tribes I will end up with seventy-two candidates, two above the required number. If on the other hand, I choose five elders from each tribe, I will fall ten candidates short of the necessary seventy. Finally, if I choose five representatives from some tribes and six from others, I will create jealousy among the tribes.

As a solution, Moshe selects six elders from each tribe, for a total of seventy-two, and then sets aside seventy-two corresponding lots. He inscribes seventy of the lots with the word *elder* and leaves the remaining two lots blank.

When the contenders for positions on the first Sanhedrin gather around the Sanctuary, Moshe instructs each candidate to draw one lot. He informs those who select lots inscribed with the word *elder*: *You have already been sanctified by the heavens.* To those who draw blanks, on the other hand, he avows: *What can I do? The Lord has not selected you.* Through this procedure he allows the selection process to be clearly guided by God's will, thus avoiding disputes between the tribes.

Eldad and Medad are "among the recorded," originally designated to be included in the group of seventy-two elders assembled outside the Sanctuary. They refuse, however, to participate. The Talmud offers two antithetical explanations for their refusal: According to an anonymous opinion, Eldad and Medad do not attend the ceremony because they are fearful of not being selected. Rabbi Shimon, however, maintains that they demur because they do not feel worthy of selection.

In spite of their absence from the proceedings, however, God grants Eldad and Medad prophetic vision.

Rabbi Shimon, true to his position, maintains that God further rewards Eldad and Medad for their humility. While the prophetic ability bestowed upon those who attend the ceremony outside the Sanctuary is fleeting,[5] Eldad and Medad are divinely granted permanent prophetic vision.[6]

B

Most later scholars accept Rabbi Shimon's position that Eldad and Medad fail to participate in the selection for the Sanhedrin because they do not feel worthy of rising to leadership. God grants them prophetic vision specifically as a reward for their unassuming nature. Eldad and Medad's story thus emerges as a moral tale, underscoring the merits of humility.[7]

There is, however, another clear moral lesson that emerges from this strange narrative. Eldad and Medad are slated for leadership, whether they wish to accept it or not. Their attempt to avoid their fate is miraculously forestalled, as God seeks them out against their will. In doing so, He conveys a message that, at once, ties into Moshe's wrenching realizations

---

5. See the following study for a debate concerning this point.
6. Talmud Bavli Sanhedrin 17a.
7. Rashi, Rashbam and others, Bamidbar 11:26.

at Kivrot Hata'ava (see previous study) and, at the same time, resounds across the ages: *No matter what your motivation, you cannot avoid your God-mandated responsibilities.*

7a   A Prophetic Postscript

Context
As Moshe's prophetic spirit is shared with the elders selected to the first Sanhedrin, the Torah states: "*Va'yitnabu* [they prophesied], *v'lo yasafu*."[1]

A fascinating debate emerges among the early biblical commentaries regarding the biblical disclaimer *v'lo yasafu*. Reflected in this dispute are two diametrically opposed positions concerning the prophetic vision evidenced by the elders at this critical historical moment.

The *Sifrei* maintains that the term *yasafu* derives from the term *l'hosif*, to add or continue. The phrase *v'lo yasafu*, therefore, means "and did not continue." The gift of prophecy experienced by the elders was a transient phenomenon, specific to the moment.[2]

Targum Onkelos disagrees. Apparently maintaining that the term *yasafu* derives from the root *sof* (end), Onkelos interprets the phrase *v'lo yasafu* to mean "and did not end." The prophetic vision granted to the elders, Onkelos argues, was permanent and did not cease with their ascension to leadership.[3]

Questions
Why do these scholars stake out such widely varying positions concerning the nature of the elders' prophetic vision? Is this dispute simply a linguistic argument, or does it mirror a deeper philosophical divide?

---

1. Bamidbar 11:25.
2. Sifrei, Bamidbar 95.
3. Targum Onkelos, Bamidbar 11:25.

Approaches

— A —

A case can perhaps be made that the debate between the *Sifrei* and the Targum reflects a fundamental tension in our approach to the very process of halacha, a tension mirrored at the pivotal moment of the Sanhedrin's creation.

— B —

Reflecting the normative approach to halachic jurisprudence, the *Sifrei* maintains: *Lo ba'shamayim hi*, the law is not in the heavens.[4] Once transmitted to the Jewish nation at Sinai, Jewish law is to be decided by sages, not by prophets. The tools of the *posek* (halachic decisor) are the *posek*'s own scholarship, his intellectual acumen, his loyalty to the halachic process, his familiarity with the vast repository of earlier halachic discussions, and his understanding of his people and his times. Prophecy has no continuing place in this process, for at Sinai God hands the law over to man.

The *Sifrei* is therefore adamant. A transient prophetic event launches the inauguration of the Sanhedrin, granting that central legal body its divine approbation. After that moment, however, prophetic vision is no longer a component in the Sanhedrin's continued functioning.

— C —

There is, however, another, spiritual dimension to the unfolding of Jewish law. For all its intellectual character, the law remains our most direct mode of communion with the mystery of God's will. Sparks of *ruach hakodesh*, holy or divine spirit, are therefore seen by many as guiding the decisions of the rabbis across the ages.[5]

How strongly one perceives the presence of this sanctified spirit in the workings of halacha depends on one's background and philosophical outlook.

---

4. Devarim 30:12, as interpreted in Talmud Bavli Bava Metzia 59b and elsewhere.
5. Ramban, Shmot 21:6; Ramban, Devarim 19:19.

Those with an intellectual bent will, of course, minimize any sense of mystery in the halachic process. To their view, as indicated above, the beauty of the law is specifically reflected in its human character, in its definition as a divine law given to the hands of man. Others, however, approaching Jewish tradition from a more mystical perspective, will see the guiding hand of God clearly in the halacha's unfolding. True, they maintain, the track of the law is determined by the sages; but the decisions of those sages mirror the will of God. Perhaps Onkelos roots his understanding of the events surrounding the birth of the Sanhedrin upon this latter approach to Jewish law. The gift of prophecy, he insists, remains with the elders throughout their lives, a precursor of the *ruach hakodesh* that will shape the decisions of their spiritual heirs in every generation.

D

A linguistic debate emerging from the moment of the Sanhedrin's birth may be just that: a simple dispute over the translation of a biblical term.

Or this debate may be much more: a foreshadowing of the tension that will characterize our approach to Jewish law across the ages.

Shelach

CHAPTER 13:1–15:41

פרק יג:א–טו:מא

Parsha Summary

The end of the line, and the beginning of another...

From the border of the Promised Land of Canaan, Moshe sends twelve spies to tour the land and bring back a detailed report to the people.

Upon their return, the spies, with the exception of Calev ben Yefuneh and Yehoshua bin Nun, offer overwhelmingly discouraging testimony concerning the nation's inability to conquer the inhabitants of Canaan. In despair, and ignoring the counterarguments of Calev and Yehoshua, the nation rises in rebellion against God, Moshe and Aharon.

God threatens to destroy the nation....

In response to Moshe's heartfelt pleas, God relents and agrees to forgive the people, with one critical caveat: This generation will perish in the wilderness. Their children will enter the land in their stead.

The ten spies who brought back the evil report are immediately struck down. Forty years of wilderness wandering are decreed upon the entire nation; Calev and Yehoshua, the two spies who remained loyal to God, are designated as the sole survivors from this generation to enter the land.

Reacting to the devastating news of their projected demise in the desert, the people attempt, against God's will, to enter Canaan. They are immediately and roundly defeated.

God commands Moshe to instruct the nation concerning two sets of laws that will become obligatory upon their entering the land: meal offerings and libations, and the separation of challa. Moshe is also commanded to instruct the people concerning the atonement process for unintentional communal idolatry, the atonement process for unintentional individual idolatry, and the punishment for intentional blasphemy.

An individual is discovered publicly desecrating the Shabbat. God orders that he be put to death.

As the parsha draws to a close, God commands Moshe to instruct the people concerning the mitzva of tzitzit, *the fringes that must be worn on a four-cornered garment.*

1 *Chet Hameraglim* 1: Unfair Blame?

Context
As the nation stands poised to enter the land of Canaan, Moshe selects twelve *meraglim*, spies, to tour Canaan and bring back a detailed report concerning the land and its inhabitants.

Upon their return, the spies issue an initial report:

> We came to the land to which You sent us and indeed it flows with milk and honey, and this is its fruit.
>
> But the nation that resides in the land is powerful, and the cities are fortified and very great, and also the descendents of the giant we saw there.
>
> Amalek resides in the Southland; the Hittites, the Yevusites and the Emorites reside in the mountains; and the Canaanites reside by the sea and on the bank of the Jordan.[1]

Reacting to this report and to the spies' further arguments, the Israelites descend into despair, openly rebelling against God, Moshe and Aharon.

Questions
What exactly is the sin of the spies? Charged with the responsibility of collecting accurate intelligence concerning the land of Canaan and its inhabitants, why are they now apparently blamed for fulfilling their mission? To quote the Ramban: "Did [Moshe] send them for the purpose of testifying falsely?"[2]

Why does this revolt, in contrast to all previous rebellions, seal the fate of the generation of the Exodus? This time, confronted with the specter of

---
1. Bamidbar 13:27–29.
2. Ramban, Bamidbar 13:2.

overwhelmingly powerful adversaries, the Israelites arguably have cause for despair. What aspect of the nation's reaction does God apparently find unforgivable?

Approaches

— A —

A close look at the text reveals that the spies' report to the Israelites unfolds in three distinct stages. With the unfolding of each stage, the culpability of the spies increases.

1. *The initial report.* While the spies' initial report (see above) seems to be a faithful fulfillment of Moshe's directives, one word changes everything. When the *meraglim* preface their remarks concerning the inhabitants of the land with the word *efes* (but), they endeavor to change the parameters of their role. No longer satisfied with simple intelligence gathering, the spies unilaterally assume an advisory capacity.

Rabbi Isaac Arama, in his *Akeidat Yitzchak*, offers a simple analogy. A servant, sent by his master to determine the quality and cost of a garment, oversteps his boundaries if, upon his return, he proffers an opinion concerning the reasonableness of the asking price.[3]

In the case of the spies, however, this seemingly simple overstepping of boundaries has a devastating effect. The implication of their report becomes: *The land is indeed beautiful;* but *the inhabitants are (too) strong (to conquer).* Suddenly, what had been a certainty now becomes an open question. The spies, after all, had been sent to determine *how* to conquer the land, not to offer an opinion as to *whether or not* the land should be conquered. By venturing an opinion concerning the latter issue, the *meraglim* sow seeds of doubt concerning the Israelites' very entry into the land.

Against this backdrop, the spies' unusual use of the Hebrew word *efes* to introduce their doubts becomes particularly telling. *Efes* (literally "zero") connotes total negation. Through their choice of language, the spies deliberately transmit a sense of profound hopelessness, striking to the core of the nation's heart.

---

3. Akeidat Yitzchak, Bamidbar, sha'ar 77.

2. *The second stage.* No sooner do the ten spies conclude their initial report, than Calev courageously rises to neutralize the effect of their words: "We can certainly ascend and conquer it, for we can surely do it!"[4]

Calev's erstwhile colleagues, however, counter his efforts by immediately moving from oblique suggestion to open assertion: "We cannot ascend against that people for they are stronger than we [*mimenu*]."[5]

Nehama Leibowitz explains the devastating double entendre within this seemingly straightforward declaration. The Hebrew word *mimenu*, she notes, can either connote the first-person plural, "than we" (as explained above, in line with the *pshat*), or it can be read as the third-person singular *mimeno*, "than he." This dual meaning serves as the basis for the Midrashic tradition that a secondary, even more disturbing message courses through the words of the spies: *Not only are the nations of the land more powerful than we, but they are more powerful "than He," than God Himself.*[6]

3. *The third stage.* Although the third section of the *meraglim*'s report follows immediately upon the second, this stage is set apart in the text by an introductory statement: "And they brought forth an evil report concerning the land they had spied upon, saying…"[7]

Finally, the true colors of the spies emerge as their tactics change. No longer do they issue pessimistically shaded reports. No longer is their full intent concealed in suggestion and double entendre. Instead, they now embark upon an open, deliberate, calculated campaign, using any means possible to discourage the people from entering Canaan. For the first time, the land itself is cast in a negative light as a "land that consumes its inhabitants."[8] The nations within are no longer simply characterized as

---

4. Bamidbar 13:30.
5. Ibid., 13:31.
6. Leibowitz, *Iyunim Chadashim B'Sefer Bamidbar*, p. 170.
7. Bamidbar 13:32.
8. Ibid. The rabbis debate the exact meaning of this phrase. Rashi, citing the Midrash, explains that God had protected the spies by causing an unusual number of deaths among the Canaanite nations. Preoccupied with their mourning, the inhabitants of the land do not notice the spies. The spies, however, misinterpret the phenomenon to mean that the land somehow "endangered its inhabitants." Sforno, on the other hand, striving to remain in the realm of *pshat*, interprets the spies' statement as an effort to disabuse the nation from the assumption that the strength of the Canaanite nations was a result of the bounty of the land. Instead, they claim, the opposite is

strong and powerful, but instead are now described as "*nefillim* [giants],⁹ the descendents of giants."

Most revealing of all, however, are the final, culminating words of the spies: "And there we saw the *nefillim*, the sons of the giant from among the *nefillim*; and we were in our own eyes as grasshoppers and so were we in their eyes!"¹⁰

A careful reading of this sentence reveals a striking "Freudian slip," millennia before Freud. "We were *in our own eyes* as grasshoppers," the spies proclaim, and only then "so were we in their eyes." *Only once we felt our own worthlessness did we become worthless in the eyes of others.*

Here then, in their own closing words, the bottom line, the true failure that lies at the core of the sin of the spies: when all is said and done, the spies are guilty of *a loss of faith in themselves.*

How overwhelmingly devastating their implied message to the Israelites must thus have been!

Do you know how we felt and what we realized when we saw ourselves matched against the nations of Canaan?

We realized that it's all been a lie – all that we have experienced and all that we have been promised over these last months – the plagues, the Exodus, the parting of the Reed Sea, the Revelation at Sinai…

We are not a conquering nation; we are not a fledgling, divinely chosen people. We are grasshoppers! We are still the servile slaves who endured centuries of servitude to Egyptian masters. We haven't changed; we haven't moved an inch.

We simply cannot do it. We will never enter that land; we will never possess that land; we will never become a nation; we will never achieve our "promised" destiny.

---

true. Only the strongest are to be found in Canaan because only the strongest are able to survive the "deleterious effects" of the land.
9. Numerous commentaries explain that the spies, by using the term *nefillim* (lit.: the fallen ones) to describe the enormous inhabitants of the land, connect those inhabitants to a mysterious group first mentioned in Parshat Bereishit (see *Vayikra*: Acharei Mot 1, *Approaches* C). This association only serves to further strengthen the fearsome mystique of the Canaanite nations.
10. Bamidbar 13:33.

B

We can now understand why the sin of the spies emerges as the turning point for the generation of the Exodus. Less a story of sin and punishment, the *chet hameraglim* reflects *a frightening but inescapable reality*: this generation simply cannot enter the Land of Israel.

By accepting the arguments of the *meraglim*, the Israelites negate the very journey that has brought them to this point. Their loss of faith in themselves clearly demonstrates that God's attempt to forge them into a confident, conquering nation has failed (see *Points to Ponder*).

The generation of the Exodus cannot make the transition from slavery to freedom. A generation will have to pass before that transition can be made.

Points to Ponder

Two disparate areas of consideration rise out of our discussion of the sin of the spies.

I. Making the Leap

According to our analysis, the sin of the spies underscores the inability of the generation of the Exodus to make the leap from slavery to freedom. An entire generation will have to pass before the Israelites enter the land.

Our own current national experience proves powerfully instructive in helping us understand this biblical narrative on a human level. After all, the miracle of return to the Land of Israel in our day has certainly not been seamless. In many cases the full acclimation of new immigrants from disparate backgrounds has waited until the second generations truly become citizens of their newfound home.

Returning to the biblical narrative, however, a serious problem emerges as we examine the unfolding events. Doesn't God know from the outset that the generation of the Exodus will fail in its transition to freedom? Why, then, does He allow the tragedy of the *meraglim* to unfold? Why not short-circuit the process and simply inform the Israelites at Sinai that their children, not they, will inherit the land?

This question, of course, brings us back to an issue that we have explored before (see *Bereishit*: Noach 1, *Approaches* A; *Shmot*: Teruma 1, *Approaches* B). How are we to understand the biblical narrative when God seems to change His mind; when out of apparent necessity, God discards Plan A in favor of Plan B? Why should a perfect God require the experience of trial and error?

The answer lies, as we have noted, in recognizing that God creates a world predicated upon the existence of free will, and that free will, in turn, is predicated on the possibility of human failure. God knows that man will fail, but He retreats to allow for man to learn from that failure.

Had God informed the Israelites of their fate from the outset, they, justifiably, would have felt that they had never been given the chance to prove themselves. They (and we) would never have learned the extent of their own limitations and the ramifications of their missteps. By giving the generation of the Exodus the opportunity to succeed and to (unfortunately) fail, God allows the unfolding events to transmit critical lessons across the ages.

II. Facts or Opinions?

A careful reading of the report of the spies reveals that they overstep another critical boundary – one easily crossed in our own experience as well.

From the outset, the meraglim *offer their opinions as fact.*

Had the spies stated upon their return, *we believe that the nations that reside in the land are too strong for us to conquer*, or even, *it seems to us that we cannot enter the land*, the Israelites might not have despaired so deeply. Opinions, after all, can be debated. Once, however, the spies offer their subjective report as fact, they leave no room for dispute. This phenomenon of transforming opinion into fact becomes more pronounced as the spies continue to speak.

The question could well be raised: How often are we – in our own dialogues, discussions and debates – guilty of the same sin as the spies? How easily do we slip from the realm of opinion into the realm of "assumed fact," convinced of our correctness, unable to recognize the validity of other points of view?

The strength of our convictions, however strong they may be, does not have the power to transform opinion into fact. This lesson, tragically taught through the sin of the spies, should not be forgotten in our day.

2 Chet Hameraglim 2: Please, God, Forgive Someone Else

Context
Following the sin of the spies, God responds to Moshe's impassioned pleas on behalf of the nation by proclaiming, *Salachti ki'dvarecha*, "I have forgiven, according to your words."[1]

In the very next moment, however, God decrees that, aside from Yehoshua and Calev (the two loyal spies), the entire generation of the Exodus will die in the desert. Only their children will inherit the land.[2]

Questions
What kind of "forgiveness" is God offering the people?

One can almost imagine the Israelites protesting: *If Your definition of forgiveness is that we are all doomed to die in the wilderness, then, please, O Lord, forgive someone else!*

Approaches

— **A** —

Our quest to understand God's "forgiveness" for the sin of the spies provides us with the opportunity to apply a critical rule of Torah study.

If a word in the Torah appears superfluous – if the inclusion or omission of that word seems to make no difference in the way that we understand the text – our comprehension of the narrative is incomplete and must be reexamined.

---

1. Bamidbar 14:20.
2. Ibid., 14:21–35.

In this case, why does God inform Moshe, *Salachti ki'dvarecha*, "I have forgiven, *according to your words*"? Why not simply say, "I have forgiven," and stop there?

The "extra" word *ki'dvarecha* directs us back to Moshe's own *devarim* (words), to the substance of Moshe's pleas on behalf of the people. And, indeed, a review of those pleas reveals a striking omission. *Moshe's words are absent any argument based on the people's merit.*

Moshe contends:

> And Egypt – from whose midst You have raised this nation with Your power – will hear....
>
> That You, the Lord, are in the midst of this nation; that eye to eye You appeared to them; in a pillar of cloud You traverse before them by day and in a pillar of fire at night.
>
> Yet You killed this people as a single man!
>
> And all the nations that have heard of Your fame will say: "*Because the Lord lacked the ability to bring this nation into the land that He had promised to them, He slaughtered them in the wilderness.*"[3]

Seen in perspective, Moshe's supplications boil down to one single argument: *Given the personal attention and care that You have shown to this fledgling nation to this point, how can You possibly destroy them now? Such a precipitous act would cause surrounding nations to conclude that You failed to bring this people into their land, because You simply could not do so. Imagine the desecration of Your name that would (God forbid) result.*

In short, God, how can You do this? What will the other peoples of the world say?

B

Moshe's limited petitions at this juncture stand in stark contrast to an earlier set of prayers offered under similar circumstances. On the summit of Sinai, after the sin of the golden calf, Moshe turns to God and begs forgiveness for the nation. On this previous occasion, however, in addition to raising concern over the impact of God's actions on world opinion, Moshe offers another critical plea:

---

3. Ibid., 14:13–16.

Remember for the sake of Avraham, Yitzchak and Yisrael Your servants, to whom You swore by Yourself, and You told them, "I shall increase your descendents as the stars of heaven, and this entire land of which I spoke I will give to your descendents, and it shall be their heritage forever.[4]

Clearly, by the time we arrive at the *chet hameraglim*, something has changed. Moshe is no longer comfortable using both lines of reasoning in the people's defense. Faced with the nation's total loss of self-confidence, Moshe feels that he cannot argue based on the merit of this generation, even in their role as heirs to the legacy of their forefathers. The only argument that he has left concerns the potential effect that God's actions will have on the attitude of surrounding nations.

C

Once Moshe's constraints at the scene of the *chet hameraglim* become clear, God's response becomes understandable, as well....

Moshe, I have forgiven, but only according to your words. Your own limited arguments reflect a clear recognition of this generation's inability to enter the land. They will, therefore, perish in the wilderness.

As far as world opinion is concerned, however, you need not worry. My power will soon be evident to all. The next generation of Israelites will successfully enter the land in place of their parents.

As you can see, Moshe, I have completely forgiven – according to your words.

D

Through his unfolding interchange with God following the sin of the spies, Moshe demonstrates a full awareness of the tragic reality confronting him. The generation that he has led out of Egypt has not made – and cannot make – the transition from slavery to freedom. God's attempt to forge them into a conquering nation has failed (see previous study). Recognition of this reality forces Moshe to limit his arguments on the people's behalf and shapes the boundaries of God's "forgiveness."

---

4. Shmot 32:13.

E

One final point, however, must be made....

As is often the case, the most tragic moments of Jewish experience carry within them the seeds of optimism and redemption.

By "forgiving" the generation of the Exodus even as He dooms them to perish in the wilderness, God redefines the concept of success and shapes the Jewish nation's future expectations.

I can call this edict "forgiveness," He informs the Israelites, *because your success as a people is measured in intergenerational terms. Just as your patriarchal ancestors live on in you, so, too, you will enter the land through your children.*

Each generation of your people lives on in those that follow. This ongoing truth will power your people across history and represents the substance of My "forgiveness" for your sin.

Points to Ponder

From the depths of devastating tragedy, God fashions the extended sense of personal mission that has sustained our people through their darkest hours. More than a belief in destiny, more than a hope for the future, it is a concrete vision of participation in a grand experiment that we know will ultimately succeed, if not in our time than in our descendents'. We are all present at each step of this intergenerational journey and we will all be there to share in our people's final redemption.

Our generation, blessed with the return of the Jewish people to their homeland, does not stand alone. Sacrifices of countless individuals and communities long gone were required to enable us to achieve this goal. Through their hopes, dreams and aspirations, those generations accompany us on our passage. Any successes we achieve are theirs, as concretely as they are ours.

And we will accompany our children, and their children after them, on the continuing journey towards the culminating moments of our people's destiny.

3 Chet Hameraglim 3: A Tale of Two Sins

Context
The Jewish calendar contains two extraordinary fast days that are, at once, powerfully similar, yet vastly different.

These occasions, Yom Kippur and Tisha B'Av, share fundamental characteristics as the only full twenty-five-hour[1] fast days in Jewish tradition and as the only fasts that include the five halachic *inuyim* (afflictions): the prohibitions on eating and drinking, washing, anointing, the wearing of leather shoes and marital relations.

Yet as similar as these days are, they are also poles apart. Yom Kippur is a biblical fast day; Tisha B'Av, of rabbinic origin. Tisha B'Av remains immersed in sorrow while Yom Kippur is cautiously, solemnly optimistic.

As if to further highlight the connection and contrast between these two fast days, the calendar links them in a multi-week spiritual journey. Beginning with the three mournful weeks preceding Tisha B'Av, this passage continues through the Shiva D'nechemta, the seven weeks of consolation that lead to the high holidays, culminating with Yom Kippur.

Questions
Clearly, our tradition sees Yom Kippur and Tisha B'Av as connected, but how? What can be learned from the comparison and contrast of these two fast days?

---
1. Approximately one hour is added to each day to account for the uncertain period of twilight.

Approaches

— A —

The answer may well emerge from the mists of history. Intriguingly, the rabbis draw yet another link between Yom Kippur and Tisha B'Av. Each of these occasions, they say, originates in a seminal sin committed at the dawn of Jewish history.

— B —

Yom Kippur is born as a result of the *chet ha'egel*, the sin of the golden calf.

In the shadow of Revelation at Mount Sinai, the nation, frightened by the specter of abandonment by Moshe, creates and worships a golden calf. Moshe, upon descending the mountain, witnesses the nation's backsliding and smashes the divinely given Tablets of Testimony. God, upon forgiving the nation at Moshe's behest, commands Moshe to once again ascend the mountain and receive a second set of tablets (see *Shmot*: Ki Tissa 2).

The rabbis relate that Moshe descends with the second tablets on Yom Kippur.[2] This biblical fast day, the holiest day of the Jewish year, thus rises out of the forgiveness granted by God for the sin of the golden calf.

— C —

Tisha B'Av emerges as a consequence of the *chet hameraglim*, the sin of the spies.

As we have seen (see the two previous studies), a short time after their departure from Sinai, the Israelites find themselves at the southern border of the Promised Land of Canaan. Twelve spies are sent to observe the land and its inhabitants preparatory to the nation's entry. Upon their return, ten of the twelve spies deliver a pessimistic report, citing the Israelites' inability to conquer the land through battle. In reaction to the account of the spies, the nation despairs, weeping through the night and rising up in rebellion against Moshe and Aharon.

Based upon calendar computation, the rabbis maintain: "That very night [when the Israelites wept in response to the report of the spies] was the eve of Tisha B'Av. Said the Holy One Blessed Be He to them [the

---

2. Rashi, Shmot 18:13.

Israelites]: 'You have cried for naught – and I shall establish for you crying across the generations.'"³

Rooted in the nation's despair over the report of the spies is the tragedy and sorrow that will visit their descendents, over and over again, throughout the ages, on the mournful day of Tisha B'Av.

—— D ——

Although the rabbis support their contentions concerning the origins of Yom Kippur and Tisha B'Av through calendar computation, their intended message obviously strikes deeper. There are no coincidences on the Jewish calendar. *To the rabbinic mind, concrete philosophical bonds link these two fast days, respectively, to tragic transgressions deep in our nation's past.* What are these connecting links and how can they help deepen our understanding of two of the most important observances in Jewish tradition?

—— E ——

We have suggested in the past that the sin of the golden calf reflects the Israelites' *desperate desire for distance from the demands of an omnipotent God* (see *Shmot*: Ki Tissa 2, *Approaches* C for a more complete analysis).

From the outset, the Israelites are unable and/or unwilling to face the new responsibilities thrust upon them at Sinai, and they respond with immediate retreat: "And the entire people saw the thunder and lightning and the sound of the shofar and a smoking mountain and they trembled and stood from afar. And they said to Moshe, 'You speak with us and we will listen; and let not God speak with us, lest we die.'"⁴

And when, forty days later, Moshe apparently fails to return from the summit of the mountain at the expected time, and the people face the fact that they will now be required to interact with God directly, without the benefit of Moshe as their intermediary, their desperate desire for *distance from God* becomes an overwhelming fear. The Israelites create a golden calf to take Moshe's place, to stand between them and their Creator.⁵

---

3. Talmud Bavli Ta'anit 29a.
4. Shmot 20:15–16.
5. Ibid., 32:1–6.

In the aftermath of the sin, after punishing those most directly involved, God moves to educate the nation to the ramifications of their crime. Threatening to distance Himself from the people, as per their expressed desire, He forces them to glimpse the emptiness that would result from such distance. The nation, in response, falls into mourning.[6]

God thus reminds the Israelites of a fundamental truth that courses through all human relationships. While safety can be found in emotional distance, the desire for such distance produces a life of emptiness. Only those willing to risk the pain and heartache that can result from nearness to others will ultimately experience the potential beauty of friendship and love.

God's message to the people in the aftermath of the *chet ha'egel* is powerful and clear: *If I am absent from your lives you will be safe, as through distance you avoid the vulnerability that would accompany My close connection with you.*

You will also miss out, however, on the grandeur that would have resulted from our closeness.

— **F** —

We can now begin to understand why the rabbis perceive a fundamental connection between the sin of the golden calf and Yom Kippur, the holiest day of the Jewish year.

Yom Kippur is the day when, yearly, we move to repair the inevitable distance that has developed between us and our Creator. We mourn our loss of perspective, explore our missteps and admit our failings. We atone for our consistent tendency to pull away from God through our practice of *comfortable* rather than *confrontational* Judaism (see *Shmot*: Ki Tissa 2, Points to Ponder). We pledge to move close again – close enough to allow divine law to challenge our lives and test our commitments.

The message of this holiest of days is clear. *The distance that develops between man and God can be repaired.* Just as God ultimately forgives the Jewish nation at Sinai and invites them, once again, fully into His presence; so, too, through the process of *tshuva* on Yom Kippur we can reconnect intimately with our Creator.

---

6. Ibid., 33:1–4.

G

At the core of the *chet hameraglim*, on the other hand, lies a profoundly different failing, yielding a profoundly different divine response (see previous two studies).

Ultimately the spies and the nation are guilty of a loss of faith in themselves. Not only do they doubt God's ability to bring them into the land, but, even more importantly, they lose trust in their own capacity for change. They see themselves still as the slaves who toiled under Egyptian rule, and they negate the transformative impact of all that has occurred during and after the Exodus.

To this failing, God responds with harsh judgment. Intergenerationally, the nation is forgiven and will ultimately enter the land. The generation of the Exodus, however, remains irredeemable. When man loses sight of his own majestic potential, he simply cannot achieve.

H

The connection drawn by rabbinic thought between the sin of the spies and the mournful day of Tisha B'Av now becomes abundantly clear.

In stark contrast to the ultimately optimistic, reparative day of Yom Kippur, Tisha B'Av remains, each year, an occasion rooted in mourning and sorrow. We bemoan our own replication of the sin of the spies, our loss of personal and national vision, our inability to rise above our pettiness and spite, our failure to glimpse the majestic potential in others and in ourselves.

Because of these continued failings, Tisha B'Av rings, over and over again, to the divine decree that, according to the rabbis, was delivered as the Jews wept over the report of the spies: *You have cried for naught, and I shall establish for you crying across the generations.*[7]

I

When you draw away from Me, God says on Yom Kippur, the anniversary of the *chet ha'egel, our relationship can yet be repaired.*

When you lose faith in yourselves, however, He decrees on Tisha B'Av, the anniversary of the *chet hameraglim, you and your generation will fail*

---

7. Talmud Bavli Ta'anit 29a.

to achieve your potential, and the realization of your dreams will be further delayed.

Points to Ponder

A strange liturgical anomaly emerges in light of the rabbinic association of the sin of the spies with Tisha B'Av and the sin of the golden calf with Yom Kippur.

Each year, a powerful and poignant body of prayers known as Selichot, Prayers of Forgiveness, is recited on the days leading to and during the Days of Awe (Rosh Hashana and Yom Kippur).

Central to these prayers is a section containing Moshe's plea to God for forgiveness: "Forgive please the iniquity of this people according to the greatness of Your kindness and as You have borne this nation from Egypt until now."[8]

And God's response: *Salachti ki'dvarecha*, "I have forgiven, according to your words."[9]

The problem is, however, that this interchange is found in the Torah in conjunction with the sin of the spies, not the sin of the golden calf. Given the vastly different nature of these two fast days, why would our tradition choose a source connected to the origin of Tisha B'Av as a central piece of the Yom Kippur liturgy?

The answer may well lie in the universal application of God's words in this interchange with Moshe (see Shelach 2).

Salachti ki'dvarecha, "I have forgiven, according to your words." *My forgiveness, Moshe, is shaped by your own vision of the people's potential. Given that your own words reflect recognition of their inability to change, My forgiveness will reflect that reality, as well.*

Each year, as we approach the holiest season of our calendar, God turns to each of us and proclaims: *Salachti ki'dvarecha*, "I have forgiven, according to your words." *My judgment of you will be based upon your own vision of yourself. The higher you reach, the greater you see your own potential, the greater My capacity for forgiveness, the greater the promise for the coming year.*

Each year, we, together with God, determine the parameters of God's forgiveness.

---

8. Bamidbar 14:19.
9. Ibid., 14:20.

4 Fringe Element

Context
Parshat Shelach closes with a discussion of the mitzva of *tzitzit*, the commandment to place fringes on the corners of all four-cornered garments worn by men. While the majority of the *tzitzit* threads are to be white in color, each bundle of *tzitzit* is to contain at least one thread of *techeilet*, a shade of blue.[1]

As mandated by the Torah, the mitzva of *tzitzit* is obligatory only if one happens to wear a four-cornered garment. The rabbis decree, however, that such a garment (a *tallit katan*, a small *tallit*) should be worn throughout the day in order to fulfill this mitzva continuously. The eventual institution of the *tallit gadol*, the large *tallit*, into Jewish practice, worn as a prayer shawl during the morning prayers and on other occasions, further reflects the significance of this mitzva.

The Talmud maintains that the mitzva of *tzitzit* is equivalent in importance to the sum of all other mitzvot combined.[2]

Questions
What is the meaning of the mitzva of *tzitzit* and why do the rabbis attach such significance to its performance? What possible purpose could there be in placing fringes on our garments?

---

1. Ibid., 15:37–38. According to rabbinic tradition, the *techeilet* color is derived from a dye produced from an aquatic creature known as the *chilazon* (Rashi, Talmud Bavli Sanhedrin 91a). For centuries, the method of *techeilet* production was considered by most authorities to have been lost to the mists of history. Some contemporary scholars and scientists, however, claim to have rediscovered the identity of the *chilazon* and have produced a color that they maintain is *techeilet*. Halachists are divided in their opinions as to whether this color is reliably *techeilet* and should be incorporated into the *tzitzit*. The mandated ratio of white to blue in the *tzitzit* is also the subject of debate among the halachic authorities.
2. Talmud Bavli Menachot 43.

Is there any underlying philosophical significance to the white and blue threads of the *tzitzit*?

Why is this mitzva recorded in the text at this point, specifically in the aftermath of the tragic sin of the spies?

Approaches

— A —

Rabbinic discussion concerning this mitzva begins at the most basic level, as the rabbis debate the very meaning of the Hebrew term *tzitzit*.

Rashi offers two alternative interpretations, each of which he supports with textual evidence. The term *tzitzit*, he says, refers either to the fringes themselves or to their role as a visible symbol meant to "be seen" (based on the root *l'hatzitz*, to see).[3]

A number of commentators, including the Rashbam, view Rashi's two approaches not as alternatives but as complementary interpretations. The term *tzitzit*, they maintain, defines, at once, both the physical structure of the mitzva and its ultimate purpose.[4]

This dual meaning of the term *tzitzit*, these scholars claim, is reflected in the strange textual flow surrounding the mitzva. The Torah first states: "and they shall make for themselves *tzitzit* on the corners of their garments,"[5] and then continues, "and it shall be for you as *tzitzit* and you shall see it."[6] Why would the Torah find it necessary to state that the *tzitzit* will serve for the Israelites as *tzitzit*?

Applying Rashi's two interpretations simultaneously, the Rashbam explains the flow of text as follows: "and they shall make for themselves *tzitzit* [fringes on the corners of their four-cornered garments]…and it shall be for you as *tzitzit* [visible symbols] and you shall see it and you will remember *et kol mitzvot Hashem*, all of the mitzvot of the Lord."[7]

The mitzva of *tzitzit* thus consists of more than making and wearing fringes on four-cornered garments. To properly fulfill this mitzva, the

---

3. Rashi, Bamidbar 15:38.
4. Rashbam, Bamidbar 15:38–39.
5. Bamidbar 15:38.
6. Ibid., 15:39.
7. Rashbam, Bamidbar 15:38–39.

fringes must "be seen"; they must serve as a visible symbol, inspiring the wearer to remember the entirety of Jewish law.

A fundamental question, however, remains: the text does not clearly explain how the *tzitzit* are meant to work. In what way will "seeing" these fringes remind the observer of "all the mitzvot of the Lord"?

B

In one of the earliest references to the symbolism of the *tzitzit*, the Talmud begins to answer this question by comparing the fringes to a "seal of clay" placed upon a slave as permanent confirmation of his status.[8]

Numerous later commentaries pick up on this theme, explaining that God commands Jewish males to wear *tzitzit* on their four-cornered garments as a lasting reminder of their subservience to divine will.

The Sforno thus maintains: "When you see [the *tzitzit*], which are as a seal placed by a master upon his servants, you will remember that you are servants to an exalted God Whose commandments you accepted through an oath and a promise. Through this you will refrain from 'straying after your hearts.'"[9]

The Ba'al Hachinuch similarly notes: "No tool in the world is more effective for the purpose of remembrance than the seal of the master fixed upon [his servants'] everyday garments…which are before [the servant's] heart and eyes throughout the day."[10]

To these and other scholars, the mechanism by which the *tzitzit* remind their wearer of "all the mitzvot of the Lord" is straightforward and concrete. These fringes comprise the uniform of an *eved Hashem*, a servant of the Lord. The individual who wears this uniform throughout the day will be constantly reminded of his role in God's service and of its incumbent responsibilities. He will thus be encouraged not to stray in the direction of sin.

Why, however, are *tzitzit* specifically chosen as a reminder of servitude to God? Is the selection of these fringes arbitrary, similar to a ribbon tied around an individual's finger as a prod to memory? Or, does some physical aspect of the *tzitzit* recommend them for their divinely ordained purpose?

---

8. Talmud Bavli Menachot 43b; see Tosafot there.
9. Sforno, Bamidbar 15:39.
10. Sefer Hachinuch, mitzva 386.

Once these questions are raised, a variety of approaches to the specific symbolism of the *tzitzit* are suggested by the sages, running the gamut from *pshat* to Midrash and from the simple to the complex.

C

An early Midrashic source quoted by Rashi, for example, views the symbolism of the *tzitzit* in mathematical terms. The numerical value of the word *tzitzit* is six hundred.[11] By adding the eight strands and five knots found in each set of fringes to that base number, we arrive at a total of six hundred thirteen, the sum of the mitzvot contained in the Torah. In this way, the Midrash maintains, the *tzitzit* serve as a reminder of "all the mitzvot of the Lord."[12]

After attacking Rashi's approach on a number of grounds, the Ramban argues that the symbolic message of the *tzitzit* is specifically contained in the thread(s) of *techeilet*, the blue strand(s) found in each set of fringes. The color *techeilet*, the Ramban states, alludes to the *tachlit* (purpose) of all creation. The goal of the mitzva of *tzitzit* is not simply to remind the observer of "*all* the mitzvot," but to remind the observer of the divine attribute of *kol* (all), the totally inclusive nature of God.[13]

The Ramban finds support for his approach in a well-known Talmudic observation concerning *techeilet*: "Why is *techeilet* different from all other colors? Because *techeilet* resembles the [color of the] sea, and the sea resembles the [color of the] heavens, and the heavens resemble the [color of God's] throne of glory."[14]

Symbolism of a vastly different nature is attributed to the *techeilet* by Rabbi Elazar the son of Rabbi Shimon in another early Midrashic source. Noting that the root word *kalla*, to complete or finish, is contained in the term *techeilet*, this scholar argues that the blue thread of the *tzitzit*

---

11. Each letter of the Hebrew alphabet is assigned a numerical value. By computing the respective values of various Torah words and phrases, the Midrash will often derive messages from the text. This mathematical Midrashic approach is known as the study of *gematria*.
12. Rashi, Bamidbar 15:39, quoting the Midrash Tanchuma Korach 12.
13. Ramban, Bamidbar 15:39. The Ramban notes additional significance in the fact that the letters of the Hebrew term *kol* are contained in the word *techeilet*. See also Ramban, Bereishit 24:1, for a fuller explanation of this scholar's approach to the divine attribute of *kol*.
14. Talmud Bavli Menachot 43b.

is designed to remind the observer of the "complete" destruction of the Egyptians through the plague of the firstborn and the closing waters of the Reed Sea.[15] Rashi adds that the blue shade of *techeilet* specifically resembles the color of the heavens as they darken towards night, the appointed time of the plague of the firstborn.[16]

Other commentaries discern practical, moral lessons reflected in the blue thread of the *tzitzit*. The Ba'al Akeida, for example, maintains that *techeilet* lies midpoint on the color spectrum between the extremes of black and white. *Techeilet* is, therefore, included in each set of *tzitzit* to reflect the desirability of a balanced life path that eschews extremes.[17]

Entering the kabbalistic, mystical realm, the Zohar perceives in the blended colors of the *tzitzit* a reflection of the attributes of God. The white threads represent *midat harachamim*, the divine attribute of compassion. The strand(s) of *techeilet*, on the other hand, signify *midat hadin*, the divine attribute of strict justice (see *Shmot*: Va'eira 1, *Approaches* E for a discussion concerning the divine attributes).[18]

Finally, Rabbi Joseph Soloveitchik suggests that the white threads of the *tzitzit* symbolically denote "clarity, rationality and that which is self-evident." *Techeilet*, on the other hand, "focuses our thoughts on the grand mysteries of human experience which elude our precise understanding."[19] With inimitable eloquence, the Rav applies the symbolic balance created by the colors of the *tzitzit* to three distinct areas of human experience:

1. *In the scientific realm.*

In scientific inquiry, the physical sciences, i.e., physics, chemistry, biology, etc., lend themselves to mathematical precision....

It is when the focus of inquiry changes to man's psyche and abstract verities that inexactitude and uncertainty intrude....

The universe will yield its secrets to the organized scientific pursuit. But the one thread of *techeilet* pertains to the spiritual realm,

---

15. Sifrei, Bamidbar 15:37.
16. Rashi, Bamidbar 15:41.
17. Akeidat Yitzchak, Bamidbar, sha'ar 77.
18. Zohar Shelach 175.
19. Besdin, *Reflections of the Rav*, vol. 2, *Man of Faith in the Modern World*, pp. 29–30.

where man is humbled by the mystery of existence. Here he needs the guidance of revelation and the religious perceptions of the soul.[20]

2. *In our personal lives.*

We have all had periods, even of an extended nature, which are rational, planned, and predictable, when we feel that we have a hold on events. At other times, however, mystery and puzzlement intervened, dislocating the pattern of our lives and frustrating all our planning....

Inexplicable events render us humbled. This is the *tekhelet* [*techeilet*] of human experience.[21]

3. *The enigma of Jewish history.*

If Jewish history operated solely with white, we would not be fighting for Israel today. From the standpoint of reason and logistics, our efforts against imponderable odds are insane....

Only people sustained by *tekhelet* could be motivated to constitute a state after two thousand years of exile. Nations governed only by white mock us incredulously and derisively....

The garment of Jewish life will yet possess both blue and white, and our historical yearnings and sacrifices will be vindicated.[22]

To the mind of the Rav, the *tzitzit* serve as a constant reminder of those elements of our existence that lie within man's comprehension, as well as those that lie beyond.

Countless other approaches are suggested by the scholars as they struggle to unravel the mysteries behind the ever-present symbol of the *tzitzit*.

— D —

One final insight into the mitzva of *tzitzit* can be derived from an enigmatic linguistic connection between this mitzva and the tragic event with which the parsha opened.

---

20. Ibid., pp. 30–31.
21. Ibid., p. 31.
22. Ibid., pp. 30–33.

As the curtain rose on Parshat Shelach, Moshe sent twelve spies *latur et Eretz Canaan*, "to *explore* the land of Canaan."[23] Now, at the end of the parsha, the Torah summarizes the purpose of the *tzitzit* by declaring: *V'lo taturu acharei levavchem v'acharei eineichem asher atem zonim achareihem*, "And you shall not *explore* after your heart and after your eyes after which you stray."[24] The Torah's repeated use of the uncommon verb *latur*, to explore, seems to link the disparate themes found at the endpoints of the parsha. What, however, is the thrust of this association? What possible link can be suggested between the sin of the spies and the mitzva of *tzitzit*?

Perhaps the answer lies in Judaism's overall attitude towards exploration of the physical world. For while the Torah here warns, "you shall not *explore* after your heart and after your eyes after which you stray," investigation of our physical surroundings is not only generally permitted by most halachic authorities, but encouraged. No less a luminary than the Rambam maintains:

> And what is the path that will lead to the fear and love [of God]? At the moment when an individual considers His wondrous and great creations and works and perceives within them His matchless and infinite wisdom, he immediately loves, praises, glorifies Him and is seized with an overwhelming desire to know His great name.[25]

Such exploration becomes hazardous, however, when we forget the basic assumptions that are meant to guide our journey. Like the spies sent by Moshe on a legitimate mission to explore Canaan, we stumble off course in our own "explorations" when we lose sight of God's presence in our lives and when we despair of our own self-worth.

The mitzva of *tzitzit* is necessary specifically because *we do not* close ourselves off from the outside world. As we traverse our own physical surroundings, the *tzitzit* serve as an ever-present reminder of our regal role as *avdei Hashem*, servants of the Lord.

---

23. Bamidbar 13:17.
24. Ibid., 15:39.
25. Rambam, *Mishneh Torah*, Hilchot Yesodei HaTorah 2:2.

Korach

CHAPTER 16:1–18:32

פרק טז:א–יח:לב

Parsha Summary

Rising rebellion, devastating response…

Moshe and Aharon face their greatest personal challenge to date: under the leadership of Korach, Datan, Aviram and On, two hundred fifty prominent members of the community rebel against their authority.

In response to the uprising, Moshe instructs the rebels to appear the next morning with burning censers filled with incense. God, he proclaims, will then "make known who is His own."

As the divine trial approaches, Moshe attempts to reason with various factions of the insurgent camp. When the rebels respond with defiance, Moshe beseeches God to reject their offerings. He then reissues instructions for the divine trial, this time including Aharon among those who are to appear "before God" with incense-laden censers.

The stage for the trial is set, as Korach's two hundred fifty followers assemble together with Moshe and Aharon at the entrance to the Sanctuary.

The entire nation, at the urging of Korach, gathers to witness the events. God, appearing in His glory, commands Moshe to instruct the people to distance themselves from the tents of Korach, Datan and Aviram. The people comply, while Datan, Aviram and their families remain standing defiantly at the entrances of their tents.

Moshe proclaims that God will attest to Moshe's leadership by miraculously causing the earth to swallow the instigators of the rebellion together with all that is theirs. No sooner does Moshe finish speaking than his prediction is dramatically fulfilled. God causes the ground to split open and swallow the households of Korach, Datan and Aviram. As the nation flees in fear from the scene, a heavenly fire consumes Korach's two hundred fifty followers.[1]

---

1. The text later states that the children of Korach do not perish during these cataclysmic

In the aftermath of the conflagration, God commands Moshe to instruct Elazar, Aharon's son, to collect the censers used by the insurgents and to create from them hammered-out sheets to be used as a covering for the Altar. In that sanctified location, they will serve to remind the nation that incense may only be offered by the Kohanim.

The next day, the people rise against Moshe and Aharon, accusing them of killing the insurgents. When, in response, a heaven-sent plague breaks out among the people, Moshe commands Aharon to offer atonement by entering the crowd with a burning censer of incense. Aharon complies and the plague is checked – only after, however, claiming one thousand seven hundred victims.

As further proof of Aharon's selection for the kehuna, *God commands Moshe to collect twelve staffs, one from each of the tribes of Israel; to inscribe the name of each tribal leader upon his respective staff – with Aharon's name etched on the staff of the tribe of Levi – and to place the staffs overnight in the Sanctuary. The staff of the tribal leader chosen for the* kehuna, *God explains, will miraculously blossom.*

Moshe complies and the staffs are collected, inscribed, and placed in the Mishkan overnight. Upon entering the Sanctuary the next day and finding Aharon's staff to have blossomed; Moshe brings the staffs out for all to see. God then commands him to return Aharon's staff to the Mishkan and to place it before the Ark, as a continuing sign of the divine selection of Aharon and his descendents.

In the aftermath of these cataclysmic events, the people express fear over their continuing vulnerability to punishment for careless entry into the Sanctuary. God responds by reiterating the responsibility of the Kohanim and Levi'im to safeguard the Sanctuary against unauthorized trespass.

The parsha ends as God outlines specific gifts that must be given by the people to the Kohanim and Levi'im, in return for their divinely appointed service.

---

events (Bamidbar 26:11). The Talmudic scholars debate (Talmud Bavli Sanhedrin 110a) whether Korach himself is swallowed by the earth, perishes by the fire, dies in a plague (see Rashi there) or, as the instigator of the rebellion, is forced to endure both the earthquake and the fire.

1 Korach's Rebellion 1: Dramatic Devastation

Context
Under the leadership of Korach and his colleagues, Datan, Aviram and On, two hundred fifty prominent members of the nation rise in rebellion against the authority of Moshe and Aharon.

At Moshe's request, God responds to this uprising with devastating power, punishing the perpetrators through a divinely targeted earthquake and a heaven-sent firestorm.[1]

Questions
What is the catalyst for Korach's rebellion and what is the substance of the rebels' complaints?

Why does Moshe abandon his customary role as the people's defender and instead request that God publicly and severely punish the perpetrators? What danger posed by this rebellion could possibly warrant such a transformation in this great leader?

No punishment recorded in the Torah is more devastatingly dramatic than the punishment meted out by God to Korach and his followers. Why does God respond so harshly to this uprising?

Approaches

—— A ——

Rabbinic argument erupts over the Korach story even before it begins, as the scholars debate the temporal position of this narrative in the Torah text.

Utilizing the broad exegetical rule that the Torah does not necessarily follow chronological order, the Ibn Ezra argues that Korach's rebellion

---

1. Bamidbar 16:1–35.

actually occurs earlier than recorded. Central to the uprising is the deep discontent rising out of an event rooted at Sinai: the transfer of ritual privileges from the firstborn Israelites to the Levi'im as a result of the firstborns' participation in the sin of the golden calf. The rebels are able to play upon the nation's suspicion that Moshe reassigned these powers on his own in order to benefit his own Levite relatives.

Although a Levi himself, Korach is also a firstborn and, therefore, a viable leader of the rebellion. Datan, Aviram and On join the uprising because, as members of the tribe of Reuven, they continue to harbor resentment over Yaakov's transfer of firstborn privileges from their tribal ancestor Reuven to Yosef, at the end of the patriarchal era. Even concerning this complaint, the Ibn Ezra suggests, the rebels effectively cast suspicion upon Moshe. Yehoshua, Moshe's designated successor, belongs to the tribe of Ephraim, one of the two tribes descending from Yosef. Ignoring the evidence from the patriarchal era, the rebels suggest that Moshe unilaterally bestows the birthright upon Yosef in order to raise Yehoshua's political standing.

Finally, a number of Levi'im join the rebellion, frustrated over their forced subordination to Aharon and his sons, the Kohanim.[2]

Agreeing with the Ibn Ezra that the rebels' lust for power plays a central role in the uprising, the Ramban also perceives a varied list of personal motives within the insurgent camp. He strongly opposes, however, the Ibn Ezra's claim that the rebellion occurs earlier than recorded in the text.

Only now, says the Ramban, after the devastating tragedies of Taveira, Kivrot Hata'ava and above all *chet hameraglim*, is Moshe vulnerable to attack. As the entire nation reels from these multiple crises, general questions naturally begin to emerge concerning Moshe's leadership. Against this turbulent backdrop, the malcontents in the people's midst feel empowered to raise the multiple grievances that they have patiently nurtured to this point.

In his disagreement with the Ibn Ezra, the Ramban uses this very episode to underscore his belief that the Torah narrative always unfolds chronologically unless otherwise indicated in the text.[3]

---

2. Ibn Ezra, Bamidbar 16:1.
3. Ramban, Bamidbar 16:1.

B

While agreeing with both the Ibn Ezra and the Ramban that a varied list of personal motives powers Korach's uprising, the Chatam Sofer goes one step further and maintains that the goals of the insurgents actually conflict with each other. Korach, on the one hand, objects to the investiture of communal and priestly authority solely in the family of Moshe and Aharon and demands an equal sharing of that authority among all the Levite families. The two hundred fifty firstborn rebels, on the other hand, oppose the overall transfer of power to the Levi'im in the first place and pine for a return of that authority to their own hands.[4]

Other scholars, including the Malbim, agree with the Chatam Sofer's claim of simmering internal conflict within the rebel camp but offer differing opinions as to the actual motivations of the insurgent subgroups.[5]

The Chatam Sofer and the Malbim both incisively apply this vision of tension in the rebel camp towards the resolution of a mystery surrounding a well-known Mishna in Pirkei Avot:

> Any dispute that is for the sake of Heaven will ultimately yield a constructive outcome; but one that is not for the sake of Heaven will not yield a constructive outcome. What sort of dispute was for the sake of Heaven? The dispute of Hillel and Shammai. And which was not for the sake of Heaven? The dispute of Korach and his assembly.[6]

At first glance, this Mishna reflects a striking imbalance. After citing "the dispute of Hillel and Shammai," the rabbis should have referenced "the dispute of Korach and Moshe." Why refer to this second conflict as "the dispute of *Korach and his assembly*"? The Chatam Sofer and the Malbim explain that, through this twist of phrase, the rabbis subtly allude to the underlying flaw that dooms Korach's rebellion from the start. Far from an idealistic, principled effort, this is an insurrection rooted in the conflicting personal ambitions of its participants. The only cause uniting the rebels is their opposition to the leadership of Moshe and Aharon. Had *Korach and*

---

4. Torat Moshe, Parshat Korach.
5. Malbim, Bamidbar 16:1–3.
6. Pirkei Avot 5:20.

C

One common thread unites the views of all these authorities, from the Ibn Ezra and the Ramban, who see converging positions within the rebel camp, to the Chatam Sofer and the Malbim, who discern simmering conflict among the insurgents. The rebellion confronting Moshe and Aharon represents a union of *convenience*, rather than *conviction*. Tapping into the nation's deep frustrations, protagonists of all sorts seize the opportunity to further their own vastly varied agendas.

D

Other commentaries perceive an even deeper subtext to Korach's rebellion. Agreeing with the Ramban's chronology that this insurrection follows the sin of the spies, these scholars discern within the rebels' claims a concrete perpetuation of that recent devastating episode. Support for this position can be found in Datan and Aviram's harsh refusal to Moshe's offer to confer:

> "We shall not ascend! Is it not enough that you have taken us out of a land flowing with milk and honey to cause us to die in the wilderness, yet you now seek to rule over us, even to rule over us further?
>
> "Moreover, you have not brought us to a land flowing with milk and honey nor given us a heritage of field and vineyard! Even were you to gouge out the eyes of these men, we shall not ascend!"[8]

With these declarations, Datan and Aviram raise the stakes of the rebellion, cunningly building upon the people's natural discontent in the wake of their failure to enter the land of Canaan. The uprising no longer centers solely on the personal grievances of a select few. At issue is the totality of Moshe's political leadership. He has taken the nation, the rebel leaders argue, from the security of Egypt (a land that Datan and Aviram

---

7. Malbim, Bamidbar 16:1.
8. Bamidbar 16:12–14.

now ironically refer to as a land "flowing with milk and honey") to die in the wilderness: Moshe has failed the entire people.

The Sforno maintains that the accusations leveled against Moshe by Datan and Aviram are even more devastating: "It is not enough that you have done us evil by taking us out a land flowing with milk and honey into the wilderness; *but you also mock us* concerning your very failure to bring us into the land.... By commanding us concerning laws that only apply in the land of Canaan[9]...[you speak of the land] as if it were already ours and we had within it 'a heritage of field and vineyard.'"[10]

Others see Datan and Aviram's proclamation, "We shall not ascend," as a direct reference to Canaan. *Under no circumstances*, they say, *will we ascend to that land! Like the spies before us, we have no desire to face the challenges that entry into Canaan would entail.*[11]

---— E ———

Finally, two dramatic confrontations recorded in the Midrash suggest what may well be the most significant element to Korach's rebellion.

The Midrash relates that Korach, accompanied by two hundred fifty communal leaders dressed in robes of pure *techeilet* (a specific shade of blue associated with the mitzva of *tzitzit*; see Shelach 5, footnote 1), approaches and challenges Moshe: "Does a four-cornered, completely blue garment require *tzitzit* or is it exempt?"

When Moshe replies that such a garment does indeed require *tzitzit*, the rebels mockingly retort: "*One blue thread* fulfills the *tzitzit* requirement of any four-cornered garment, yet a garment that is totally blue is not, by dint of its basic color, automatically exempt?"[12]

Korach then challenges Moshe a second time: "Does a house filled with holy texts require a mezuza on its doorpost?"

When, once again, Moshe answers in the affirmative, Korach mocks: "The two scriptural sections found in a mezuza fulfill a home's requirement, yet the two hundred seventy scriptural sections of the entire Torah text do

---

9. Ibid., 15:1–31.
10. Sforno, Bamidbar 16:14.
11. An anonymous position quoted by the Abravanel, Bamidbar 16:1.
12. Midrash Rabba Bamidbar 18:2, as quoted by Rashi, Bamidbar 16:1.

not? *These [illogical] precepts could not have been divinely commanded to you, Moshe; clearly you fabricated them yourself.*"¹³

Whether or not we accept these recorded confrontations as literal, the intent of the Midrash is clear. The rebellion of Korach is not simply a political power grab, nor solely a revolt against entry into the land. To the rabbinic mind, this uprising constitutes *a direct attack on Moshe's overall halachic authority.*

Once raised by the Midrash, this theme resonates in rabbinic sources across the ages, finding eloquent voice in our day in a powerful exposition by Rabbi Joseph Soloveitchik. The Rav maintains that Korach's rebellion is best perceived as "a 'common sense' rebellion against Torah authority" – an attack on Torah law based on man's limited logic.

The Rav explains that Korach's error lies in his failure to appreciate the two levels of intelligence involved in the application of Jewish law. While the path of halacha is partially guided by *da'at*, basic intelligence and practical judgment, its primary determinant is *chochma*, specialized knowledge and scholarship. The primacy of *chochma* in the determination of law, says the Rav, rises out of another basic truth. *While inner religious experience is a critical component of Jewish religious practice, the concrete act of a mitzva's performance is primary. The divinely inspired mitzvot have intrinsic value, independent of their effect upon those who perform them.* The development of these mitzvot, therefore, cannot be left to the subjective common sense of "everyman." Only those possessing *chochma* – trained in the intricacies of Jewish thought and scholarship – can determine the path of the law:

> The objective act of performing the mitzva is our starting point. The mitzva does not depend on the emotion; rather, it induces the emotion. One's religious inspiration and fervor are generated and guided by the mitzva, not the reverse.... In teaching law and its proper application, the *chochma* dimension of knowledge is decisive.... [O]nly the Torah scholar is the authority and common sense can be misleading.¹⁴

---

13. Midrash Rabba Bamidbar 18:2.
14. Besdin, *Reflections of the Rav*, vol. 1, *Lessons in Jewish Thought*, pp. 143–144.

Korach argues the case for religious subjectivism; believing that an individual's personal feelings should be the overriding determinant of his religious practice. He argues that a mitzva itself has no objective value; all that matters is how the act affects the participant. Within Korach's religious rubric, therefore, *da'at* (common sense) and not *chochma* (scholarship and expertise) defines the course of Jewish law: anyone, no matter his background, can decide what the law should be. Furthermore, mitzvot should be modified according to changing times and tailored to the spiritual needs of each person. *In Korach's world there is no inherent value or constancy to God-given law; all that matters is man's own sensibilities.*

Korach's dangerous rebellion, continues the Rav, serves as the prototype for challenges to halachic authority in our day:

> Today, many individuals claim the right to exercise their own common sense in determining the relevance and format of contemporary Judaism, despite the fact that they are hardly Biblical and Talmudic scholars. Synagogue ritual committees and popular magazine articles debate the continued usefulness of various religious practices and explore the possibilities of reformulating Judaism in line with modern thought. These self-styled "*poskim* [halachic authorities]" concede their lack of formal training in Jewish texts and sources, but they insist nonetheless on their right to decide fundamental religious questions on the basis of "common sense."…
>
> Today, reasonable people concede the authority of mathematicians, physicists, and physicians in their areas of expertise, and would not think of challenging them merely on the basis of common sense. Why, then, are so many well-intentioned people ready to question the authority of the Torah scholar, the *lamdan*, in his area of specialized knowledge?[15]

From the Rav's vantage point, our own experience, in our own time, sheds light on the dangers of Korach's rebellion against Moshe Rabbeinu, Moshe our teacher, the progenitor of rabbinic authority across the ages. Without the defining force of that authority, Jewish law cannot survive. Unfettered,

---

15. Ibid., pp. 139, 141.

in his time or in ours, Korach's path of religious subjectivism leads to the destruction of the legal process begun at Sinai.[16]

F

No matter which approach we adopt in our analysis of Korach's rebellion – whether we view his uprising as a personal grab for power, a revolt against entry into the land, a rebellion against halachic authority or an amalgam of all the above – it is easy to understand the force with which the uprising is addressed by both God and Moshe. Left unanswered, Korach's public effort to undermine the leadership of Moshe and Aharon would have dealt a devastating blow to the newly developing fledgling Jewish nation.

God must therefore respond, swiftly and harshly.

Points to Ponder
I. Direction in the Darkness

As I write this study, my Englewood community is reeling from a number of devastating tragedies. The most recent of these, the sudden death of a wonderful twenty-one-year-old college student, has left many within the community searching for spiritual direction. Particularly affected, of course, have been the young man's many friends.

On the morning following this young man's tragic death, a number of those friends appeared in unexpected numbers at one of our synagogue's daily prayer services. When I spoke to them after the service, it became clear to me that their personal search for direction had led them back to the "familiar": to the *shul* (synagogue) and to its daily prayers. Not knowing exactly what the experience would offer them at this difficult moment, they nonetheless felt that this was the thing to do, that their attendance would somehow provide them with a sense of structure and solace, a feeling of coming home.

Here then, is yet another argument against allowing the performance of mitzvot to be subject to the performer's feelings and whims. Had these young men not attended services countless times under less dramatic circumstances, had they not come regularly even when they didn't feel like it – even when it didn't seem to make logical sense – they would not have known where to turn in the face of tragedy. Ongoing involvement

---
16. Ibid., pp. 139–148.

in mitzvot, observed even at times when their observance seems routine and pro forma, changes and shapes our religious outlook and provides a structure that we can depend on when we need it most. While personal meaning should always be sought in daily observance, the regular performance of mitzvot itself will one day aid us, even when that daily meaning is absent.[17]

As these young men from my community clearly learned, Torah law affords us with a structure to which we can turn when answers elude us – a structure that, in turn, provides direction through the darkness.

II. It's Not about Us

At the core of Korach's rebellion lies another issue that finds real resonance in our day.

By definition, the decision to live a "Jewish life" requires the ceding of center stage to an entity larger than ourselves. We concede that everything is not about us, our needs, or our desires. We align ourselves with a higher life purpose that, in our estimation, is determined by God and demands our allegiance.

This pledge of loyalty to the Divine, however, can be subtly undermined through our own actions, without our realization. By demanding that every aspect of religious law "make sense," by insisting that only rules understandable to us are truly meaningful, we place ourselves, rather than God, center stage. Religious observance becomes yet another aspect of our lives that we insist on subjugating to our design and control. What we think becomes important, rather than what God demands.

The fact remains, however, that surrender of authority to a higher power is the first essential step on the path to meaningful religious life. Only upon taking that step can we begin to benefit from the humbling yet empowering sense of belonging to a much greater whole.

Unlike many other faith traditions, Judaism does not demand that our surrender to God be totally "unconditional." As we have often noted, our tradition openly invites us to struggle with its details in a search for meaning. In the end, however, when understanding eludes us, the moment

---

17. It goes without saying that Jewish tradition maintains that an individual's regular performance of mitzvot always has a global positive effect – not just for the individual himself, but for the world at large.

of surrender to the Divine arrives. We must then set our logic aside and commit ourselves to the observance of the law, simply because we are so commanded.

This ceding of control to a higher authority has never been more difficult or more important than it is today. In our culture of personal entitlement, where we misguidedly tend to see ourselves – and teach our children to see themselves – as centers of the universe, true religious perspective becomes an essential and healthy counterbalance, reminding us that our own lives acquire their greatest significance within the context of a much greater, God-determined whole.

Where Korach lost his way, we must find ours, if we are to assume our proper place in God's universe.

2 Korach's Rebellion 2: Give and Take

Context
The Torah opens the narrative of Korach's rebellion with the following statement: *Va'yikach Korach ben Yitzhar ben Kehat ben Levi...*, "And Korach the son of Yitzhar the son of Kehat the son of Levi *took*, as did Datan and Aviram the sons of Eliav and On the son of Pelet, the offspring of Reuven...."[1]

Questions
The Torah states that Korach and his colleagues "took" but fails to tell us what was "taken." What is the meaning of this puzzling omission?

Approaches

— A —

A variety of suggestions are offered by the classical authorities as they attempt to explain the mysterious opening of Parshat Korach.

Rashi, for example, adopts Onkelos' translation of the text rendering the phrase *va'yikach Korach*, "and Korach took," as *va'etpaleg Korach*, "and Korach separated."[2] The Torah, Rashi explains, informs us that Korach, through his actions, "took himself out of" (separated himself from) the community.[3]

According to most manuscripts of his commentary, Rashi quotes a second possibility based on Midrashic sources.[4] Korach "took" others with him. Through the persuasive power of his words and the strength of

---

1. Bamidbar 16:1.
2. Targum Onkelos, ibid.
3. Rashi, Bamidbar 16:1.
4. Midrash Rabba Bamidbar, Korach 1; Midrash Tanchuma Bamidbar, Korach 1.

his personality, he convinced the legal leaders of the community to join his insurrection.[5]

The Chizkuni offers a slight variation on Rashi's second approach. Korach "took" Datan, Aviram and On. Korach launched his rebellion by convincing the coconspirators mentioned in the text to join him. This interpretation of the text, the Chizkuni admits, requires that we ignore the Hebrew letter *vav* (meaning "and") that portrays Datan, Aviram and On as "takers" along with Korach, rather than as "being taken." In defense of his position, the Chizkuni notes a series of other locations in the Torah where the letter *vav* seems superfluous.[6]

Citing the passage from Bereishit "And Avraham *took* Sarai, his wife, and Lot, his nephew, and all of their possessions and the souls they made in Charan…," the Rashbam follows the Tanchuma and Chizkuni's lead and explains that the first sentence of Parshat Korach refers to Korach's general gathering of his followers.[7]

In a lengthy exposition, the Ramban rejects Rashi's interpretations and instead quotes an alternative position cited by the Midrash Tanchuma.[8] The language of "taking," the Ramban argues, is often associated in the Torah with matters of the heart. In this case, the phrase *va'yikach Korach* implies that Korach "took" the advice of his heart in moving against Moshe and Aharon.[9]

After defending Rashi's interpretation against the Ramban's critique, however, Rabbi Eliyahu Mizrachi challenges the latter's understanding of the Tanchuma. A careful reading of this opinion in the Midrash, says the Mizrachi, reveals that its authors view Korach as the *object* rather than as the *subject* of the phrase *va'yikach Korach*. The phrase does not mean "and Korach took," but rather "and Korach was taken." Korach is overcome by the desires of his heart. His doomed journey begins when he falls sway to his own destructive desires.[10]

---

5. Rashi, Bamidbar 16:1.
6. Chizkuni, Bamidbar 16:1.
7. Rashbam, Bamidbar 16:1.
8. Midrash Tanchuma Bamidbar, Korach 2.
9. Ramban, Bamidbar 16:1.
10. Mizrachi, Bamidbar 16:1.

---- **B** ----

In addition to these and other classical interpretations, a creative approach to the introductory sentence of Parshat Korach can be suggested. This approach, somewhat Midrashic in nature, rises out of one powerful fact: *Korach's rebellion is dangerous not because it is devoid of truth but because it is a manipulation of the truth.*

Kol ha'eida kulam kedoshim…, "the entire assembly – all of them – are holy, and in their midst is the Lord," Korach argues, "and why do you exalt yourselves over the congregation of the Lord?"[11] *If we are all equally holy before God, Moshe, what gives you and Aharon the right to hold sway over us?*

The populist call for equality resonating in Korach's words finds clear support in God's prior directive to the people: *Kedoshim tihiyu*, "Holy shall you be."[12] *In matters of sanctity, you are all potentially equal…* (see *Vayikra*: Kedoshim 1, *Approaches* C).

Had Korach's call for equality remained in the sphere of sanctity, in the realm of our personal relationship to God, his ideas would have posed no threat. Concerning the individual quest for sanctity, Korach is, after all, correct. *Kol ha'eida kulam kedoshim*, "The entire assembly – all of them – are holy." Each of us is challenged to forge a unique relationship with the Divine. In the realm of this relationship, we are all potentially equal because the only yardstick against which we are each judged is ourselves. Whatever our life journey may be, the sanctity we each achieve is determined by how well we travel the road and by the personal qualities we demonstrate along the way.

Korach's big lie emerges, however, when he makes the leap from the area of *relationship* to the area of *role* in religious life. For while it is true that in the sphere of relationship to our Creator we are all potentially equal, in the roles we play, we clearly are not. We cannot all be a Moshe or an Aharon, nor are we meant to be. Many life positions within Jewish experience are automatically assigned at birth. Even earned roles, technically open to all, are not, on a practical level, *equally* open to all. Genetics, environment, the time periods in which we each live, the choices made by those who precede us – and more – all help determine, together

---

11. Bamidbar 16:3.
12. Vayikra 19:2.

with our own personal choices, the unique ultimate role that each of us plays in our nation's story (see *Vayikra*: Tzav 2; Kedoshim 1, *Approaches* D for a fuller discussion of this topic).

When Korach deliberately and seamlessly moves from the realm of *relationship* to the realm of *role* in religious life by challenging the deserved authority of Moshe and Aharon, he threatens to undermine the delicate, critical balance meant to shape the Israelites' connection to their Creator, and God must respond.

Perhaps then, the Torah leaves the phrase *va'yikach Korach*, "and Korach took," ambiguous, specifically because the phenomenon it describes is amorphous. *Korach "took" pieces of his world. He selectively chose and manipulated elements of the truth in order to create his own narrative and fashion his own reality.* Cynically, he plays upon the ambitions of those around him, building on a kernel of legitimacy, to convince them of the righteousness of his unjust claims.

Korach's story thus becomes a cautionary tale, alerting us to demagogues across the ages and to the powerful narratives they painstakingly weave. Using the truth selectively as a tool, tailoring that truth to suit their purposes, playing on the weaknesses of their contemporaries, the Korachs of the world skillfully create their own persuasive realities, designed to lure the unsuspecting into their camp.

Points to Ponder

Beyond the false realities consciously created by Korach and his philosophical heirs, the concept of personal worlds has greater, more universal application.

Over many years in the rabbinate, I have developed my own informal, straightforward gauge of mental health. This measurement is based on the principle that we each live in individual worlds, unique realities unconsciously created out of our own personalities, perceptions and outlooks. *No two of these worlds are exactly the same.*

An individual's mental health can be determined by how closely his own personal world matches the baseline of the "real world." The closer his world to that baseline (the worlds will never match perfectly), the healthier, by definition, he will be. Conversely, the further his world from the baseline, the more problems he will encounter.

While this equation may seem obvious and self-understood, it is often forgotten in the breach.

My colleagues and I are frequently approached by individuals indignantly wrestling with the thoughts and actions of others that, to them, defy comprehension. In situations ranging from practical disputes to wrenching personal crises, the basic questions we hear are constant: *How could he/she act this way? What is he/she thinking? What gives him/her the right?*

When confronted with such situations, my first counsel, more often than not, is to recognize that *the actions of others make sense to them*. In the individual worlds that they occupy, they find logic to their thoughts and deeds.

In circumstances where the perceptual disparity between the protagonists is not that great, when the individual worlds in question are not that distant from the "real world baseline," the simple acceptance of divergent perspectives is often the first step towards reconciliation. When we recognize another's right to see things his way, we set our feet squarely on the path towards mutual respect.

In more difficult, even tragic circumstances when the world of at least one protagonist is so distant from the "real world baseline" as to create aberrant behavior, the acceptance of the existence of that individual's personal world is, nonetheless, instructive. At the very least, such acceptance frees others from the futile attempt to comprehend the individual's behavior in their own terms, enabling them to turn their energies to more productive goals. Optimally, particularly in cases involving a family unit, such recognition leads to the pursuit of professional help both for the individual in question and for those who deal with him directly.

3 Korach's Rebellion 3: Pushing God's Hand

Context

The Torah describes Moshe's immediate reaction to the rebellion led by Korach, Datan, Aviram and On, as follows:

> And Moshe heard and fell on his face. And he spoke to Korach and to his entire assembly, saying: "Come morning and God will make known who is His own....
>
> "This shall you do: Take for yourselves censers – Korach and his entire assembly – and put fire in them and place incense upon them, before God tomorrow. And it will be the man that God will choose, he is the holy one. You presume too much, children of Levi!"[13]

Later in the narrative, after attempting to reason with the rebels and after receiving instructions from God to separate the onlookers from Korach's camp, Moshe proclaims to the watching nation:

> "With this you shall know that the Lord sent me to perform all of these deeds; that it was not from my heart. If these [the rebels] die like all men and the destiny of all men is appointed for them, the Lord has not sent me.
>
> "But if the Lord will create a new phenomenon, and the ground will open its mouth and swallow them up with all that is theirs, and they will descend alive into the pit, then you will know that these men have provoked the Lord."[14]

---

13. Bamidbar 16:4–7.
14. Ibid., 16:28–30.

Questions

A careful reading of the text reveals a powerfully puzzling question that we could easily miss.

How can Moshe devise a supernatural test without prior consultation with God?

All other paranormal miracles in the Torah are divinely ordained. What gives Moshe the right, in this one instance, to respond to Korach's rebellion by first constructing a supernatural trial and only then apparently requesting/demanding God's participation?

Approaches

— A —

A number of commentaries, including Saadia Gaon and the Rashbam, avoid the questions raised by Moshe's reactions to Korach entirely by claiming that Moshe's seemingly independent actions are not independent, at all.

Upon hearing the rebels' accusations, Moshe "falls on his face." This response, these scholars maintain, is an attempt on Moshe's part to communicate with God through prayer and a request for prophetic vision. During his supplications, Moshe receives divine instructions as to how to respond to the challenges before him. The steps outlined in the passages that follow, therefore, are determined by God, not by Moshe.[15]

— B —

Other authorities, however, including Rashi, mirror an earlier Midrashic tradition that interprets Moshe's reaction to the insurrection differently. Moshe falls on his face, they maintain, not in prayer, but in shame and despair. Confronted with the Israelites' repeated rebellions, Moshe now finds himself incapable of interceding on their behalf.[16]

According to these authorities, however, our original questions remain. If God does not communicate with Moshe at the outset of the rebellion, how does Moshe know what to do? Is it possible that Moshe, on his own, devises the test by which Korach and his followers will be tried

---
15. Saadia Gaon, Bamidbar 16:4; Rashbam, ibid.
16. Rashi, Bamidbar 16:4; Midrash Tanchuma Bamidbar, Korach 4.

and then requests/demands God's acquiescence? If so, by what right does he do so?

C

Perhaps the answer lies in the overarching threat presented by Korach's rebellion. As we have noted, this insurrection is not only a grab for personal power on the part of the rebels, but a fundamental challenge to Moshe's overall halachic influence. Left unchecked, Korach's efforts would undermine the very concept of rabbinic authority at its infancy, dealing a death blow to the halachic process and to the ability of the Jewish nation to survive across the ages (see Korach 1, *Approaches* C).

Moshe must, therefore, respond comprehensively – not only to the open rebellion, but to its underlying agenda. Central to the concept of rabbinic authority and to the halachic process as a whole is the revolutionary partnership forged between God and man in the development of the law. Within the context of this partnership, God effectively cedes the determination of the law to man through His authorization of the rabbis to interpret and apply the divine decrees. He does so with the implicit promise that as long as a scholarly effort to reach the truth is made and full loyalty to the halachic process is shown, he will agree with whatever conclusions the rabbis reach. Relinquishing His infallible control over the course of the law, God thus allows man, with all his limitations, to determine its path (see *Shmot*: Yitro 5).

Moshe recognizes, however, that with Korach's rebellion, the halachic God-man partnership already stands at a critical crossroads – almost before it begins. He concludes that, to protect the integrity of the halachic process, he must not only prove himself to be the divinely selected progenitor of rabbinic authority, but he must also openly demonstrate the divinely mandated underpinnings of that authority. He therefore turns to God and takes a calculated risk:

Dear Lord, at this critical moment Your very plans for us hang in the balance. If this challenge to my leadership is successful, if the questions raised by this rebellion take root in the hearts of the people, more will be lost than my leadership alone. All respect for rabbinic authority will dissipate and chaos will reign in the transmission of the law.

We must, therefore, show the nation the nature of our joint agreement concerning the halachic process. Across the ages, the rabbis will be challenged to make legal decisions and to take concrete action without the benefit of Your prior approval. They will do so with the full confidence that You will retroactively accept the legal decisions they make.

Now, I ask that You do the same, in a different realm. Allow me, this one time, to dictate the terms of this trial to Korach and his followers, to develop the supernatural test by which they will be tried. If the people see that You retroactively agree with my stipulations, they will accept not only my leadership but also the partnership with You upon which it is based. They will come to appreciate and respect the nature of rabbinic authority – the authority destined to guide them across the ages.

Moshe, risking everything on a bold experiment that he feels must succeed, publicly "pushes God's hand" in response to Korach's rebellion. God's positive response, in the face of open challenge, reinforces the partnership lying at the core of the halachic process and ensures the stability of Jewish law at its inception.

4 Korach's Rebellion 4: Making Sense of the Incense

Context

As indicated in the previous study, Moshe responds to Korach's accusations by instructing Korach and his followers to "Take for yourselves censers…and put fire in them and place *ketoret* [incense] upon them, before God tomorrow. And it will be the man that God will choose, he is the holy one."[1]

Later, in the aftermath of Korach's rebellion, when plague erupts within the nation as a result of their continuing complaints against Moshe and Aharon, Moshe commands his brother: "Take the censer and place upon it fire from the altar and place *ketoret* – and go quickly to the assembly and provide atonement for them…." Aharon complies and the plague is checked.[2]

Questions

Whether we view God or Moshe as the initial architect of the supernatural trial by which Korach and his followers will be tested (see previous study), the question remains: Why is *ketoret* chosen as the centerpiece of that trial?

Furthermore, how does Moshe know that the *ketoret* will be an effective mechanism in checking the spread of the plague that afflicts the Israelites later in the narrative?

What is the source of this symbol's apparent power?

---

1. Bamidbar 16:6.
2. Ibid., 17:11.

Approaches

── **A** ──────────────────────────────

Before attempting to interpret the specific role that the *ketoret* plays in this episode, a brief exploration of the incense itself, its place in the Temple service and its importance in later rabbinic thought will prove instructive.

First mentioned in Parshat Teruma during the instructions for the creation of the Sanctuary and its utensils,[3] the *ketoret* was offered in the Temple twice daily by a Kohen, once in the morning and once in the evening, on a special golden altar reserved for that purpose.[4] On Yom Kippur, the incense assumed an extraordinary role, accompanying the Kohen Gadol on his solitary journey into the *Kodesh Kadashim*, the Holy of Holies, where its smoke filled this most sanctified space.[5]

Even during the daily service, the *ketoret* was presented by the designated Kohen in private, with all onlookers removed from the area.

While the Torah lists only four ingredients for the *ketoret*,[6] rabbinic tradition maintains that the incense was actually manufactured from eleven different component spices specified to Moshe at Sinai.[7] The manufacture of the *ketoret* was reserved for Temple use only. Any individual who deliberately prepared this formula for another purpose became subject to the severe punishment of *karet*, excision from the community at the hands of God.[8]

As a symbol, the *ketoret* captures the imagination of the rabbis, many of whom view the incense as being invested with extraordinary atoning and curative powers.[9] Other sources speak of the ability of the *ketoret* to materially enrich those involved in its service. To ensure that its powerful benefits could be shared by all, no Kohen was given the opportunity to offer the daily incense more than once in his career.[10] Some authorities maintain that, in the absence of the Temple service, great merit accrues

---

3. Shmot 25:5.
4. Ibid., 30:7–8.
5. Vayikra 16:12–13.
6. Shmot 30:34.
7. Talmud Bavli Kritot 6b.
8. Rambam, *Mishneh Torah*, Hilchot Klei Hamikdash 2:9.
9. Talmud Bavli Yoma 44a.
10. Ibid., 26a.

to those who simply recite the passage of Pitum Haketoret,[11] which discusses the production of the incense. For these and other reasons, many communities include this passage at the end of the daily morning prayer service.

At the opposite end of the spectrum lie those authorities who perceive utilitarian goals in the offering of the *ketoret*. The Rambam, for example, explains that the incense served to protect the honor due to the Sanctuary by countering the odors created by the slaughtering, preparation and burning of the many animal sacrifices offered daily. "For the soul feels elevated in the presence of spices and a good odor, and is attracted to them, just as it abhors and avoids a bad odor."[12]

The questions, however, remain. What is the source of the mystical powers attributed by many authorities to the incense? Is there any logical explanation for these powers? And, again, why does the symbol specifically play such a central role in the Korach story?

B

As we have noted in the past, we venture into "turbulent waters" with questions such as these. The mysterious mitzvot of the Temple worship, like all *chukim* (edicts whose purpose is not evident from the text), may well forever remain beyond our ken. Some authorities, in fact, reject any attempt to interpret *chukim* from a logical perspective. Such exploration, they believe, undermines the very purpose of these commandments which are specifically designed to cultivate man's unquestioning loyalty to God. Other authorities, however, encourage intellectual examination of all mitzvot as a necessary component in the quest to reach a more complete understanding of God's will. Even these scholars, however, caution that the explanations derived for *chukim* may or may not be accurate and should never become the reason for their observance. (See *Shmot*: Teruma 3; *Vayikra*: Vayikra 2, Approaches II A; *Vayikra*: Shmini 4, Questions, Approaches F; *Vayikra*: Tazria-Metzora 1, Questions; *Vayikra*: Acharei Mot 1, Approaches; *Vayikra*: Kedoshim 5b.)

---

11. Talmud Bavli Kritot 6a.
12. Rambam, *Moreh Nevuchim* 3:45.

C

If we accept, for the purpose of this study, that the search for meaning in all mitzvot is commendable, a powerful Talmudic tradition points the way towards a deeper understanding of the *ketoret* and its central role in the Korach narrative: "Rabbi Chana bar Bizna said in the name of Shimon Chasida: 'Any fast day that does not include the participation of sinners from within the Jewish community is not a fast; for the galbanum had a repugnant odor and yet the Scripture counted it among the *ketoret* spices.'"[13]

Rabbi Shimon's moral lesson, derived allegorically from the *ketoret*, underscores the unique nature of this offering. The *ketoret* is, by definition, a "blend," its aromatic "sweet savor" achieved through the interaction of its combined ingredients. Each carefully measured element of the incense is critical to its composition; even the absence of the galbanum, unusable in isolation, invalidates the mixture. Similarly, every individual plays a decisive role in determining the nature of the collective. The "sinners of Israel" not only achieve personal atonement when they join their brothers in the penitential experience of a fast day, but they contribute to the combined communal endeavor. They become central to the "blend."

From this vantage point, the *ketoret* emerges not only as the *medium*, but as part of the *message* of the trial of Korach.

Korach and his followers directly challenge this overarching concept of community as they move against the authority of Moshe and Aharon. Their line of attack, Nehama Leibowitz notes, is subliminally reflected in the rebels' own words: *Kol ha'eida kulam kedoshim*, "The entire assembly – all of them – are holy."

Tellingly, the rebels do not say, "The entire assembly [as a unit] is holy," but, rather, "The entire assembly – all of them [individually] – are holy."

The rebels' desire for personal aggrandizement overwhelms any sense of collective responsibility. The recent call of Sinai, mandating the creation of a "kingdom of priests and a holy nation," is drowned out by a cacophonous chorus demanding personal privilege and power.[14]

The centrality of the *ketoret* in the unfolding drama thus conveys a powerfully appropriate response to Korach and his followers:

---
13. Talmud Bavli Kritot 6b.
14. Leibowitz, *Iyunim Chadashim B'Sefer Bamidbar*, p. 206.

Your rebellion, rooted in unfettered ambition and a lust for power, threatens to undermine the fundamental phenomenon that grants this nation its strength. We are powerful as a "blend" – individuals with unique attributes and singular roles, working in concert to achieve God's will. No two of us are the same. Our unique individual contributions are all essential, but we attain our full strength, both as individuals and as a nation, only through personal interaction with the community.

As certainly as the ketoret *is a* ta'arovet *(a mixture), we achieve greatness through our* areivut, *our interaction with each other.*

5 Korach's Rebellion 5: A Misunderstanding?

> **Context**
> As the Korach narrative moves towards its dramatic and violent climax, God turns to Moshe and Aharon and commands: "Separate yourself from amid this *eida* [assembly], and I shall destroy them in an instant!"[1]
>
> Immediately Moshe and Aharon fall on their faces and object: "O God, God of the spirits of all flesh, shall one man sin, and You be angry with the entire *eida*?"[2]
>
> God responds: "Speak to the *eida*, saying, 'Get yourselves up from all around the dwelling places of Korach, Datan and Aviram.'"[3]

Questions

What exactly transpires in this strange interchange between God, Moshe and Aharon? Apparently we must accept one of two possibilities. Either God changes His mind as the conversation unfolds or His use of the term *eida* changes contextually.

Specifically, to which *eida* (assembly) does God refer when He warns Moshe and Aharon, "Separate yourself from amid this *eida*, and I shall destroy them in an instant"?

Is the entire nation initially imperiled by God's wrath, as Moshe and Aharon apparently assume? This approach allows for a consistent understanding of the term *eida* throughout the dialogue but requires an acceptance that God "changes His mind," for He first threatens to destroy the *eida* (the entire nation), but relents upon hearing the objections of Moshe and Aharon. He then commands these leaders to move the *eida* away from the rebel camp.

---

1. Bamidbar 16:21.
2. Ibid., 16:22.
3. Ibid., 16:23–24.

Or…do Moshe and Aharon actually misunderstand God's intent? Perhaps all along God threatens to punish only the participants in Korach's rebellion. This approach allows for consistency in God's plan but requires accepting a shift in God's use of the term *eida*. God initially threatens to destroy the *eida*, referring to *the rebel camp*. When Moshe and Aharon erroneously assume that the entire nation is imperiled, God explains His intent more clearly and commands these leaders to separate the *eida*, *the nation*, from the rebels.

Approaches

A

A number of classical commentaries, including Rabbeinu Chananel and the Kli Yakar, maintain that Moshe and Aharon initially misunderstand God's intent. God, from the outset, only intends to punish the rebels. When God proclaims, "Separate yourself from amid this *eida*, and I shall destroy them in an instant," he is threatening to destroy only Adat Korach, Korach's assembly.

Moshe and Aharon, however, misinterpret God's threat to destroy the *eida* as referring to the entire nation and they, therefore, object: "…shall one man sin, and You be angry with the entire *eida*?"

In response, God adopts Moshe and Aharon's use of the word *eida* (referring to the entire nation), and clarifies His aim: "Speak to the *eida* [nation], saying, 'Get yourselves up from all around the dwelling places of Korach, Datan and Aviram.'" *I never intended to destroy the entire nation. As long as the people move out of harm's way, they will be safe.*[4]

B

Raising a series of objections to Rabbeinu Chananel's approach, the Ramban exclaims: "Far be it [from us to say] that Moshe failed to understand his own prophecy and drew a mistaken conclusion."[5] Instead, the Ramban, Rashi and numerous other authorities adopt the position that Moshe and Aharon are correct in their initial assessment of the danger facing the Israelites. God fully intends to punish the entire nation

---

4. Rabbeinu Chananel, quoted in Ramban, Bamidbar 16:21; Kli Yakar 16:21.
5. Ramban, Bamidbar 16:21.

in response to Korach's rebellion and only relents after hearing Moshe and Aharon's plea. According to these scholars, the meaning of the word *eida* remains consistent through the entire passage and refers to the nation as a whole.[6]

Rashi and the Ramban do disagree, however, on one critical point.

Reflecting an earlier Midrashic tradition, Rashi maintains that Moshe and Aharon object to the fundamental inequity in God's intended punishment of the nation. *The people have done nothing wrong*, they argue, *and there is no excuse for a knowing God to inflict punishment upon the innocent.* This argument, Rashi explains, courses beneath the surface of the terse conversation recorded in the text:

> Moshe and Aharon: "O God, God of the spirits of all flesh…" Thou Who knows all thoughts: Yours is not the way of flesh and blood. A king of flesh and blood is unable to fully determine the identity of those who rebel against him. When angered, therefore, he exacts retribution upon all. To You, however, all thoughts are revealed and You know who the sinner is. Therefore, "Shall one man sin, and You be angry with the entire assembly?"
>
> God: You have spoken well. I know and shall make known who has sinned and who has not sinned.[7]

The Ramban, on the other hand, in contrast to Rashi, insists that the Israelites fully deserve their threatened punishment. At the onset of Korach's rebellion, this scholar maintains, the Israelites are solidly supportive of Moshe and Aharon. As the rebellion progresses, however, Korach skillfully convinces the people that, in attempting to regain the privileges of the firstborn, he is defending the entire nation's honor as well as his own. By the time the trial of the rebels begins, the Israelites' support of Moshe and Aharon has waned and the entire nation stands in grave peril.

---

6. Rashi, Bamidbar 16:22; Ramban, Bamidbar 16:21.
7. Rashi, Bamidbar 16:22, referencing the Midrash Tanchuma Bamidbar, Korach 7.

Confronted with this looming disaster, Moshe and Aharon successfully focus God's attention on Korach as the principal perpetrator and, thereby, protect the people.[8]

[Note: According to both Rashi and the Ramban, this event emerges as one of several in the Torah where God seems to change direction in response to the prayers of man. See *Bereishit*: Noach 1, *Approaches* A; *Shmot*: Teruma 1, *Approaches* B; Ki Tissa 5, *Approaches* D; Shelach 1, *Points to Ponder* B; for discussions of some of the philosophical issues raised by this phenomenon.]

─── **C** ───────────────────────────────

Another approach to this dramatic interchange between God, Moshe and Aharon can be suggested if we accept the possibility that while God does indeed threaten the entire nation with destruction, He does so with an ulterior motive. Over the course of this cataclysmic episode, God deliberately sets out to educate the Israelites to a lesson critical to their continued national development: *the lesson of involvement.*

Perhaps, as the confrontation between Moshe and the rebels reaches its climactic moments, the people see themselves as innocent, neutral bystanders. Unwilling to take a stand between the powerful protagonists, the Israelites "hedge their bets": *Let us watch this drama unfold and we will reap the benefit of the results. If Moshe and Aharon emerge victorious, we will remain loyal to them. Nothing will have changed. If, on the other hand, Korach and his followers triumph, they will gain our allegiance.*

Perceiving the Israelites' collective neutrality, God threatens the entire people. "Separate yourself from amid this *eida* [entire nation]," he commands Moshe and Aharon, "and I shall destroy them in an instant!"

Moshe and Aharon reply, "O God, God of the spirits of all flesh, shall one man sin, and You be angry with the entire *eida*?" *O Lord, the people are not guilty. They have done nothing wrong.*

God responds: "Speak to the *eida*, saying, 'Get yourselves up from all around the dwelling places of Korach, Datan and Aviram.'" *Moshe and Aharon, you are mistaken. At critical times like these there is no place for neutrality. There can be no innocent bystanders. Choices must be made.*

---

8. Ramban, Bamidbar 16:21.

Tell the people to vote with their feet. Let them move away from the tents of Korach, Datan, Aviram and their followers; and, by doing so, let them publicly reject the rebels and their cause. The moment has come for the people to decide and, through their decision, determine their own fate.

This approach preserves both linguistic and thematic uniformity over the course of the conversation between God, Moshe and Aharon. The term *eida* consistently refers to the entire nation as God sensitizes the people to the moral imperative of involvement. God does not "change His mind." Instead, he instructs the people to change. *At critical moments in human experience*, He informs them, *there are no innocent bystanders. Decisive choices must be made and acted upon....*

Points to Ponder

"All that is necessary for the triumph of evil is for good men to do nothing."

This statement, often attributed to the Anglo-Irish statesman Edmund Burke,[9] has certainly been painfully proven over the long, turbulent course of Jewish history. Throughout the centuries, the horrific evil perpetrated against the Jewish people has been directly enabled by the apathy of those who stood and watched. The silence of the world in the face of the Holocaust is only the most dramatic iteration of this tragically recurring phenomenon.

While, however, we are quick to point to this failing in others, the lesson rooted at the scene of Korach's trial cuts both ways.

We can justifiably demand the active pursuit of justice from others only if we are willing to engage in that pursuit ourselves. While we, as Jews, clearly have the right to dedicate our greatest energies and efforts towards securing the welfare of our own global Jewish family, we cannot become so insular that the legitimate struggles of others escape our notice and support.

A number of years ago, at the height of the crisis in Macedonia, as the airwaves were filled with images of Albanian refugees languishing in refugee camps, I received an unexpected call from a member of my

---

9. Although this statement is widely attributed to Burke (1729–1797), no definite original source in his writings has been found. Some authorities suggest that it may have been adapted from his statement "When bad men combine, the good must associate; else they will fall one by one, an unpitied sacrifice in a contemptible struggle" (*Thoughts on the Cause of the Present Discontents*, 1770).

congregation, himself the son of Holocaust survivors. "My parents were interned," he said, "in a refugee camp following World War II. My father clearly remembers the kindness of a stranger, a visitor, who brought him a blanket against the cold. In the aftermath of my father's experiences in the Shoah, that simple act of compassion made such a profound impression that it stayed with him for the rest of his life.

"Given my father's experiences, I cannot daily watch the pictures of suffering refugees without doing something. Rabbi, would you be willing to join with me on a mission to aid Albanian refugees in a Kosovar refugee camp?"

Not fully believing that my congregant was serious, I agreed, and, to my vast surprise, soon found myself traveling to Skopia, Macedonia, along with over a dozen other volunteers. There, we joined with young Israeli youth leaders in bringing much-needed supplies, programs and human contact to the refugees.

Among the many aspects of that experience that will remain with me always is the memory of a quiet meeting prior to our departure. We sat around a table in the synagogue library as the participants shared their motivations for joining the mission. The remarks of one member of the group were particularly telling: "For years," she said, "I've heard stories of the actions of a select few 'righteous Gentiles' who courageously acted on behalf of Jews. Now, *I want to be a righteous Jew.*"

6 Is this Miracle Really Necessary?

Context

In the aftermath of Korach's rebellion, after harsh punishments have been meted out to the perpetrators, God turns to Moshe with one final set of instructions. He directs him to collect a staff from each of the tribes of Israel, to inscribe the name of each tribal leader upon his respective staff – with Aharon's name etched onto the staff of the tribe of Levi – and to place the staffs overnight in the Sanctuary.

These staffs, God explains, will serve as miraculous indicators of His own divine will: "And it shall be that the man whom I [God] shall choose, his staff will blossom; and I shall cause the complaints of the children of Israel to subside from upon Me."[1]

Moshe complies with God's instructions, and twelve staffs, each emblazoned with the name of a tribal leader, are brought to the Sanctuary where they remain overnight. On the morrow, when Moshe enters the Sanctuary, he finds that Aharon's staff alone has "brought forth a blossom, sprouted buds and mature almonds."[2] God has, once again, made known His selection of Aharon for the role of Kohen Gadol, High Priest.

After Moshe brings the twelve staffs out for the people to see, God commands him to return Aharon's staff to the Sanctuary where it will serve as a continual reminder, an impediment to further rebellion against God's choices for leadership.[3]

Questions

Why is this miracle necessary?

---

1. Bamidbar 17:20.
2. Ibid., 17:23.
3. Ibid., 17:16–24.

Hasn't God, in the most decisive ways possible, already declared His clear choice of Moshe and Aharon for leadership? Weren't the targeted earthquake, the heaven-sent fire and the devastating plague that punished Korach, his followers and the rebellious Israelites powerful enough indications of God's resolve?

If the Israelites have not been convinced by now of God's choices, will the quiet additional miracle of Aharon's flowering staff really make the difference?

Approaches

— A —

Perhaps the key to understanding the miraculous coda of the Korach narrative lies in focusing not on the final miracle in isolation but, instead, on that miracle's contextual message. The flowering staff of Aharon could hardly be more different from the preceding phenomena that marked God's response to Korach's rebellion. Gone, suddenly, are the terrifying images of earthquakes, fires and plagues. In their place, in stark contrast, now appears the peaceful vision of a budding staff.

As God, over the course of Korach's rebellion, moves from death and destruction towards this culminating miracle of quiet beauty, He conveys a powerful message to the Israelites:

Although I was forced to respond to the uprising against Moshe and Aharon with overwhelming force and power, I do not want the election of these leaders to remain forever rooted in those tragic, necessarily destructive events. Let, instead, the flowering of Aharon's staff become the enduring symbol of his priesthood. Let the leadership of "this lover of peace and pursuer of peace" be forever associated in your minds with a quiet final miracle of creation. And, through this miracle, let both leaders and disciples alike learn that there is no more powerful force in God's arsenal, nor in their own, than the force of creation.

— B —

The transition towards the quiet miracle of Aharon's staff may well herald the onset of an even greater global transition in the nation's development. If we accept that Korach's rebellion occurs, as recorded in the text, after the *chet hameraglim*,[4] the Israelites now stand on the threshold of major changes in the nature of their relationship with God.

Over the course of the next forty years in the wilderness, as one generation of Israelites gives way to the next, the nation will move from the relational level of yira, *fear and awe, to the level of* ahava, *love.*

The generation of the Exodus and Revelation will inexorably disappear, erstwhile slaves whose ability to relate to God is limited to the primitive plane of fear. Heirs to a legacy of torment under Egyptian rule, this generation innately responds only to overwhelming power. God, therefore, speaks to them in a language they can understand. Through events such as: the ten plagues, the parting of the Reed Sea, the thunder and lightning of Sinai and the earthquake, fire and plague of Korach's rebellion, God becomes their new master, to be held in awe and to be feared.

The children of these slaves, however, will experience God differently. Raised for nearly four decades in the bosom of God's continual protection, surrounded by the clouds of glory, nurtured on the heaven-sent manna, this second generation will learn to relate to God through the more mature dimension of love. To this generation, God will emerge as a loving, benevolent parent Who, with kindness and sensitivity, sustains His people on their continuing journey.

The first step in the monumental transition from *yira* to *ahava* may well take place in the quiet of the night, in the solitude of the Sanctuary, as Aharon's staff begins to blossom. With this miracle, God deliberately moves from destruction to creation, heralding a journey that will bring His people close.

Points to Ponder

Our people's formative national journey from *yira* to *ahava* in its relationship with God creates the paradigm for the individual religious passage we each are meant to experience over the course of our lives.

If as children we necessarily begin with *yira*, perceiving God as a mysterious, distant and fearsome power, impassively controlling our destiny, a mature relationship with God requires that we successfully

---

4. Ramban, Bamidbar 16:1; see Korach 1, *Approaches* A for a discussion of the differing opinions concerning the temporal position of the Korach narrative in the Torah.

transition to the dimension of *ahava*, as well. The sense of awe that underlies our perception of the divine should certainly never be lost. As the years pass, however, a growing, more pervasive sense of love is meant to fill our hearts, as we learn to believe in an approachable, benevolent deity Who desires our welfare and cares deeply for our concerns.

Fearing God is easy. Loving Him can, at times, be difficult. Inevitably, there will be moments in our lives when God seems distant, when His will and intentions remain unclear, when our relationship with Him is strained. Nonetheless, we are challenged to cultivate a deep, abiding trust that He is with us even then – perhaps particularly then – watching over us and caring for us as a parent would a child.

The journey towards God experienced by our nation at its infancy should be experienced by each of us, as well. Only then can our relationship with God be complete.

Chukat

CHAPTER 19:1–22:1

Parsha Summary

Mysterious ritual, sad passings, tumultuous passages…

Parshat Chukat opens as God commands Moshe and Aharon concerning the mysterious ritual of the para aduma *(red heifer)*, designed to effect the purification of an individual contaminated by close proximity with a human corpse.

The text then records Miriam's death, as the historical narrative resumes towards the end of the nation's forty-year sojourn in the wilderness.

Finding themselves without water, the people rise in protest against Moshe and Aharon. God instructs Moshe to take his staff, to join with Aharon in gathering the nation and to speak to a specific rock in order to bring forth water. Moshe complies with God's initial requests, but then deviates by chastising the people and striking the rock twice, causing water to flow forth. God informs Moshe and Aharon that, as a result of their failure to publicly sanctify Him during this episode, they will not merit bringing the Israelites into the Promised Land of Canaan.

Moshe sends emissaries to the king of Edom, asking for right of passage through his territory. When the Edomite king refuses and responds by massing his army, the Israelites turn from his border.

Upon the nation's arrival at the mountain of Hor Hahar, God commands Moshe to accompany Aharon and Elazar, Aharon's son, to the mountain's summit. There he is to remove the priestly garments from Aharon and place them on Elazar, in preparation for Aharon's death on the mountaintop. The three leaders obey and Aharon dies on the summit of Hor Hahar. The Israelites descend into mourning.

The nation responds to an attack by the Canaanite king of Arad, and, with God's help, defeats the enemy.

The people rise in complaint against God and Moshe over the rigors of the continuing journey and God responds by releasing an attack of poisonous serpents. The Israelites turn to Moshe, beseeching him to pray for their salvation. In response to Moshe's prayers, God commands him to fashion a copper serpent and place it on a pole in full view of the people. God instructs all victims of the serpents' bites to gaze upon the copper serpent and thereby survive.

The text chronicles the nation's continuing journeys.

When the Israelites request right of passage through the territory of the Emorites, Sichon, the Emorite king, responds by massing his people and attacking. The Israelites roundly defeat the Emorites in battle. When subsequently Og, the king of Bashan, launches an attack, the Israelites are once again victorious.

1 An Abundance of Mystery

Context
With the phrase *Zot chukat haTorah*, "This is the statute of the Torah,"[1] God introduces the laws surrounding the purifying ritual of the *para aduma*, the red heifer.

In summary, the Torah mandates that an individual who comes into close proximity with a human corpse enters a seven-day state of *tuma*, ritual impurity. On the third and seventh day of this period, as an essential step in the process of purification, a solution containing spring water and the ashes of a red heifer are sprinkled upon the contaminated individual. At the end of the seven-day period, after immersing in a mikva, a natural pool of water, the individual completes his process of purification.

In a perplexing turnabout, the Torah also mandates that those involved in the manufacturing of the red heifer solution and its application upon the impure individual experience their own brief period of *tuma* (ritual impurity).[2] The ashes of the red heifer thus possess the unique, puzzling capacity *l'taher et hateme'im u'l'tamei et hatehorim*, "to purify the defiled [the subjects of the ritual] and to defile the pure [the performers of the ritual]."

Questions
Fundamental questions emerge as we confront one of the deepest mysteries of the Torah.

What is the significance of the red heifer and why do its ashes, mixed in a solution with spring water, effect purification?

Why does the *para aduma* solution "defile the pure even as it purifies the defiled"?

---

1. Bamidbar 19:2.
2. Ibid., 19:1–22.

Are we consigned to accept the ritual of the *para aduma* as a commandment without rational basis or can lessons be learned even from this seemingly "magical" mitzva?

Approaches

—— A ——

Once again we find ourselves squarely in the realm of *chukim* (statutes), laws of the Torah that seem to defy logical explanation. While we have entered this arena in our studies before, for the first time we find ourselves at the core of this mysterious realm. More than any other set of Torah laws, the ritual of the red heifer, introduced by the text itself as *chukat haTorah*, "the statute of the Torah," has come to symbolize God's will at its most unfathomable.

Numerous sources in rabbinic literature attest to the depth of the mystery surrounding the *para aduma*. To cite a few:

1. King Solomon, the wisest man in history, was able to unravel all the mysteries of the Torah, with the exception of one. Concerning the laws of the red heifer, he was forced to admit, "I thought I would become wise, but it is beyond me."[3]

2. In response to the challenges of an idolater, Rabbi Yochanan ben Zakai offered an explanation of the laws of *para aduma*. Afterwards, his students objected: "Our teacher, you have pushed him away with a reed [you have given a weak argument]. What, however, will you say to us?"

Rabbi Yochanan responded, "By your lives, the dead do not defile and the waters [of the red heifer] do not purify. Rather, the Holy One Blessed Be He has decreed: 'I have forged a statute and enacted a decree and you have no right to transgress my decree.'"[4]

3. Knowing full well that the nations of the world will challenge the Jews concerning the unfathomable laws surrounding the *para aduma*, the Torah introduces these laws with the phrase *Zot chukat haTorah*, "*This is the statute of the Torah. This is an edict decreed by Me, and you have no right to question it.*"[5]

---

3. Kohelet 7:23; Midrash Rabba Bamidbar 19:3.
4. Midrash Rabba Bamidbar 19:8.
5. Rashi, Bamidbar 19:2.

CHUKAT – AN ABUNDANCE OF MYSTERY

How then are we to approach the puzzling edicts surrounding the *para aduma*? Can logical analysis offer any insight into their mysteries? Do we even have the right to try?

B

Before we continue our analysis, it will be helpful to review a series of conclusions reached in earlier studies concerning *chukim* (for a more detailed discussion of these points complete with references, see *Shmot*: Teruma 3; see also *Vayikra*: Vayikra 1, *Approaches* II A; Shmini 4, *Questions*, *Approaches* F; Tazria-Metzora 1, *Questions*; Acharei-Mot 1, Approaches; Kedoshim 5b).

1. Rabbinic opinion is divided concerning the value of intellectual search within the realm of *chukim*. At one end of the spectrum lie those authorities who insist that *chukim* must be viewed not only as laws beyond our comprehension but as edicts that have no individual intrinsic purpose. The primary role of these laws, as a group, is to develop man's loyalty to God through the cultivation of unquestioning obedience to His will.

At the opposite end of the spectrum are those scholars who insist that each of God's laws is uniquely purposeful and that the search for meaning within all mitzvot is not only allowed but encouraged. Man should make every effort, these authorities believe, to determine the fundamental reasons for each mitzva. Such study can only help us attain a more complete understanding of God's will.

Intermediate positions along the spectrum of rabbinic opinion maintain that, while every mitzva has a reason, blind obedience to the commandments represents the highest level of relationship with the Divine. Only those unable to relate to God on this elevated plane, these scholars feel, should engage in rational investigation of the mitzvot.

2. Even those scholars who encourage rational examination of *chukim* clearly recognize the potential dangers of such search. Failure to determine the reason for a specific commandment, they emphasize, should never lead us to treat that mitzva lightly. We must also recognize that any rationale we do arrive at may or may not be accurate, given the limitations of our own intellectual abilities.

3. When we deal with issues related to the biblical constructs of *tuma* and *tahara* we must also overcome the problems presented by the terms themselves (see *Vayikra*: Tazria-Metzora 1, *Approaches* A). No

appropriate English translation exists for the Hebrew words *tuma* and *tahara*. The commonly suggested translations "pure and impure" or "clean and unclean" carry value judgments that are not necessarily applicable.

For want of a better option, in the course of this study, we will continue to translate these terms in the usual manner, while recognizing the limitations of such translation.

C

As the rabbis focus on the core issues of the *para aduma*, their comments naturally reflect the range of opinion concerning logical analysis of divine law in general.

At one extreme are those scholars who not only acknowledge the inexplicable nature of the red heifer, but view its mystery as a commentary on the Torah as a whole.

Rabbi Yitzchak Arama, for example, lists various possible approaches to mitzvot in general, including the approach of rational search. He concludes, however, that the highest level of Torah observance is reflected in Rabbi Yochanan's response to his students concerning the red heifer: "By your lives, the dead do not defile and the waters [of the red heifer] do not purify. Rather, the Holy One Blessed Be He has decreed 'I have forged a statute and enacted a decree and you have no right to transgress my decree.'"

Blind obedience to God's law without the need for rational explanation represents the pinnacle of religious devotion. The very inclusion of *chukim* in the panoply of mitzvot, Arama argues, is designed to convey this lesson and to apply it to the entire Torah. Just as we observe *chukim* without comprehending them, so too, we should observe all mitzvot, even those we think we understand, specifically because we are so commanded by God and not on the basis of any supposed rationale.[6]

In a similar vein, the Hasidic master Rabbi Levi Yitzchak of Berdichev is among those who note that the Torah does not introduce the laws of *para aduma* with the statement "This is the statute of the red heifer," but rather, "This is the statute of the Torah": "In principle, the reasons for the Torah and its laws are hidden from mankind. Man must perform and observe [the mitzvot of] the Torah simply because God commands us to

---

6. Akeidat Yitzchak, Bamidbar, sha'ar 99.

perform and observe them. This truth is hinted at in the phrase 'this is the statute of the Torah.' *The entire Torah and its mitzvot are to be considered by us as chukim.*"[7]

Another Chassidic master, Rabbi Tzvi Elimelech of Dinov, goes a major step further, maintaining that "belief does not require the concurrence of rational interpretation. Instead, rational interpretation requires the concurrence of belief." To support his point, Rabbi Tzvi Elimelech notes that the Talmud uses a Torah phrase to prove that an object with a three-cubit circumference also possesses, by definition, a width of one cubit. At face value, this Talmudic exercise seems superfluous. Why should a fact easily verified by physical measurement require scriptural proof? Because, Rabbi Tzvi Elimelech argues, the Torah does not require logical support. *Logic, however, requires the support of the Torah.*[8]

— D —

In stark contrast to those who are willing to accept the mystery of the *para aduma* without question, other scholars struggle to find rational meaning in this strange ritual.

An early Midrashic tradition, for example, views the red heifer as an atoning rite for the sin of the golden calf.[9] In interpreting this Midrash, the Kli Yakar explains that full atonement can only be achieved by "digging up the roots of sin." Only by addressing the underlying cause of a transgression can one hope to avoid its recurrence. The burning of the red heifer symbolizes the destruction of wealth, the abundance of which was a fundamental cause of the sin of the golden calf.[10]

While the Rambam also views the *para aduma* as a ritual of atonement, he parts company with the Midrash concerning the sin for which the ritual atones:

> The red heifer is called a sin offering because it effects the purification of persons who have become impure through contact with a human corpse and enables them to enter the Sanctuary.... Once a person

---

7. Kedushat Levi, Bamidbar, Chukat.
8. Rabbi Tzvi Elimelech of Dinov, as quoted in Nachshoni, *Hagot B'parshiot HaTorah*, Vol. 2, p. 644.
9. Midrash Rabba Bamidbar 19:2.
10. Kli Yakar, Bamidbar 19:2.

became impure he would have been forever forbidden to enter the Sanctuary and to eat hallowed foods had it not been for this heifer which bore the burden of his sin.[11]

Apparently, according to the Rambam, the very phenomena of *tumat met* and the distance from God caused by such impurity create the need for atonement. Even when caused for valid reasons, distance from God is a "sin."

Comparing the ashes of the red heifer to the sent goat of Yom Kippur (see *Vayikra*: Acharei Mot 1) and other similar rituals, the Rambam also suggests a logical explanation for the *para aduma*'s puzzling capacity to "purify the defiled and defile the pure." Just as the sent goat acquires the taint of sin by symbolically acquiring the transgressions of the Israelites during the Yom Kippur service, so too, during the ritual of the red heifer, sin is figuratively removed from the defiled individual and transferred to the waters of the *para aduma* solution. To underscore this symbolic transference, the solution now gains the potential to convey its own "acquired impurity" to anyone with whom it comes into contact.[12]

Numerous other commentaries offer extensive and imaginative interpretations of the ceremonies associated with the red heifer. The Sforno, for example, suggests a pedagogic approach. Through the combination of the antithetical symbols of ashes (fire) and water in the *para aduma* solution, the Torah teaches that the path of *tshuva*, return from sin, sometimes requires bold counterbalancing action. An individual who falls into a pattern of extreme behavior may need the temporary corrective of acting at the other extreme in order to return to the desired middle path. The union of physical opposites in the "waters of the red heifer" thus symbolizes that the balance between behavioral excesses will produce the "golden mean." Many other details surrounding the *para aduma*, the Sforno maintains, can also be explained by this approach.[13]

For his part, Rabbi Shimshon Raphael Hirsch builds a complex explanation of the *para aduma* ritual based on his general approach to *tuma* and *tahara* throughout the Torah.

---

11. Rambam, *Moreh Nevuchim* 3:47.
12. Ibid.
13. Sforno, Bamidbar 19:2.

The "first and irreplaceable condition for living our lives on a higher plane," Hirsch maintains, is "freedom of will in moral matters."[14] Man's perception of such freedom, however, is endangered when he confronts the fact of his own inevitable death. If death destroys the entire human being; if man, like all other organic creatures, lives under the spell of this "irresistible, overpowering force,"[15] then moral freedom is only an illusion and moral laws become meaningless.

Only by recognizing that he operates simultaneously in two arenas – a limited physical sphere and an unlimited moral, immortal sphere – can man transcend his confrontation with death.

The laws of *tuma* and *tahara* throughout the Torah serve as correctives, designed to sensitize man to his moral freedom whenever he is challenged by physical limitations. In effect, God exhorts man: "Be not deceived by corpse and death, become free, become immortal not in spite of, but together with all that is physical…remain immortal master of your mortal body…."[16]

Hirsch explains that the various details of the *para aduma* ritual are constructed to help man regain his equilibrium after a close encounter with death. The unblemished red heifer, for example, having never borne a yoke, represents the uncontrolled physical-animal nature of man. The handing over of the animal to the Kohen represents an individual's free-willed, conscious choice to integrate his physical nature into a world governed by the laws of the Torah. Both the body's eventual return to the earth, symbolized by the burning of the red heifer into ash, and the eternal continuity of the soul lie within the scope of God's plan for mankind.

With great detail and care, Hirsch proceeds to show how each aspect of the *para aduma* ceremony further teaches that *gaining proximity to God on earth requires the joining of both aspects of man's existence.* "The laws of God's Torah always presuppose the mortal body joined to the immortal part of man's being."[17]

---

14. Rabbi Shimshon Raphael Hirsch, Bamidbar 19:22.
15. Ibid.
16. Ibid.
17. Ibid.

E

No scholarly exercise within our tradition more clearly showcases the relationship of the Jewish people to the totality of Jewish law than our age-old, continuing struggle with the ritual of *para aduma*.

Both those who accept this mysterious rite with blind obedience and those who strive to pierce its mysteries view this difficult section of Torah text as relevant to our lives, transmitting lessons concerning our relationship with God, our world and ourselves.

Points to Ponder

Another observation concerns the *para aduma*'s unique capacity *l'taher et hateme'im u'l'tamei et hatehorim*, "to purify the defiled and to defile the pure."

Perhaps what we have labeled as a unique phenomenon is not really so unique, after all. Our world is, in fact, filled with phenomena that can cut both ways – phenomena that, dependent upon the situation and the players involved, can give rise to either positive or negative results, and sometimes even to both simultaneously.

As a case in point, I have often felt that many "open," heterogeneous Modern Orthodox communities, such as the ones that I have been privileged to serve, have the capacity, for want of better terminology, *l'taher et hateme'im u'l'tamei et hatehorim*.

Tolerant, welcoming and nonjudgmental, these congregations carry the real potential to draw individuals and families of varied religious backgrounds closer to Judaism and its practices. Many individuals who might well have felt uncomfortable in more rigidly Orthodox communities find themselves at home in these congregations, drawn in by the warm friendship and acceptance shown to them and by the acts of communal kindness and sharing that they observe. Their developing congregational affiliation often leads to a growing interest in Jewish tradition, resulting in greater personal study and observance.

At the same time, however, "open" Orthodox communities can prove challenging at the other end of the spectrum. The communal "tolerance" that proves to be such an asset in attracting the less affiliated can encourage diminished observance among the "already affiliated." Communal standards of religious practice are invariably relaxed, as an atmosphere of "live and let live" is fostered. Behaviors that might be seen as questionable in other Orthodox communities become commonplace, even among those who would have adhered more strictly to the letter of the law had they lived elsewhere.

Don't get me wrong....

I love the communities in which I have served as rabbi. Even more, I consider such communities essential to the fabric of Jewish life, presenting Orthodoxy in a welcoming fashion and providing a rich, dynamic religious texture that cannot be experienced elsewhere.

Nonetheless, these communities also offer an ongoing challenge to rabbis and congregants alike. Together, they must work to maintain a healthy balance between the tolerance that defines the community's character and the potential relaxation of religious standards that can threaten its spiritual growth.

2 My, How Time Flies…

Context
Immediately after outlining the laws of the *para aduma*, the Torah resumes its historical narrative with the statement "And the children of Israel, the whole assembly, arrived in the Wilderness of Tzin in the first month, and the nation settled in Kadesh; and Miriam died there and was buried there."[1]

Questions
Something astonishing has occurred in the Torah that could easily escape our notice. *Nearly thirty-eight years have passed without comment from the text.*

The last historical event recorded in the text, the rebellion of Korach and its aftermath, took place at the beginning of the nation's forty-year period of wilderness wandering.[2] The death of Miriam, however, occurs at the end of this period, in the fortieth year of wandering.[3] From this point in the text until the end of the book of Devarim and the close of the Torah, the Torah deals solely with the final year in the wilderness and with the commandments transmitted by Moshe during that year.

What happened to the bulk of the forty-year period of wilderness wandering? Clearly these have been important, formative years. An entire generation, the generation of the Exodus, has perished and a new generation has risen, destined to enter the land. According to numerous commentaries that is why the Torah now states, "And the children of Israel,

---

1. Bamidbar 20:1.
2. Note: Although there is disagreement among the rabbis as to the exact temporal position of the rebellion of Korach (see Korach 1), the latest posited time for this event is shortly following the sin of the spies, at the beginning of the forty-year period in the wilderness.
3. Seder Olam Rabba 9; Rashbam, Bamidbar 20:1; Ibn Ezra, Bamidbar 20:1 and numerous other sources.

the whole assembly, arrived in the Wilderness of Tzin…." The entirety of the nation that will enter the land is now present and accounted for.[4]

Why, then, do all the wilderness years passed without any comment in the text at all – without, in fact, even a note that they have passed?

Approaches

— A —

Strangely enough, the Torah's silence concerning the missing thirty-eight years is matched by a similar silence from the classical commentaries. While some of the scholars, such as the Chizkuni, are clearly aware of the phenomenon of the missing years,[5] they make no attempt to explain why the Torah does not chronicle this period of time more fully.

— B —

Perhaps the key to this mystery lies in the answer to another, more technical question.

What is the symbolism of the repeated appearance of the number forty at critical moments of the biblical text? Why are there forty days of rain that create the flood, forty days repeatedly spent by Moshe on the summit of Mount Sinai over the course of Revelation, forty days during which the spies tour the land of Canaan, forty years of wandering in the wilderness…?

A possible answer emerges from an unexpected source.

In commenting on the development of a human fetus, the Talmud states that, until the passage of forty days from conception, the embryo is considered to be *maya b'alma*, mere water. From that point on, the fetus enters a new, more advanced stage of development.[6] Clearly, to the rabbinic mind, *the fortieth day marks a critical point in the birthing process.*[7]

---

4. Rashi, Bamidbar 20:1; Ibn Ezra, ibid.
5. Chizkuni, Bamidbar 20:1.
6. Talmud Bavli Yevamot 69b.
7. A word of caution: This rabbinic statement concerning the developmental stages of the human fetus should not be misinterpreted as an automatic acceptance of abortion during the early forty-day period of gestation. While the laws of abortion in Jewish law are complex and detailed, the general rule remains that abortion is

C

If the number forty represents a critical juncture in the biological birthing of a human being, perhaps the number forty plays a similar role throughout Jewish tradition. Upon consideration, *each time a phenomenon appears in units of forty in the Torah text, a new reality is about to be born*. The forty days of rain in Noach's time mark not only the destruction of the old world but *the birth of a new one*; Moshe's forty days on the summit of Mount Sinai signal *the birth of a new nation* forged on the foundation of God's law; the forty-day tour of the spies through Canaan gives rise to *the birth of a new, devastating reality* for the generation of the Exodus; and the forty years of wilderness wandering give *birth to a new generation of Israelites* who will enter the land.

D

The forty-year period of wilderness wandering, therefore, carries no intrinsic independent significance. The significance of these years emerges instead as a period of incubation, a time when, step by step, a new generation is forged through a crucible of experience. The value of the wilderness years will be determined by the nature of the generation born, by the product created during the passing years.

Will this new generation of Israelites avoid the missteps of their fathers? Will this people, surrounded by clouds of God's protection, sustained on the heaven-sent manna, live in their journeys through God's manifest will, effectively transitioning from the fear of God to the love of God (see Korach 6)? Will the forty years have done their job?

These questions can only be answered in retrospect, as the story of this generation unfolds, after the wilderness years have passed. The Torah therefore remains silent concerning the passage of the years themselves, allowing us to draw our conclusions concerning their value after the fact, on the basis of the generation born.

Points to Ponder

Often, we attribute automatic power to time's passage: Give it time…. Things will get better…. Time heals…. Things get better over time….

---

prohibited at any time after conception unless the life of the mother is threatened. Under all circumstances, appropriate rabbinic authority should be consulted.

And yet, when we consider our own experience and the experience of those around us, we are forced to admit that the passage of time doesn't always "make things better." In fact, often the reverse is true. As time passes, unaddressed psychic wounds can fester, perceived slights can grow in intensity and misunderstandings can turn into hostility.

As a rabbi, I have experienced the tragedy of families unwilling to sit together even at the funeral of a loved one. When asked, however, as to the origin of the problem, family members often cannot remember. A small slight, a minor insult lost in the mists of memory turns, over time, into a permanent rift that can no longer be repaired.

The Torah's silence concerning the Israelites' forty-year wilderness passage reminds us of a lesson too often forgotten: *The passage of time, in and of itself, is immaterial. What matters is what takes place during that time, and how those events impact upon our lives.*

If, over the years, problems are ignored and reconciliation avoided, then the passage of time will work against us. If, on the other hand, we use our time wisely and constructively, confronting our shared issues squarely and with sensitivity, then time will surely be our ally.

3 Punishment Fitting the Crime?

Context

Immediately following the death of Miriam, the nation rises in complaint against Moshe and Aharon due to a lack of water. When Moshe and Aharon turn to God at the entrance of the Sanctuary, God instructs Moshe: "Take the staff and gather together the assembly – you and Aharon, your brother – and speak to the rock before their eyes and it will give forth its waters. And you shall bring forth water from the rock and you shall give drink to the assembly and to their animals."

Moshe takes his staff, gathers the people facing the rock and says to them, "Listen now, rebellious ones, from this rock shall we bring forth water for you?"

Raising his arm, Moshe then strikes the rock with his staff twice, and abundant water pours forth, providing for the people and for their livestock.

God turns to Moshe and Aharon and proclaims, "Because you did not believe in Me to sanctify Me in the eyes of the children of Israel, *therefore you shall not bring this assembly to the land that I have given them.*"

The Torah concludes this tragic event with the statement "These are *mei meriva*, the waters of strife, where the children of Israel contended with God, and He was sanctified through them."[1]

On three other occasions in the text, God explicitly identifies the events at *Mei Meriva* as the source of His refusal to allow Moshe and Aharon to enter the land of Canaan.[2]

---

1. Bamidbar 20:1–13.
2. Ibid., 20:23–24; 27:12–14; Devarim 32:48–51.

Questions

A number of years ago, on one of my synagogue's numerous missions to Israel, we traveled to locations in Jordan, as well. Among the sites we visited was the mountain believed to be Har Nevo, the peak from which Moshe viewed the land of Canaan from afar, and upon which he died.

Like so many of us, I have long been troubled by God's refusal to allow Moshe to enter the land of Canaan. As I stood alone, however, on that windy summit in Jordan, looking out, as once did Moshe, on a view that spans from the Dead Sea to the Galilee, I was struck as never before by the ultimate tragedy that marked Moshe's life.

This humble, reluctant leader – pressed into service by divine command, pushed to the limit repeatedly by his backsliding flock, ever the defender of the nation before God – manages to lead his people successfully to the very border of their Promised Land. Yet, apparently because of a misstep at the scene of the waters of strife, he is denied the opportunity to enter that land himself. He leads the people to the realization of their dreams, but is denied the realization of his own.

Why does Moshe deserve this fate?

What specific sin does Moshe commit at the scene of *Mei Meriva* that is beyond forgiveness? And why, in addition, is Aharon punished simply for being a bystander?

In what way do the actions of these great leaders indicate a "lack of belief in God" and a "failure to sanctify Him"?

Approaches

—A—

Some scholars, upon careful review of the narrative, cannot find any action taken by Moshe and Aharon at *Mei Meriva* that merits the severe punishment they receive. Disputing the overwhelming evidence of the text, therefore, these authorities claim that the guilt of Moshe and Aharon actually emerges from other, more powerful sources.

The Abravanel, for example, maintains that Aharon's sin lay in his involvement in the fashioning of the golden calf,[3] while Moshe's

---
3. Shmot 22:2–5.

transgression consisted of expanding the mandate given to the spies prior to their entry into the land of Canaan.[4] The actions of these great leaders were well-intentioned, the Abravanel argues, and yet in each case they inadvertently contributed to the national disasters that ensued. God therefore balances His responses carefully. To protect Moshe and Aharon's reputation, He does not punish them immediately, together with those guilty of intentional rebellion. He instead waits for them to commit an intentional sin, however minor, and then punishes them for their original transgressions. When Moshe deviates from God's commandment and strikes the rock, God seizes the opportunity to exact retribution upon these leaders for their previous, more substantial failings.[5]

── **B** ──────────────────────────

The vast majority of commentaries, however, find the clear testimony of the text incontrovertible. As noted above, God explicitly and repeatedly identifies the events at *Mei Meriva* as the source of His refusal to allow Moshe and Aharon to enter the land of Canaan.

Rashi reflects the position of these authorities when, commenting on the sentence "Because you did not believe in Me to sanctify Me in the eyes of the children of Israel, therefore you shall not bring this assembly to the land that I have given them," he adamantly argues, "The text openly reveals that had it not been for this sin alone, they [Moshe and Aharon] would have entered the land."[6]

Clearly, something specific happens at *Mei Meriva* to seal the fate of these great leaders. The question, however, is what?

The rabbinic search for an answer gives rise to one of the most heated debates in biblical interpretation to this day.

── **C** ──────────────────────────

Building upon an earlier Midrashic source, Rashi chooses the most obvious explanation for Moshe's sin. *Moshe is punished for his failure to obey God's explicit commandment.*[7] Commanded by God to *speak* to the

---

4. Bamidbar 13:17–20.
5. Abravanel, Bamidbar 20:1–14.
6. Rashi, Bamidbar 20:12.
7. Ibid.

rock, Moshe instead *strikes* the rock twice. This deviation from God's instructions, although perhaps mitigated by circumstances,⁸ diminishes the sanctification of God's name.

Had water rushed forth as a result of Moshe's verbal command, the people would have concluded: *If this rock, which neither speaks, hears, nor requires sustenance, fulfills the word of the Lord, how much more then should we!*

Because Moshe does not follow God's commandment to the letter, the Israelites lose an opportunity to glean a lesson critical to their developing relationship with God. Moshe thus fails to sanctify God's name and loses his right to enter the land of Canaan.⁹

— D —

While agreeing with Rashi's contention that Moshe's failure lies in striking rather than speaking to the rock, numerous other commentaries offer alternative insights into the significance of that failure.

The Rashbam, for example, defends Moshe's misstep as resulting from a logical misunderstanding of God's intent. Because God specifically instructs him to "take the staff," Moshe assumes that he is meant to strike the rock, as he had been commanded to do under similar circumstances, years earlier, at Refidim.¹⁰ Despite the inadvertent nature of Moshe's actions, God nevertheless punishes him severely because, as the Talmud notes, "God is exacting with those nearest to Him to the point of a hair's breadth."¹¹

The Sforno, for his part, relates the problem raised by Moshe's striking of the rock to the essential character of divine miracles. All supernatural events recorded in the text, this scholar claims, can be divided into three categories, in increasing order of intensity:

---

8. Rashi explains that Moshe becomes confused as to the rock specified by God. After speaking unsuccessfully to the "wrong" rock, Moshe reasons that, perhaps, he is meant to strike the rock as he had been commanded to do by God, under similar circumstances, years earlier at Refidim (Shmot 17:1–7). As fate would have it, Moshe then turns to the "right" rock and strikes it twice. In another source (Bamidbar 31:21), Rashi adds that Moshe's error in judgment in striking the rock is caused by his anger at the nation.
9. Rashi, Bamidbar 20:10–12.
10. Shmot 17:1–7.
11. Rashbam, Bamidbar 20:10; Talmud Bavli Yevamot 121b.

1. Hidden miracles, performed by God through natural means.

2. Open miracles that can occur naturally but only through powerful forces and over a long period of time.

3. Open miracles that cannot occur at all through natural means.

The full extent of God's power, the Sforno explains, is demonstrated only through miracles from the third, highest category. Such events also attest to the worthiness of the earthly messenger through whose agency the wonder is performed.

In response to the complaints of the Israelites, God decides to demonstrate His own full power to the people and to reestablish Moshe's credentials with them. He therefore commands Moshe specifically to perform a miracle that cannot occur through natural means: "*Speak to the rock* before their eyes and it will give forth its waters."

Moshe, however, has his doubts.

Unable to believe that God would perform a miracle at the highest level on behalf of the rebellious Israelites, *Moshe consciously deviates from God's commandment* and strikes the rock, splitting it in a manner that can occur through natural forces, over time. By deliberately lowering the caliber of the miracle performed at *Mei Meriva*, Moshe thus fails to sanctify God's name to the fullest possible extent.[12]

― E ―

In his ethical work *Shmoneh Prakim*, the Rambam breaks from Rashi completely, choosing an entirely different interpretive path to Moshe's sin at *Mei Meriva*. In the midst of a lengthy discussion encouraging a golden mean of personal conduct, the Rambam cites Moshe's actions at the scene of *Mei Meriva* as proof of the dangers of immoderate behavior: "*Moshe's entire sin lay in erring on the side of anger and deviating from the mean of patience.*"

This anger, the Rambam claims, is clearly evidenced in Moshe's declaration: "*Listen now, rebellious ones*, from this rock shall we bring forth water for you?"

Unwarranted anger, in and of itself, is considered sinful. Moshe's public rage at *Mei Meriva*, however, constitutes an even more dangerous failing in God's eyes. Not only does Moshe set a dangerous example for

---

12. Sforno, Bamidbar 20:8.

the entire people, but he also potentially causes the nation to erroneously conclude that God is "enraged" by their complaints. There is, in fact, no indication in the text of such divine wrath. While God is indeed "angered" on a number of other occasions by the people's groundless complaints, at *Mei Meriva*, the Israelites, suffering from thirst, are justified in their protests.[13]

— **F** —

The Ramban strongly disagrees. In a lengthy exposition, this scholar disputes the approaches of Rashi, the Rambam and others to Moshe's sin. Concerning Rashi's suggestion that Moshe is punished for striking rather than speaking to the rock, the Ramban insists that God would not have commanded Moshe to "take the staff" had He not intended him to strike the rock. The Ramban also harshly rebuts the Rambam's interpretation on a number of counts, pointing out, most fundamentally, that God never chastises Moshe for anger, and that, in fact, God Himself must have been angered by the Israelites' bitter complaints.

The Ramban therefore quotes Rabbeinu Chananel in offering an entirely different perspective on the events at *Mei Meriva*. Moshe and Aharon's failings are reflected not in the first half of the passage quoted by the Rambam, but in its second half: "Listen now, rebellious ones, from this rock *shall we bring forth water for you?*"

The problem is at once clear and startling. In place of stating, "*Shall God bring forth water?*" Moshe instead proclaims, "*Shall we bring forth water?*" Moshe and Aharon's public assumption of credit for the miracle, although obviously inadvertent, cannot go unanswered. Absent a strong response from God, the nation might erroneously conclude that Moshe and Aharon had produced the water on their own, through magical powers. Such an interpretation would undermine the very tenets of belief in divine authority that these leaders themselves had worked so hard to instill in the nation.

God's accusation, "Because you did not believe in Me to sanctify Me in the eyes of the children of Israel…," can, the Ramban explains, be interpreted to mean: *You failed to instill belief in Me in the people's hearts.*

---

13. Rambam, *Shmoneh Prakim*, chapter 4.

Even further, through your incautious words, you undermined My sanctity in their eyes.[14]

The Ramban concludes his remarks concerning the events at *Mei Meriva* by acknowledging the limitations of rational explanation for what is "one of the great mysteries of the Torah" and by offering an additional kabbalistic interpretation for the episode, which remains outside the scope of our discussion.[15]

── G ──────────────────────────────

Moving in yet another, totally different direction, the Ibn Ezra maintains that the sin of Moshe and Aharon lies in their initial undignified reaction to the people's complaints. Instead of demonstrating confidence in God's ability to provide for the people, these great leaders approach the Sanctuary "as fugitives," fleeing before the nation's threats.[16]

Centuries later, Rabbi Joseph Albo elaborates on the Ibn Ezra's approach by arguing that Moshe and Aharon should have directly asked God to perform a specific supernatural act in response to the people's complaints. "The failure of a prophet to perform miracles," Albo explains, "is liable to make people doubt the truth of the text that the Lord establishes the words of his servants."[17]

God therefore accuses these great leaders of a "failure of belief." In their humility, Moshe and Aharon do not trust that God will respond to their direct request for miraculous intervention.[18]

── H ──────────────────────────────

Many years ago, Rabbi Harold Kanatopsky, a brilliant teacher and orator who served as rabbi of my community during my teenage years, offered a new, innovative approach to the events at *Mei Meriva*. So profoundly did

---

14. Ramban, Bamidbar 20:7.
15. Ibid.; see also Rabbeinu Bachya, Bamidbar 20:8, for further elaboration.
16. Ibn Ezra, Bamidbar 20:6; 20:8.
17. Rabbi Yosef Albo, *Sefer Ha'ikrim*, 4:22.
18. This approach contradicts our earlier suggestion that Moshe's invoking of a specific miracle during the rebellion of Korach was an exception to the rule. I would argue, however, as do commentaries such as Rabbeinu Chananel and the *Akeidat Yitzchak*, that Moshe does not generally initiate specific miraculous events. He instead waits for instructions from God.

this approach impress me that I have not only remembered it and quoted it over the years, but I have also added some thoughts of my own. I can no longer remember where Rabbi Kanatopsky's ideas end and mine begin, but the foundation of this approach is certainly his.

To understand the events at *Mei Meriva*, we first must add to the puzzle.

As the Rashbam notes (see above), this is not the first time that Moshe finds himself in the circumstances presented at *Mei Meriva*. An almost parallel event occurs earlier in Moshe's career. Shortly after the Exodus, at a location known as Refidim, the Israelites find themselves without water and converge in complaint against Moshe. On that occasion God distinctly commands Moshe: "And you shall *strike* the rock and water will issue forth from it and the people will drink."[19]

This seems to make our questions concerning the events at *Mei Meriva* even more troubling. How can Moshe be blamed, as Rashi and so many others claim, for striking the rock at *Mei Meriva* when that was exactly what he was told to do – with success – on a previous occasion? Even more importantly, why does God command Moshe at Refidim to *strike* the rock and at *Mei Meriva* to *speak* to the rock? Given the similarity between these two parallel episodes, why does God change His instructions in such seemingly arbitrary ways?

Upon consideration, there is one powerful variable between the episodes at Refidim and *Mei Meriva*: *the Israelites themselves.*

At Refidim, Moshe and Aharon are confronted by the generation of the Exodus. At *Mei Meriva*, forty years later, they are confronted by the wilderness generation.

As we have noted (see Korach 6, *Approaches* B; *Points to Ponder*; Chukat 2, *Approaches* D), the transition between these two generations marks a major paradigm shift in God's relationship with His people. Over a forty-year period, the nation moves from the relational level of *yira*, fear and awe, to the level of *ahava*, love.

The erstwhile slaves who comprised the generation of the Exodus and Revelation were able to relate to God only on the primitive plane of fear. Shaped by their decades under the taskmaster's whip, they responded to brute force and power. God, therefore, commanded Moshe at Refidim to

---

19. Shmot 17:6.

speak to this generation in a language that they could understand. *Strike the rock*, He commanded, *and let the Israelites recognize the power of their new heavenly master.*

Forty years later, at *Mei Meriva*, a new generation has emerged that has not known slavery on an adult level. Nurtured under God's watchful care, this generation has learned to relate to their Creator through the more mature dimension of *ahava*.

God therefore commands Moshe: *Take the staff. Show the people that you can use it, but that you deliberately will not. Instead, speak to the rock and, in doing so, "speak" to the people. Demonstrate to them, at this critical moment, that the power of love is infinitely stronger than the power of brute force. Through love, I will provide for them now; through love, we will relate to each other across the pages of time.*

Moshe, however, slips….

Confronted again by the bitter complaints of the Israelites, he flashes back to Refidim. He sees before him not the Israelites of the day, but their parents and grandparents of yesteryear. *Nothing has changed*, he concludes. *These people still understand only the power of the staff.*

And in that one fell instant, as Moshe lifts his staff to strike the rock, he fails to transition with his people from one generation to the next, from one relational level to another. This failure seals his fate. He and Aharon (who makes no move to stop his brother) will remain forever part of their generation, consigned to perish in the desert without entry into the land.

Far from a minor misstep, Moshe's actions at *Mei Meriva* emerge as a fundamental failure of leadership. This greatest of leaders remains rooted in the past, unable to respond to the internal changes that have transformed his people. God's seemingly drastic response to Moshe's failure at *Mei Meriva* now becomes understandable. Sadly, Moshe's time has come and gone. A new leader must now emerge – a leader who will be able to transition with the next generation in its march towards a glorious future.

4 The Nature of Natural Events

Context
Following the death of Aharon and the battle against the Canaanites of Arad, the nation rises in complaint over the conditions of their continuing journey. God responds with a punishing attack of poisonous serpents, causing a multitude of deaths among the people. When Moshe, responding to the desperate pleas of the nation, prays that this devastating attack be suspended, God commands him, "Make for yourself a fiery serpent and place it upon a high pole and it shall come to pass that anyone who has been bitten shall see it and live."[1]

Moshe obeys and the Torah states: "And Moshe made a copper serpent and set it on a high pole; and it came to pass that if a serpent bit a man, he would look upon the copper serpent and live."[2]

Questions
God's instructions to Moshe concerning this incident seem abundantly strange. What is the import of the serpent that Moshe is commanded to fashion?

How can the God Who commanded at Sinai "You shall not make for yourself a graven image nor any likeness of that which is in the heavens above or that which is on the earth below or that which is in the water beneath the earth"[3] now instruct Moshe to create what seems to be divinely sanctioned idolatry?

Why doesn't God simply suspend the attack of the serpents without the introduction of this strange symbol?

---

1. Bamidbar 21:8.
2. Ibid., 21:9.
3. Shmot 20:4.

Approaches

— A —

Rabbinic recognition of the serious philosophical issues raised by this episode is evidenced by a dramatic departure from the norm in the Mishna. In the third chapter of the tractate of Rosh Hashana, the Mishna interrupts its halachic discourse to raise two philosophical questions. The second of these reads as follows: "Does a [copper] serpent cause death; or does a [copper] serpent grant life? Rather, when Israel glanced heavenward and submitted their hearts to their Father in the heavens they were cured; and if not they perished."[4]

Clearly, to the rabbinic mind, no supernatural powers can be attributed to the copper serpent. *Any cure granted to the Israelites could only have issued from God Himself.*

The rabbis of the Mishna, however, seem to beg the central question. If the Israelites were cured when they "submitted their hearts to their Father in the heavens," why was the copper serpent necessary at all? If this event is simply an example of divine response to mortal prayer, what role does the copper serpent play?

— B —

Some commentaries consider the episode of the copper serpent to be beyond the realm of human understanding. The Ibn Ezra, for example, connects our questions concerning this event to the shroud of mystery that envelops all divinely ordained miracles. Even during moments of clearest divine revelation, God's ways remain beyond our ken. We can no more comprehend why God commands Moshe to perform a miracle through the medium of a manufactured serpent than we can understand why a tree branch should sweeten the waters of Mara[5] or why, much later in Jewish history,[6] date honey should cure King Chizkiyahu's affliction of boils.[7]

---

4. Mishna Rosh Hashana 3:8.
5. Shmot 15:22–25.
6. Melachim II 20:7.
7. Ibn Ezra, Bamidbar 21:8.

Other scholars, however, unwilling to accept this episode at face value, struggle to find logical meaning in the symbol of the copper serpent. Rabbi Meir ben Baruch of Rothenberg (the Maharam) and the Ba'al Haturim, for example, maintain that the copper serpent is designed to prevent further sin on the part of the Israelites. Just as a father might leave his disciplining rod in full view to deter his children from further mischief, so too, God commands Moshe to display the copper serpent to the Israelites as a clear reminder of the potential ramifications of their actions.[8]

The Chizkuni suggests that the copper serpent illustrates God's extraordinary ability to afflict and to cure through the same medium. Only He can punish the nation through an attack of serpents and then heal them through a copper serpent.[9] The Sforno, on the other hand, finds reference to the nature of the Israelites' sin in the symbol of the "fiery serpent." Just as a mythical fire-breathing serpent damages through its breath, so too, the Israelites sin through their complaints against God – complaints carried on their breath.[10]

Finally, the Ramban argues that the creation of the copper serpent enables God to further demonstrate His power through the performance of a "miracle within a miracle." Usually, this scholar argues, the condition of an afflicted individual will worsen if that individual is openly confronted with the source of his malady. By nature, therefore, the victim of a snake bite will suffer a setback if he sees the image of a snake. Miraculously, however, during the episode of the copper serpent, God causes the suffering Israelites to heal upon symbolic confrontation with the source of their illness.

---- C ----

Most intriguing, perhaps, is the approach to this episode mapped out by Rabbi Shimshon Raphael Hirsch. Hirsch notes a powerful linguistic detail in the Torah's introduction to the serpents' attack: *Va'yishalach Hashem ba'am et hanechashim haserafim*, "And God let the fiery serpents loose against the people."[11]

---

8. Maharam, Bamidbar 21:9; Ba'al Haturim, ibid.
9. Chizkuni, Bamidbar 21:9.
10. Sforno, Bamidbar 21:9.
11. This detail is further elaborated upon by Nehama Leibowitz in her study on this parsha.

There is a significant difference between the words *va'yishlach* (conjugated in the Hebrew *kal* form) and *va'yishalach* (conjugated in the Hebrew *pi'el* form). The former term indicates an act of "sending," while the latter term implies an act of "setting free" or "letting loose." By introducing the attack of the serpents with the term *va'yishalach* as opposed to *va'yishlach*, the Torah conveys that God does not "send" a supernatural plague of serpents to attack the Israelites. The nation is, after all, already traveling through a land of "snake, fiery serpent and scorpion."[12] God simply lifts His divine protection from the people and, by doing so, "lets loose" the dangers that are already there.

The copper serpent can therefore be seen, Hirsch boldly suggests, not as a symbol of God's miraculous intervention, but as a reminder of what can occur *when God fails to intervene*.

As each afflicted Israelite lifts his eyes to the copper serpent, he recognizes anew the hidden dangers that have dogged the heels of his people throughout their wilderness journeys. *He realizes that only God's protection has enabled them to reach this point.* This new grateful awareness lends fervency to his prayers, granting them the capacity to awaken God's compassion.

The symbol of the copper serpent, Hirsch concludes, speaks with clarity across the ages, reminding us of the unseen dangers that surround us each day: "Nothing is so thoroughly calculated to conciliate us in the everyday disappointments in life which so easily sting us to impatience… than the conviction of the abyss on the narrow edge of which the whole path of our life treads [and] which the loving hand of God veils from our sight."[13]

There but for the grace of God go we…. If the copper serpent is held in view, the petty disappointments that regularly afflict us will be kept in perspective, as we realize, with gratitude, the gifts that God bestows upon us daily.

— **D** —

Hirsch's original approach to the episode of the copper serpent, however, opens the door to a powerfully perplexing philosophical question.

---

12. Devarim 8:15.
13. Rabbi Shimshon Raphael Hirsch, Bamidbar 21:8.

God is, after all, the Creator of the very dangers that He potentially protects us from. What, then, is the character of God's continued involvement in these "natural" forces that surround us daily? Is every event that occurs in our environment divinely ordained, or do some forces in the natural world proceed on "automatic pilot," affecting man automatically and arbitrarily unless God steps in? Are the calamities that rock our world, from illness to earthquakes, to be viewed as punishment or, at the least, messages from God? Or can we view some of these phenomena as arbitrary, deliberately placed by God outside the realm of His own conscious control?

And what about the "good things" that happen to us – are they all, in every detail, deliberately divinely sent our way? Or, once again, can we attribute some of these events to good fortune that just happens to cross our path?

While recognizing that a full understanding of God's divine justice can only emerge when we become privy to the whole picture – including the character of the spiritual "world to come" after death – the question remains: *How clearly can we perceive God's hand in this world*?

To put the question in other words, what is the relationship between the natural order of the world around us and the concept of Divine Providence (God's direct governance of the world and His active providential care of man)?

— **E** ————————————————————————

A full discussion of the nature of Divine Providence in Jewish thought is well beyond the scope of this limited study. A brief review of some fundamental issues involved, however, will help us understand the intellectual honesty with which these questions have been debated across the ages.

At first glance, one might wonder what the fuss is all about. A faith tradition that, on the one hand, fully believes in God's omniscience and omnipotence, and, on the other hand, considers Divine Providence an essential philosophical principle, must certainly maintain that God ordains every last detail of our lives. And, without question, this approach of direct divine control is reflected in numerous foundational sources in Jewish tradition.

The Torah itself is replete with passages underscoring God's use of natural forces as mediums of reward or punishment. The most familiar of these sections, the second paragraph of the Shma, openly speaks of "rain in your land at its proper time" and "grass in the field for your cattle" in response to man's obedience to God's laws and of "restraint of the heavens so that there will be no rain," "failure of the ground to yield its produce" and "banishment from the land" in response to disobedience.[14] Numerous other biblical sections, including the two *tochachot* (sections of rebuke), feature warnings concerning the various natural and man-made calamities that will befall the nation if they stray from God's mandated path.[15] God's providence on both an individual and a national scale is further evidenced in the narratives concerning early man, the flood, the patriarchal era, the Exodus, and more.

While the Torah applies no definitive label to the concept of God's ongoing oversight of the world, the Hebrew term for providence, *hashgacha*, does emerge from a passage in Psalms that proclaims: "From his lofty throne *hishgiach* [(God) looks down upon] all the inhabitants of the earth."[16] As discussion continues across the ages, God's personal care for his creations becomes more specifically known as *hashgacha pratit*, specific providence.

F

Moving to rabbinic sources, no systematic analysis is found in the Talmud or Midrash concerning the issue of Divine Providence (or, for that matter, any other major philosophical issue). Instead, the opinions of the rabbis emerge from disparate statements scattered across various tractates and volumes. The clearest of their observations support the vision of a God Who is actively involved in all aspects of the world's functioning, down to the smallest detail. In the Talmudic tractate of Chullin, for example, the rabbis proclaim, "No man bruises a finger on earth unless it is decreed in heaven";[17] while, in the tractate of Avoda Zara, God is described as sitting and nourishing the entire world, from "the horns of a wild ox to

---

14. Devarim 11:13–17.
15. Vayikra 26:14–43; Devarim 28:15–68.
16. Tehillim 33:14.
17. Talmud Bavli Chullin 7b.

the ova of lice."[18] God is viewed as the arbiter of man's fate and fortune, "creating ladders upon which He casts one individual down while He raises another";[19] and He serves as a divine matchmaker, "sitting and pairing couples: the daughter of so-and-so to so-and-so."[20]

The rabbis are quick to recognize the need to carve out space for man's independent free will within the context of this deterministic worldview. They therefore proclaim: "Everything is in the hands of heaven, except the fear of heaven,"[21] and "All is foreseen, but freedom of choice is given; and the world is judged with goodness, and all is in accordance with the works."[22] Ultimately, even man's mortal character is not an automatic reality, but rather a divinely ordained response to man's actions: "There is no death without sin and there is no suffering without transgression."[23]

G

These and other rabbinic statements seem to leave little room for belief in natural events and forces occurring without the benefit of God's active manipulation. Nonetheless, a discordant note is struck by another, less obvious series of Talmudic and Midrashic observations. Here, the rabbis seem to reflect discomfort with a world in which each and every event is directly and individually attributable to God's direct intervention. No one would argue, of course, God's power to control the forces of nature at will. The question is whether or not He chooses at times to allow the world to follow a natural course, absent His immediate involvement.

Literally dozens of references, for example, are found in the Talmud and Midrash concerning the role of *mazal* (fortune), an arbitrary force associated with the constellations, in determining the world's fate. Even man, some authorities maintain, comes under its sway. The famous Talmudic sage Rava proclaims, "The life of my son and my sustenance are not dependent upon merit but upon *mazal*";[24] while in the tractate of Shabbat the Talmud states: "*Mazal* increases wisdom and *mazal* engenders

---

18. Ibid., Avoda Zara 3b.
19. Midrash Rabba Bereishit 68:4.
20. Ibid.
21. Talmud Bavli Brachot 33b.
22. Pirkei Avot 3:19.
23. Talmud Bavli Shabbat 55a.
24. Ibid., Moed Katan 28a.

wealth."25 One opinion in the Zohar goes so far as to claim: "Everything is dependent upon *mazal*, even the Torah scroll in the Sanctuary."26

Of particular interest is a Talmudic debate concerning the vulnerability of the Jewish nation to the power of *mazal*, with Rabbi Chanina maintaining, *Yesh mazal l'Yisrael*, "The Jewish people are susceptible to *mazal*," and Rabbi Yochanan arguing, *Ein mazal l'Yisrael*, "The Jewish people are not susceptible to *mazal*."27 While numerous other Talmudic authorities support Rabbi Yochanan's position, excluding the Jewish nation from the vagaries of fortune,28 the debate itself is noteworthy, reflective of the rabbinic struggle to balance God's ongoing care for His chosen people with the arbitrary forces that might impinge on their fate.

In addition to the many discussions concerning the impact of *mazal*, Talmudic sources reflect recognition of other arbitrary forces that can potentially affect man's destiny. Some scholars, for example, note that when Moshe repeats God's instructions to the nation concerning the night before the Exodus, he adds the warning "And, as for you, let no man go out from the entrance to his house until morning."29 Moshe's admonition, these scholars maintain, is motivated by a desire to keep the Israelites safe from the plague of the firstborn and reflects the recognition that "Once permission has been given to the 'destroyer' [to act], he does not distinguish between the righteous and the wicked."30 *Even if an individual does not "deserve" death, he should not place himself in potential danger, lest he be caught in the conflagration.*

Further in this Talmudic passage, the same sentiment is echoed in more pedestrian yet practical fashion by scholars who observe, "If pestilence is in the city, bring your feet in [go indoors to avoid infection]."31 The rabbis conclude with a series of similar advisories, including the general warning, often found in rabbinic literature, that an individual should travel only during the day in order to avoid nightly dangers.32 These and

---

25. Ibid., Shabbat 156a.
26. Zohar Bamidbar, Naso 134.
27. Talmud Bavli Shabbat 196a.
28. Ibid., 196 a–b.
29. Shmot 12:22.
30. Talmud Bavli Bava Kama 60a.
31. Ibid., 60b.
32. Ibid., 60a–b.

other admonitions reflect rabbinic awareness that naturally occurring forces can seriously endanger an individual's safety.

H

By the time we arrive at the medieval period of Jewish history, complex comprehensive theories concerning the parameters of Divine Providence begin to emerge. Some scholars, such as the Ramban, set forward the deterministic position that "an individual does not have a stake in the Torah of Moshe, our teacher, until he believes that our affairs and chance occurrences are all miraculous, that there is no 'natural order' or 'routine working' within the universe."[33] Other authorities offer alternative positions.

As a case in point, the approach of the Rambam in his *Guide to the Perplexed* proves particularly instructive. After discussing a series of theories concerning God's governance of the world – from the Epicurean model that perceives the universe as totally governed by chance, to the view of the fatalists that any event in the universe is the direct result of God's intervention – the Rambam sets forth what he considers to be the Jewish approach to Divine Providence. In a lengthy exposition, this scholar remains true to form. A supreme rationalist in all areas of theology, here he posits the view that

> Divine Providence is connected with divine intellectual influence, and the same beings which are benefited by the latter so as to become intellectual, and to comprehend things comprehensible to rational beings, are also under the control of Divine Providence, which examines all their deeds with a view of rewarding or punishing them.[34]

According to the Rambam, *hashgacha pratit*, God's direct individual care, extends only to human beings, who as creatures of intellect can themselves relate directly to God. Divine care for species other than man, on the other hand, remains in the realm of *hashgacha klalit*, general (rather than specific) providence, and is limited to the preservation of the species as a whole. God does not directly determine by specific decree whether "a

---

33. Ramban, Shmot 13:16.
34. Rambam, *Moreh Nevuchim* 3:17.

certain leaf drops from a tree" or "a certain spider catches a certain fly." These events are the result of chance, in a world that continues to follow natural rules set in place by God at Creation.

Even when it comes to His relationship with man, however, God's gift of providence is not universally applied. Since divine influence reaches man through man's own intellectual strivings, the greater man's intellectual and spiritual perfection, "the greater the effect of Divine Providence upon him."[35] Man thus plays a direct role in determining the impact of Divine Providence on his own life. God's care over man will be commensurate with man's own religious search. Those individuals whose lives are unfortunately animalistic and brutish in nature will find themselves largely governed by the forces of chance that rule the nonhuman species. Those, on the other hand, who aspire to human perfection will find Divine Providence playing a much greater role in their lives.[36]

I

Centuries later, in his classic work *Halakhic Man*, Rabbi Joseph Soloveitchik (the Rav) elucidates the full implications of the Rambam's approach to Divine Providence:

> *The fundamental of providence is here transformed into a concrete commandment, an obligation incumbent upon man* [my italics]. Man is obliged to broaden the scope and strengthen the intensity of the individual providence that watches over him; it is all in his hands. When a person creates himself, ceases to be a mere species man, and becomes a man of God, then he has fulfilled that commandment which is implicit in the principle of providence.[37]

To the Rav, providence is not only a divinely granted gift, but an explicit imperative. Afforded the opportunity to establish an association with God, man is *obliged* to do so. The Man-God relationship, however, is a two-way street. When an individual reaches out to God, God reaches out

---

35. Ibid., 3:18.
36. Ibid.
37. Rabbi Joseph B. Soloveitchik, *Halakhic Man*, translated by Lawrence Kaplan (Philadelphia: Jewish Publication Society, 1983).

in return, bestowing upon that individual, in ever-increasing measure, the personal gift of Divine Providence.

The Rav, however, recognizes that this model of personal providence can fall short in the face of the episodes of overwhelming tragedy that periodically engulf mankind. While the phenomenon of individual personal suffering is difficult enough to comprehend in a world governed by Divine Providence, even more difficult are those national moments such as the Holocaust, when God's presence seems to disappear entirely.

Such moments can best be approached, the Rav maintains, by turning to the difficult biblical concept of *hester panim*, the hiding of God's face. The Torah prophesies that at particular moments in history, God, in response to sin, will take the radical step of hiding His face from the world.[38]

The phenomenon of *hester panim*, the Rav maintains, connects to the Torah's narrative of creation at the beginning of time. As described in the Torah, creation emerges as a process by which God, step-by-step, imposes order upon *tohu va'vohu* (primordial chaos). Such chaos, however, the Rav explains, never disappears, but continues to course beneath the surface of existence, held at bay only by God's constant renewal of creational order. When God "hides His face," He withdraws from direct maintenance of that order and, as He backs away, the world reverts to its original state of *tohu va'vohu*. During such tragic times, Divine Providence seems to disappear and the violent forces of nature and chance hold sway, engulfing righteous and non-righteous alike (see *Bereishit*: Bereishit 1, *Approaches* A).[39]

— J —

A myriad of other scholars, from medieval to modern, posit their own theories concerning Divine Providence. Some of these authorities emphasize God's control over all world events, while others limit such control in various ways. All, however, struggle to find a balance between the care of a thinking God towards man and the arbitrary forces that often seem to govern our lives.

---

38. Devarim 31:18.
39. Besdin, *Reflections of the Rav*, vol. 2, *Man of Faith in the Modern World*, pp. 34–37.

Points to Ponder

As I write these words, Japan is reeling from the effects of a powerful earthquake and tsunami that, to date, have claimed over twenty thousand lives, devastated countless others and prompted an ongoing nuclear emergency that is still out of control.

In the aftermath of this unfathomable tragedy, some individuals from within the Jewish community, including at least one prominent Israeli rabbinic authority, have publicly pointed to Japan's continued incarceration of two yeshiva students on charges of drug running as the source of God's wrath against that country. By way of proof, they cite a seemingly prescient Talmudic passage in the tractate of Brachot that maintains: "When the Holy One Blessed Be He recalls His children immersed in misery among the nations of the world, He causes two tears to drop into the Great Sea, and the resultant sound is heard from one end of the earth to the other, and that is [what we perceive as] an earthquake."[40]

A Jewish music video, professionally produced in the weeks following the earthquake, features two prominent Jewish musical artists issuing a poignant plea on behalf of the youthful prisoners. Towards its close, this video, *The Japan Song*, also contains dramatic footage of the tsunami. While the video's producers have issued the disclaimer "The tsunami footage in the clip was implemented as a sign of solidarity with the tragedy that struck the great Japanese nation,"[41] numerous observers continue to interpret the video as supporting the position that tragedy struck Japan because of its treatment of the two yeshiva students.

These public statements should come as no surprise in light of similar pronouncements by various Jewish communal leaders over the years, blaming world tragedies on the global community's mistreatment of the Jews, and Jewish tragedies upon the Jews' own sinfulness.

If only things were so simple....

Our analysis of the Jewish philosophical approaches to the issue of Divine Providence, albeit brief and incomplete, is detailed enough to make one point clear: Across the centuries, the rabbis recognized the deep and difficult questions raised by the clash between a belief in God's governance of the world, on the one hand, and man's practical experience, on the

---

40. Talmud Bavli Brachot 59a.
41. Http://thejapansong.com.

other. Eschewing simplistic solutions, they posited complex approaches towards a reconciliation of Jewish philosophy with the evidence emerging from a surrounding world.

We do ourselves and others a disservice when, in place of such serious, balanced analysis, we respond to powerfully difficult issues with sound bites; when, from among a myriad of possible sources, we selectively quote and apply rabbinic statements to support predetermined points of view.

Do we really possess intimate enough knowledge of God's ways to propose, with any degree of certainty, reasons for His actions? What do we say about ourselves, to ourselves and to others when we publicly explain away the death of innocent thousands as a divine response to the imprisonment of two yeshiva students, even if their continued incarceration may be unjust? Such sentiments not only demonstrate a profound insensitivity to the Japanese victims and to their families but also ignore the many sources in Jewish literature that speak of the value of all human life before God.

Each year, we close the Pesach Seder in a very odd way, with the singing of *Chad Gadya*, a Hebrew folk song of apparent medieval origin, chronicling a chain of seemingly arbitrary (and, to be truthful, violent) events that only culminate with God's obvious intervention. Across the ages, many theories have been posed as to why this strange song, with no clear reference to the Exodus story, serves as a coda to the Seder. In light of our discussion of Divine Providence, we can, perhaps, propose yet another explanation.

We specifically close the rituals of the Seder night by giving a nod to the reality of the world around us. We acknowledge that the divinely driven historical order (lit.: *seder*) that shapes our nation's journey – an order to which we have testified through the Seder ritual – may not always be apparent, and that God's hand in both our national and personal lives may not always be clearly seen. *In short, we prepare to leave the Seder evening – during which we have celebrated God's presence in our national history from its earliest footfalls – and reenter a world where that presence, although real, can be difficult to discern.*

Living in such a world, we must approach the mysteries surrounding the nature of God's providence in our lives with the humility, hesitation and thought-filled analysis that they deserve.

Balak

CHAPTER 22:2–25:9

בלק

פרק כב:ב–כה:ט

Parsha Summary

Of curses and blessings…

Balak, the king of Moav, fearing the apparent strength of the Israelites, attempts to secure the services of Bilam, a Midianite sorcerer, to curse the nation. Bilam, upon God's instructions, initially refuses the invitation. When a second group of messengers arrives from the king, however, Bilam inquires again and gains God's permission to travel to Balak. God informs the sorcerer, however, that he will be limited in his actions by God's further instructions.

Angered by some aspect of Bilam's decision to participate in Balak's plan, God causes an angel, initially invisible to Bilam, to block the sorcerer's path. Bilam's donkey, however, perceives the angel's presence and moves off the path to avoid an encounter. This action launches one of the strangest episodes in the Torah, during which both the donkey and the angel verbally communicate with Bilam. The episode ends with the angel reiterating that Bilam may continue his journey, but "only the word that I [God] shall speak to you – that you shall speak."

Bilam completes his journey, arrives in the presence of the Moabite king; warns the king that he (Bilam) will be bound by God's will but, nonetheless, endeavors to fulfill the king's wishes by cursing the Israelites. The sorcerer's first two attempts, however, are thwarted when God transforms Bilam's words from curses into blessings. On his third attempt, Bilam has an apparent change of heart, recognizing that "it was good in God's eyes to bless Israel."[1] Turning his face towards the wilderness, the sorcerer again blesses the people.

---

1. Bamidbar 24:1.

Angered by Bilam's failure to curse the Israelites, Balak orders the sorcerer to return to Midian. Bilam explains his own behavior by reminding the king that he had stipulated from the outset that he would be bound by God's will. The sorcerer then shares a prophecy with Balak concerning Israel's ascendancy over its enemies in the "end of days." The king and the sorcerer part, as Bilam returns to his home and Balak goes on his way.

The Israelites dwell in Shittim, where they begin to consort with the women of Moav and are drawn towards the idolatrous worship of Ba'al Pe'or. (The Midrash and the Talmud attribute these events to a scheme contrived by Bilam; see Balak 1, Approaches G and Balak 5.*) As a result, God's anger is kindled against the nation.*

When an Israelite brazenly sins with a Midianite woman in full view of Moshe and the nation, near the entrance of the Sanctuary, Pinchas, the son of Elazar and grandson of Aharon, rises to slay the perpetrators. This act of zealotry causes the God-sent plague afflicting the people to cease, but not before twenty-four thousand of their number tragically perish.

1 Look Who's a Prophet Now!

Context
Fearing the apparent strength of the Israelites, Balak, the king of Moav, attempts to secure the services of Bilam, a Midianite sorcerer, to curse the nation.

God intervenes and transforms Bilam's intended curses into blessings.[1]

Questions
Who was Bilam and what was the nature of his apparent powers? Was he a divinely appointed prophet or simply a gifted sorcerer? If he was a prophet, by what merit did he earn his heavenly bestowed gifts?

Approaches

A

The evidence concerning Bilam that emerges from the Torah is contradictory and confusing.

Bilam enters the biblical stage as a spiritual mercenary, ready for hire to the highest bidder for destructive purposes. And yet, he evidences a clear concern for God's will, refusing to accept Balak's summons until he receives express divine consent.[2]

Once granted permission to participate in Balak's plot, Bilam seems to set his concerns for God's preferences aside. Over and over again, he persists in his attempts to curse the Israelites, against God's express desires. Although Bilam informs Balak from the outset, "Am I empowered to say anything [on my own]? *Whatever word God places in my mouth, that I*

---

1. Bamidbar 22:2–24:25.
2. Ibid., 22:7–20.

*shall speak,"*³ both the sorcerer and the king attempt to sway God's mind through ritual and sacrifice.⁴

Only after these repeated unsuccessful efforts does the Torah testify to a change of heart on Bilam's part: "And Bilam saw that it was good in God's eyes to bless Israel, and he did not go as every other time towards divinations, and he set his face towards the wilderness."⁵

The Torah thus portrays Bilam as a personality in conflict, an individual who accepts God's authority, yet actively chafes against and attempts to undermine that authority.

--- B ---

Confusing as well is God's relationship to Bilam. On the one hand, the connection between God and the sorcerer is clearly close and personal. Few individuals, after all, are granted the gift of direct communication with the Divine. At the same time, however, God appears to toy with the sorcerer, first refusing his request to participate in Balak's plot, then granting that request, then chastising Bilam for actually acceding to the request, then ultimately controlling the very words that emerge from Bilam's mouth. [Note: God's changing posture concerning Bilam's request will be discussed in Balak 3.]

Is Bilam a prophet or a puppet? The picture painted by the Torah is ambiguous.

--- C ---

Given the lack of clarity emerging from the text, we should not be surprised by the plethora of views concerning Bilam found in rabbinic literature.

In spite of the fact that a passage in the book of Yehoshua retroactively refers to Bilam as a sorcerer,⁶ the Talmud lists Bilam among seven prophets who prophesy to the nations of the world.⁷ A number of early Midrashic sources make surprising claims concerning the extent of Bilam's prophetic ability. Commenting on the statement towards the end of the Torah "And

---

3. Ibid., 22:38.
4. Ibid., 22:40; 23:1–4, 14–15, 29–30.
5. Ibid., 24:2.
6. Yehoshua 13:22.
7. Talmud Bavli Bava Batra 15b.

never again did there arise *in Israel* a prophet like Moshe,"[8] the *Sifrei* maintains that only "in Israel" was Moshe a singularly supreme prophet. *Among the nations of the world, however, there did arise a prophet "like" Moshe, and that prophet was Bilam.*[9] Additional Midrashic sources go even further, attributing to Bilam specific powers that surpass even Moshe's.[10]

Other authorities limit Bilam's prophetic abilities in comparison to the abilities of the prophets of Israel. The Midrash notes, for example, that the Torah repeatedly chronicles God's interaction with Bilam through the use of the unusual term *va'yikar*, "and [God] happened upon."[11] This term, explains the Midrash, connotes a relationship rooted in impurity.[12] Later scholars clarify that God's relationship with Bilam is the product of happenstance and chance, and does not reflect the constancy of a meaningful bond. This stands in contrast to the divine connection with prophets such as Moshe, about whom the Torah states, *va'yikra*, "and [God] called."[13] God's encounters with Moshe are constant, conscious and deliberate, while His encounters with Bilam are random and sporadic.[14] Another Midrashic source notes that God initially communicates with Bilam specifically during the darkness of the night,[15] because "[Bilam] was not truly worthy of receiving the divine spirit."[16]

— **D** —

In her analysis of the Bilam-Balak narrative, Nehama Leibowitz points to two other distinctions between Bilam and the classical *nevi'im*, prophets of Israel.

Firstly, she explains, *Bilam seeks prophetic vision*. He builds altars, offers sacrifices and performs rituals in an attempt to "force" God's gift of prophecy. In stark contrast, the classical *nevi'im* do not seek divination. In many cases, in fact, the *nevi'im* actually attempt to flee the overwhelming

---

8. Devarim 33:10.
9. Sifrei, Devarim 33:10.
10. Tanna d'Vei Eliyahu Rabba 28; Midrash Rabba 14:20; Midrash Aggada Bamidbar 24:17.
11. Bamidbar 23:4, 16.
12. Vayikra Rabba 1:13.
13. Vayikra 1:1.
14. Rashi, Vayikra 1:1.
15. Bamidbar 22:9–10, 19–20.
16. Midrash Rabba Bamidbar 20:12.

responsibilities thrust upon them by God, as did Moshe at the burning bush, and as will the prophet Yona, centuries later, in the face of God's commandment to preach to the evil Gentile city of Ninveh. A true *navi*, in his humility, invariably considers himself unworthy of direct contact with God.

Secondly, the prophets of Israel consistently underscore the divine authorship of their visions, the phrase "saith the Lord" punctuating their pronouncements like a refrain. Only God's involvement, they believe, lends veracity to their visions and justifies their claim to be heard. Bilam, on the other hand, takes personal credit for his visions, opening his last two declarations with the introduction "saith Bilam the son of Be'or…"[17]

E

Other commentaries move to limit Bilam's prophetic abilities even further. Possibly mirroring earlier suggestions in the Talmud and Midrash,[18] the Ramban maintains that Bilam begins and ends his career as a sorcerer and only experiences a fleeting episode of prophecy during his involvement with Balak's plot. This temporary gift of prophecy, in addition, is only granted by God to enable Bilam to participate in an episode that will bring eventual honor to the Israelites.

Bilam's spiritual transformations, from sorcerer to prophet and back again, explains the Ramban, are actually reflected in the text. The Torah's unusual contention that Balak summons Bilam from "the land of the members of his people"[19] implies that Bilam originates as a sorcerer "from a land where all were sorcerers."[20] Bilam attains temporary prophecy during his interactions with Balak, as God "opens the sorcerer's eyes."[21] After parting company with the Moabite king, however, Bilam reverts to

---

17. Bamidbar 24:4, 15.
18. The Midrash Hagadol (Bamidbar 3:22) traces Bilam's career as beginning with gambling, idolatry and sorcery. The Midrash Rabba (Vayikra 1:12) maintains that Bilam was granted prophecy only for the benefit of Israel. The Talmud (Sanhedrin 106a) claims that he began as a prophet and became a sorcerer.
19. Bamidbar 22:5.
20. Ramban, Bamidbar 22:5. Note: Once again the Ramban seems to be building upon earlier Midrashic sources that trace Bilam's ancestry to a line of sorcerers. One midrash goes so far as to identify Bilam as Lavan, the patriarch Yaakov's manipulative father-in-law.
21. Bamidbar 22:31.

his original status as a sorcerer. This reversion is attested to by the earlier noted passage from the book of Yehoshua: "And Bilam, the son of Beor, *the sorcerer*, did the children of Israel slay with the sword."[22]

The Ramban also goes out of his way to review the earlier mentioned Midrashic claim that some of Bilam's powers surpassed those of Moshe (see above). He argues that, properly understood, the attributes mentioned in the Midrash do not indicate any real superiority on Bilam's part.

F

Returning to the textual narrative, whatever the extent or limitations of Bilam's prophetic abilities, his purported activities remain problematic. A prophet's fundamental role, after all, is to reflect God's will and transmit His message to the people. The issuance of blessings and curses is not contained in a prophet's job description. While a *navi* is granted the ability to predict future events in order to warn, encourage and educate his audience, nowhere is he given the power to unilaterally shape those future events. Why then is Bilam presented as an individual about whom it is known, "Those you bless shall be blessed and those you curse shall be cursed"?[23] [Note: The general question as to why God finds it necessary to forestall Bilam's curses of the Israelites (whatever the nature of Bilam's powers) will be discussed in the next study.]

Following, as is his wont, the path of *pshat*, the Rashbam suggests that Bilam's powers of blessing might well have been perceived rather than actual. Balak knows of Bilam's reputation as a prophet and sorcerer. The Moabite king, therefore, assumes that these abilities will lend efficacy to Bilam's prayers and sacrifices, as well.[24]

If, on the other hand, we accept that Bilam's powers to bless are real, perhaps they simply represent a refinement of a general gift granted by God to man, at the dawn of Jewish history. According to Midrashic tradition, God transmits the power of interpersonal blessing to Avraham with the statement "and you will be a blessing."[25] The Midrash explains God's words to mean "blessings are given to your hand. Until now they

---

22. Yehoshua 13:22.
23. Bamidbar 22:5.
24. Rashbam, Bamidbar 22:6.
25. Bereishit 12:2.

were in My hand. I blessed Adam and Noach. From this time on you will bless whom you wish."[26] With this proclamation to Avraham, God indicates that as part of the divine partnership agreement with humanity, He will respect the words spoken by man and reckon with them when He makes His decisions. Man thus acquires the power of blessing and prayer (see *Bereishit*: Toldot 3, *Approaches* A).

The question, however, remains: Why would Bilam be granted special abilities within this God-man partnership? It would stand to reason that the more saintly the individual, the closer he grows to God, the more powerful his blessings. Conversely, Bilam's evil tendencies should distance him from God and preclude his being granted extraordinary powers to curse or to bless.

Sensitive to this issue, a number of rabbinic sources make an astounding claim. Bilam's unique powers of blessing are based neither on merit nor on spiritual authority. *These powers are instead the product of Bilam's singular ability to tap into preexisting conditions in his environment* (see Chukat 4, *Approaches* E–J for a discussion of the relationship between ongoing forces in the fabric of creation and the phenomenon of Divine Providence). The Talmud postulates, for example, a split second each day when God is angered and man stands at his most vulnerable. Alone in creation, Bilam is capable of calculating and using that moment to pronounce his curses, so that he can strike at the point of his victims' greatest exposure.[27]

For its part, the Zohar, noting Bilam's self-description as "the man with the open eye," attributes to Bilam the attribute of an "evil eye," the ability to draw independent destructive powers against anything he gazes upon.[28] For this reason, as the story progresses, Balak repeatedly goes out of his way to ensure that Bilam looks down upon the Israelite camp as the sorcerer prepares to pronounce his curses.[29]

---

26. Midrash Rabba Bereishit 39:11.
27. Talmud Bavli Brachot 7a, Avoda Zara 4a.
28. Zohar 1:68b.
29. Bamidbar 22:41; 33:13, 28.

G

Finally, dissatisfied with the paucity of information concerning Bilam's background, character and powers, Midrashic authorities also elaborate on his possible origins and life story. The Zohar, for example, traces the sorcerer's tutelage to the "fallen angels" Aza and Azael, obliquely referenced (according to some authorities) in a mysterious passage in the book of Bereishit[30] (see *Vayikra*: Acharei Mot 1, *Approaches* C for a discussion of the puzzling Midrashic tradition concerning these angels).[31]

As noted above, some authorities see Bilam as originating from a land immersed in sorcery. Other scholars are even more specific, tracing his ancestry to different possible negative historical figures. Targum Yonatan goes so far as to identify Bilam as none other than Lavan the Aramite, who plagues the patriarch Yaakov[32] – and now, apparently, his descendents – through trickery and deceit.[33]

Numerous sources in the Talmud and Midrash place Bilam in Egypt before the Exodus, in the role of a trusted adviser to Pharaoh; and some sources even name him as the author of several harsh decrees against the Israelites, including the decision to drown the male Israelite infants in the Nile.[34]

A strong tradition builds on a later brief textual source[35] identifying Bilam as the architect of the seemingly unrelated events that bring the Israelites to their knees at the end of Parshat Balak.[36] Upon failing to curse the nation, Bilam designs, in great detail, a plot to defeat the Israelites by leading them down a path of licentiousness and immorality.[37] His efforts bring about the tragic events at Ba'al Pe'or (see Balak 5).

These and other observations reflect a familiar tendency within Midrashic literature to attribute to the villains of the Torah greater evil than appears outright in the text (others treated similarly by the Midrash include Yishmael, Esav and Lavan). In mirror fashion, the Midrash

---

30. Bereishit 6:1–2.
31. Zohar 1:126.
32. Bereishit 29:13–32:1.
33. Targum Yonatan, Bamidbar 22:5.
34. Talmud Bavli Sota 11a; Yalkut Shimoni, Shmot 166; Midrash Hagadol Shmot 2:23.
35. Bamidbar 31:16.
36. Ibid., 25:1–9.
37. Talmud Bavli Sanhedrin 101a.

elaborates greatly on the righteousness of biblical heroes, once again adding a great deal of biographical information not contained in the text. The interpretation of this far-ranging information depends, in large measure, on one's general approach to Midrash. Those who view Midrash in literal terms will accept this biographical material literally, as personal details concerning familiar figures handed down over the centuries. Those, on the other hand, who interpret Midrash figuratively will view this material more flexibly, as a rabbinic attempt to fill in the blanks, and as a vehicle, like all Midrashim, for the transmission of critical lessons and ideas.

— H —

A multitude of other sources concerning Bilam's character, power and background are found in rabbinic literature. Like the opinions that we have reviewed, these observations paint a complicated, often contradictory picture of one of the most mysterious characters of the Bible.

A final quote from the Zohar perhaps sums up this sorcerer/prophet in all of his mystery and complexity: "There is no evil that does not contain a tiny spark of sanctity, and Bilam understood this."[38]

As our next study will show, the distinction between Bilam's intended curses and his pronounced blessings was often subtle and nuanced. Bilam tried to walk a thin line between spiritual splendor and depravity. He will forever be remembered, however, as a man who, granted God-given gifts beyond comprehension, tragically chose to use those gifts towards the destruction of others.

Points to Ponder

God talks to them, too? Bilam's story raises a series of serious questions....

From a Jewish perspective, what does the existence of Gentile prophets say about God's relationship with the nations of the world? What does it say about the uniqueness (or lack of uniqueness) of His relationship with the Jewish people? What exactly was the role of the seven prophets who, according to the Talmud, preached to the nations of the world?[39]

---

38. Zohar 2:69b.
39. Talmud Bavli Bava Batra 15b.

Some Jewish authorities view the phenomenon of Gentile prophecy ethnocentrically, as yet another phenomenon underscoring the spiritual superiority of the Jewish nation.

The Ramban, for example, quotes the *Sifrei* as maintaining that prophetic vision is granted to the nations of the world only in order to level the playing field, as it were: to remove the possible complaint on their part that had they been given the same opportunities as the Israelites, they too would have been loyal to God's law. For this reason, individual Gentiles are granted the gift of prophecy. Like Bilam, however, they fail to take advantage of the opportunity.

Bilam's story, however, may well carry a different message. As we have noted before, *the chosen nature of the Jewish nation does not connote exclusivity*. While the Torah attests to a unique connection between God and the Jewish people, numerous sources within Jewish tradition reflect recognition of a continuing relationship between God and all the nations of the world (see *Bereishit*: Noach 4). The existence of Gentile prophets early in world history may simply be another manifestation of that relationship.

2 Why Bother?

Context
Fearing the apparent strength of the Israelites, Balak, the king of Moav, attempts to secure the services of Bilam, a Midianite sorcerer, to curse the nation.

God eventually allows Bilam's participation in Balak's plot, but warns the sorcerer: "Only the thing that I shall speak to you – that you shall do."[1]

Bilam's repeated attempts to curse the Israelites are thwarted as God transforms the sorcerer's curses into blessings.

Questions
No story in the Torah is stranger then the story of Balak and Bilam.

Why does God find it necessary to intervene in order to prevent Bilam from cursing the Israelites? We can certainly understand a divine move to preempt a physical threat against the nation. What danger, however, is potentially carried by a verbal threat such as Bilam's curses? Why does it matter what this sorcerer says? Why can't God simply choose to ignore him?

Deepening the puzzle is a fascinating fact concerning the story of Balak and Bilam: *this is the only story in the Torah – since the patriarch Avraham enters the historical stage – that takes place totally out of view of the Israelites, their emissaries or their ancestors.*

This narrative is comprised of a series of events, interactions and conversations at which no Israelite is present. Had God not informed us of these events, we would never have even known that they happened. Bilam would have pronounced his curses, God would have simply ignored them, and the Israelites would have gone blissfully on their way, forever unaware of Bilam's words. Who knows how many other unnoted verbal

---
1. Bamidbar 22:2–20.

threats were directed against the Israelites during the biblical era, their echoes fading into the mists of history. What makes this episode worthy of God's or our notice? Why is the narrative of Balak and Bilam included in the Torah at all?

Approaches

A

One perspective on the issues we raise is reflected in our discussion concerning Bilam's power to bless or curse (see previous study). According to this approach, *the threat posed by Bilam's words emanates from God's own decision to grant strength to man's speech.*

At the dawn of Jewish history, at the launch of Avraham's journey, God promises the patriarch: "And you will be a blessing."[2] This statement is understood by the Midrash to mean "Blessings are given to your hand. Until now they were in My hand. I blessed Adam and Noach. From this time on you will bless whom you wish."

As a result of this heavenly decree, every word spoken by man about another, for good or for bad, acquires power. God therefore moves to abort Bilam's curses before they can acquire the power of spoken words.

We further suggested that Bilam's words might have carried singular strength, either due to his close, albeit mysterious relationship with God, or as a result of his singular ability to tap into preexisting conditions in his environment and direct them against his enemies (see previous study, *Approaches* G).

God's own self-imposed limitations in the face of man's speech and/or Bilam's ability to manipulate the very rules created by God to govern His universe may well have enabled the sorcerer to seriously threaten the Israelites through his words. God therefore moves to stop those words from ever being spoken.

This approach to Bilam's threat is underscored in the Midrashic pronouncement "There were no days, from the day that the world was created, when the Holy One Blessed Be He needed to be with [the people

---

2. Bereishit 12:2.

of] Israel as much as the time when Bilam wanted to destroy [them] from the world."³

---- B ----

Other commentaries are unwilling to consider the possibility that Bilam's words could have directly threatened a people protected by "the righteousness of the patriarchs and the merit of the Revelation at Sinai."⁴ God is compelled, these scholars argue, to change Bilam's words for other reasons.

The Ibn Ezra, for example, suggests that God acts to prevent the surrounding nations from arriving at an erroneous conclusion that would damage the nation's honor. In the aftermath of Bilam's efforts, the Israelites endure a devastating plague as a result of the sin of Ba'al Pe'or. Had Bilam been allowed to curse the nation, observers would have mistakenly concluded that this plague had actually been caused by the sorcerer's curses.⁵

Similar explanations are offered by later authorities who, likewise, maintain that God intervenes so that observers will not attribute later failings of the Israelites to the effect of the sorcerer's curses.⁶

The Abravanel, however, rejects the Ibn Ezra's approach, failing to see within it any compelling threat against the Israelites. How then, the Abravanel asks, are we to view the textual sources⁷ clearly testifying that, had it not been for God's merciful intervention, Bilam's curses would indeed have had devastating impact upon the people?

The Abravanel therefore posits a real, albeit indirect, threat potentially presented by Bilam's words. As Balak himself clearly testifies, by the time the story begins, Bilam has earned public renown for his perceived powers in the area of blessing and curse. Had the sorcerer been allowed to pronounce his intended curses, surrounding nations would have heard and would have been encouraged to attack the "newly vulnerable" Israelites. "Open season" would have been called on the fledgling nation. Once God transforms Bilam's curses into blessings, however, the special status of the

---

3. Zohar Chadash, Balak 54.
4. Abravanel, Bamidbar 22:7.
5. Ibn Ezra, Bamidbar 22:9.
6. Shadal, Bamidbar 22:2; *Midrashei Torah* (Anselm Astruc), Bamidbar 22:15.
7. Devarim 23:6; Yehoshua 24:9–10; Micha 6:5.

nation in God's eyes becomes readily apparent to all, rendering the people safe from attack.[8]

A similar interpretation is suggested by Rabbi Meir Simcha Hacohen of Dvinsk, who maintains that God intervenes in the Balak/Bilam story in order to "thrust the fear of Israel upon all the kings of the nations."[9] Once someone of Bilam's stature blesses the Israelites, surrounding nations will be fearful of moving against them in any way.

A creative approach to the impact of Bilam's words is offered by Rabbi Shimshon Raphael Hirsch, the pivotal rabbinic leader of nineteenth-century German Jewry whose emphasis on the universal role of the Jewish nation serves as a foundation of his religious philosophy. God visits specific individuals, whether Jewish or Gentile, with prophetic vision, to enable them to bring forward His message to the world. *In this case, God wants Bilam to bless the Israelites in his role as a prophet, not for their sake, but for the sake of the surrounding nations.* He wants the world to recognize that this is a "blessed people," whose very character and mission reflect God's will for mankind as a whole. When Bilam attempts to subvert this prophetic mandate by cursing rather than blessing the Israelites, God steps in to ensure that the intended divine message to mankind will be properly transmitted and received.[10]

― C ―

Another possible approach to the significance of Bilam's words can be gleaned from a puzzling rabbinic observation that, at first, seems only to deepen the mysteries before us. In the book of Devarim, as Moshe recounts the Bilam-Balak episode in retrospect, he relates: "And God transformed, on your behalf, the curse into a blessing."[11]

Why, ask the rabbis, does Moshe speak of a singular transformation of "the curse into a blessing"? Weren't *multiple curses* transformed into blessings during this episode?

The answer suggested by the scholars threatens to undermine the thrust of the entire Balak/Bilam narrative:

---

8. Abravanel, Bamidbar 22:2–25:9.
9. Meshech Chochma, Bamidbar 22:20–22.
10. Rabbi Shimshon Raphael Hirsch, Bamidbar 22:12.
11. Devarim 23:6.

> Rabbi Yochanan stated: From the blessings pronounced by Bilam, one can determine what was in his heart…. Rabbi Abba bar Kahana [further] maintained: [due to the sins of the Israelites] *all of them [the blessings] reverted back to the original curses* [my italics], with the exception of the blessing concerning synagogues and houses of study, as the Torah states, "And God transformed, on your behalf, the curse into a blessing": *"the curse" and not "the curses"* [my italics].[12]

How astounding! The rabbis would have us understand that, in the final analysis, God's intervention in the Bilam story has limited effect. After God "troubles Himself" to change the sorcerer's curses into blessings (an act whose necessity we have already questioned), *almost all of those blessings turn back into curses*. Perplexingly, the Balak/Bilam story now seems to make even less sense. Why does God bother to transform Bilam's words if, in practical terms, those words are not truly "transformed" at all?

Perhaps the rabbis, in their own inimitable style, answer all of our questions at once. Fundamentally, they maintain, God's message through the Balak/Bilam narrative is surprising but clear: *It does not matter what Bilam says!*

Phenomena like Bilam's words ultimately have no independent power. Although God may grant credence to words spoken by man, such words are not the primary determinants of an individual's fate.

This sorcerer can curse you or bless you; it makes no difference. Your destiny will be decided not by outside forces, but by your own merit. Your own actions will determine whether you are "cursed" or "blessed."

Had God allowed Bilam to proceed with his intended curses, the Israelites, upon hearing of the sorcerer's words (or barring that, upon learning of similar phenomena) could have claimed them as justification for their failings: *How could we be blamed? Were we not doomed from the start?*

God therefore decides to use the Balak/ Bilam episode as a teaching opportunity. He intervenes, changes the sorcerer's curses to blessings and reveals the entire episode to the Israelites from the start. In doing so, He effectively proclaims: *Now I have removed any possible excuse. The words pronounced upon you by the sorcerer are positive. The final significance and*

---

12. Talmud Bavli Sanhedrin 105b.

impact of those words, however, like so much else in your lives, is in your hands. If you are meritorious, Bilam's blessings will remain intact. If not, those very "blessings" will be turned against you.

Always remember that your story will be defined by no one else. You can blame no outside force. Ultimately, it's all up to you....

3 If I Could Talk to the Animals

Context

As the opening segments of the Balak/Bilam narrative unfold, God's communication with Bilam grows increasingly strange.

1. In response to Bilam's first inquiry concerning participation in Balak's plans to curse the Israelites, God clearly declares, "*Do not go with them*; do not curse the nation, for it is blessed!"[1]

2. When Bilam persists in his inquiries after receiving a second set of messengers from the Moabite king, God states, "If the men have come to summon you, *arise, go with them*; but only the thing that I shall speak to you – that you shall do."[2]

3. Finally, when Bilam complies with God's instructions and journeys towards a meeting with Balak, one of the strangest narratives in the Torah begins to unfold: "*And God's anger was kindled because he [Bilam] was going*, and an angel of the Lord stood on the road to impede him…."[3]

The angel, at first, remains unseen to Bilam. The sorcerer's donkey, however, perceives the angel's presence and turns off the road to avoid an encounter. When Bilam strikes the animal in an attempt to turn it back to the road, the angel again blocks the way. The donkey, in a continuing effort to avoid the angel, presses Bilam's leg against the wall, injuring the sorcerer and causing him to strike the animal again in anger. Suddenly, God grants the donkey the power of speech and the animal objects to its master: "What have I done to you that you have struck me three times?… Am I not your donkey that you have ridden upon me all your life until this

---

1. Bamidbar 22:12.
2. Ibid., 22:20.
3. Ibid., 22:22.

day? Have I been accustomed to behaving towards you in such a manner?"[4]

Bilam concedes the point and God opens the sorcerer's eyes, allowing him to see the angel, with sword unsheathed, standing before him.

The angel defends the donkey's actions and informs Bilam that had the animal not turned off the path, Bilam's life would have been forfeit. The sorcerer replies that he had been unaware of the angel's presence. He informs the angel that he will now willingly abort his journey if God does not want him to proceed.

The angel, however, replies, "*Go with the men*, but only the word that I shall speak to you – that you shall speak."[5]

Questions

Bewilderment best describes our reaction as we confront the opening stages of the Balak/Bilam narrative.

Through the growingly strange media of conflicting instructions, a semi-visible angel and, ultimately, a talking donkey, God clearly conveys significant messages to Bilam and, through him, to us. What, however, are those divine communications?

Why does God first tell Bilam not to participate in Balak's plan, yet subsequently grants the sorcerer permission to go to the king, when Balak persists in his invitations?

What is the meaning of God's conditional response to Bilam's second request, "*If the men have come to summon you*, arise, go with them?" Isn't it clear by now that the king's messengers have come to summon him?

After giving Bilam permission to travel to Balak, why does God become angry with the sorcerer "because he was going"? And, if God is now angry, why not simply order Bilam to return home? Why place an angel in Bilam's path "to impede him" and then, ultimately, allow him to continue on his journey?

---

4. Ibid., 22:28–30.
5. Ibid., 22:35.

Most perplexing of all, of course, is the entire episode of the talking donkey. What is the significance of this event? Why is the angel initially visible only to the donkey, creating conflict between Bilam and his "steed"? Why does God enable the donkey to talk? And what message does the animal actually deliver? Ultimately, other than complaining over its treatment at the hands of its master, the donkey doesn't seem to say much at all. Why then, does God enable the donkey to speak in the first place?

Approaches

— A —

As the scholars attempt to understand this strange introduction to a strange story, they focus first on the conflicting instructions issued by God to Bilam. The Ohr Hachaim, for example, explains that the changes in God's instructions to the sorcerer are designed to address two different divine concerns.

On the one hand, if God allows Bilam to participate in Balak's scheme, observers will mistakenly conclude that the sorcerer is acting independently and is not under divine control. On the other hand, continued divine refusal will give rise to the erroneous conclusion that God is preventing Bilam's participation because He fears the sorcerer's powers. In order to balance these concerns, God initially prohibits Bilam from traveling to Balak, thereby demonstrating His complete control over the sorcerer's actions. With the arrival of the second set of messengers from the king, however, God shows his disdain for Bilam's assumed powers by allowing the sorcerer to embark on the journey. When Bilam awakens the next morning, however, and, without a word of explanation, hurries to join the messengers, he contravenes God's original intent. By failing to inform the king's emissaries that his compliance with their request had been contingent upon receiving divine consent, Bilam creates the impression that he is acting as an independent agent – and thereby incurs God's wrath.[6]

---

6. Ohr Hachaim, Bamidbar 22:20, 22.

B

In contrast to the Ohr Hachaim, the Ramban argues that God's position remains completely consistent throughout the seemingly conflicting instructions to Bilam.

God does not object to the sorcerer's proposed journey – only to its stated purpose. When the king's messengers first approach the sorcerer, God therefore states, "Do not go with them; do not curse the nation, for it is blessed!" *You are prohibited from cursing the Israelites. If that is the sole purpose of your proposed journey, why would you go at all?*

Once Balak persists, however, and sends a second set of messengers to Bilam, God informs the sorcerer, "If the men have come to summon you, arise, go with them; but only the thing that I shall speak to you – that you shall do." *I have no objection to your taking the journey, only to its stated purpose. Inform the king's emissaries that you are prohibited from cursing the Israelites and that you will, in fact, bless them if I so command you. If the messengers have, nonetheless, "come to summon you" – if they want you to journey with them in spite of My clear stipulations – then "arise, go with them."*

Driven by his deep desire to participate in Balak's plan, however, Bilam fails to convey God conditions. He instead awakens in the morning, saddles his donkey and eagerly begins to journey with the messengers as if he fully intends to fulfill Balak's requests without constraint. The Torah therefore testifies, "God's anger was kindled because he [Bilam] was going...."[7] *God is angered because He knows that had Bilam informed Balak's emissaries of the divine restrictions placed upon him, this journey would have never taken place.* Absent Bilam's ability to curse the Israelites, the king has no reason to demand the sorcerer's presence.[8]

Later commentaries adduce textual support for the Ramban's position by pointing to the distinction between the Hebrew terms *itam* and *imahem*, both of which literally mean "with them." *Itam*, they maintain, implies a separation between the participating parties, the retention of independent purpose. *Imahem*, on the other hand, suggests a total sharing of thought and intent between those involved.

---

7. Bamidbar 22:22.
8. Ramban, Bamidbar 22:20.

God initially commands Bilam, *Lo telech imahem*, "Do not go with them,"⁹ *do not join them in their stated goals.* He later permits the sorcerer to travel with the king's emissaries by stating, *Kum lech itam*, "Arise, go with them,"¹⁰ *but maintain your own independent counsel.*

Ultimately, however, Bilam incurs God's wrath when he goes *im sarei Moav*, "with the officers of Moav,"¹¹ philosophically, as well as physically.¹²

Nehama Leibowitz suggests that this linguistic distinction may well be the basis of an early Midrashic comment quoted by Rashi that, without explanation, interprets the phrase *im sarei Moav* as reflecting Bilam's joining of purpose with the emissaries of the king.¹³

--- C ---

For his part, Rashi interprets the divine instructions given to Bilam as underscoring the sorcerer's own freedom of choice.

Although God originally prohibits Bilam from acceding to the king's requests, he later tells the sorcerer, *Im likro lecha ba'u ha'anashim*, "If the men have come to summon you" – *if, in spite of my earlier statements, you really believe that the invitation proffered by these men will accrue to your benefit* – "arise, go with them."¹⁴

The existence of free choice, however, does not protect an individual from the consequences of the "wrong choices" that he makes. While God allows Bilam to choose freely, He is ultimately angered by the sorcerer's decisions.¹⁵

---

9. Bamidbar 22: 12.
10. Ibid., 22:20.
11. Ibid., 22:21.
12. *Haktav V'hakabala*, Bamidbar 22:12; Malbim, Bamidbar 22:21.
13. Leibowitz, *Iyunim Chadashim B'Sefer Bamidbar*, p. 306; Midrash Rabba Bamidbar 20:10; Rashi, Bamidbar 22:21.
14. This interpretation is consistent with Rashi's approach to an earlier, linguistically similar but vastly different textual passage rooted at the dawn of Jewish history. When God commands the patriarch Avraham *Lech lecha…*, "Leave your land, your birthplace and the home of your father…," Rashi explains, "[Leave] for your good and for your benefit" (Rashi, Bereishit 12:1).
15. Rashi, Bamidbar 22:20, 22.

D

These and other rabbinic observations shed light on God's initial instructions to Bilam. The next phase of the narrative, however, the episode of the "talking donkey," clearly demands and receives its own independent, careful attention and analysis across the ages.

E

Some authorities accept this episode at face value, as a miraculous intervention on God's part, overturning the familiar laws of a physical world in order to convey powerful lessons to Bilam and those around him.

Rabbi Shimshon Raphael Hirsch, for example, sees Bilam's encounter with the "talking donkey" as a humbling experience, designed both to break the sorcerer's arrogant spirit and to demonstrate God's absolute control over the unfolding events: "He [Bilam] wants to amend God's plan for the world and is blinder than his own animal, he wants to vanquish God's resistance and must accommodate himself to the wish of his own animal, he wants to ruin an entire nation by his word and has to confess the impotence of his wrath against an animal, he wants to be arrogant towards lords and princes and becomes a laughing-stock before his own attendants. He [God] Who can vouchsafe speech to an animal can also use the mouth of a Bilam to proclaim His Word."[16]

The Kli Yakar views the miracle of the talking donkey as conveying an even more humiliating lesson to Bilam. The donkey possesses no innate verbal capability but, instead, acquires the temporary power of speech for the sole purpose of participation in God's plan. Similarly, Bilam enjoys no independent prophetic ability. God's gift of vision will be fleeting, and will exist only so that honor may be bestowed upon the Israelites.[17]

The Sforno interprets the entire episode in more positive terms, as a divine attempt to move Bilam towards repentance and change. Even as he eagerly travels towards participation in Balak's evil plan, Bilam remains potentially redeemable.[18]

In contrast to these interpretations, the Meshech Chochma argues that this strange miracle is directed towards the king's messengers rather than

---

16. Rabbi Shimshon Raphael Hirsch, Bamidbar 22:22, 28.
17. Kli Yakar, Bamidbar 22:28.
18. Sforno, Bamidbar 22:28.

towards Bilam himself. As we have noted before, the Meshech Chochma maintains that God's primary purpose throughout the entire Balak/Bilam narrative is to "thrust the fear of Israel upon all the kings of the nations" (see previous study, *Approaches* B). By ensuring that Bilam blesses the Israelites, God intends to increase their stature in the eyes of surrounding nations and protect them from potential attack. This plan will only work, however, if observers are convinced that Bilam's words mirror divine truth and are not the result of collusion between the sorcerer and the Israelites themselves. God therefore performs "an astounding wonder," an event "beyond the boundaries of nature," in full view of Balak's distinguished officers. The miracle of the talking donkey will thus serve as a clear demonstration of divine control over the unfolding events, including Bilam's eventual pronouncements.[19]

— F —

Other scholars, less willing to accept the episode of the talking donkey as a miraculous physical event, choose to explain this puzzling episode in less literal fashion.

Consistent with his approach to angelic encounters throughout the biblical text, the Rambam, for example, views neither the angel's appearance nor the donkey's speech as physical phenomena (see *Bereishit: Vayishlach 2, Approaches* D). This entire episode unfolds, the Rambam maintains, in the realm of a prophetic vision or dream granted by God to Bilam.[20]

Centuries later, Rabbi Shmuel David Luzatto (Shadal) offers an even more revolutionary suggestion. This scholar notes the "surprising" lack of surprise on the part of Bilam and his servants to the phenomenon of the "talking donkey." Confronted with such bizarre behavior on the part of the animal, argues Shadal, the sorcerer and those with him should have been struck dumb. Yet the Torah describes Bilam responding to the donkey as if nothing untoward has occurred. In addition, Shadal notes, the term *daber*, the usual specific term for human speech, is absent from this episode.

---

19. Meshech Chochma 22:20–22.
20. Rambam, *Moreh Nevuchim* 2:42.

Based on these observations, this scholar maintains that the donkey never actually utters a word. When struck by its master, the animal begins to plaintively bray, as if to say, *What have I done to you…?* When Bilam continues to react angrily, the donkey brays again, as if arguing, *Am I not your donkey…; have I acted this way on any previous occasion…?* Faced with such strange reactions from his usually "faithful steed," Bilam is forced to acknowledge that something untoward must be causing the animal's aberrant behavior. The phrase "and God opened the mouth of the donkey," explains Shadal, references the unusual (but totally natural) cries that flowed from the donkey's mouth. Similarly, in the introductory plea to the Amida (the central silent prayer in Jewish liturgy), a Jew regularly requests: "O Lord, open my lips, and my mouth will tell of Thy praises." *God, grant me the power of potent but totally natural speech.*[21]

---- G ----

These and other rabbinic sources mirror the wide range of opinion concerning the opening events of the Balak/Bilam narrative. Consensus is reached, however, on one significant point. No passage within the text, even those that seem abundantly strange to us, should be dismissed without careful analysis.

Viewed through the prism of rabbinic thought, each and every detail of God's complex communication with Bilam becomes significant, setting the stage for the dramatic story that has begun to unfold.

Points to Ponder
We learn in Pirkei Avot:

> Ten things were created at twilight on the eve of the Shabbat [of creation]…[:] the mouth of the earth [that swallowed Korach and his followers]; the mouth of [Miriam's] well; the mouth of [Bilam's] donkey; the rainbow; the manna; [Moshe's] staff; the *shamir* [a worm with the strength to cut stones, used by King Shlomo in the building of the Temple]; the letters, the writing and the tablets [of Sinai].[22]

---

21. Shadal, Bamidbar 22:2.
22. Pirkei Avot 5:9.

The Rambam comments on this passage as follows:

> We have already remarked that [the sages] do not believe in the continued renewal of [God's] creative will. Rather [they maintain] that, during creation, God implanted in nature the potential power to bring forth all that will be.
>
> Whether a phenomenon is recurrent and is therefore perceived as natural, whether a phenomenon is rare and is therefore perceived as a miracle – all is equal.[23]

The Ramban further comments:

From a recognition of the large-scale, public miracles, man comes to acknowledge the hidden miracles, which are the foundation of the entire Torah. For an individual does not have a stake in the Torah of Moshe, our teacher, until he believes that our affairs and chance occurrences are all miraculous; that there is no "natural order" or "routine working" within the universe.[24]

The above passages raise two points for our consideration:

1. Through the eyes of the Rambam and other commentaries, the Mishna in Pirkei Avot reflects the position that there is "nothing new under the sun."[25] Embedded in God's original acts of creation are the seeds for all that is to come. Both "natural events" and "miracles" rise out of the fabric of the existing universe.

2. In spite of widely differing viewpoints on the general issue of Divine Providence (see Chukat 4, *Approaches* H) both the Rambam and the Ramban agree, as do many other authorities, that the term *miracle* is subjectively based. We refer to a phenomenon as miraculous, not because it differs substantively from other phenomena around us, but because we find it extraordinary within our experience. Objectively, a talking donkey is no more miraculous than a sunrise, the flight of a butterfly, the human brain.... Were we to see these phenomena anew, we would marvel at their existence. We would certainly consider them "miraculous."

---

23. Rambam, Commentary on Pirkei Avot 5:9.
24. Ramban, Shmot 13:16. Note: This passage reflects the Ramban's deterministic view concerning the workings of the universe. For an examination of this and other approaches to the issue of Divine Providence, see Chukat 4.
25. Kohelet 1:9.

Our sages would have us remember that the God Who can create the wonders around us each day can certainly, if He desires, enable a donkey to talk.

4 Does the Leopard Change Its Spots?

Context
Twice, Bilam has endeavored to curse the Israelites only to have his words transformed into blessings through divine intervention. As the sorcerer now rises for a third attempt, the text signals a sea change in his personal attitude: "And Bilam saw that it was good in God's eyes to bless Israel, so he did not go as every other time towards divinations; and he set his face towards the wilderness. And Bilam lifted his eyes and saw Israel dwelling according to its tribes; and the Spirit of God was upon him."[1]

Questions
What is the nature of Bilam's shift in attitude at this point in the story? Has he truly set aside his own desire to harm Israelites in favor of fulfilling God's wishes?

What is the significance of the phrase "and he set his face towards the wilderness"? Does this action inform in any way the sorcerer's changed approach towards the Israelites?

Once Bilam decides on his new course, he is apparently struck by the vision of "Israel dwelling according to its tribes." What is it about this scene that so moves the sorcerer?

Approaches

— A —

The rabbis' natural suspicion of changing motives on the part of biblical villains (see, for example, the rabbinic debate concerning Esav's apparent

---

1. Bamidbar 24:1–2.

reconciliation with Yaakov[2]) surfaces again at this pivotal moment in the Balak/Bilam story, stirring debate across the ages.

Some scholars are willing to accept a true change in attitude on Bilam's part. The Ramban, for example, maintains that the sorcerer has become convinced of the futility of his efforts to curse the Israelites by the very words that he, himself, was earlier forced to utter: "There is no divination in Yaakov and no sorcery in Israel."[3] Charting a new path, Bilam, therefore, "set his face towards the wilderness."[4] He turns towards the site of the Israelite encampment, hoping that a gaze upon the nation itself will spur his effort towards true communication with God.[5]

Likewise, the Rashbam, with his usual allegiance to textual *pshat*, simply declares: "From this point on, [Bilam] intended to bless them [the Israelites] with a full heart."[6]

—— B ——

Accepting the possibility of real, albeit temporary, transformation on Bilam's part allows us to consider an additional explanation for the phrase "and he [Bilam] set his face towards the wilderness."

The *midbar*, wilderness, serves as the backdrop for almost all pivotal events in the early development of the Jewish nation. Moshe's initial encounter with his Creator, the revelation at Sinai, the birth of Jewish nationhood and the forty-year period of national wandering and developmental growth all take place in the wilderness. God's choice of the *midbar* for these seminal national experiences is far from accidental. The wilderness is, at once, isolating, equalizing, humbling and imposing. The unique sense of perspective that can be gained in the *midbar* – an awareness of man's limitations balanced with a feeling of closeness to his Creator – can scarcely be replicated in any other geographic terrain.

The Torah's picture of the arrogant sorcerer, Bilam, turning his face towards the wilderness as he tries to change his ways thus carries tremendous power. At least for a moment, Bilam casts his eyes upon the *midbar*. Setting aside his pride-filled attempts to sway God's will, his sense

---

2. Sifrei, Beha'alotcha 69.
3. Bamidbar 23:23.
4. Ibid., 24:1.
5. Ramban, Bamidbar 24:1.
6. Rashbam, Bamidbar 24:1–2.

of superiority over his fellow man, the sorcerer seeks a different path. This path will be filled not with magical incantations and enchantments, but with a feeling of oneness with others and obedience to his Creator. For once, Bilam enters the *midbar* and, in doing so, momentarily and with humility assumes his proper place in the human race.

C

Other authorities, however, question the authenticity of Bilam's apparent transformation. Rashi, for example, basing his position on a version of Targum Onkelos that the Ramban claims was not properly edited,[7] imputes negative motives to the sorcerer's gaze "towards the wilderness." Bilam, Rashi maintains, deliberately gazes towards the site of the sin of the golden calf as he readies his next pronouncement. *If I cannot curse the Israelites through divination and sorcery*, he reasons, *I will cause a curse to rise against them out of their own iniquity.*[8]

Quoting the well-known Talmudic adage "Better the curse uttered by Achiya the Shilonite against Israel[9] than the blessing directed towards them by Bilam,"[10] the Sforno argues that Bilam's shift at this point in the narrative is solely tactical. He decides to attack the Israelites while playing by God's rules. Convinced that he will once again be forced to bless the nation, Bilam deliberately constructs a blessing containing an implicit curse.[11] This attempt is reflected in the rabbinic observation "From the blessings pronounced by Bilam, one can determine what was in his heart…"[12] (see Balak 2, *Approaches* C).

Finally, Rabbi Shimshon Raphael Hirsch charts an intermediate course between the opposing interpretations of Bilam's mindset. In spite of Bilam's failed attempts to curse the Israelites, Balak argues that one

---

7. Rashi, Bamidbar 24:1.
8. Ramban, Bamidbar 24:1.
9. Kings I 14:15.
10. Talmud Bavli Ta'anit 20a. Note: Achiya, a prophet from the city of Shilo, prophesies that God will "strike the kingdom of Israel as a reed is shaken in the water" (Kings I 14:15), while Bilam blesses the Israelites by comparing them to "cedars by water" (Bamidbar 24:6). The rabbis, however, note the "blessing" in Achiya's curse and the "curse" in Bilam's "blessing." A reed, they note, will bend in the face of a strong wind but will not break. A cedar, on the other hand, will be uprooted by a strong wind.
11. Sforno, Bamidbar 24:1.
12. Talmud Bavli Sanhedrin 105b.

potent avenue of attack still remains. He urges the sorcerer to move to "another place" from which to view the nation. When Bilam agrees, Balak instructs the sorcerer to ascend "the summit of Pe'or which looks out on the face of Yishimon." *Come look at the nation from a different vantage point*, the king argues, *with a gaze that includes the moral wasteland of Peor* (a geographic location associated with immoral cults and rites). *Let us see if there is a flaw in the moral fiber of this people; whether or not their own failings can serve as the source of their downfall.*

Bilam accedes to the king's request, but remains neutral in his own outlook. He "looks towards the wilderness" to see whether or not the king's hopes of finding moral weakness on the part of the Israelites will bear fruit.[13]

— D —

Whatever Bilam's true intent as he prepares to announce his next vision, the text testifies that he is deeply moved by something that he sees: "And Bilam lifted his eyes and saw Israel dwelling according to its tribes; and the Spirit of God was upon him."[14]

What is it about the Israelite encampment "dwelling according to its tribes" that can penetrate even Bilam's heart?

— E —

The *pshat* of the text would seem to direct us back to the opening scenes of the book of Bamidbar, where the nation prepares for its journey from Sinai. There, as we have noted, God balances the unity of Revelation with the enforced diversity of the nation's desert encampment.[15] By ordering the Israelites to surround the Sanctuary, tribe by tribe, family by family, God conveys the clear message that *unity does not mean uniformity*. Different ideas, different views, different backgrounds will power a people united by a common purpose and dream (see Bamidbar 2, *Approaches* I, J).

Now, almost forty years later, Bilam looks down upon the Israelite encampment and, against his will, is impressed by the results of God's blueprint for His nation. The sorcerer sees before him a people peaceably

---

13. Rabbi Shimshon Raphael Hirsch, Bamidbar 23:28; 24:1.
14. Bamidbar 24:2.
15. Ibid., 1–4.

"dwelling according to its tribes," a united nation that has learned to respect and appreciate its own natural diversity. Such a people, he realizes, will be immune to his spiritual attacks. Such a people will not be easily defeated.

Points to Ponder

A well-known Talmudic tradition, quoted by Rashi, suggests an additional dimension to Bilam's perception of the Israelites "dwelling according to its tribes": "[Bilam noted] that the doors of their tents were not directed towards each other."[16] In other words, *the Israelites afforded each other the privacy of their own homes.*

Today, in contrast, the doors of our tents face each other directly. We live in a world where the very concept of private space is increasingly endangered, where our invasive curiosity has morphed from tabloids to Twitter, where nothing is beyond the bounds of public scrutiny. Everything is fair game; from the unveiling of personal secrets to the flaunting of the human body, everything is open, readily accessible for the entertainment of all....

In such a world, the observant Jew is enjoined to swim against the tide. He is challenged to carve out sacred personal space for himself and to respect such space in the lives of others, as well. He must struggle to educate his children towards the importance of confidentiality and the value of personal dignity and modesty. These tasks form the foundation of an easily misunderstood series of laws in Jewish tradition known as the laws of *tzniut*.

Too often, even within the observant Jewish community, these important laws are treated cavalierly, their mere mention conjuring up images of "old world" etiquette and archaic societal regulations. Such misjudgments allow us to facilely dismiss the entire rubric of *tzniut* out of hand, as laws that spoke to a different place and time.

The sad truth is, however, that these laws have never been needed more.

At a time when man's very image is cheapened in the marketplace, the laws of *tzniut* speak of the dignity and self-respect meant to lie at our core. Each person has the right to those parts of his life that he feels are solely his

---

16. Talmud Bavli Bava Batra 60a; Rashi, Bamidbar 24:2.

own. Modesty in dress and demeanor is a way of silently demanding those rights, a way of drawing the boundaries beyond which others, without permission, cannot cross.

Finally, the laws of *tzniut* remind us that obsessive interest in the lives of others damages not only the "observed" but the "observer" as well. *The more time we spend looking into the tents of others, the less time we have to look constructively into our own.*

The prophet Micha says it better than we ever could as he outlines the bottom line: "He [God] has told you, man, what is good; and what does the Lord require of you, but to do justice and the love of righteousness, *v'hatzneiʾa lechet im Elokecha*, and to walk with *tzniut* [modestly] with your God?"[17]

---

17. Micha 6:8.

5 A Devastating Epilogue

Context
Following Bilam's failed attempts at cursing the nation, the Israelites are seduced by the "daughters of Moab" and fall prey to the licentious idolatry of Ba'al Peor. God responds with a devastating plague that tragically claims twenty-four thousand victims from among the people.

Although no clear connection is immediately drawn in the text between the main story of Parshat Balak and the devastating episode of Ba'al Peor, a brief reference found later in the book of Bamidbar lays blame for this tragic event squarely at the feet of the sorcerer Bilam: "Behold! It was they [the Midianite women] who caused the children of Israel, *by the word of Bilam*, to commit a betrayal against the Lord regarding the matter of Peor; and the plague occurred in the assembly of the Lord."[1]

Questions
If the episode of Ba'al Peor can be directly traced to the scheming designs of Bilam, why doesn't the Torah immediately say so?

Why record this tragic episode as an apparent epilogue to the Balak/Bilam narrative, omit any connection between the two stories, and then subsequently affirm such a connection, in a textual aside, much later in the text?

---

1. Bamidbar 31:16.

Approaches

— A —

A solution to these puzzles can be found if we recognize the tragic episode of Ba'al Peor not only as the textual epilogue to the Balak/Bilam narrative, but as the event that drives the message of that entire story home.

As we have noted before, the Talmud maintains that God's transformation of Bilam's curses into blessings ultimately has very limited practical effect. Due to the sins of the Israelites, the majority of these blessings revert back to their original curses. From this rabbinic perspective the Balak/Bilam story conveys a powerful, counterintuitive lesson: *Bilam's words, and other similar phenomena, do not matter at all. Ultimately our fate is determined by our own merit or guilt* (see Balak 2).

— B —

Suddenly, the strategically placed episode of Ba'al Peor is invested with new, devastating significance. As the Israelites emerge unscathed from Bilam's external threat, only to fall prey to their own shortcomings, the flow of events mirrors in practice what the Balak/Bilam narrative preaches in theory: *We can blame no one else for our failures; our destiny is in our hands.*

The Torah's immediate omission of Bilam's pivotal role in the episode of Ba'al Peor now becomes completely understandable. Any mention of the sorcerer's involvement would have diminished the Torah's consistent message of personal responsibility. Through its silence, the Torah effectively robs us of the ability to blame anyone else for our people's descent into idolatry. We are forced to realize the uncomfortable truth: Bilam's machinations would never have succeeded had he not found the Israelites willing, easy prey.

Any mention of connection between Bilam and his successful plot against the nation will wait for another time and place. For now, the Torah is intent on bringing Parshat Balak to a cohesive close. From start to finish, this parsha is designed to sensitize us to the role that we play in determining our own fate.

Pinchas

CHAPTER 25:10–30:1

פרק יט:א–כב:א

Parsha Summary

Heavenly rewards, critical transitions, daily ritual…

As the curtain rises on Parshat Pinchas, God delineates the divine reward to be bestowed upon Pinchas for his act of zealotry during the episode of Ba'al Pe'or. This reward is to include a "covenant of peace" and a "covenant of eternal priesthood."

God then commands Moshe concerning the new state of enmity that is to exist between the Israelites and the nation of Midian, due to the devastating damage caused by the Midianites during the episode of Ba'al Pe'or.

As the attention of the people begins to turn in earnest towards entry into the land of Canaan, God commands Moshe and Elazar to conduct a census of all male Israelites over the age of twenty. The results of this census, recorded in the text, are to be used in the division of the land. God then commands Moshe concerning the procedure for that division.

The text lists the census of the Levi'im separately.

The four daughters of Tzelaphchad approach Moshe protesting the fact that, because their father "died of his own sin in the wilderness" without leaving sons, their family would not receive its rightful land portion. When Moshe seeks divine counsel, God informs him that the daughters of Tzelaphchad are justified in their claims. In the absence of sons, daughters will inherit their family's land.

When God again informs Moshe of his impending death, Moshe beseeches God to appoint a leader in his stead. God designates Moshe's student, Yehoshua bin Nun, as Moshe's successor. He then commands Moshe to publicly appoint Yehoshua, in full view of the nation, to his new leadership role.

God instructs Moshe to command the Israelites concerning the daily Tamid offering and the Shabbat, Rosh Chodesh and festival Musaf (additional) offerings.

1 Yes and No

Context
During the tragic episode of Ba'al Pe'or, recorded at the end of Parshat Balak, Pinchas ben Elazar slays the two perpetrators of an act of public defamation. In response to Pinchas' precipitous actions, God suspends the deadly plague that has already claimed twenty-four thousand Israelite lives.

As Parshat Pinchas opens, God details the divine reward to be bestowed upon Pinchas for his courageous actions.

Questions
Through the suspension of the deadly plague and through the bestowal of divine reward, God clearly indicates his approval of Pinchas' apparent vigilantism.

One could well ask, however, by what right does Pinchas take the law into his own hands? How does Jewish law, in general, view such solitary acts of zealotry?

Approaches

A

The halachic verdict concerning Pinchas' actions can best be described as one of striking ambivalence.

On the one hand, the Talmud includes the circumstances facing Pinchas in its list of situations in which Jewish law permits zealots to enter the breach and summarily execute perpetrators in the very act of their crimes.[1] This legal allowance for zealotry is even identified as one of the few regulations directly transmitted by God orally to Moshe at Sinai.[2]

---
1. Mishna Sanhedrin 9:6.
2. Talmud Bavli Sanhedrin 82a.

On the other hand, the rabbis also maintain that this right of zealotry falls into a small, puzzling category of laws described as *halacha v'ein morin kein*, "law that one may not teach."[3] Had Pinchas sought halachic advice before acting, he would have been instructed to refrain.[4] Furthermore, had Pinchas' victim, Zimri, turned and killed Pinchas in self-defense, Zimri would not have been liable for prosecution and punishment.[5] These puzzling legal rulings indicate that, while actions like those performed by Pinchas may be halachically *allowed*, they are not uniformly halachically *embraced*.

Midrashic comments concerning Pinchas' actions reflect a similar ambivalence. The Jerusalem Talmud maintains that Pinchas acted "against the will of the sages," while Yehuda ben Pazi goes so far as to suggest that only heavenly intervention prevented Pinchas from being excommunicated by authorities of the time.[6]

— B —

The complex, seemingly contradictory rabbinic attitude towards Pinchas' actions rises out of the delicate balance struck by Jewish law as it navigates between two conflicting truths:

1. The halachic system, deeply committed to the deliberate application of the rule of law, can rarely, if ever, condone the decision to move beyond due legal process.

2. A legal system that does not allow for immediate, extraordinary reaction to moments of great exigency cannot survive, certainly not across the course of a turbulent history.

To address the conundrum created by these competing realities, Jewish law creates the category of *hora'at sha'a*, emergency decrees.[7] This legal category allows for extraordinary extra-legal decisions and actions under exceptional circumstances.

---

3. Ibid.
4. Ibid.
5. Ibid.
6. Talmud Yerushalmi 9:7.
7. S. Y. Zevin, ed., *Encyclopedia Talmudit* (Jerusalem: Talmudic Encyclopedia Publishing Ltd., 1980), vol. 8, s.v. *hora'at sha'a*.

Even actions taken under the rubric of *hora'at sha'a*, however, require the approval of prophetic or legal authority.[8] Zealotry, such as that evidenced by Pinchas, pushes the envelope one step further. Here, the halacha contemplates the possibility of individual action, precipitously taken, in cases of greatest exigency. The hesitation with which Jewish law approaches such zealous acts is most clearly exhibited in the aforementioned principle, that the rules allowing and governing such acts are *halacha v'ein morin kein*, law that one may not teach. This principle reflects a startling halachic posture. *So ambivalent is the rabbinic attitude towards acts of zealotry that even though such acts are legal, we may not convey their legality even to someone seeking halachic guidance. Were someone to request a halachic psak (ruling) prior to the performance of an act of zealotry, he would be told not to act.*

Some commentaries suggest that this halachic hesitation rises out of the fact that zealotry is an *allowance*, rather than an *obligation*. Respecting the zealot's deep visceral reaction to the crime, God *allows* him to respond. He is, however, not commanded to do so.[9] If the zealot asks for halachic guidance before acting, therefore, he will not be instructed to proceed.

Other authorities perceive the halachic hesitation concerning zealotry as reflective of uncertainty concerning the motives of the zealot. To qualify as a zealot, one "must be animated by a genuine, unadulterated spirit of zeal to advance the glory of God."[10] Such purity of motive, however, is rare. Most often, other, less legitimate factors influence an individual's decision to act under the cover of zealotry. The sages of Pinchas' time, therefore, suspicious of their hero's motives, move to excommunicate him, only to be stopped by a divine decree attesting to his genuineness.[11]

Some scholars, however, see the complex halachic approach to zealotry as reflective of an even more basic issue.

Zealotry can be acceptable, suggest these authorities, only when it is true zealotry – when the act is emotionally driven, performed in the heat of the moment, without hesitation or calculation. *If an individual, at the moment of crisis, pauses to ask for halachic guidance, he is by definition*

---

8. Rambam, *Mishneh Torah*, Hilchot Yesodei HaTorah 9:3; Hilchot Sanhedrin 24:4.
9. Rabbeinu Yerucham, Talmud Bavli Sanhedrin 82a.
10. Torah Temima, Bamidbar 25:13.
11. Ibid.

no longer a zealot and therefore forfeits any halachic allowance for his precipitous actions.

An act of zealotry thus emerges as the singular exception to the general rule of Jewish law. *To qualify as a permissible act of zealotry, the deed must be performed without, rather than with, halachic consultation.*[12] Judgment can only take place in retrospect, as the halacha determines, after the fact, whether or not this individual is a true zealot, justified in his actions.

— C —

Finally, another potential objection to acts of zealotry rises, according to some commentaries, from an additional, secondary source.

A zealot is open to criticism, these scholars maintain, not only because of his precipitous actions, but because of the personal danger to which he exposes himself. Rabbi Meir Dan Plotski, in his commentary on the Torah, *Kli Chemda*, notes that the Talmudic allowance for zealotry is recorded in the plural. Zealots are permitted to act in concert, this sage maintains, because of the safety provided by their numbers. The authorities of Pinchas' time, Rabbi Plotski argues, specifically opposed Pinchas' behavior because, by acting alone, he exposed himself to mortal danger.[13]

— D —

These and other observations in Jewish scholarly literature reflect the deep legal and philosophical complexities raised by actions like those of Pinchas at Ba'al Pe'or.

At the dawn of Jewish history, at a time of great crisis, a solitary man courageously steps forward to defend God's name. In doing so, he not only responds to the needs of the moment, but challenges us across the ages to confront the place of the zealot in Jewish thought and law.

---

12. See Rashi, Talmud Bavli Sanhedrin 82a.
13. Kli Chemda, Bamidbar 25:11–13.

2 Righteous Reward

> **Context**
> As Parshat Pinchas opens, God details the divine reward to be bestowed upon Pinchas for his courageous defense of God's honor during the episode of Ba'al Pe'or: "Therefore, proclaim: Behold! I give him My covenant of peace. And it shall be for him and his offspring after him a covenant of eternal priesthood, because he took vengeance for his God and he atoned for the children of Israel."[1]

Questions

The reward granted by God to Pinchas seems to be completely counterintuitive. During the episode of Ba'al Pe'or, Pinchas defended God's honor by summarily executing an Israelite man and a Midianite woman who were engaged in an act of public desecration.[2] Pinchas' violent act of zealotry, while apparently warranted, could hardly be construed as a "peaceful" act. Why then does God go out of His way to specifically reward Pinchas with a divine "covenant of peace"?

In the same vein, why is ascension to the priesthood an appropriate practical reward for Pinchas? The paradigm of the priesthood is, after all, Pinchas' grandfather Aharon, famously identified as a "lover of peace and a pursuer of peace."[3] Pinchas' violent actions seem to be strange qualifications for his grandfather's priestly mantle.

Are the "covenant of peace" and the "covenant of eternal priesthood" mentioned in the text synonymous, or does God grant this hero multiple rewards? If these rewards are separate, what is the exact nature of the "covenant of peace"?

---

1. Bamidbar 25:12–13.
2. Ibid., 25:5–8.
3. Pirkei Avot 1:12.

Finally, the concrete implications of Pinchas' priestly reward are equally unclear. Why must God bestow upon Pinchas a "covenant of eternal priesthood"? Isn't Pinchas already a Kohen simply by dint of the fact that he is Aharon's grandson?

Approaches

— A —

While some scholars, notably Rashi, perceive only one reward accruing to Pinchas,[4] other authorities view the two covenants as separate pledges.

One group of commentaries, for example, including the Abravanel, interprets the divinely ordained "covenant of peace" as a concrete commitment on God's part to ensure Pinchas' personal safety. In the aftermath of the violent events at Ba'al Pe'or, God pledges to protect Pinchas from any retribution that might be taken against him by the powerful family and friends of his victim, Zimri.[5]

The Sforno agrees that the "covenant of peace" granted by God to Pinchas is fundamentally a pledge of divine protection. The protection God pledges, however, is not protection from Zimri's supporters but from death itself. Citing a series of textual and Midrashic sources indicating that Pinchas far outlives his contemporaries,[6] the Sforno maintains that with this first covenant, God promises Pinchas the gift of personal longevity.[7]

Moving in a completely different direction, the Netziv, Rabbi Zvi Yehuda Berlin, offers a powerfully stirring interpretation of the "covenant of peace." This blessing, the Netziv maintains, is designed to counteract the destructive internal tendencies that Pinchas' violent deed might have aroused:

> He [God] blessed him [Pinchas] with the attribute of peace, that he should be neither quick-tempered nor easily angered. For it is only natural that the act performed by Pinchas, the slaying of a soul by his hand, would leave in his heart a powerful unrest....

---

4. Rashi, Bamidbar 25:12.
5. Abravanel, Bamidbar 25:11–15.
6. Shoftim 11:26, 20:28; Midrash Rabba Bereishit 60:3.
7. Sforno, Bamidbar 25:12.

Therefore, divine blessing is bestowed upon him, that he should continually experience tranquility and the attribute of peace, and that his own actions should not haunt him.[8]

Through a divine "covenant of peace," the Netziv claims, God ensures that Pinchas' personal encounter with violence will not leave him permanently scarred.

Equally beautiful is the approach of Rabbi Shimshon Raphael Hirsch, who suggests that the definition of "peace" is very much in the eye of the beholder. From a Torah perspective, however, the definition is clear:

> *True peace of men rests on the peace of all of them with God* [my italics]. He who dares to wage war with people who are against divine Goodness and Truth is…fighting for the "covenant of peace" on earth. He who, for the sake of so-called peace, quietly leaves the field to people who are really at variance with God, his love of peace is at one with the enemies of the "covenant of peace" on earth."[9]

Pinchas' violent actions in defense of God's name, Hirsch argues, are actually "peaceful acts." As he fights to preserve God's will, Pinchas brings the world one step closer to the "covenant of peace," to the true state of tranquility resulting from the attainment of harmony between God and man.

--- **B** ---

Turning to the second of the two covenants mentioned in the text, the "covenant of eternal priesthood," we are immediately confronted with the technical questions surrounding Pinchas' status as a priest before and after the fateful events of Ba'al Pe'or.

If Pinchas is already a Kohen by dint of his identity as Aharon's grandson, why must he now be blessed with "a covenant of eternal priesthood"?

---

8. Ha'ameik Davar, Bamidbar 25:12.
9. Rabbi Shimshon Raphael Hirsch, Bamidbar 25:12.

Two basic approaches are suggested by the commentaries, both based on the early Midrashic dictum "Pinchas was not appointed as Kohen until he killed Zimri…."[10]

Rashi maintains that Pinchas, although a descendent of Aharon, is not a Kohen at all until these events unfold. The *kehuna*, this scholar explains, is granted to those descendents of Aharon who are born after Aharon and his sons are themselves inaugurated into the priesthood. Because Pinchas was born before the moment of Aharon's ascension, he can only enter the priesthood in an exceptional fashion, as a result of God's blessing in the wake of his heroic act.[11] A slight alternative to this approach is suggested by a group of scholars who maintain that while Aharon and his sons were originally inaugurated into the *kehuna*, his grandsons were not. Pinchas is, therefore, not a Kohen until God confers such status upon him following the events at Ba'al Pe'or.[12]

Both the Ibn Ezra and the Ramban, on the other hand, interpret the "covenant of priesthood" as referring specifically to the High Priesthood. Although Pinchas is a Kohen from the outset, his heroism catapults him to a new, higher status. God now commands Moshe to publicly proclaim that the chain of High Priesthood will, in the future, emerge directly from Pinchas.[13]

C

Whichever approach we accept, however, the question remains: In what way is the granting of priesthood, in any form, an appropriate reward for Pinchas' violent actions?

A number of commentaries, including the Abravanel, answer this by suggesting that the "covenant of priesthood" is a *confirmation*, rather than a *conferral*, of Pinchas' *kehuna*. Through this covenant, God allays the zealot's fears concerning his own current status. In the aftermath of the events at Ba'al Pe'or, Pinchas is concerned that he will lose his status as a Kohen because of the law invalidating any individual guilty of murder or manslaughter from the priesthood. God, therefore, grants Pinchas the

---

10. Yalkut Shimoni, Shemini 247:531.
11. Rashi, Bamidbar 25:13.
12. Da'at Zekeinim Miba'alei Hatosafot, Bamidbar 25:13.
13. Ibn Ezra, Bamidbar 25:13; Ramban, ibid.

"covenant of priesthood," reassuring him that, because his courageous actions served the greater good, his current status as a priest remains intact.[14]

D

The Ktav Sofer, however, chooses an interpretive path that skillfully weaves the two covenants bestowed upon Pinchas into one cohesive whole.

God, this scholar maintains, confers priesthood upon Pinchas after the events at Ba'al Pe'or specifically because the character exhibited by Pinchas during those events recommends him to the priesthood.

As teachers of the nation, the Kohanim are required to instruct the people with unbending strength and unyielding commitment. There is to be no compromise when it comes to matters of the law and ritual. The zeal demonstrated by Pinchas in his defense of God's name, therefore, will serve him well in his priestly role.

At the same time, however, the passion for God's law, meant to be part of every Kohen's psyche, must be balanced by a warmth that discourages strife and brings others close. This is the warmth of Aharon, "the lover of peace and the pursuer of peace." God, therefore, blesses Pinchas with *both* a "covenant of peace" and a "covenant of eternal priesthood."

There will be times when, as a priest, Pinchas will have to be an Aharon, and times when he will have to be a zealot. Together, the two covenants will provide Pinchas with the balance essential to his success.[15]

---

14. Abravanel, Bamidbar 25:10–13.
15. Ktav Sofer, Bamidbar 25:12–13.

3 Keeping Things Complicated

Context
As the focus of God's instructions turns towards the entry of the Israelites into Canaan, God commands Moshe concerning the division of the land among the tribes. Clear definition of the geographic boundaries of each tribe's portion from the outset will prevent internal conflict upon entry into the land.

> To these shall the land be divided as an inheritance according to the number of names. To the many shall you give the greater inheritance and to the few shall you give the lesser inheritance; to each one according to his count shall his inheritance be given.
> Only by lot shall the land be divided, according to the names of their fathers' tribes shall they inherit. According to the lot shall one's inheritance be divided, between the many and the few.[1]

In the Talmudic tractate of Bava Batra, the rabbis take note of an apparent contradiction in this text concerning the division of the land.

On the one hand, the phrase "to these shall the land be divided" indicates that the division of Canaan should take place according to the Israelite population on the eve of entry into the land. On the other hand, the phrase "according to the names of their fathers' tribes shall they inherit" seems to imply that the previous generation, the generation of the Exodus, must somehow be factored into the equation.

---

1. Bamidbar 26:53–56.

In response to this apparent contradiction, three positions are outlined in the Talmud:[2]

1. Rabbi Yoshea maintains that the land is to be divided according to the tally of those leaving Egypt and transmitted as an inheritance to their children entering the land. Each individual over the age of twenty at the time of the Exodus "receives" a portion of land which he "bequeaths" to his child(ren). If he has one child, that child receives the entire portion. If he has numerous children they divide the portion equally between them.

2. Rabbi Yonatan disagrees and postulates a more complicated equation based on a unique formula of "reverse inheritance." "In regard to all other inheritances the living inherit the deceased," Rabbi Yonatan explains, "while here, the deceased inherit the living."

The distribution process posited by Rabbi Yonatan runs as follows:

a. An initial division takes place according to those entering the land, with each individual receiving one land portion.

b. All portions are then symbolically "bequeathed back" one generation and pooled by family. Each family pool is then redivided according to the number of those leaving Egypt and then bequeathed back to the next generation. [Illustration: Reuven and Shimon are brothers who participate in the Exodus from Egypt. Reuven has nine sons, while Shimon has one. Reuven's nine sons and Shimon's one son each receive one land portion, respectively, for a total of ten portions. The portions of the sons are then "bequeathed in reverse" to their fathers to create one pool consisting of the ten portions. The pool is then redivided into two blocks of five portions each, one block "belonging" to Reuven and one block "belonging" to Shimon. The blocks are then inherited by the children, with Reuven's nine sons receiving one block of five portions to divide among them and Shimon's one son receiving a block of five portions, all his own.

3. Finally, Rabbi Shimon ben Elazar argues that the land is distributed both to those leaving Egypt and to those entering the land. Each individual among those leaving Egypt receives one

---

2. Talmud Bavli Bava Batra 117a–b.

> portion (which he bequeaths to his children); each individual among those entering the land receives one portion; each individual satisfying both criteria (i.e., he is among those leaving Egypt *and* among those entering the land) receives two portions.³

Questions

Sound confusing? Certainly does! Whichever position we take in this Talmudic dispute concerning the division of the land, why does God deliberately, and seemingly unnecessarily, complicate a process that should, at first glance, be simple? Why not divide Canaan in a straightforward manner among those Israelites who are entering and will be living on the land? Why must the Torah go out of its way to factor in the generation of the Exodus, a generation that, as a whole, will never step foot on the soil of Canaan?

Complicating matters further is the fact that the division of the land is at once the most important and the most sensitive internal issue facing the Israelites as they prepare to enter Canaan. By creating an equation that grants larger parcels of land to certain individuals and smaller parcels to others, isn't God setting the stage for jealousy, controversy and dispute? Why is God willing to risk such tension by insisting that the generation of the Exodus be factored into the equation?

---

3. Numerous scholars wrestle with the difficulty presented by Rabbi Shimon's third category. All those who were over the age of twenty at the time of the Exodus perished in the desert and did not enter the land (with the exception of Yehoshua and Calev). How, then, can Rabbi Shimon speak of a category satisfying both criteria? The Rashbam suggests that, according to Rabbi Shimon, an individual over the age of twenty entering the land who had a father who, himself, was over the age of twenty at the time of the Exodus inherits two portions. Others maintain that individuals who were over the age of sixty at the time of the Exodus were not subject to the divine decree of death in the desert and could, therefore, participate in the entry into the land.

Approaches

— A —

Although the generation of the Exodus forfeits its right to enter Canaan, God clearly wants its tangible presence to be concretely felt during the distribution of the land. Divine insistence on the involvement of this doomed generation in this historic process adds further dimension to lessons that we have encountered in our studies before. So important are these lessons, it appears, that God is willing to risk controversy in the distribution of the land in order to convey them.

— B —

The legacy of the land. By the time we leave Egypt and become a nation at Sinai, we already possess a history and a sense of legacy. Due to the events of the patriarchal era, the Land of Israel is not a destination unknown to us, but a cherished land of which we have heard countless tales, the land promised to our ancestors, centuries before (see *Bereishit*: Vayechi 4, *Approaches* C).

Now, however, God goes one step further and makes this national legacy personal….

Through a divinely mandated formula, each individual entering Canaan receives his parcel of land not as a gift, but as a direct inheritance from his parents. A powerful sense of ownership, therefore, ties the people to the land. Each Israelite sees his entry into Canaan no longer only as the realization of age-old promises, but as a tangible opportunity to participate in the fulfillment of his parents' dreams.

— C —

Success is determined in intergenerational terms. The message strikes deeper still, as the definition of success introduced with the sin of the spies is now crystallized (see Shelach 2, *Approaches* E).

Success, God again emphasizes, is determined for the Jew in intergenerational terms. Although the members of the Exodus generation perish in the desert, they are nonetheless "present" as the nation prepares to enter the land. Their struggles and accomplishments have not only paved the way for this moment, but have made them part of this moment. The very distribution of Canaan cannot take place without them.

As each Israelite prepares to meet the unknown challenges that lie on the path leading to Canaan, he learns the extraordinary truth concerning his nation's eternal journey: *Your parents are with you; they accompany you on this historic passage, as you take your first steps into your land. And just as certainly, you and your ancestors will be with your children, and with your children's children, each step of the way, until the end of days.*

4 Teaching Moshe

Context
A dramatic interchange between God and Moshe concerning Moshe's impending death concludes with the public appointment of Yehoshua as Moshe's eventual successor.

The text immediately moves to a lengthy description of daily, Shabbat, Rosh Chodesh and festival communal offerings.[1]

Questions
Rarely is the textual transition in the Torah so abrupt. What if any connection is there between the death of Moshe and the appointment of Yehoshua, on the one hand, and the litany of communal *korbanot*, on the other? Why are these sections juxtaposed in the text?

Approaches
The commentaries are divided in their approaches to this sudden textual transition....

--- **A** ---

Some scholars struggle mightily to discern a thematic connection between the seemingly disparate passages.

Rashi, for example, quoting an earlier Midrashic tradition,[2] maintains that God now demands from Moshe what Moshe has just demanded from Him.

Just a moment ago, Moshe, you directed Me towards the concerns of the people with the request that I appoint a successor to lead the nation after your death. I responded with the appointment of Yehoshua.

---

1. Bamidbar 27:12–30:1.
2. Sifrei, Bamidbar 28:1–2.

Now, Moshe, direct the people towards My concerns by listing the ongoing communal offerings that they will be responsible to bring.[3]

The Ohr Hachaim, on the other hand, suggests that the Torah lists the communal offerings specifically at this point in order to forestall a potential misunderstanding on Yehoshua's part. Yehoshua might erroneously assume that his new leadership role will authorize him to donate communal sacrifices on the people's behalf. God therefore emphasizes that such offerings must come from the communal coffer.[4]

The Ibn Ezra, for his part, adopts a more straightforward approach. In the aftermath of the discussion concerning Moshe's death, God commands Moshe to instruct the people concerning the communal offerings because Moshe will not be there to do so after they enter the land.[5]

— B —

Other scholars perceive references within the offerings themselves to specific challenges that will accompany the leadership transition from Moshe to Yehoshua.

The Malbim argues that the daily Tamid offerings, the first *korbanot* listed in the parsha, are brought morning and evening, at critical points in the sun's journey through the sky, in order to counteract the cult of sun worship prevalent at the time. Had Moshe entered the land with the people, the Malbim continues, his powerful presence would have quelled the nation's desire to participate in such idolatrous practices. The Tamid offerings would, consequently, have become unnecessary. With the inevitability of Moshe's absence, however, these offerings are rendered essential and they are, therefore, now enumerated in the text.[6]

The Ralbag, for his part, adopts a broader approach. The listing of the communal sacrifices at this point in the text, this scholar maintains, foreshadows a looming shift in the nation's ability to communicate with God. As the mantle of leadership passes from Moshe to Yehoshua, the level of prophetic vision guiding the people will inexorably weaken. Moshe's singular relationship with the Divine, described in the Torah as

---

3. Rashi, Bamidbar 28:2.
4. Ohr Hachaim 28:2.
5. Ibn Ezra, Bamidbar 28:1.
6. Malbim, Bamidbar 28:1–12.

"face-to-face,"⁷ will not be replicated by any other prophet.⁸ Yehoshua and leaders to follow will be compelled to augment their own more distant prophetic vision through consultation with the Urim and Tumim, the miraculous mechanism on the Kohen Gadol's breastplate designed to facilitate dialogue with the Divine.⁹

The Urim and Tumim will only operate properly, however, when the priests fulfill their overall ritual functions in the Temple to the letter. God therefore commands the nation concerning an area of the Kohanim's activities that is dependent upon the community's largesse. Failure on the part of the people to provide adequate funds for the purchase of the communal offerings will hamper the performance of the priests and ultimately lead to a weakening in the functioning of the Urim and Tumim. Communication with God through this miraculous mechanism will thus be threatened at a time when the nation needs it the most.

By textually connecting the nation's ritual obligations to the leadership transition from Moshe to Yehoshua, the Torah subtly underscores the high stakes now attached to the community's performance.¹⁰

C

In contrast to the scholars who struggle with the strained textual flow between these two passages, others either ignore or avoid the questions raised by this phenomenon entirely.

The Ramban, for example, sidesteps the issue by connecting the litany of offerings to earlier passages in the text discussing the division of the land. The offerings now listed, he explains, become obligatory upon the people only with their entry into Canaan. Now that the nation is preparing to enter the land, therefore, God instructs Moshe to command them concerning these *korbanot*.¹¹

---

7. Shmot 33:11.
8. Devarim 34:10.
9. Shmot 38:30; Talmud Bavli Yoma 73b.
10. Ralbag, Bamidbar 27:15–28:39.
11. Ramban, Bamidbar 28:2.

D

Perhaps, however, another connection can be proposed between the passage concerning Moshe's death and the list of *korbanot* that immediately follows.

Having again informed Moshe of his impending demise, God faces the challenge of consoling this great leader. What solace, however, can God offer in the face of Moshe's personal tragedy? What consolation can possibly ease this great leader's pain as he helplessly confronts the divine decree prohibiting him from leading his people into the Promised Land?

The same solace and consolation, perhaps, that God has offered to the Israelites themselves.

You will be there when your children succeed.

Through the complex formula governing the distribution of the land, God has just reiterated to the nation that success for the Jew is to be measured in intergenerational terms (see previous study). Now, He conveys that same lesson to their leader.

You have successfully laid the groundwork, Moshe, for an eternal people that will transcend the boundaries of time in its journey across the face of history. One generation will inexorably lead to the next, but each generation will be present every step of the way.

You will be there, Moshe, each day as your people perform the ongoing ritual that you have taught them. Day in and day out, no korban *will be offered without you.*

And when your people's journey takes a tragic turn, and the realm of korbanot *is denied them; you will be there to witness the rituals that survive. For you will accompany this people until the end of days.*

Therein lies your solace, as you confront the difficult personal journey that lies before you.

Points to Ponder

The Torah narrative draws much of its power from the multiplicity of layers overlaid throughout the text. Personal stories seamlessly interweave with the unfolding saga of a nation, foreshadowing the experience of a people that, throughout history, will build its collective narrative upon the personal stories of countless individuals.

To read the closing sections of the book of Bamidbar and the entire book of Devarim without recognizing the private and public drama coursing beneath the surface of the text is to miss a great deal of the Torah's beauty.

As the nation prepares to enter the land, a generation fades into memory, yet, somehow, remains on the scene; a new generation rises to assume its rightful place in history; an elderly leader struggles to accept the reality of his journey's end; a new leader nervously prepares to take the reins; a people ready themselves to bid farewell to the only leader that they have known….

Real people, experiencing real challenge, triumph and tragedy…

Reading the Torah this way allows us to touch their lives and to view our own lives in perspective. Reading the Torah this way allows us to see this timeless narrative as the harbinger of all that is to follow.

Matot-Masei מטות-מסעי

CHAPTER 30:2–36:13 פרק ל:ב–לו:יג

Parsha Summary

Vows, vengeance, victory, voyages to the border and a book's end…
   Moshe instructs the heads of the tribes concerning the laws of nedarim, personal vows. Particular emphasis is placed on the limited power of repeal granted to a father or a husband over a woman's vows.
   God commands Moshe to take vengeance before his death against the Midianites for their actions during the tragic episode of Ba'al Pe'or. Moshe assembles an army with Pinchas at its head and a successful attack is launched against the Midianites. Upon the army's return, however, Moshe angrily chastises the officers for sparing the women who, he reminds the nation, were the real perpetrators of the episode of Ba'al Pe'or. He commands the people to put all male children and all females old enough to be sexually active to death by the sword. All female children, he explains, may remain in captivity. The people comply.
   Confronted with the booty taken by the victorious Israelite army, Elazar the Kohen commands the people concerning the kashering and immersion of vessels.
   God conveys the formula to be used in dividing the captured wealth of Midian between the returning soldiers and the entire people. Specific portions are also to be separated as a tribute to God and given to the Kohanim and Levi'im. Spontaneously, an additional tribute is also offered by the officers of the Israelite army, in gratitude for the safe return of the entire army from the battle.
   Representatives of the tribes of Reuven and Gad approach Moshe with the request that they be allowed to remain on the East Bank of the Jordan River. Moshe responds indignantly, expressing deep-seated fears that the refusal of these tribes to enter Canaan will prompt the entire nation to

question their own entry into the land. Such an eventuality, he warns, might well lead to a national tragedy similar to the sin of the spies, a generation earlier.

The representatives of Reuven and Gad counter with an offer to fight in the vanguard of the Israelite army, returning to their homes and families only after the conquest of the land. Moshe agrees, and the territory on the East Bank of the Jordan is set aside for the tribes of Reuven and Gad and one-half the tribe of Menashe.

The Torah segues into Parshat Masei, the last parsha of the book of Bamidbar, with a recording, in retrospect, of the details of the nation's wilderness wonderings.

God then commands Moshe concerning the conquest of Canaan, exhorting him to remind the nation of the physical and spiritual dangers that will continue to abound, if their conquest of the land's inhabitants is incomplete.

The impending entry into Canaan becomes more concrete as God instructs Moshe concerning the borders of the Promised Land, the leaders who will represent the tribes during the distribution of the land, and the forty-eight cities to be set aside for the Levi'im. Six of these forty-eight cities will also serve as "cities of refuge," to which individuals guilty of negligent homicide will be exiled.

The book of Bamidbar closes as God, responding to the concerns of the elders of the tribe of Menashe (the tribe to which the daughters of Tzelaphchad belong; see parsha summary, Pinchas), mandates that a woman who inherits land from her father must marry within her tribe.[1] This edict balances a daughter's right of inheritance with the rights of a tribe to retain its land allotment.

---

1. The Talmud explains that this limitation applied only to the generation that entered the land (Talmud Bavli Bava Batra 120a).

1 Changing World, Unchanging Law

Context
As Parshat Matot opens, Moshe outlines the laws governing *nedarim*, personal vows. These edicts underscore the seriousness with which such verbal commitments are to be treated.

In contrast to men, who remain personally responsible for all vows taken,[1] a woman's vows can be summarily rescinded by her father or her husband, depending upon her status.

In general terms: A father is granted the right to rescind the *nedarim* of a single daughter until she reaches the status of a *bogeret* (six months after puberty), while a husband is granted the right to revoke his wife's vows. The vows of an underage betrothed woman can only be canceled by her father and her husband-to-be, acting jointly.[2]

Questions
In our "liberated society," some aspects of the laws of vows seem difficult to accept.

---

1. Note: The only avenue of redress for a man who undertakes a vow that he subsequently regrets is a process known as *hatarat nedarim*, annulment of vows. The individual must profess his regret to a court and must present sufficient evidence that the vow was taken hastily, without proper consideration, or that unexpected circumstances have arisen that would have originally restrained him from having taken the vow. If the court determines, upon careful examination, that his arguments have merit, the court may, under strict guidelines, annul the vow retroactively. The edicts concerning *hatarat nedarim* are complex and detailed and are, according to the Talmud, a classic example of laws that are only hinted at in the Torah, with most of the details left for the oral tradition.
2. Bamidbar 30:2–17.

Why should the Torah draw a distinction between the vows of men and women? Is a woman any less capable of responsibly committing herself to specific behaviors than a man?

How should the woman of today view laws that seem to place her in a subservient position to the male figures in her life? Aren't such edicts proof positive of the Torah's bias against women?

Approaches

— A —

We find ourselves, once again, entering turbulent waters....

On the one hand, we could well ask from the outset: Do we even have the right to ask these questions, to assume that the laws of the Torah must always conform to our modern sensibilities? Almost every society in human experience feels that it has finally arrived at a communal structure that most closely reflects the desired social reality. And yet, how many such societies and their structures have come and gone, while Torah law has endured? God clearly has His reasons for distinguishing between men and women in halachic areas such as the laws of vows. Perhaps those reasons are destined to remain elusive to the "modern mind."

On the other hand, should the natural limitations of our perspective cause us to shy away from confrontation with any aspect of the Torah text? Many authorities, as we have seen, are even willing to delve into the mysteries of *chukim*, ritual laws for which no apparent reason is evident in the text (see *Shmot*: Teruma 3). Certainly societal laws, such as the laws of vows, should be fair game for our philosophical exploration. All laws of the Torah, after all, are meant to inform and shape our lives. If we can succeed in better understanding those edicts that, at first glance, seem foreign to us, we may well uncover new life lessons that we have missed before. And, if we fail, we will be no worse off. We can always back away, accepting the existence of mysteries that lie beyond our ken.

— B —

As a first step, we might be tempted to approach the laws of vows as we have approached other issues in the text before, by noting the tension between eternality and temporal context in the study of the Torah text. *While our tradition clearly maintains both the divine origin and the eternal applicability of Torah thought and law, we cannot deny that the Torah was revealed to a specific people in a specific era.*

Noting this double-edged reality, we have wondered aloud whether or not we can understand specific phenomena in the Torah, such as the biblical allowance for slavery, as products of the times (see *Shmot*: Mishpatim 1, *Points to Ponder*). We have also seen that historical context serves as the basis for such classical approaches to the text as the Rambam's explanation of the origin of *korbanot* (in his *Guide to the Perplexed*) and the Ramban's understanding of the character of the priestly garments (see *Shmot*: Mishpatim 1, *Points to Ponder*; Tetzave 3, *Approaches* A; *Vayikra*: Vayikra 1, *Approaches* II A).

Attempts to apply the approach of historical context to the laws of vows prove, however, to be less satisfying. The laws of slavery have fallen into disuse with the disappearance of the institution itself from our society. Even the laws of *korbanot* and the priestly garments, which we expect to be reinstated at some point in our history, are distant from our current experience and make no apparent comment on the status of any group within the community.

The laws of vows, however, while seldom applied, remain on the books to this day. With the continuing drive towards women's equality in so many spheres of the society surrounding us, we confront the challenge of explaining these and similar laws to an increasingly sophisticated audience. Failure to do so adds fuel to the accusations that such edicts are either outdated or unfairly prejudicial.

C

A review of the halachic literature regarding the laws of *nedarim* reveals that, from the outset, the rabbis derive severe limitations from the text over the rights of a husband or a father to revoke a woman's vows.

Based on the Torah's statement "Any vow and any oath-prohibition *to cause affliction of the soul*, her husband may let it stand and her husband may revoke it,"[3] the Mishna maintains that a husband may only rescind vows that would deny his wife one of life's permitted pleasures.[4] The Talmud, noting a second defining phrase, "These are the statutes that God

---

3. Ibid., 30:14.
4. Talmud Bavli Nedarim 79a.

commanded Moshe, *between a man and his wife…,*" expands the rights of the husband to include the cancellation of any vow that can affect the marital relationship.[5]

While the Rambam maintains that a father's rights over his daughter's vows extends to all vows taken,[6] numerous other authorities disagree and restrict the father's rights, as well, only to those vows that would deny his daughter one of life's permitted pleasures.[7] Furthermore, the biblical phrase "in her youth, in her father's house"[8] is understood by the rabbis as limiting a father's rights over his daughter's vows to the six-month period following the onset of puberty. Before that point, the young woman is considered underage and any vows she takes are automatically nonbinding. After the six-month period following puberty, she is considered to be mature enough to be responsible for her own commitments.[9]

The rights of a father or a husband over a woman's vows are limited to the day that he first hears of the vow. This period of time is not defined as a twenty-four-hour period but is determined by the day itself. If a father, for example, hears of his daughter's vow late in the day and wishes to revoke that vow, he must respond immediately, before that day ends.[10]

These and other technical boundaries, rooted in the text and discussed extensively in the Talmud and later halachic works, severely restrict the rights of a father or a husband to rescind a woman's vows. Clearly, the Torah is not granting open-ended control over a woman's verbal commitments to the male figures in her life. Instead, the text constructs a narrowly targeted allowance, restricted to specific types of vows and carefully regulated by a detailed network of laws.

---

5. Ibid., 79b.
6. Rambam, *Mishneh Torah*, Hilchot Nedarim 12:1.
7. Rosh, Talmud Bavli Nedarim, beginning of chapter 11; Ran, ibid.; Ramban, Bamidbar 30:14; see Tur, Yoreh Deah 234 and Beit Yosef there; see also *Shulchan Aruch*, Yoreh Deah 234:58. Note: A third position grants the father complete rights over the vows of a daughter who has never been betrothed. If, however, the young woman was betrothed and her intended died, resulting in her return to her father's home, her father can now only annul those vows that would prohibit an otherwise permissible pleasure (see Tur, Yoreh Deah 234; *Shulchan Aruch*, Yoreh Deah 234:58).
8. Bamidbar 30:17.
9. Talmud Bavli Nedarim 70a; Rambam, *Mishneh Torah* 11:1–7.
10. Talmud Bavli Nedarim 76b; Rambam, *Mishneh Torah* 12:15–16.

D

In sharp contrast to the extensive halachic literature dealing with the technical boundaries of these laws, almost no information is found in the classical commentaries concerning their rationale. Why does the Torah grant a woman's father or husband the right of repeal over even a limited category of her vows? What explanation can be offered for the clear asymmetry between the roles of men and women reflected in these laws?

The silence of the classical commentaries concerning these issues can, of course, be interpreted in a number of ways. Perhaps the scholars did not see these edicts as troubling at all and were comfortable accepting them, without question, as God's will. Perhaps the commentaries felt no discordance between these laws and the societies of their day, which were marked by a myriad of clear public differentiations between men and women.

E

It is not surprising that the first real attempt (at least that I could find) to explain the rationale behind these laws is made by Rabbi Shimshon Raphael Hirsch; the towering nineteenth-century German scholar whose religious philosophy envisions a relationship between traditional observant Judaism and the modern world. Hirsch, as might be expected, bases his interpretation of the laws of *nedarim* on the distinct roles that, in his view, are mandated by Jewish tradition for men and for women.

A man, this scholar explains, "is the independent maker of his position in life."[11] If, therefore, a man vows to take abnormal restrictions upon himself, he, alone, must make the necessary arrangements to allow these conditions to be met.

The greatness of a woman's calling in life, however, lies in her entering and assuming a position that is not of her own creation. "The woman herself does not provide the house. She enters the home provided by the man and rules in it as the happiness-bringing administrator of all that is to be found there, in the sanctity of manners, the morals and feelings directed towards God."[12]

---

11. Rabbi Shimshon Raphael Hirsch, Bamidbar 30:4.
12. Ibid.

As the spiritual guardian of the Jewish home, the woman occupies a central role upon which others become clearly dependent. To fulfill her responsibilities, a woman must be free of external constraints that could "permanently stand in the way of the fulfillment of her calling."[13] The Torah, therefore, grants limited veto rights to a woman's father or husband over any vows that might prevent her from fulfilling her primary religious role.[14]

--- **F** ---

Recognizing that Rabbi Hirsch's approach might not resonate with some modern readers and failing to find other serious attempts in the literature to explain these laws, I decided to try something different. Through the listserv of the Rabbinical Council of America I asked my colleagues whether any of them had either encountered or independently arrived at a rational approach to the laws of vows. The thoughtful, varied answers I received served to reinforce ideas that I had been considering on my own.

Some of my colleagues maintained that, in a general sense, these laws can only be understood against the backdrop of the Torah's general resistance to vows. The potential sources of this resistance are manifold, and include a rejection of asceticism; a belief in the transformative power of Torah law without the need for added constraints; a recognition that Torah values can be distorted through the addition of individually authored rules; and an aversion to the creation of situations where, due to the acceptance of supplemental restrictions, individuals are increasingly likely to fail.

Nonetheless, the Torah does acknowledge that certain vows can enhance an individual's religious and spiritual growth. Instead of mandating, therefore, a blanket prohibition on vows, the Torah institutes a selective process of annulment (see the first footnote in this study, in the *Context* section) or revocation under very specific conditions. The prerogatives of the father and the husband are part of this selective process.

While this approach grants us context, however, it fails to address the asymmetry between men and women in the area of *nedarim*.

---

13. Ibid.
14. Ibid.

G

Confronting this issue squarely, a number of my colleagues readily opened the door to an obvious, potentially explosive area of consideration that I, myself, had been approaching with caution. Perhaps the asymmetry in Torah law concerning vows, they suggested, reflects naturally existing perceptual and behavioral differences between men and women (à la *Men Are from Mars, Women Are from Venus*).

Once this door is opened, the possibilities before us are manifold and understandably controversial. To suggest a few…

Can it be, for example, that these laws are partially necessary, not because of a woman's limitations, but specifically because of the emphasis that men place upon physical attraction? Clearly, neither men nor women can completely see their relationship through the eyes of the other. A woman might, therefore, take upon herself specific restrictions in the quest for greater spirituality without fully understanding how those restrictions could make her less attractive to a potential suitor or a mate. In order to forestall the damage possibly caused to crucial relationships by such an act, the Torah grants a woman's father and/or husband a limited opportunity to rescind such vows.

Perhaps, by granting a father the right to cancel his daughter's vows during the six-month period following the onset of puberty, the Torah provides him with a unique opportunity to exercise parental control and direction during a particularly turbulent time in her life. Buffeted by the physical and psychological changes that mark her emergence into womanhood, the young woman confronts her inner conflicts and begins to develop the worldview and the personal skills that will carry her through life. Specifically at this time, the Torah grants significance to the young woman's verbal commitments, but only with parental oversight, enabling her to safely and securely test her limits under a watchful eye.

Some of my colleagues suggested that a woman's greater emotionality, compounded by her historically vulnerable status in society, makes her more prone to extreme threats and vows. While there are certainly exceptions to this rule, the Torah operates in general categories. The woman must recognize that, even under duress, her verbal commitments will be treated seriously. She is offered, however, the safeguard of limited oversight.

Finally, there are times when the father or husband's very act of canceling a daughter or wife's vow can itself be constructive. Given the nature of the vows that can be revoked, the cancellation conveys to the woman the ongoing concern of a "significant other" in her life for her continuing welfare and/or his desire to maintain a healthy, unburdened relationship between them. Such assurances can be particularly significant to a woman, young or old, at various stages in her life.

There may be those who feel that, with suggestions such as these, we have crossed the line of "political correctness." And, certainly, we can offer no proof that any of these explanations, or any others that we might offer in this vein, actually form the basis of the laws of *nedarim* found at the beginning of Parshat Matot. Even those individuals, however, who adamantly insist on equality between men and women must admit to natural differences between the sexes. Is it not conceivable that those differences may play a role in the formulation of God's law?

── H ──

In the final analysis, answers to our questions concerning the laws of *nedarim* may be found in all, some or none of the above explanations. Perhaps other sources that we have not cited at all contain keys to understanding. When the Torah itself provides no explanation for its laws, we are left with possibilities, rather than certainty.

We return, therefore, full circle, to where we stood as our study opened. The eternal law of the Torah has withstood the test of centuries and will, we believe, withstand that test until the end of days. While there will certainly be those, in each generation, who will demand that its edicts conform to the thinking of the time, there can be no guarantee of such correlation. Our task is to remain loyal to the law, even as we struggle with its meaning.

Points to Ponder

While the asymmetry between men and women reflected in the laws of *nedarim* has little practical impact on our daily lives, other social distinctions drawn in the Torah between men and women can have major effect. The tragic plight of the *aguna* (lit.: the chained woman), a woman unable to obtain a *get* (Jewish decree of divorce), results from one such distinction.

At the core of the issue lies the one sentence in the book of Devarim that serves as the basis for divorce proceedings in Jewish law: "And he [the husband] wrote her [the wife] a bill of divorce, presented it to her and sent her from his house."[15]

As clearly indicated by this passage, the husband is the active party in the halachic events that effect a Jewish divorce. He (or his agent) must initiate the proceedings by writing the document of divorce and he (or his agent) must deliver that document to his wife. She, in contrast, plays a passive role as the recipient of the divorce decree. So passive is her role, in fact, that she need not even be a willing participant in the process. According to biblical law, as long as a man delivers a *get* to his wife's personal domain, she is automatically divorced, even absent her agreement.[16]

By the time we reach the Middle Ages, however, Rabbeinu Gershom, one of the greatest luminaries of the Ashkenazic community, issues a *takana*, a rabbinic decree (see *Shmot*: Yitro 5, *Approaches* C), designed to even the playing field somewhat in the area of divorce. He prohibits, upon pain of excommunication, the divorce of women against their will.[17] This *takana* does allow for exceptions in cases of great exigency, as determined by the decision of one hundred rabbis.

The Torah-mandated centerpiece of Jewish divorce, however, remains inviolate, beyond the reach of Rabbeinu Gershom's *takana* or any other. *The husband must, of his own free will, initiate and participate in the divorce process.* This fact gives rise to a tragic possibility. If a husband is unable or unwilling to effect divorce proceedings, in spite of the clear need for severance, his wife becomes an *aguna*. She remains "chained" to her husband, still married and thus prohibited from moving on to another relationship.

In the past, this tragic eventuality usually resulted from a man's disappearance due to accident, war or the like. To avoid the creation of *agunot* in such cases, Talmudic authorities adopted halachic leniencies,

---

15. Devarim 24:1.
16. *Shulchan Aruch*, Even Ha'ezer 119:6.
17. Rema, ibid.

wherever possible, in their acceptance of evidence concerning the husband's death.[18]

A different type of *igun* (*aguna* status) however, has also always existed, created by recalcitrant husbands who deliberately refuse to grant a *get* to their wives. These women remain trapped in a state of limbo, held hostage, often for financial ransom, by bitter, angry, manipulative men. By all accounts, such *agunot* have become more prevalent in recent times.

Cognizant of the deep personal pain caused by this situation, halachists have struggled to develop halachically acceptable ways to counteract the actions of recalcitrant husbands. The stakes, the authorities understand, cannot be higher, and the balance that needs to be struck cannot be more delicate. On one side lies the personal pain of the *aguna*, chained to an unloving partner, unable to move forward with her life. On the other side lies allegiance to the halachic system in one of the most critical areas of Jewish law, defining the nature of the marital bond and of the Jewish family itself.

Faced with the challenge of striking this balance, the solutions proposed by the rabbis are varied and imaginative. They consider, for example, the possibility of "unfriendly persuasion." While all agree that a *get* must be granted *willingly* by the husband, sources as early as the Mishna allow for a certain degree of "pressure": "We coerce him [the recalcitrant husband] until he says, 'I am willing.'"[19]

Few halachic statements, however, are as open to interpretation as this one. How much coercion is allowed? At what point does a *get* become invalid because the pressure applied has crossed over the line? No less an authority than the Rambam maintains that in a situation where a *get* is clearly warranted, a husband can even be *physically pressured* into becoming a "willing participant" in divorce proceedings.[20] Other coercive steps, such as social pressure, communal ostracism, public humiliation and, where possible, even imprisonment have been used effectively in convincing recalcitrant husbands to relent.

Recent years have seen other proposed solutions. In certain cases, authorities such as Rabbi Moshe Feinstein have invalidated marriage

---

18. Talmud Bavli Gittin 3a.
19. Mishna Erachin 5:6.
20. Rambam, *Mishneh Torah*, Hilchot Gerushin 2:20.

ceremonies retroactively and allowed women to remarry, on the basis of halachic defects (such as unacceptable witnesses) in the original ceremonies.[21] The Rabbinical Council of America and other groups have taken a proactive step, advocating the signing of a halachic prenuptial agreement. This agreement, a legal document designed to pass muster in civil court, obligates both the bride and groom to appear before a *beit din* (Jewish court) in the sad eventuality of a decision to divorce.

The document further obligates the husband to a fixed sum of daily support from the time the *beit din* determines that a *get* should be given until the time the divorce proceedings actually take place. This payment is not constructed as a fine, which would create an invalid "forced *get*," but as a continuation of the customary support a husband is obligated to provide for his wife throughout marriage. The authors and proponents of the halachic prenuptial agreement hope that its widespread use will greatly minimize the incidence of *igun* throughout the Jewish community.

In spite of these and other rabbinic attempts to mitigate the phenomenon of *igun*, the problem understandably remains a vexing one for the Jewish community. One case of *igun* is one case too many; and, if anything, as we have noted, the number of cases in the Jewish community seems to be increasing. Given the deep pain that marks each instance, many observers feel frustrated with what they perceive as the inability of the rabbinate to simply "solve the problem." Why can't Jewish law find a way, they ask, to equalize the process of divorce?

While such protestations are certainly understandable, the move towards solutions at all costs can prove damaging, even to the *agunot* themselves. As a case in point, in 1996, a number of rabbis, including one of the leading thinkers of the Modern Orthodox movement, established an independent *beit din*, Beit Din Zedek L'Ba'ayot Agunot, specifically designed to deal with the plight of *agunot*. The centerpiece of this *beit din*'s approach to the problem was the halachic concept of *mekach ta'ut*, false sale.

Marriage, these rabbis reasoned, is fundamentally a contract between two individuals, and, like any other contract, must be marked by full disclosure at the time of the "deal." According to Jewish law, if a participant in an agreement discovers that a critical detail was not shared with him

---

21. Igrot Moshe, Even Ha'Ezer 4:80.

at the time of a contract's formalization, that individual may claim his rights as the victim of a false sale and abrogate the contract retroactively.[22] A woman victimized by a recalcitrant husband, reasoned the founders of this *beit din*, can easily claim that at the time of her marriage, the true character of her husband to be was hidden from her. Had she known his true nature, as an individual who could now, consciously and sadistically, cause her such pain, she never would have married him. Under the laws of contracts, this claim alone should be enough to annul her marriage and render a *get* unnecessary.

As attractive as this solution seemed, however, it failed to garner support even in the most liberal corners of the Orthodox community. The activities of the Beit Din Zedek L'Ba'ayot Agunot were roundly condemned by a myriad of halachic authorities and by major Orthodox organizations including the Beit Din of America, affiliated with the Rabbinical Council of America and the Orthodox Union; Agudath Israel of America; the National Council of Young Israel and many others.[23] In 1998, a petition signed by scores of Modern Orthodox rabbis warned that women remarrying on the basis of divorces obtained by this court would be considered adulterers according to Jewish law and that their children would be considered halachically illegitimate. "We are certain that virtually no Orthodox rabbi would be willing to officiate at weddings of women who wish to remarry based upon [the court's annulments]," the authors of the petition proclaimed.[24]

The strenuous and nearly unanimous criticism of the actions of the Beit Din Zedek L'Ba'ayot Agunot was based on the conviction that, although in selected cases the argument of *mekach ta'ut* can be used to annul a marriage,[25] the criteria applied by this court for the revocation of marriages failed to approach even the most minimal legal standards for the determination of *mekach ta'ut*.

Of even greater concern was the potential impact of these decisions on the legality of future marriages. If a woman could cancel her nuptials retroactively in such facile fashion, the critics reasoned, what would

---

22. Rambam, *Mishneh Torah*, Hilchot Mechira 15.
23. "Full-Court Press against New Bet Din," *Jewish Week*, February 27, 1998.
24. "Divorce Court Battle Heats Up," *Jewish Week*, June 5, 1998.
25. "Where Divorce Can Be Denied, Orthodox Jews Look to Prenuptial Contracts," *New York Times*, March 17, 2012.

prevent cancellation of marriages for a myriad other reasons, as well? Literally any husband or wife could seek an annulment on the basis of newly discovered "damaging" information concerning his/her spouse not known at the time of their marriage. "Had I only known…I never would have married him/her." The very sanctity of the marital bond was at stake, and the battle had to be waged.

In hindsight, the argument can well be made that, in spite of the best of intentions, the Beit Din Zedek L'Ba'ayot Agunot performed a real disservice to the hundreds of women who obtained divorces under its auspices. Few, if any, authorities within the Orthodox community accepted the divorced status of these women and, consequently, their ability to remarry either in Israel or the diaspora was severely curtailed. So controversial were the actions of this *beit din* that even a leading Orthodox feminist and activist for *agunot* proclaimed that the actions of the Beit Din Zedek L'Ba'ayot Agunot had actually made the situation worse for the women involved.[26] The efforts of the Beit Din Zedek L'Ba'ayot Agunot proved to be, at best, a classic case of good intentions gone awry.

The controversy surrounding the actions of the Beit Din Zedek L'Ba'ayot Agunot underscores the complexities that the Orthodox world faces as it struggles to ease the plight of *agunot*. Without question more can be done to address this tragic problem. Communities should certainly unite behind the efforts to identify and socially ostracize each individual who refuses to grant his wife a *get*. The use of proactive techniques such as the halachic prenuptial agreement should be made universal. Continued exploration of imaginative new approaches within the law to resolve the tragedy of every *aguna* should take place.

We must, however, also recognize the dangers of precipitous action. As deeply painful as the plight of each *aguna* may be, and as difficult as the law that gives rise to these situations may be to understand, the divinely inspired legal system that has preserved us as a people must, itself, be respected and preserved. An inauthentic approach, however appealing, can undermine that very system and cause unexpected, damaging consequences.

---

26. Soriya Daniels, "Potential Solutions to the Agunah Problem," MyJewishLearning. com.

2 Jewish Jihad?

Context
God commands Moshe to respond to the devastation caused by the Midianites during the tragic episode of Ba'al Pe'or (see Balak 5): "Carry out the avenging of the Israelites from the Midianites; afterward you will be gathered unto your people."[1]

Moshe reacts by instructing the nation to assemble an army, with Pinchas ben Elazar the Cohen at its helm, for the purpose of carrying out "the vengeance of the Lord upon Midian."[2]

The Israelites are victorious in battle, killing all the male Midianites, capturing the women and children and plundering the enemy's wealth and livestock.

Upon the victorious army's return, however, Moshe angrily chastises its officers: "Did you let every female live? Behold, they were the ones who caused the children of Israel, by the word of Bilam, to commit a betrayal against the Lord regarding the matter of Pe'or; and the plague occurred in the assembly of the Lord."[3]

Moshe commands the nation to put all the male Midianite children and all females old enough to be sexually active[4] to death by the sword. All female children, he explains, may remain in captivity.

The people comply....

Questions
Few if any episodes in the text are more disturbing than the battle against Midian and its aftermath.

---

1. Bamidbar 31:1–2.
2. Ibid., 31:3.
3. Ibid., 31:15–16.
4. Sifrei, Bamidbar 31:17.

What explanation, if any, can be offered for the violent acts committed in this episode? Why would God command the death of noncombatant woman and children?

How can we respond to those who point to this and similar passages in the text as proof of the violent nature of the "Old Testament God"? Even more importantly, how can we ourselves address our own discomfort with narratives such as this?

How does the Torah's overarching message of compassion and human dignity correlate with God's commandments concerning the battle of Midian and His instructions relating to warfare, in general? Under what conditions is warfare sanctioned under Jewish law? What legal limits are placed upon a soldier's conduct in the course of halachically permitted conflict?

Our questions are heightened by the events of our day. We are quick to criticize terrorist attacks and the targeting of innocent civilians in the name of "jihad." Such acts, we passionately argue, become even more despicable when they are purportedly perpetrated in the pursuit of "religious" goals. In what way, however, are the commandments issued by God to the Israelites in this narrative different? Can it be that the Midianite civilians are not "innocent"? If they are guilty, what is the nature of their crime?

Approaches

— **A** —

I approach this particular study with a great deal of trepidation, not only because a full treatment of the topic of warfare in Jewish thought remains well beyond the scope of our discussion, but because the Torah's description of the battle against Midian has troubled me for years.

Can we possibly explain God-ordained violence in a way that will satisfy our modern sensibilities? Recognizing the limitations of our understanding, should we even try? We have no right, after all, to expect that Torah law will always correlate with the mores of our day (see previous study). Would we, therefore, be better served by turning the page and avoiding the frustration of unanswered questions? Or should we delve deeper and face the questions head-on?

An early Midrashic source indicates that the conflicts confronting us were keenly felt by the rabbis, as well. The Talmud suggests that Shaul, the first king of Israel, engages God in poignant debate after receiving the divine command to utterly destroy the nation of Amalek and all of its wealth:

> When God said to Shaul, "Go and smite Amalek"…
> Shaul responded, "And behold, concerning one [slain] soul, the Torah mandates the [atoning ritual] of the Axed Heifer,[5] concerning these countless [Amalekite] souls, how much more so [will atonement be necessary if I slay them]? And, if the people have sinned, how have the animals sinned? And if the adults have sinned, how have the children sinned?"
> A heavenly voice emerged and responded: "Do not be overly righteous!"[6]

If the rabbis imagine that the first king of Israel, in direct communication with God, receives no clear answer to his deep-seated questions, what chance have we of answering our own?

From the outset, however, we have argued in our studies in favor of confrontation with the difficult challenges that emerge from the text. To ignore the questions raised by the battle against Midian – and by the issue of biblical warfare in general – would be to shy away from some of the most obvious of these challenges.

We will, therefore, once again enter a complex arena, allowing the battle against Midian to serve as our point of entry into a brief examination of the general rules of warfare in biblical thought.

B

Based on evidence from the text, the halachists delineate two general categories of armed conflict in Jewish law.

1. Milchemet mitzva, *obligatory warfare.* Combat that is commanded by God and is, therefore categorized as a mitzva.

---

5. Devarim 21:1–9.
6. Yoma 22b.

This category of conflict is limited to wars waged against the seven indigenous nations residing in the land of Canaan before the Israelite conquest; to the ongoing battle against the nation of Amalek, the sworn enemy of the Jewish people; and to wars waged in the nation's self-defense. A Jewish king need not consult with the Sanhedrin before ordering the nation to engage in a *milchemet mitzva*. During the course of obligatory conflict against the seven nations or Amalek, no living enemy soul is to be spared.[7]

2. Milchemet reshut, *optional warfare.* Combat that is permitted by divine law but is not obligatory.

This category of combat includes wars waged by the nation in order to increase its borders, power and renown. The approval of the Sanhedrin is required before a king can involve the nation in such a conflict. During the course of optional combat, the Jewish nation must spare the lives of enemy women and children.[8]

C

The Torah clearly states that before engaging in battle, the nation must present its adversaries with formal terms of peace.

"When you draw near to a city to wage war against it, and you shall call out to it in peace. And it shall be that if in peace it responds to you, then all the people that are found therein shall be tributaries to you, and they shall serve you. But if it does not make peace with you, but makes war with you, you shall besiege it."[9]

The extent of this requirement to offer peace overtures, however, is hotly debated by scholars across the ages.

Numerous commentaries, including Rashi and the Ra'avad, maintain that the obligation to offer peace prior to battle is limited to circumstances of *milchemet reshut*, optional warfare. When facing Israel's inveterate adversaries – the seven indigenous nations of Canaan or the nation of Amalek, upon whom it is a mitzva to wage war – peace may not be offered under any terms. The destruction of these nations is obligatory.[10]

---

7. Rambam, *Mishneh Torah*, Hilchot Melachim 5:1–2.
8. Ibid.
9. Devarim 20:10–12.
10. Rashi, Devarim 20:10; Ra'avad, *Mishneh Torah*, Hilchot Melachim 6.

Proponents of this position derive support from the text itself. The biblical passage that opens with the directive cited above, requiring the offering of peace terms, later declares, "So shall you do to all the cities that are distant from you, that are not of the cities of these [the seven] nations."[11] This delineation seems to exclude the seven indigenous nations of Canaan from any possible peace agreement.

Another group of scholars, however, led by both the Rambam and the Ramban, interpret the text differently. Peace must be offered to a potential adversary, these authorities argue, under any circumstances, even before the onset of a *milchemet mitzva*, an obligatory conflict. The Ramban explicitly includes the seven Canaanite nations in this mandate[12] but stops short of mentioning the nation of Amalek, the paradigm of evil within Jewish tradition. In contrast, the Rambam openly insists that the Amalekites must, as well, be given the opportunity to accept terms of peace. "One may not wage war against any human being in the world," the Rambam declares, "unless he has first called out to him in peace."[13] *No one*, the Rambam maintains, *not even an Amalekite, is irredeemable.*

As proof of his position that peace overtures must precede even an obligatory conflict, the Rambam cites the claim in the book of Yehoshua, "There was no city [in the land of Canaan] that sued for peace with the children of Israel other than the Hivites who lived in Givon…."[14] Clearly, argues the Rambam, had other cities sought peace with the Israelites, their overtures would also have been accepted.[15] The Ramban further quotes a Midrashic tradition explicitly maintaining that, prior to the Israelites' entry into Canaan, Yehoshua offered three choices to the inhabitants of the land: to vacate their cities, to accept peace terms or to engage in battle.[16] Even the Ra'avad, who argues that peace may not be offered to an adversary before engaging in an obligatory war (see above), accepts the Midrashic tradition that Yehoshua offered peace terms to the inhabitants of the land. Prior to the Israelites' entry into the land, the Ra'avad argues, the conflict with the seven nations had not yet been joined. Up to that

---

11. Devarim 20:15.
12. Ramban, Devarim 20:10.
13. Rambam, *Mishneh Torah*, Hilchot Melachim 6:1.
14. Yehoshua 11:19.
15. Rambam, *Mishneh Torah*, Hilchot Melachim 6:1, 4.
16. Ramban, Devarim 20:10; Talmud Yerushalmi Shevi'it 6:1.

point, therefore, even members of those nations could have opted for peace.[17]

D

In his formulation of the terms of peace offered to an adversary, the Rambam adds a far-reaching provision that does not appear explicitly in the relevant Torah passage. Any peace agreement established, this scholar maintains, must obligate the surrendering nation to the seven Noachide laws of fundamental morality.[18] These seven laws, elucidated in the Talmud, form a baseline ethical expectation for all world societies[19] (see *Bereishit*: Noach 4, *Context*). To the Rambam, the establishment of peace with other peoples is not an independent event, but must serve to advance Israel's overall mission of raising the ethical standard of the world community. *While peace must be offered to even the most entrenched enemies of Israel, the Rambam argues, Israel cannot and should not live in peace with any nation unwilling to live by a basic moral code.*

Other authorities, however, maintain that acceptance of the Noachide code is only a prerequisite for nations who will continue to dwell within the boundaries of the Land of Israel. The ethical commitments required from those who will live in close proximity to the Jewish nation are higher, lest they lead the Israelites astray. For all others, the acceptance of the peace terms outlined in the Torah itself is sufficient.[20]

E

A puzzling phrase in the Torah's description of the battle against Midian serves as the source for yet another critical halachic stipulation concerning warfare, recorded in the *Sifrei* and codified by the Rambam.

Describing the onset of the battle, the text states: "And they [the Israelites] massed against Midian, *as the Lord had commanded Moshe.*"[21]

God's commandment launching this encounter (see above), however, contains no explicit instructions as to how the battle should be fought.

---

17. Ra'avad on Rambam, *Mishneh Torah*, Hilchot Melachim 6:4.
18. Rambam, *Mishneh Torah*, Hilchot Melachim 6:1.
19. Bereishit 9:2–6; Talmud Bavli Sanhedrin 56a–b.
20. Ramban, Devarim 20:10; Radbaz on Rambam, *Mishneh Torah*, Hilchot Melachim 6:1.
21. Bamidbar 31:7.

What is the implication, therefore, of the phrase "as the Lord had commanded Moshe"?

In a surprising stroke, the *Sifrei* explains that God's instructions to Moshe prior to the battle against Midian include an orally transmitted imperative: *A Jewish army may besiege an adversary from only three sides, leaving one side unguarded as an avenue of escape for those who wish to flee.*[22]

The *Sifrei* thus transforms our understanding of the Jewish attitude towards war. *The victims of war, this Midrash maintains, are given the opportunity to choose their fate even after the battle is joined.*

The scholars quoted in the Midrash actually argue as to whether this divine oral "escape clause" applied to the battle of Midian itself, or whether, given the heinous nature of the Midianites' crimes, this battle was the exception from which no flight was allowed.[23]

The Rambam, however, is decisive:

> When siege is laid to a city for the purpose of capture, it may not be surrounded on all four sides but only on three. And place is granted to those who would flee and to all who wish to escape with their lives. As the text states, "And they massed against Midian, as the Lord commanded Moshe." It has been learned by tradition that that was the instruction given to Moshe.[24]

Even in the battle against Midian, the Rambam maintains, the Israelites are commanded to provide an escape route for those who wish to flee. The captives who are ultimately brought before Moshe are individuals who, when given the choice, opted to stand and fight.

── **F** ──────────────────────────────

Moving past the battle against Midian, however, the question still remains. Under what conditions must this escape route be provided? Is this allowance limited to situations of optional conflict or does it extend to obligatory conflicts, as well? Are we required to afford even members

---

22. Sifrei, Bamidbar 31:7.
23. Ibid.
24. Rambam, *Mishneh Torah*, Hilchot Melachim 6:7.

of the seven Canaanite nations and Amalekites with the opportunity to flee the battlefield?

At face value, the Rambam makes no distinction between optional and obligatory conflicts and seems to apply this allowance to all battles in which the Jewish people are involved.[25] Some authorities, however, including the Radbaz, maintain that even the Rambam agrees that once the battle is joined, inveterate enemies of the Jewish nation (such as the members of the seven nations) cannot be allowed to flee.[26]

G

Our discussion to this point has shown that the Torah's approach to warfare, as seen through the eyes of the rabbis, is much more nuanced and complex than first meets the eye. Opportunities for peaceful resolution to potential conflict and for personal avoidance of war are woven into the very fabric of the law. Even the most historically inveterate enemies of the Jewish nation are, according to many authorities, to be afforded these opportunities.

H

Another rabbinic decision, however, made centuries after the close of the Bible, may have even greater practical implications concerning the conduct of Jewish wars in our day.

The Mishna records the debate over and the eventual acceptance of a potential convert of supposed Ammonite descent, in spite of the biblical injunction, "An Ammonite or a Moabite may not enter the congregation of the Lord, even their tenth generation…to eternity."[27]

This allowance is made, the Mishna explains, because of the actions of the ancient Assyrian king Sancheriv (sixth century BCE), who, upon embarking on a campaign of conquest in the ancient Middle East, completely subdues his enemies by exiling them from their homelands and scattering them across the face of his empire. This practice prevents conquered peoples from regrouping, reclaiming their own identity, and threatening the Assyrian empire from within. Tragically, Jewish history is

---

25. Ibid.
26. Radbaz on Rambam, *Mishneh Torah*, Hilchot Melachim 6:7.
27. Devarim 23:4.

indelibly altered when the Kingdom of Judah is conquered[28] and treated in this fashion by Sancheriv.[29] As a result, ten tribes of Israel assimilate into surrounding cultures and disappear from the historical stage. The remaining tribes, who populate the Kingdom of Judah, escape a similar fate only through miraculous intervention and become, in the main, the ancestors of the continuing Jewish nation.[30]

Like the "Ten Lost Tribes" of Israel, the Mishna claims, other ancient biblical nations, including the Ammonites and the Moabites, were scattered by Sancheriv, resulting in the loss of their independent identity. Even someone claiming to be of Ammonite descent, therefore, is not treated as such and may become a full-fledged member of the Jewish people.[31]

The Rambam codifies this law broadly:

> When Sancheriv, the king of Assyria, rose, he confused all the nations and commingled them one with another and exiled them from their places. Therefore, Egyptians in the land of Egypt today are different people [than before]. And, so too, the Edomites in the field of Edom.... Therefore, a convert who comes in our time, in all places, whether he [claims to] be Egyptian, Ammonite, Cushite or of any other nationality, both men and women, are immediately permitted to join the congregation.[32]

Even further, some commentaries see the concept of commingled nations as the basis for the Rambam's practical ruling concerning obligatory conflict against the seven Canaanite nations. Commenting on our ongoing responsibilities in this area, the Rambam states:

> It is a positive commandment to destroy the seven [Canaanite] nations, as it states, "You shall utterly destroy them."[33] And anyone who encounters an individual from among [these nations] and fails

---

28. Melachim II 17.
29. Ibid., 18:11–12.
30. Ibid., 19:35.
31. Mishna Yada'im 4:4.
32. Rambam, *Mishneh Torah*, Hilchot Issurei Bi'ah 12:25.
33. Devarim 20:17; Rashi, ibid.

to kill him, transgresses a negative commandment, as it states, "You shall not allow a soul [from among them] to live."³⁴ *And their memory has long since perished* [my italics].³⁵

The Radbaz explains that the Rambam's disclaimer, "And their memory has long since perished," is based on the fact that "Sancheriv arose and confused the world."³⁶ *The seven nations are, therefore, no longer identifiable and the practical obligation to destroy them no longer applies.* [Note: The Rambam's apparent failure to extend this exemption to the nation of Amalek will be discussed below. See *Approaches* I.]

— I —

Centuries later, the concept of commingled nations again becomes part of the halachic discourse concerning obligatory warfare when a number of halachists revisit the biblical commandment to blot out the nation of Amalek.³⁷

The Torah's approach to Amalek is straightforward. Identified as the archenemy of God's will in the world, Amalek must be treated with unremitting enmity by the Jewish nation across the face of time. The Jew, God commands, must remember Amalek's vicious attack upon him until he succeeds in "erasing the remembrance of Amalek from under the heavens."³⁸

While the biblical commandment concerning Amalek seems clear, however, the practical application of this law becomes the subject of debate across the ages. At the core of the rabbinic dispute lies the continuing identity of Amalek itself. For some authorities, over time, Amalek is increasingly seen as a conceptual rather than as a physical entity.³⁹ For other scholars, however, the focus on the literal, concrete commandment remains important. What is the status, they wonder, of our obligation to seek out and destroy the actual nation of Amalek in our day? Faced with the obvious practical and moral problems inherent in this

---

34. Devarim 20:16.
35. Rambam, *Mishneh Torah*, Hilchot Melachim 5:4.
36. Radbaz, ibid.
37. Chaim Palagi, *Einei Kol Chai*, Sanhedrin 96b.
38. Devarim 25:19.
39. Rav Shimshon Raphael Hirsch, Shmot 17:14, Devarim 25:18.

question, many adopt the approach elucidated by Rabbi Yosef Babad in the *Minchat Chinuch*, his renowned commentary to the *Sefer Hachinuch*: "And today we are no longer commanded in this [commandment to blot out the remembrance of Amalek] because Sancheriv has already risen and confused the whole world."[40]

From the perspective of these scholars, the entire notion of obligatory warfare based on national identity becomes moot after the sixth century. Due to Sancheriv's policies of conquest, our classical enemies are no longer identifiable. Obligatory wars in our day are thus limited to cases of self-defense.

── J ──

A fascinating "blended" position concerning the nature of Amalek in our day is offered by Rabbi Joseph Soloveitchik, based upon a subtle discrepancy in the rulings of the Rambam.[41]

As we have seen, the Rambam notes in his codification of the law that the obligation to destroy the seven Canaanite nations no longer applies because "their memory has long since perished."[42] In contrast to the later scholars cited above, however, the Rambam makes no such allowance concerning the obligation to destroy the nation of Amalek.[43] This omission would seem to indicate that, in the Rambam's eyes, *Amalek, unlike the seven nations, continues to exist to this day, incurring our continuing enmity.*

Why, asks the Rav, would the Rambam assume that Amalek survives, while the memory of other ancient nations "perishes"?

To explain this legal disparity, the Rav suggests that *two distinct commandments concerning Amalek emerge from Torah text, reflecting two different categories of Amalek.*

1. The verse "You shall blot out the remembrance of Amalek"[44] mandates the destruction of each individual genealogical descendent of Amalek. This commandment loses its force when Sancheriv's method of conquest robs the ancient nations of their independent identities.

---

40. Minchat Chinuch, mitzva 604.
41. Rabbi Joseph B. Soloveitchik, *Fate and Destiny* (New York: Ktav, 2000), pp. 65–66, 92–95.
42. Rambam, *Mishneh Torah*, Hilchot Melachim 5:4.
43. Ibid., 5:5.
44. Devarim 25:19.

2. The verse "The Lord will have war with Amalek from generation to generation"[45] establishes the obligation to obliterate *any nation across the face of history that seeks to destroy the Jewish people*. This second commandment, which defines Amalek in broad conceptual rather than biological terms, remains unaffected by Sancheriv's actions. Within the context of this commandment, Hitler and the Nazis were the Amalekites of the 1930s and '40s, while "the mobs of Nasser and the mufti"[46] were the Amalekites of the 1950s and '60s.

"There still exists," the Rav explains, "a category of Amalek [as a people] even now after the peoples have been intermingled [and there are no longer any individual Amalekites]."[47]

We can safely assume that the Rav would similarly identify the members of Hamas, Hezbollah and the Iranian Revolutionary Guard as Amalekites in our day.

The Rav goes on to suggest that the Rambam's ruling categorizing any defensive war as an obligatory conflict may well rise out of this second commandment concerning Amalek. Any nation that attacks the Jewish people automatically falls into the category of Amalek, and is governed by the verse "The Lord will have war with Amalek from generation to generation."

The Rav agrees that the concept of obligatory warfare based on genetic national identity becomes moot after Sancheriv's conquests. He maintains, however, that a second type of national identity emerges from the Torah's commandments concerning Amalek – *an identity determined by behavior rather than by bloodline*. This national identity remains intact to this day, obligating the Jewish people in each generation to ongoing struggle against the Amalekites of their day.

K

We have traveled far in our discussion from the stark biblical passages describing the battle against Midian. Nonetheless, some of the most troubling questions raised at the beginning of our study still demand our attention and analysis.

---

45. Shmot 17:16.
46. Rabbi Joseph B. Soloveitchik, *Fate and Destiny*, p. 65.
47. Ibid., p. 95.

Why does God command the execution of the captive Midianite women and children? How can we correlate this directive with the Torah's overarching messages of compassion and human dignity? If, as we have seen in our studies, Torah law concerning warfare is actually deeply nuanced and complex, why isn't that complexity reflected in this phase of the battle against Midian?

— L —

The Torah, it would seem, discusses extraordinary circumstances – a time when the Israelites are locked not only in an ongoing battle for their own survival but also *in a seminal struggle to determine the moral course of mankind.*

In this continuing conflict, dangerous threats extend well beyond the battlefield, and even those who appear to be noncombatants often present unexpected mortal threats. By the time God commands Moshe to attack Midian, the battle has already been joined. The first salvo, launched against the Israelites in the plains of Shittim – where the Midianite women deliberately seduced the Israelites towards the licentiousness and idolatry of Ba'al Pe'or – clearly demonstrated the unconventional nature of the threat. Midian would not be content with the clash of troops on the field of battle, but would make all its citizens combatants. Once joined in this manner, the struggle against Midian can only end for the Israelites with the destruction of the enemy in all of its forms.

Through edict and example, the Torah prepares us for those times in human experience when humanity will confront pure, unmitigated and unrepentant evil: times when the only response can be the recognition and total eradication of that evil from the world.

Our brief journey through biblical and rabbinic thought on the topic of warfare has clearly demonstrated, however, that *exceptional conflicts such as the events at Midian do not serve as templates for the general conduct of war throughout Jewish history.* The practical halachot that have governed this critical and tragic area of human experience across time are complex, thoughtful, nuanced and, wherever possible, humane.

Points to Ponder

At some level, one might argue, the proof is in the product….

Fast-forward centuries to the present day. With the passage of time, what kind of battlefield ethic has Torah law and thought produced? How does this ethic compare to that adopted by the current adversaries of the Jewish people?

For the first time since the Bar Kochba revolt, a litmus test is available for the assessment of these issues. The Jewish nation once again occupies the battlefield in defense of its home, and the conduct of its troops in the realm of warfare can be readily assessed.

Over the past decades in the face of intractable foes, the defense forces of the State of Israel have adopted a formal code of battlefield conduct. This code is summarized on a card carried by each soldier and includes the following provision concerning "purity of arms":

> The IDF servicemen and women will use their weapons and force only for the purpose of their mission, only to the necessary extent and will maintain their humanity even during combat. IDF soldiers will not use their weapons and force to harm human beings who are not combatants or prisoners of war, and will do all in their power to avoid causing harm to their lives, bodies, dignity and property.[48]

These and other commitments govern the IDF's conduct during the course of their battles with the enemy, often at great cost to the Israelis themselves. During the Second Intifada in 2002, for example, twenty-three Israeli soldiers perished when the decision was made to send in ground forces to root out terrorists in the refugee camp in Jenin. The alternate, safer approach of bombing the camp had been rejected out of concern for the potential collateral damage to the Arab civilian population.

The Israeli army regularly warns civilians via leaflets, radio broadcasts and even SMS messages to leave their homes prior to the use of firepower in their area, and the IDF is the only army in the world to maintain a map of locations such as churches, mosques, schools and hospitals in order to avoid attacking these locations, whenever possible.

Contrast these ethical practices to the behaviors exhibited by Israel's enemies. Hamas, Hezbollah and other terrorist groups deliberately blur the distinction between civilians and soldiers by making all Israelis

---

48. Israel Defense Forces Code of Ethics.

targets, and regularly protect themselves by embedding their troops and leaders in their own civilian populations. The Palestinian Authority, while ostensibly conducting "peace talks" with Israel, allows for (and, in fact, encourages) the demonization of all Jews, in mosques, over the airwaves and even in children's textbooks. Terrorist murderers of innocent civilians are extolled and glorified by Arab governments, in the perpetuation of a culture of senseless hatred against Israel and world Jewry.

What has produced this contrast? What is the source of the ethical culture of the Israel Defense Forces? Is it the centuries of thoughtful halachic discussion concerning the morality of warfare, conducted when the battlefield was beyond our reach? Is it the Jew's recognition of the pain of the victim, born out of the millennia of his own victimization and pain?

Whatever the answer, one thing is clear: given the opportunity to once again affect the fate of others on the field of battle, the Jewish nation, in contrast to its adversaries and at its own cost, chooses the ethical path. This choice, more than anything else, testifies to the moral fabric of Jewish law. For the Jew, the way is not the way of jihad.

3 Falling Short

Context

With the Promised Land in sight, the tribes of Reuven and Gad approach the leaders of the nation and request that they be allowed to remain on the East Bank of the Jordan. "If we have found favor in your eyes, let this land be given to your servants as a heritage; do not bring us across the Jordan."[1]

Indignantly, Moshe responds: "Will your brothers go out to war while you settle here?"[2]

Moshe expresses deep-seated fears that this proposal will cause the entire nation to doubt their entry into the land. How tragic it would be, he argues, if this generation were to fail at the last moment, as their fathers failed a generation earlier, in response to the report of the spies.

The representatives of Reuven and Gad counter with a pledge to fight in the forefront of the nation during the conquest of Canaan, only returning to their homes in the Transjordan after the full subjugation of the land.

"Pens for the flock shall we build here for our livestock and cities for our small children. And we shall arm ourselves swiftly in the vanguard of the children of Israel until we have brought them to their place…. We shall not return to our homes until the children of Israel will have inherited – each man his inheritance."[3]

Moshe accepts this pledge, announces the agreement to the nation and designates the land on the East Bank of the Jordan as the heritage of the tribes of Reuven, Gad and half of the tribe of Menashe.[4]

---

1. Bamidbar 32:5.
2. Ibid., 32:6.
3. Ibid., 32:16–18.
4. Ibid., 32:1–33.

Questions

Numerous textual and conceptual questions confront us as we consider this pivotal event on the border of the land of Canaan.

The Torah repeats the particulars of the agreement forged between Moshe and the tribes of Reuven and Gad *no less than five times*, in varying levels of detail: once when the deal is first proposed by the tribes, once when Moshe repeats the agreement back to the tribes, once when Reuven and Gad respond, once when Moshe announces the accord to the entire nation and a final time when the tribal representatives publicly commit themselves to the agreement.

Why are all these repetitions necessary? The details of the agreement are clearly stipulated in the original presentation made by the tribes to Moshe. The Torah, in each successive instance, could have avoided needless duplication by simply stating: *And Moshe* (or the tribal leaders, depending upon the context) *conveyed the details of the agreement….*

Furthermore, by what right does Moshe independently agree to the proposal offered by the two tribes? On numerous occasions during the tenure of his leadership, Moshe turns to God for guidance in resolving challenging situations. Why in this case, confronted with a radical departure from the divinely ordained plan of full entry into the land, does Moshe feel comfortable acting on his own? Why doesn't he consult God for guidance before allowing two tribes to settle outside the land of Canaan?

On a different note, the request for a heritage on the East Bank of the Jordan is made only by the tribes of Reuven and Gad. Why, then, does Moshe ultimately include half the tribe of Menashe in the agreement concerning the Transjordan?

Finally, what is the eventual verdict of history concerning the actions of the tribes of Reuven and Gad? Do they fulfill their responsibility completely when they fight in the forefront of the nation during the conquest of the land; or do they remain culpable for their refusal to join their brothers in the inheritance of Canaan? And what is the status of the East Bank territory in which these tribes ultimately dwell? Does this area acquire the holiness reserved for the Land of Israel; or are Reuven and Gad forever on the outside looking in?

Approaches

—A—

As we have noted before, whenever the Torah repeats a conversation, the different versions of that conversation must be carefully scrutinized and compared. Invariably, subtle and not-so-subtle disparities emerge that prove critical to our understanding of the narrative.

In the case before us, significant divergences of perspective between Moshe and the tribal representatives become evident as their conversation unfolds – differences that Moshe consciously addresses in an attempt to reframe the worldview of the leaders standing before him.

1. Reuven and Gad's proposal to Moshe: "Pens for the flock shall we build here for our livestock and cities for our small children. And we shall arm ourselves swiftly in the vanguard of the children of Israel until we have brought them to their place…. We shall not return to our homes until the children of Israel will have inherited – each man his inheritance."[5]

2. Moshe's response: "If you do this thing, if you arm yourselves before the Lord for battle; and every armed man among you shall cross the Jordan before the Lord until He drives His enemies before Him; and the land is conquered before the Lord, and then you shall return and you will be vindicated before the Lord and before Israel; and this land shall be for you as a heritage before the Lord. But if you do not do so, behold, you will have sinned to the Lord and know your sin that will encounter you. Build for yourselves cities for your small children and pens for your livestock; and that which you have spoken shall you do."[6]

3. Reuven and Gad's response: "Your servants shall do as my Lord commands. Our small children, our wives, our livestock and all our animals shall remain here in the cities of the Gilead. And your servants shall cross over, every armed person of the legion before the Lord, to do battle as my Lord speaks."[7]

4. Moshe's announcement to the nation's leaders: "If the children of Gad and the children of Reuven will cross the Jordan with you, all armed for battle before the Lord, and the land is conquered before you, you shall

---

5. Bamidbar 32:16–18.
6. Ibid., 32:20–24.
7. Ibid., 32:25–27.

give them the land of Gilead as a heritage. And if they do not cross over, armed with you, then they shall take their heritage in the land of Canaan."[8]

5. Reuven and Gad's public assertion: "That which the Lord has spoken to your servants, so shall we do. We will cross over armed before the Lord to the land of Canaan and ours shall be the heritage of our inheritance across the Jordan."[9]

B

The verbal duel begins with the very first words of the tribes' proposal to Moshe: "*Pens for the flock* shall we build here for our livestock and cities for our small *children*…."

Moshe in his response, deliberately changes the order of the text: "Build for yourselves *cities for your small children* and *pens for your livestock*…."

Rashi, reflecting an earlier Midrashic tradition, offers the obvious explanation for this discrepancy:

> They [the tribal representatives] showed greater concern for their wealth than for their sons and daughters, as they placed their cattle before their small children.
> Said Moshe to them: *Not so! Keep the primary primary and secondary secondary. First build for yourselves cities for your small children, and, after that, pens for your cattle.*[10]

Only someone blinded by an overwhelming desire for material gain could stand on the banks of the Jordan, on the very eve of his nation's entry into the Promised Land, and ignore the call of history. Only someone who considers the protection of his cattle more important than the protection of his children could turn his back on the spiritual heritage in which those children had been destined to share.

Foreshadowing the materialistic motivations of the two tribes, the Torah introduces this entire episode with a sentence that, as Nehama

---

8. Ibid., 32:29–30.
9. Ibid., 32:31–32.
10. Rashi, Bamidbar 32:16.

Leibowitz notes,[11] begins and ends with the word *livestock*: "And *livestock* in great multitude was possessed by the children of Reuven and Gad; and they saw the land of Yazher and the land of Gilead, and behold, the place was a place for *livestock*."[12]

Given the priorities of the tribes of Reuven and Gad, the stage is set for failure from the outset....

C

A striking anomaly in Moshe's response to the two tribes alerts us to an even more pervasive philosophical divergence between the protagonists in this episode. As Moshe reviews the tribes' proposal to participate in the conquest of the land, he inserts the phrase "before the Lord" no fewer than five times in four short sentences (see above, *Approaches* A). Why does Moshe find such reiteration necessary? Wouldn't one mention of God's involvement have sufficed?

The answer becomes clear upon viewing Moshe's words in the context of the entire discussion. Moshe repeatedly stresses God's involvement in the conquest of the land because *the representatives of the tribes, in their original proposal to Moshe, do not mention God's name even once.*

The tribes of Reuven and Gad define their responsibility at this juncture solely in interpersonal terms. In order to counter Moshe's objections to their remaining on the Jordan's East Bank, they must find a way to satisfy their obligation towards the rest of the nation. They offer to do so by fighting at the forefront of the Israelite army.

Moshe, however, sees things differently. The nation's entry into Canaan is not solely a nationalistic enterprise but is, even more fundamentally, a fulfillment of God's will. The two tribes' primary obligation, therefore, lies not towards their brothers but, rather, towards God. Ever the teacher, Moshe brings God into the picture over and over again, hoping the tribes will come to realize the nature of their true responsibilities.

A similar perceptual disparity may actually be mirrored at a parallel moment, a generation earlier, during the nation's first attempt to enter the land. There, two heroes, Calev ben Yefuneh and Yehoshua bin Nun (actually mentioned by Moshe, in our narrative, in his response to the two

---

11. Leibowitz, *Iyunim Chadashim B'Sefer Bamidbar*, p. 355.
12. Bamidbar 32:1.

tribes), emerge from among the spies as the sole defenders of the mandate to enter Canaan. Although both of these champions exhibit extraordinary courage and strength, only one is chosen as the next leader of the people, the successor to Moshe.

Calev is the first to speak against the spies: "And Calev *stilled the people towards Moshe* and said: 'We shall shortly go up and take it [the land] into possession; for we can certainly do it!'"[13]

When Yehoshua publicly enters the fray, however, the substance of the argument changes entirely:

> And Yehoshua bin Nun and Calev ben Yefuneh, of those who spied the land, tore their garments. And they said to the entire assembly of the children of Israel: "The land that we passed through, to spy out, the land is very, very good. *If the Lord desires us*, then He will bring us to this land and give it to us, a land that flows with milk and honey. *Only against the Lord do not rebel!* And you, do not fear the people of the land, for they are our bread. Their protection has departed them; *and the Lord is with us*. Do not fear them!"[14]

Although Calev rises first to speak against the spies, his argument is limited, rooted in political support of Moshe's leadership. It remains for Yehoshua to raise the bar by clearly identifying the sin of the spies as a rebellion against God. Only an individual who is acutely aware of God's involvement in the conquest of Canaan can lead the people into the land.

— **D** —

Returning to our narrative a generation later, a basic question emerges. Do the tribes of Reuven and Gad "get" Moshe's implicit messages? Do they pick up on this great teacher's repeated attempts to reshape their worldview?

On the surface, the tribes' reply to Moshe indicates both a clear reorientation of priorities and a newfound recognition of the need to fulfill God's will. "*Our small children, our wives, our livestock and all our*

---

13. Ibid., 13:30.
14. Ibid., 14:6–9.

animals shall remain here in the cities of the Gilead. And your servants shall cross over, every armed person of the legion *before God*...."[15]

Even more telling is the public assertion of the tribes to the nation: "*That which the Lord has spoken* to your servants, so shall we do."[16] Moshe has apparently not consulted with God during this entire process, yet the tribes openly consider the bargain he constructs with them to be reflective of God's will.

The text thus seems to testify that the tribes have come around to Moshe's position on all issues underlying this negotiation. *We hear you*, they implicitly proclaim, *and accept the critical life lessons that you have taught us.*

E

On a deeper level, however, one can argue that the tribes of Reuven and Gad ultimately miss the point. Moshe's "real message" falls on deaf ears. Had these tribes truly heard Moshe, they would have completely withdrawn their request to remain in the Transjordan. Although they are willing to assist in the conquest of Canaan, the tribes of Reuven and Gad steadfastly turn their backs on their divinely mandated destiny to settle the land.

The judgment of history concerning the actions of these tribes is, therefore, complex and inconsistent.

After the tribes of Reuven and Gad successfully fight alongside their brothers, their own territory in the Transjordan becomes part of the national heritage of the Jewish people and acquires the sanctity reserved for the Land of Israel.[17] Nonetheless, Reuven and Gad are the first tribes to be exiled, centuries later, during the Assyrian conquest of the Kingdom of Israel.[18] This tragic fate, the rabbis claim, is a measure-for-measure payback for their original rejection of the land at the time of its conquest.[19]

---

15. Bamidbar 32:26–27.
16. Ibid., 32:31.
17. Rambam, *Mishneh Torah*, Hilchot Terumot 1:2–3. Note: See explanation offered by Rabbi Menachem Leibtag, Tanach Study Center "Nevi'im Rishonim" series, Yehoshua 22, www.tanach.org.
18. Divrei Hayamim I 5:26.
19. Midrash Rabba Bamidbar 22:6.

On a practical level, when the subjugation of the land is complete and the tribes of Reuven and Gad do return to the Transjordan, a potentially dangerous rift develops between them and the rest of the nation.[20] Some commentaries suggest that Moshe's seemingly arbitrary decision to place a portion of the tribe of Menashe together with the tribes of Reuven and Gad on the Jordan's East Bank is actually an attempt to forestall such eventualities. Moshe's hope is that the two "halves" of Menashe will retain close ties, thus connecting the populations on both banks of the river.[21]

Clearly, on many levels, the decision of Reuven and Gad to remain on the East Bank of the Jordan is far from optimal....

F

If our analysis is correct, however, the most difficult question of all emerges. *Why does Moshe agree, without divine consultation, to the proposal of the two tribes?*

As noted above, on a number of occasions during his leadership tenure, Moshe turns to God for guidance when faced with difficult quandaries. Yet, on this occasion, Moshe not only makes a momentous decision independently, but reaches a conclusion that seems to contravene God's stated intent. Given God's clear desire that the Israelites dwell in Canaan, by what right does Moshe unilaterally allow two of the tribes to remain outside that land's borders?

G

An answer to this difficult question may well lie in a fundamental truth concerning our relationship to God's commandments, a truth most clearly reflected in a seemingly unrelated source rooted forty years earlier, at the beginning of the book of Bamidbar.

As the nation readies itself for the journey from Sinai, God mandates a transfer of role from the firstborn males of the nation to the males of the tribe of Levi.[22] The rabbis explain that the Israelite firstborn, originally slated to serve within the Temple, forfeit their rights through involvement

---

20. Yehoshua 22.
21. Mordechai HaKohen, Siftei Kohen Parshat Matot, p. 303.
22. Bamidbar 3:11–13.

in the sin of the golden calf. The Levites, who, in contrast, remain loyal to God during that tragic episode, are chosen to serve in their stead.[23]

Surprisingly, however, God's proclamation alone does not effect this transfer of spiritual authority. Instead, a concrete procedure must be performed in order to raise the Levites to their new status "in place of every firstborn among the children of Israel."[24]

God firsts instructs Moshe to conduct a census of all firstborn male Israelites and to reconcile the results with an earlier census of the male Levites. When a surplus of 273 firstborn Israelites is determined, God further commands Moshe to collect a redemption of 1,365 shekels from the firstborn, five shekels apiece for each of their number who does not have a corresponding Levi to "take his place."

Why, however, is this redemption ritual necessary at all? Why can't the transfer of spiritual authority to the Levites be effected simply through God's pronouncement?

By demanding this concrete ritual of transfer, it would seem, God consciously conveys a critical message: The mitzva of serving within the Temple can be broken down into the twin components of *opportunity* and *obligation*. *Opportunity can be forfeited, but obligation cannot.*

The firstborn, therefore, having lost the *opportunity of ritual authority*, must still reckon with the *remaining obligation*. Each firstborn Israelite male must ensure that a Levi takes his place in the Temple and, when that proves impossible, must find another way to contribute to the service.

H

We can now begin, perhaps, to understand Moshe's decisions as, on the very border of the Promised Land, he confronts the proposal of the tribes of Reuven and Gad. Standing before him, he realizes, are individuals voluntarily forfeiting their *opportunity* to inherit the land even as they pledge to fulfill, in large measure, their *obligation* towards that effort.

Moshe quickly recognizes the overwhelmingly delicate dilemma before him. *Opportunity*, he realizes, *cannot be forced*. Perhaps, in his mind's eye, Moshe searches for and finds halachic precedents of voluntarily forfeited opportunity. The law, for example, of the *eved Ivri*,

---

23. Bamidbar Rabba 3:3.
24. Bamidbar 20:41.

the Hebrew indentured servant who, opting to remain in servitude after his mandated tenure, must undergo a ritual designed to convince him of the error of his choice. Tellingly, the law attempts to *convince* rather than *command* the slave to choose freedom.[25] The *eved*'s opportunity for freedom cannot be mandated; it must be chosen freely (see *Shmot*: Mishpatim, *Approaches* II F).

Moshe must therefore proceed cautiously. Any attempt to force the tribes of Reuven and Gad to take an opportunity that they are determined to forfeit will backfire and may well catalyze the national rebellion that Moshe desperately fears (see above). He must, instead, attempt to convince these tribes to voluntarily reconsider their decisions.

Step by step, Moshe sets out to reshape the mindset of the tribes of Reuven and Gad, hoping against hope that he will, in the process, convince them to reverse their decision to stay outside the land. His efforts, however, fall short. While he successfully moves them to address, piecemeal, basic errors in their own perspective, their global plan nevertheless remains intact. The tribes of Reuven and Gad remain committed to fulfilling much of their *obligation* towards the conquest of Canaan. Tragically, however, they also insist on forgoing the historic *opportunity* that lies immediately before them: the opportunity to join their brothers in settling the land.

Points to Ponder

How little has changed....

The centuries-old failure of the tribes of Reuven and Gad, in full sight of their intended goal, speaks volumes to us concerning the causes of personal failure in our own lives. We often seem to fall short of our own goals for the same reasons that the two tribes fell short of theirs.

1. *Mistaken priorities.* An anonymous cleric once observed: "I have never encountered an individual who, on his deathbed, bemoaned: *I wish I had spent more time in the office*...."

Regretfully, for many of us, such recognition arrives only in retrospect. Day after day, our drive towards personal success and professional advancement regularly overwhelms our attempts to carve out time for ourselves and our families. Whatever scarce downtime we do have is marred by the demands created by instant accessibility. We become as

---

25. Shmot 21:5–7; Talmud Bavli Kiddushin 22b.

available as the closest handheld device, expected to answer an e-mail, text or call, under all circumstances and at a moment's notice. In spite of our good intentions, we inevitably find ourselves giving "pens for our livestock" precedence over "cities for our children."

To compensate for this lack of availability to our families, today's society has popularized the notion of "quality time." *Quality, we reason, is better than quantity. I can't be with my family often but I can at least ensure that the limited time we spend together is filled with value and experience.*

While such planned experiences are certainly worthwhile, however, *what our loved ones need most from us is not quality time, but time, period.* We can never know when a critical moment will arise; when a parent's spontaneous observation will shape a child's perspective; when a child's question will launch a significant discussion; when a shared instant will unexpectedly become a seminal event. In our own memories, it is often the unanticipated event that leaves the greatest impact: the stolen moment, the snow day off from school, the pickup game in the backyard, the unplanned bedtime story.

Given that we cannot predict which moment of our shared lives will be important, the better part of wisdom dictates that we optimize our opportunities. *The more time we spend in the company of those we care about, the greater the chance that we will be there when it matters.*

2. *A missing God.* The absence of God from Reuven's and Gad's calculations concerning the conquest of Canaan also strikingly foreshadows challenging patterns in our own time.

As the State of Israel has matured, she has becomes a state like all others, replete with her own faults and flaws. And, as the drama of Israel's birth and early years has receded with time, new generations of Israelis have emerged who do not automatically share the idealism of their parents and grandparents. Increasingly disillusioned by the shortcomings they see in those around them and influenced by the development of post-Zionist ideology, many of these young Israelis have understandably begun to question the need for the constant struggle and deep sacrifice that is required from those living in today's Jewish homeland. *Why, after all, is a Jewish state necessary? Why risk our lives for a nationalistic enterprise? Why not live elsewhere, where life is easier and the threat of terror and war does not cast a pall over each passing day?*

While diaspora Jews certainly have no right to criticize personal decisions made by specific Israelis, we certainly can note with interest the one Israeli population that has, in large measure, retained the Zionist fervor that marked the founding of the Jewish state. The Religious Zionist community certainly struggles with challenges of its own, yet maintains an unabated belief in the Zionist enterprise and an unyielding commitment to the building of a strong Jewish homeland. To the Religious Zionist, the return to Zion is much more than another nationalistic endeavor. It is a reflection of God's will and the fulfillment of an age-old dream kept alive across centuries of difficult diaspora wanderings.

Perhaps the most significant evidence of the commitment of this community to the State of Israel can be seen in the overwhelmingly disproportionate number of religious officers in the Israel Defense Forces. Although Religious Zionists constitute only 8 percent of the overall Jewish population in Israel, figures released by the IDF's Human Resources Department in 2008 indicate that a full 60 percent of officers in the Israeli army are followers of Religious Zionism. The numbers climb to 70 percent in the infantry brigades and to 75 percent in the special fighting units.

This phenomenon, to be sure, is not without its own accompanying challenges. The Religious Zionist movement's general commitment to Eretz Yisrael Hashleima, the whole Land of Israel (including the West Bank), inevitably brings this community into sharp conflict with those in the government and in the general population of Israel who are willing to consider the ceding of land as part of a potential peace agreement with the Palestinian Arabs. Such tensions have already surfaced dramatically, with the evacuation of Gaza serving as a deeply traumatic event for the Religious Zionist movement.

These issues aside, however, the facts seem clear. Absent a spiritual dimension, the Zionist enterprise, like all national movements, runs the real risk of weakening over time. In addition, as the spirit of the nation wanes, a growing number of Israelis may well find the personal cost of perpetuating the Zionist dream too dear.

In the face of these realities, the place of the Religious Zionist community in Israel (and, to a lesser extent, in the diaspora, as well) has never been more critical. More than ever, this community is challenged to build bridges to a surrounding population, educating them to the spiritual foundations that lie at the core of the historical return to Zion.

Absent God, the settling of Canaan was readily rejected by the tribes of Reuven and Gad. Absent God, the State of Israel runs the tragic risk of becoming a state like any other state, potentially rejected when memory fades and the going gets tough.

3. *Opportunity and obligation*. Finally, the forfeiture of opportunity on the part of the tribes of Reuven and Gad at the dawn of Jewish history speaks volumes to us about similar forfeitures in our own lives.

This narrative, for example, certainly challenges a diaspora Jewish community living at a time when the Promised Land, after thousands of years of wandering, is fully "in our sight." Will we, like the tribes of Reuven and Gad, remain on the periphery of Jewish experience as the focus of our history shifts back to the Land of Israel? Will we and our children forfeit the opportunity to live in the land of our ancestors, an opportunity for which our people have prayed for centuries? Regardless of our excuses and rationalizations, upon such forfeiture, how will history judge us?

More generally, the story of the tribes of Reuven and Gad raises important questions concerning our attitude towards religious practice as a whole. Too often, even among observant Jews, the performance of mitzvot is perceived in terms of *obligation* rather than *opportunity*. Daily practice becomes rote and automatic, with little thought given as to how that performance is meant to shape, enhance and enrich our lives. The opportunity presented by daily prayer, for example, for self-reflection and communion with the Divine; the opportunity presented by Shabbat for spiritual replenishment and the gaining of personal perspective; the opportunity presented by the festivals for reconnection with eternal ideals are just a few of the countless examples of opportunities missed when we fail to appreciate the rich rewards of meaningful, thoughtful Jewish observance.

In remarks on the evening of November 13, 2011, upon being honored by Yeshiva University for fifty years of service to the Jewish community, HaRav Aharon Lichtenstein, Rosh Yeshiva of Yeshivat Har Etzion and one of the preeminent thinkers of today's Modern Orthodox community, spoke eloquently of the balance between obligation and opportunity in Jewish life. He noted that Judaism gives the lie to the philosophy of Kant, who maintains that "that which is normative cannot bring joy and that which is joyous cannot be normative."

Citing the three blessings concerning Torah study recited each day at the opening of the daily prayer service, Rabbi Lichtenstein described these blessings as creating a balance between the requisite sense of obligation towards Torah study and the sweet, joyous satisfaction that is meant to be derived from such study. "What greater opportunity is there in life," this scholar declared, "than to be an *oved Hashem*, a servant of the Lord!"

At its deepest level, the failure of the tribes of Reuven and Gad on the very border of the Promised Land serves as a cautionary tale, reminding us of the tragic results when we lose sight of the opportunities before us, inherent in each aspect of our lives as Jews.

4 In Retrospect: A Troubling Travelogue

Context
Parshat Masei, the final parsha in the book of Bamidbar, opens with a retrospective listing of the forty-two stations that marked the Israelites' wilderness wanderings.[1]

Questions
What is the purpose of this after-the-fact travelogue? Why is this dry, technical information included in the eternal Torah text?

What possible lessons can be derived from this forty-nine-sentence itinerary?

Approaches

— A —

The severity of these questions is, apparently, so deeply felt by the Ibn Ezra that he feels compelled to offer a revolutionary suggestion. *The inclusion of the itinerary in the Torah was not "God's idea."* Commenting on the passage's introductory statement, "And Moshe wrote their goings forth, stage by stage, by the commandment of the Lord,"[2] the Ibn Ezra explains that the phrase "by the commandment of the Lord" refers to the travels themselves (and not to their recording in the text by Moshe).

Towards the end of the Israelites' forty-year period of wilderness wandering, this scholar maintains, the Israelites encamp for a number of months in the plains of Moab, departing only upon Aharon's death. During that time, *apparently of his own volition* and for his own unstated purposes, Moshe records in retrospect the details of the Israelites'

---
1. Bamidbar 33:1–49.
2. Ibid., 33:2.

wilderness journeys, which had all taken place "by the commandment of the Lord."[3]

B

The vast majority of scholars, including the Ramban[4] and the Abravanel,[5] however, take serious issue with the Ibn Ezra's approach. Moshe, these authorities maintain, would never have recorded this detailed travelogue in the Torah of his own initiative. The very idea that Moshe could independently amend the text undermines our understanding of the Torah as "God's word." Additionally, the Torah does not need to tell us that the Israelites' wilderness journeys took place by God's commandment. This fact has already been clearly established in the text (see Beha'alotcha 2).

These scholars insist, therefore, in direct opposition to the Ibn Ezra, that the Torah specifically informs us that Moshe *recorded the itinerary* at God's behest. Representing this viewpoint, the Rambam asserts that the phrase "by the commandment of the Lord" is designed to emphasize the divine origin of a passage that we might have otherwise found "useless."[6]

Like every other section of the Torah, these scholars maintain, the retrospective travelogue at the beginning of Parshat Masei is part of God's message to His people. Confronted with this puzzling textual passage, we are tasked to uncover its divinely determined purpose.

C

Rising to this challenge, the authorities suggest a number of approaches to this section of text.

To cite a few…

In an opinion quoted in Rashi, Rabbi Moshe Hadarshan notes that the recorded route attests to God's benevolence even in the realm of punishment. Although God, in response to the sin of the spies, had condemned the nation to forty years of wandering in the wilderness, the Israelites' "wandering" was actually severely curtailed. Only forty-two stations are listed in the itinerary. Of these stations, fourteen served as

---

3. Ibn Ezra, Bamidbar 33:1–2.
4. Ramban, Bamidbar 33:1–2.
5. Abravanel, Bamidbar 33:1.
6. Rambam, *Moreh Nevuchim* 3:50.

stopping points during the first year after the Exodus, before the divine decree, while another eight stations were visited during the final year, before entry into the land. *Over the span of thirty-eight years, therefore, a total of only twenty journeys took place.* The Israelites' wilderness experience was remarkably stable in spite of its tragic origins.[7]

Like Rabbi Moshe HaDarshan, the Ba'al Akeida discerns indications of God's compassion within the retrospective itinerary. This scholar maintains, however, that the considerations described are specific, rather than general. Each station listed in the text references a particular divine act of kindness bestowed on the people, from the elaborate details of the Exodus to the many miracles that sustained the nation during its wanderings.[8]

Going one step further, the Tosafists detect a halachic purpose to this section of text. Jewish law obligates an individual, upon encountering a location where divine miracles occurred, to recite the blessing "Blessed art Thou, Lord our God, King of the universe, Who performed a miracle for my forebears at this place."[9] In order to facilitate the fulfillment of this obligation, the Torah now records the locations in the wilderness where such miracles transpired.[10]

Moving in a totally different direction, the Sforno argues that the wilderness itinerary does not extol God's allegiance to the Israelites but, instead, the Israelites' allegiance to God. For four decades, the people traveled at God's behest, through stark, barren terrain, moving from station to station without prior knowledge of their immediate destination. This loyalty to God's wishes now earns the nation the right to enter the Promised Land.[11]

— **D** —

The most direct explanation for the inclusion of the Israelites' wilderness itinerary in the text, however, is suggested by the Rambam in his *Guide to the Perplexed*. The Rambam maintains that this passage plays a critical role in establishing the veracity of the Torah's narrative. With the passage

---

7. Rashi, Bamidbar 33:1.
8. Akeidat Yitzchak, Bamidbar, sha'ar 86.
9. Rambam, *Mishneh Torah*, Hilchot Brachot 10:9.
10. Quoted in Nachshoni, *Hagot B'parshiot HaTorah*, vol. 2, p. 704.
11. Sforno, Bamidbar 33:1.

of time, the Rambam suggests, doubts could easily develop concerning the authenticity of the miracles that marked the nation's travels:

> Miracles are only convincing to those who witnessed them, while coming generations, who know of them only from the account given by others, may consider them as untrue….
>
> The greatest of the miracles described in the Law is the stay of the Israelites in the wilderness for forty years, sustained by the daily supply of [the heaven-sent] manna….
>
> God, however, knew that, in the future, people might doubt the veracity of these miracles…they might think that the Israelites remained in the wilderness in a place not far from inhabited land, where it was possible to live [in the ordinary way]…or that they could plow, sow and reap, or live on vegetation [naturally growing along the route]; or that the manna came down regularly in those locations as an ordinary natural product; or that there were wells of water [along the route]….
>
> In order to remove all these doubts, and to firmly establish the accuracy of the account of these miracles, Scripture enumerates all the stations [that marked the journey of the Israelites], so that the coming generations may see them and learn the greatness of the miracle[s] that enabled human beings to live in these places for forty years.[12]

By carefully describing the route followed by the nation during their extended wilderness travels, a passage through barren wasteland that could only be survived through miraculous intervention, the Torah buttresses its own narrative concerning God's miraculous care for the nation during their wilderness wanderings.

— E —

A striking observation offered by the Malbim grants a final perspective on the wilderness itinerary recorded at the beginning of Parshat Masei. This scholar notes that the parsha opens with the statement "These are

---

12. Rambam, *Moreh Nevuchim* 3:50.

the journeys of the children of Israel who went out of the land of Egypt according to their legions...."[13]

As a rule, the Malbim maintains, a journey is defined by its *destination*, not by its *point of departure*. Why, then, does the Torah describe the Israelites' journey by the fact that they "went out of the land of Egypt" and not as a journey "towards the land of Canaan."

Incisively, the Malbim argues that the wilderness journey of the Israelites *could not* be defined as a journey towards Canaan. Arrival at the border of Canaan could have been, and initially had been, accomplished without passage along this tortuous route. Instead, the lengthy wilderness sojourn was specifically designed to "take the Israelites out of Egypt," to purify the people from the defiling effects of centuries of servitude and immersion in Egyptian culture.

> For this reason, He caused them [the Israelites] to wander in the wilderness; and they underwent numerous tribulations and were tested with numerous trials and experienced refinement after refinement, until they were purified and exchanged their "soiled garments" for "sanctified vestments" of pure and holy character....[14]

Each step of the Israelites' carefully recorded journey is designed to move the nation one step further from Egypt, to further complete their transformation from servile slaves into a nation worthy of its destiny. It is this journey of the spirit, described in a detailed itinerary as the book of Bamidbar begins to close, that defines the entire book in retrospect.

---

13. Bamidbar 33:1.
14. Malbim, Bamidbar 33:1.

Sources

Abravanel – Rabbi Don Yitzchak Abravanel; biblical commentator, philosopher, statesman, diplomat (Portugal, Spain, Italy, 1437–1508).

The last great figure of Spanish Jewry, the Abravanel served during his lifetime as finance minister to the kings of Portugal, Spain and Italy. The Abravanel used his high position and great wealth to benefit his brethren and spared no effort in petitioning the Spanish king and queen, at the time of the Spanish Inquisition, to reverse the edict banishing the Jews from Spain. Failing in that effort, the Abravanel himself suffered expulsion in 1492 with the rest of the exiles.

The Abravanel authored many works including major commentaries on the Torah, other books of Tanach, *Pirkei Avot*, the Haggada and the Rambam's *Guide to the Perplexed*. His commentaries are divided into chapters, each of which is introduced by the list of questions and problems which he intends to address in the chapter. The Abravanel often applied the lessons learned from Scripture to issues confronting the Jewish society of his day.

Albo, Yosef – Rabbi, philosopher, preacher (Spain, circa 1380–1444).

A student of Rabbi Chasdai Crescas, one of the leaders of the Jewish community in Christian Spain, Albo is best known for his major work, *Sefer Ha'ikkarim*, the Book of Principles. In this treatise, Albo critiques earlier attempts, such as that of the Rambam, to identify the fundamental principles of Jewish faith. Albo suggests his own formulation, reducing Jewish dogma to three basic principles from which, he claims, all else flows: the existence of God, divine revelation at Sinai, and reward and punishment.

While many details of Albo's personal life remain unclear, his participation in specific events is recorded. He played a prominent role in the Disputation of Tortosa (1413–14) and was still active in 1433, when he delivered a sermon at a circumcision.

Alshich, Moshe – Rabbi, scholar, halachist, commentator (Turkey, Israel, Syria, 1508–1593).

Born in Adrianople, Turkey, the Alshich emigrated at a young age to Tzfat, Israel, where he studied under and was ordained by Rabbi Yosef Caro. The

Alshich gained such prominence as a teacher, orator, halachic authority and communal leader that he was granted the title *Hakadosh* (the holy one), a title reserved for a few select rabbinic figures across Jewish history. The Alshich's last years were spent in Damascus, Syria.

Among other works, the Alshich published volumes of his popular lectures and sermons relating to various sections of Tanach (Torah, Prophets and Writings). Particularly noteworthy is his commentary on the Torah, *Torat Moshe*, which follows a homiletic approach and is filled with practical lessons on ethics and morals.

Ba'al Ha'Akeida – Rabbi Yitzchak ben Moshe Arama; biblical commentator, Talmudic scholar, rabbi (Spain, 1420–1494).

Yitzchak ben Shlomo Arama served as the principal of a rabbinical academy at Zamosa and as rabbi of the communities of Tarragon, Fraya and Calatayud. He is most well known for his lengthy philosophical commentary on the Torah, *Akeidat Yitzchak*, which earned him the title Ba'al Ha'Akeida (author of the Akeida). This work consists of 105 "portals," each of which contains two sections: *derisha* (investigation) and *perisha* (exposition). In the first of these two sections, Arama examines a philosophical idea reflected in his chosen text. He then, in the second section, uses this philosophical idea to address and solve problems in the text itself.

The skillful manner in which Arama joins these two sections creates the template for Jewish preaching across the ages.

Ba'al Haturim – Rabbi Yaakov ben Asher; halachist, Talmudic scholar, biblical commentator (Spain, 1270–1340).

Third son of the major Talmudic commentator Rabbi Asher ben Yechiel (the Rosh), the Ba'al Haturim emerged to make towering contributions of his own to Jewish scholarship. His greatest work was the *Arba Turim* (Four Rows), a pivotal codification of practical Jewish law that continues to serve a basic text for the study of halacha to this day. This code was divided into four basic sections and was the precursor of Rabbi Yosef Caro's *Shulchan Aruch*.

The Ba'al Haturim wrote a comprehensive commentary to the Torah in which he included explanations from the works of previous scholars such as Rashi, Ramban, Radak, Ibn Ezra and others. To whet the reader's interest, he prefaced each section of this commentary with an "appetizer" – a segment featuring *gematria* (observations based on the assignment of numerical value to the letters of the text), acronyms and other symbolic references. In an ironic twist of fate, these "appetizers" captured popular attention and have been preserved and published to this day as a separate commentary in the Ba'al Haturim's name.

Babad, Yosef – Rabbi, Talmudic scholar, halachic authority (Poland, 1800–1874).

Few life details are known concerning Babad, who served as a rabbi in several cities in Galicia before being appointed chief of the rabbinic court in Tarnopol in 1857.

His primary work was the renowned *Minchat Chinuch*, a major commentary and expansion on the *Sefer Hachinuch*.

Bass, Shabbetai ben Yosef – Biblical and Talmudic scholar, bibliographer, printer (Poland, Czechoslovakia, Germany, Holland, 1641–1718).

Following the murder of his parents in a pogrom in Kalisz, Poland, Bass and his elder brother fled to Prague. There he received both a thorough Talmudic and general education and was appointed bass singer (hence his name) in the renowned Altneu Shul of Prague.

Bass's love of books drew him to publishing and printing. Between 1674 and 1679, he visited libraries in Poland, Germany and Holland, stopping in various centers of Jewish scholarship. In Amsterdam he studied the art of printing and proofreading and published a series of works, including his renowned supercommentary on Rashi, the *Siftei Chachamim*, as well as a Hebrew bibliography of twenty-two hundred Judaic works, citing books, authors, contents, format and place and year of printing. Subsequently, Bass established a successful printing press in Dyhernfurth, Germany, but was plagued by a series of misfortunes including anti-Semitic accusations that led to his brief arrest. The last years of his life were devoted to the second edition of his bibliographical material, which he never completed.

Caro, Yosef – Hamechaber (the author); scholar, halachist, author of the *Shulchan Aruch* (Set table), the universally accepted, authoritative code of Jewish law (Spain and/or Portugal, Turkey, Israel, 1488–1575).

Born either in Spain or Portugal, Caro fled to Turkey with his family upon the expulsion of Jews from Portugal, in 1497. Living successively in the cities of Istanbul, Adrianople, Nikopol and Salonika, Caro studied with numerous scholars, many of whom shaped his mystical life perspective.

In 1522, at the age of thirty-four, Caro began to write his monumental *Beit Yosef*, a project which would occupy him for twenty years and which he concluded only after moving to Tzfat, Israel. With this work, Caro strove to create order out of the multiplicity of codes and halachic rulings that had developed in Jewish law over the centuries. Caro traced each law to its origins, discussed the law's development through an analysis of divergent opinions and rendered authoritative practical rulings. In order to avoid unnecessary duplication, Caro fashioned the *Beit Yosef* as a commentary to the *Arba Turim* of Rabbi Yaakov ben Asher.

While the *Beit Yosef* was considered by Caro to be his most important scholarly writing, it is the more succinct digest of that work, the *Shulchan Aruch*, for which this scholar is eventually immortalized. The *Shulchan Aruch*, with its ordered, succinct presentation of practical Jewish law, quickly became the authoritative legal code for world Jewry and the point of departure for halachic works that followed.

Among Caro's other contributions was the *Kesef Mishneh*, an extensive commentary on the Rambam's *Mishneh Torah*.

Chaifetz, Rabbi Moshe – Teacher, philosopher, poet (Italy, 1663–1711).

Born in Trieste, Chaifetz moved to Venice, where he earned his livelihood as a private tutor. He was proficient in areas of Jewish scholarship as well as in mathematics, philosophy and the natural sciences.

In addition to poetry, Chaifetz's major work was a philosophical commentary on the Torah, *Melechet Machshevet*. He also wrote *Chanukat HaBayit*, a volume dealing with the construction of the Second Temple.

Chatam Sofer – Rabbi Moshe ben Shmuel Sofer; rabbinic leader, Talmudic scholar, halachist, biblical commentator (Germany, Hungary, 1762–1839).

A child prodigy, the Chatam Sofer entered yeshiva at the age of nine and was delivering public lectures by the age of thirteen. After years of intensive study, he assumed rabbinic and teaching positions in several communities before accepting, in 1807, his primary position in Pressburg, Hungary. There he established a major yeshiva which housed, at its height, five hundred students, many of whom went on to become influential leaders in their own right.

Reacting to the newly developing Reform movement, the Chatam Sofer vehemently opposed any changes or innovations in Jewish practice. He is considered by many to be one of the most influential figures in the development of Chareidi Judaism (the most theologically conservative form of Orthodox Judaism today). The Chatam Sofer authored numerous important responsa (answers to halachic questions) as well as oft-studied commentaries on the Torah and Talmud, including *Chatam Sofer al HaTorah* and *Torat Moshe*.

Chizkuni – Rabbi Chizkiya ben Manoach Chizkuni; biblical commentator (France, thirteenth century).

Almost nothing is known about the personal life of the Chizkuni, a classical biblical commentator who lived in Provence around the year 1250. The Chizkuni's commentary, which focuses on the *pshat* (simple meaning) of the text, is based, according to the author, upon a number of earlier sources. In particular, the Chizkuni often elaborates upon the observations of Rashi.

The commentary of the Chizkuni first appeared in print in Venice in 1524.

Da'at Zekeinim Miba'alei Hatosafot – A compilation of Torah commentary authored by the Tosafists (a large group of twelfth- to thirteenth-century medieval rabbis whose critical and explanatory glosses are basic to the study of Talmud).

The period of the Tosafists began after the completion of Rashi's commentaries; the first Tosafists were actually Rashi's sons-in-law and grandsons. The Talmudic commentaries of the Tosafists are characterized by lengthy analyses of difficult passages and by a willingness to critically review the positions of their predecessors, particularly Rashi.

Preserved in manuscript for centuries, the *Da'at Zekeinim Miba'alei Hatosafot* was first formally published in 1783.

Epstein, Baruch Halevi – Commentator, scholar, author (Russia, 1860–1942).

The son of Yechiel Michel Epstein, Baruch Halevi studied under the tutelage of both his father and his uncle, the Netziv.

Although he was offered numerous rabbinic positions in such major centers as Pinsk, Moscow and Petrograd, Epstein opted to earn his livelihood as a bookkeeper and to devote his free time to Torah study. The author of numerous volumes, he is best known for his monumental *Torah Temima*. In this work, he connects passages of the Talmud and Midrash to their sources in the written text and comments extensively on the topics they raise.

Feinstein, Moshe – Reb Moshe; rabbi, preeminent Torah sage and halachic authority of the twentieth century (Russia, America, 1895–1986).

After serving as rabbi of Luban (near Minsk) for sixteen years, Reb Moshe immigrated to the United States in 1937. Settling in the Lower East Side, where he remained for the rest of his life, he assumed the position of rosh yeshiva at Mesivta Tiferes Yerushalayim. Under his guidance, this institution became a leading American yeshiva.

Reb Moshe was regarded by most leading rabbinic contemporaries as the *Gadol Hador*, the greatest Torah stage of his generation, and his decisions on Jewish law were accepted as authoritative by Orthodox Jews throughout the world. He played a major role in defining the continuing interface between halacha and issues of modernity, rendering decisions on a wide range of issues including artificial insemination, transplantation surgery, end-of-life medical care, abortion, financial ethics, business and labor disputes, etc.

Close to two thousand of Reb Moshe's responsa are contained in *Igrot Moshe*, a multivolume work arranged according to the sections of the *Shulchan Aruch*. His commentary on the Torah was published posthumously under the title *Darash Moshe*.

Hacohen, Meir Simcha of Dvinsk – Rabbi, talmudic scholar, biblical commentator (Latvia, Lithuania, 1843–1926).

Renowned as a brilliant Talmudic scholar and beloved as a compassionate leader, Rabbi Meir Simcha served as rabbi of the city of Dvinsk for forty years. In 1906 he turned down a rabbinic position in Jerusalem as a result of the entreaties of the Dvinsk community who argued that his departure would "destroy" not only their community but the entire diaspora. During World War I when most of the Jewish community fled Dvinsk, leaving behind only the poorest inhabitants, Rabbi Meir Simcha remained, declaring that as long as there were nine Jews in the city he would be the tenth.

Among his most important works were the *Meshech Chochma* and *Ohr Sameach*, commentaries on the Torah and on the Rambam's *Mishneh Torah*, respectively.

Hirsch, Shimshon Raphael – Rabbi, biblical commentator, rabbinic leader, philosopher (Germany, 1808–1888).

In the wake of the emancipation, traditional Judaism was desperately in need of a powerful leader to guide the transition of Orthodoxy into a new world marked by greater freedom. Rabbi Shimshon Raphael Hirsch successfully filled that role.

In 1851, Hirsch relinquished a prominent rabbinic post to become the rabbi of eleven individuals who had separated from the general community of Frankfurt am Main in response to that community's shift towards Reform Judaism. From those humble beginnings, Hirsch built a model Orthodox community of five hundred members.

Hirsch developed a philosophy of *Torah im Derech Eretz* (lit.: Torah and the way of the land) which envisioned a relationship between traditional observant Judaism and the modern world. Much controversy exists today as to the exact dimensions of the relationship envisioned by Hirsch. There is no question, however, that Hirsch's contributions were instrumental in the development of German Orthodox Jewry and paved the way for the development of today's Modern Orthodox community throughout the Jewish world. Hirsch published many works including *Nineteen Letters*, in which he brilliantly responds to the major philosophical questions of his day; *Horeb*, a text outlining his approach to Jewish belief and practice; and an extensive, thought-provoking commentary on the Torah.

Ibn Ezra – Rabbi Avraham ben Meir Ibn Ezra; biblical commentator, philosopher, poet, grammarian, physician, astronomer/astrologer (Spain, Egypt, North Africa, Italy, France, England, Israel, 1092–1167).

Over the course of an impoverished and itinerant life, the Ibn Ezra made a profound contribution to Jewish scholarship. A prolific poet, the Ibn Ezra produced treatises on Hebrew grammar, mathematics, astronomy/astrology and philosophy.

The Ibn Ezra's greatest contribution, however, was made through his renowned commentary on the Torah and other books of Tanach (an acronym for the biblical canon – Torah, Nevi'im, Ketuvim: the five books of Moses, the Prophets and the Writings). This work, which inspired numerous supercommentaries, is singular for its strong use of grammatical principles to uncover the *pshat* of the text. While the Ibn Ezra's commentary included a great deal of exegetical material authored by his predecessors, he did not shy away from offering his own original observations.

Jacob, Benno – Rabbi, biblical commentator (1862–1955).

Born in Breslau, Jacob attended the gymnasium, university and theological seminary of his native town, earning his PhD in 1889. He served as rabbi in Gottingen from 1891 to 1929 after which he retired to Hamburg to concentrate on his writing.

Jacob's biblical commentary is noteworthy for its use of literary analysis and modern scholarship.

Kli Yakar – Rabbi Ephraim Shlomo ben Chaim of Luntshitz; *dayan*, biblical commentator, orator (Poland, Bohemia, 1550–1619).

At an early age, the Kli Yakar earned a reputation as a spellbinding speaker and traveled in that capacity through numerous cities and towns. Subsequently, he served as rosh yeshiva and *av beit din* (head of the Jewish court) in Prague.

His renowned commentary on the Torah, the *Kli Yakar*, is largely homiletic in style.

Ktav Sofer – Rabbi Shmuel Binyamin Sofer; rabbi, rosh yeshiva, commentator (Hungary, 1815–1871).

Oldest son of the famed Chatam Sofer and grandson, on his mother's side, of the renowned Rabbi Akiva Eiger; the Ktav Sofer succeeded his father in 1839, at the age of 24, as the rabbi of Pressburg, Hungary, and as the rosh yeshiva of the famed Pressburg Yeshiva.

Serving as rabbi of Pressburg for thirty-three years, the exact number of years that his father had served before him, the Ktav Sofer followed his father's legacy of opposition to radical change as he preached strict adherence to the tenets and practices of traditional Judaism. In 1868, the long nascent conflict between the Hungarian Orthodox and Reform Jews finally erupted at a Jewish congress convened in Budapest. As a result, largely under the leadership of the Ktav Sofer, a separate Orthodox community was established.

The Ktav Sofer authored a commentary on the Torah as well as volumes of responsa and Talmudic commentary all under the title *Ktav Sofer* (by which the author himself became known).

Leibowitz, Dr. Nehama – Biblical scholar and commentator, teacher (Israel, 1905–1997).

Born in Riga, Latvia, Nehama Leibowitz was awarded a doctorate from the University of Berlin in 1930 and emigrated that same year to the British Mandate of Palestine. Over the course of her career, Leibowitz taught for decades at a Religious Zionist teachers seminary, lectured at Tel Aviv University, where she was appointed full professor, delivered regular radio addresses on Voice of Israel radio and lectured in a multitude of settings throughout the country.

Leibowitz is best known for her *gilyonot* (lit.: pages), stencils on the weekly Torah reading which she distributed to all interested. Her incisive analytical approach to text made these *gilyonot* immensely popular and through their distribution she rekindled intense interest in the study of biblical text and commentary throughout the Jewish world. Later Leibowitz produced formal studies, which were eventually collected into books on the Torah. Leibowitz was awarded the Israel Prize for education in 1957.

Levi Yitzchak of Berdichev – The Kedushat Levi; rabbi, Chassidic master (Poland, Ukraine, circa 1740–1810).

One of the most famous personalities in the third generation of the Chassidic movement, Rabbi Levi Yitzchak was born into a distinguished rabbinic family in Galicia. After his marriage, he moved to his father-in-law's home in Lubartow, Poland, where he was introduced to Chassidism by Rabbi Shmuel Shmelke Horowitz of Nikolsburg. In 1766, Rabbi Levi Yitzchak went to study under Rabbi Dov Ber, the Maggid of Mezritch, becoming one of his closest disciples.

After serving in a number of prior rabbinic posts, Rabbi Levi Yitzchak became rabbi in Berdichev in the Ukraine in 1785, where he remained until his death. There he earned great renown as a rabbi, Chassidic master and scholar.

Rabbi Levi Yitzchak was known for his singular love of the Jewish people and for his stress upon ecstasy and joy in prayer and in the performance of mitzvot. His work *Kedushat Levi* – on the Torah, festivals, *Pirkei Avot* and other topics – is considered one of the essential works of Chassidic literature.

Luzzatto, Shmuel David – Shadal; philosopher, scholar, biblical commentator, poet (Italy, 1800–1865).

Over the course of a prolific literary career, Luzzatto produced a great number of works in both Hebrew and Italian including a commentary on the Torah, commentaries on numerous books of the Prophets, a treatise on Hebrew grammar, a guide to the understanding of Targum Onkelos, essays and poems.

While deeply traditional, Luzzatto was unafraid to challenge established ideas. He subjected the commentary of the Ibn Ezra to scathing attack and, while he greatly admired the Rambam for the latter's halachic contributions, he did not hesitate to criticize that great scholar for adopting elements of Aristotelian philosophy.

In 1829, Luzzatto was appointed professor at the rabbinical college of Padua. He contributed to most of the Jewish periodicals of his time, corresponded voluminously with contemporaries and wrote on an extremely wide range of Jewish topics.

Maharal – Rabbi Yehuda Loew; rabbi, Talmudic scholar, philosopher, commentator (Poland, Bohemia, 1525–1609).

Born to a noble family that traces its lineage to King David, the Maharal was one of the most influential Jewish thinkers of the postmedieval period. So expansive was his influence that Rav Avraham Yitzchak Hacohen Kook (the first chief rabbi of Israel) once proclaimed that the Maharal was "the father of the approach of the Vilna Gaon on the one hand and the father of the Chassidic movement on the other."

After serving as rabbi of Nikolsburg in the province of Moravia for twenty years, the Maharal moved to Prague in 1573, there opening a yeshiva and mentoring numerous outstanding disciples. After leaving for a brief period to serve as rabbi in the city of Posen, the Maharal returned to Prague in 1598 to assume the position of chief rabbi.

A renowned educator, the Maharal criticized his contemporaries for not heeding the advice of the Mishna which counsels that children should be taught subjects that are age appropriate. "The fools nowadays," he proclaimed, "teach boys Torah with the commentary of Rashi, which they do not understand and also Talmud which they cannot yet grasp." (The Maharal's supercommentary on Rashi is entitled *Gur Aryeh*.) While clearly rooted in the world of Torah, the Maharal embraced the study of secular subjects, particularly mathematics.

A prolific writer, the Maharal was held in high esteem by Jews and non-Jews alike. His statue was erected in 1917 at the entrance to the province town hall by the municipal authority, and his synagogue, the Altneu Shul, stands to this day.

Maharam of Rothenburg – Rabbi Meir ben Baruch; Talmudic scholar, Tosafist, halachic authority (Germany, France, 1215–1293).

Born in Worms to a family of scholars, Rabbi Meir studied under a series of renowned teachers in Germany and France. In 1242, the public burning of the Talmud in France prompted Rabbi Meir to write an elegy that is included to this day in the Tisha B'Av liturgy.

Returning to Germany, Rabbi Meir settled in Rothenburg, where he remained for more than forty years. Although he held no official communal position outside of Rothenburg, his fame as a Talmudic scholar quickly spread and he became widely known as the greatest scholar of his generation, functionally serving as the halachic "court of appeals" for Germany and surrounding countries. A myriad of questions were addressed to him from communities in Germany, Bohemia, Italy, France and Spain, to which he responded in clear, succinct and lucid style. The importance of these responsa in the formulation of Askenazic law, custom and ritual cannot be overstated.

Rabbi Meir also exerted profound influence upon a large number of illustrious students, including Rabbi Asher ben Yechiel (the Rosh) and Rabbi Asher's son, Yaakov, the author of the halachic compendium the *Arba Turim*. The works of Rabbi Meir and his students were studied thoroughly by later scholars and served as the basis for much of the work of Rabbi Moshe Isserles (the Rema), the author of the Ashkenazic glosses to Rabbi Yosef Caro's *Shulchan Aruch*.

In 1286, outraged at new persecutions of the Jews at the hands of King Rudolf I, Rabbi Meir participated in an exodus from Germany, only to be captured in Lombardy, returned to the king and imprisoned. Numerous attempts on the part of the community to secure his freedom failed and Rabbi Meir tragically died in prison. His body was returned to the community over a decade after his death, and even then, only upon payment of a large ransom.

Malbim – Rabbi Meir Leib ben Yechiel Michael; biblical commentator, community rabbi (Poland, Romania, Russia, 1809–1879).

The Malbim served as the rabbi of a series of prominent communities including Bucharest, where, for a time, he assumed the position of chief rabbi of Romania. The Malbim's strong defense of traditional Judaism and his unwavering opposition to the new rites and practices promulgated by the Reform movement provoked the resentment of many wealthy German Jews. Repeatedly, the Malbim's persecutors managed to instigate his removal from rabbinic positions and, on one occasion, their accusations actually led to his imprisonment.

The Malbim's incisive commentary on the Torah, *Hatorah V'hamitzva*, is noteworthy for projecting the unity of the Written and Oral Law and for its strong foundation in linguistic analysis.

Mecklenberg, Rabbi Yaakov Tzvi – Rabbi, biblical commentator (East Prussia, 1785–1865).

Mecklenberg began his rabbinic career in 1829 when he became the assistant to the rabbi of Koenigsberg, the capital of the German province of East Prussia. In 1831, he graduated to the role of rabbi and remained in that position until the day he died.

Mecklenberg's major work was *Haktav V'hakabala*, a commentary on the Torah which stressed the indivisibility of the Written and Oral Law. Responding to the emerging claims of the Haskala (Enlightenment) movement that the traditional explanations of the Torah were outdated and far-fetched, Mecklenberg demonstrated the authentic textual and linguistic basis for traditional interpretation.

Midrash Hagadol – Collection of Midrashim compiled in the late thirteenth century by the Yemenite scholar Rabbi David ben Avraham Adani.

This work, culled from ancient Tannaitic (Mishnaic) sources, was preserved in manuscript for centuries and studied primarily within the Yemenite community. European scholars, within the last 150 years, have printed carefully edited versions of the text. The Midrash Hagadol serves as a significant record of many teachings from the Mishnaic and Talmudic period which are found in no other source.

Midrash Rabba – A collection of Midrashic anthologies on various books of Tanach.

Although the title "Rabba" is shared by all of these anthologies, they are not a cohesive work but a series of Midrashic texts edited in different centuries and in various locales. Bereishit Rabba (Midrash Rabba Bereishit) was compiled in the sixth century and consists of wide-ranging ethical teachings, homilies, maxims, parables and metaphors all connected (albeit sometimes loosely) to the text of Bereishit.

Midrash Tanchuma – A compilation of Midrashim, many of which are ascribed to the Talmudic sage Tanchuma bar Abba.

Rav Tanchuma bar Abba, who lived in Israel during the second half of the fourth century CE, was a student of the renowned sage Rav Huna and a major author of *aggadot* (Midrashic tales). The text ascribed to his name has appeared over the centuries in various versions.

Midreshei Halacha – A group of Tannaitic expositions on the Torah designed to identify the sources of the 613 mitzvot within the Torah text.

In contrast to *Midreshei Aggada* (homiletical Midrashim such as the Midrash Rabba, Midrash Tanchuma, etc.), *Midreshei Halacha* are primarily halachic in purpose. Nonetheless, they contain much aggadic material, as well. While the contents of the *Midreshei Halacha* date to the Mishnaic period, the redaction of the extant texts apparently occurred much later. Numerous theories, in fact, concerning the categorization and dating of these Midrashim have been offered by scholars and historians.

Because practically no halachic legislation derives from the book of Bereishit, *Midreshei Halacha* are only found in connection with the books of Shmot, Vayikra, Bamidbar and Devarim. These Midrashim are referred to by various titles such as *Mechilta*, *Sifra*, *Sifrei* and *Torat Kohanim*.

Mishna – First official written summary of the Oral Law.

The editing of the Mishna by Rabbi Yehuda Hanasi at the end of the second century CE marked a major transformation in the mode of transmission of Jewish tradition. Until this time, the distinction between Written Law (*Torah She'bichtav*) and Oral Law (*Torah She'b'al Peh*) had been studiously maintained, the latter memorized and transmitted verbally across the centuries. Driven by the fear, however, that the Oral Law would be lost if not recorded in writing, Rabbi Yehuda developed the six "orders" of the

Mishna. This pioneering sage, however, preserved the character of the Oral Law by recording the Mishnaic edicts in short, cryptic style which requires immediate further oral explication.

The sages of the Mishna are known as the Tannaim.

Mizrachi, Eliyahu – Talmudic scholar, biblical commentator, rabbi, rosh yeshiva, halachic authority (Turkey, 1450–1526).

Born and educated in Constantinople, Mizrachi rose to become the foremost rabbinic authority in the Ottoman Empire of his day. Mizrachi was firm and unbending in his legal positions and responded to halachic queries addressed to him from far and wide. His grueling daily schedule encompassed communal leadership, the stewardship of a yeshiva, extensive teaching, the rendering of legal decisions and scholarly writing.

In addition to his major achievements in the area of Jewish scholarship and communal leadership, Mizrachi also studied and wrote on secular subjects, particularly mathematics and astronomy.

Mizrachi's crowning achievement – and the project which he personally considered his most important – was his monumental supercommentary on Rashi. This extensive work became the basis for continued study and analysis by later commentaries.

Nachshoni, Yehuda – Contemporary biblical scholar and commentator (Israel).

Nachshoni is the author of one of the most comprehensive works on the weekly parsha, *Hagot B'parshiot HaTorah* (available in an English translation by Shmuel Himelstein: *Studies in the Weekly Parashah: The Classical Interpretations of Major Topics and Themes in the Torah*, ArtScroll Judaica Classics [New York: Mesorah, 1989]). In this work he presents a series of essays on each parsha, raising critical questions and offering a wide array of approaches from the classical to the contemporary.

Netziv – Rabbi Naftali Tzvi Yehuda Berlin; Talmudic scholar, rosh yeshiva, biblical commentator (Poland, Russia, 1817–1893).

For forty years beginning in 1854, the Netziv served as the rosh yeshiva of the Yeshiva of Volozhin. The Netziv's scholarship, coupled with a deep personal love for all of his students, transformed the yeshiva into the largest such institution of its time and a major spiritual center for the Russian Jewish community. His opposition to the secularization of the yeshiva eventually brought him into conflict with government authorities and, according to some versions, led to the yeshiva's closing in 1892 (others suggest that the closure was due to internal upheaval). The Netziv was one of the early supporters of Jewish settlement in the Land of Israel.

Among the Netziv's publications was his popular biblical commentary, the *Ha'ameik Davar*, in which he emphasized the consonance between Talmudic interpretation and the *pshat* of the Torah text.

A son of the Netziv's first marriage was Rabbi Chaim Berlin, who became chief rabbi of Moscow and subsequently chief rabbi of the Ashkenazic community in Yerushalayim; a son of his second marriage was Rabbi Meir Berlin (later Bar-Ilan), a leader of the religious Zionist Mizrachi movement who inspired the creation of Bar-Ilan University (named in his memory).

Ohr Hachaim – Rabbi Chaim Ibn Attar; rabbi, biblical commentator, Talmudic scholar, kabbalist (Morocco, Israel, 1696–1743).

One of the most prominent rabbis in his native land of Morocco, the Ohr Hachaim decided in 1733 to resettle in the Land of Israel. He was, however, detained along the way in Livorno, Italy, by leading members of the Jewish community who established a Talmudic academy for him. Finally arriving in Jerusalem in 1742, the Ohr Hachaim served as the head of the Beit Midrash Knesset Yisrael until his death.

The Ohr Hachaim's commentary on the Torah combines textual analysis with Talmudic and kabbalistic insights. Over the years, this commentary has become particularly popular within the Sephardic and Chassidic communities.

Onkelos – Convert to Judaism, scholar and author of the seminal Aramaic translation of the Torah, Targum Onkelos (Rome, Israel, 35–120 CE).

According to tradition, Onkelos was the nephew of the Roman emperor Titus (who, as a general, was responsible for the destruction of the Second Temple).

After his conversion, Onkelos authored Targum Onkelos, a monumental interpretive translation of the Torah into Aramaic. This translation, which received the approbation of Onkelos' teachers, the Mishnaic scholars Rabbi Eliezer and Rabbi Yehoshua, offers striking insights into the text. So authoritative did this work become that the rabbis of the Talmud decreed that the weekly reading of the Torah portion should include the reading of the Targum, as well. Targum Onkelos is included in almost all published editions of the Torah today.

Pirkei Avot – Mishnaic tractate containing the ethical pronouncements of the Tannaitic sages.

Pirkei Avot is singular within the Talmud in its focus upon ethical maxims as opposed to legal stricture. Many of Judaism's best-known proverbs and moral observations are contained within this tractate.

Elsewhere, the Talmud proclaims, "He who desires to be pious, let him practice the teachings of *[Pirkei] Avot.*"

Plotski, Meir Dan – Rabbi, Talmudic scholar, rosh yeshiva, communal leader (Poland, 1866–1928).

Author of the *Kli Chemda*, a commentary on the Torah, Plotski occupied rabbinical positions in Warta and subsequently in Ostrow. In 1926, at the age of sixty, he resigned from the rabbinate and was appointed to head a large yeshiva in Warsaw, known only as "the Mesivta."

Plotski served as chairman of the executive committee of the Rabbinical Council in Poland and as the emissary of Agudat Israel in Belgium, England and the United States.

Rabbeinu Bachya – Rabbi Bachya ben Asher; biblical commentator, *dayan*, preacher (Spain, 1263–1340).

A disciple of the renowned Talmudist Rabbi Shlomo ben Aderet (the Rashba), Rabbeinu Bachya served as a preacher and a *dayan* (rabbinical judge) in Saragossa, Spain. Rabbeinu Bachya is best known for his commentary on the Torah, which combines *pshat*, Midrash, philosophy and Kabbala. Each weekly parsha is introduced by an ethical discussion citing a verse from Proverbs.

Rabbeinu Chananel – Rabbi Chananel ben Chushiel; Talmudic scholar, halachic authority, commentator (Tunisia, 990–1055).

Rabbeinu Chananel lived in the city of Kairouan, Tunisia, where he studied under the tutelage of his father, Chushiel ben Elchanan, head of the Kairouan yeshiva. Following in his father's footsteps, Rabbeinu Chananel eventually earned the title *Reish Bei Rabbanan* (chief among the rabbis), accorded by the Babylonian academies of his day.

Rabbeinu Chananel wrote the first authoritative commentary on the Talmud, great sections of which are preserved and recorded on the actual pages of specific Talmudic tractates. In contrast to the later commentary of Rashi, Rabbeinu Chananel's work is not a running interpretation of the entire text. Instead, he summarizes and explains the main arguments of the Gemara and issues halachic decisions on the matters in question. He relies greatly on the positions of the Babylonian Geonim, and thus serves as an important bridge between the teachings of the Geonim and the scholars of North Africa and those of the scholars of Europe and Israel. Many later commentaries rely heavily on his work.

Rabbeinu Chananel also wrote a commentary on the Torah, only portions of which have been preserved.

Rabbeinu Tam – Rabbi Jacob ben Meir Tam; Talmudic scholar, Tosafist, halachic authority (France, circa 1100–1171).

The grandson of Rashi and one of the outstanding members of the Franco-German Tosafist school of Talmudic study, Rabbeinu Tam was widely acknowledged as the greatest scholar of his generation. Students flocked to him from as far away as Bohemia and Russia and disseminated his teachings upon their return to their native lands. A strong personality, Rabbeinu Tam often sought to impose his halachic authority upon other communities in an effort to maintain unity of practice.

Rabbeinu Tam authored numerous works, including *Sefer Hayashar*, the Book of the Upright, consisting of two sections, one containing his responsa, the other containing Talmudic novellae. The commentary of the Tosafot on the Babylonian Talmud is replete with his explanations, glosses and decisions.

Rabbeinu Tam personally experienced the horrors of the Second Crusade and only miraculously escaped death.

Rabbeinu Yerucham – Rabbi Yerucham ben Meshulam; halachic authority (Provence, Spain, 1290–1350).

Born in Provence, Rabbeinu Yerucham moved to Spain in the wake of the Jewish expulsion from France and settled in Toledo. There he devoted himself to the study of Talmud under the tutelage of the Rosh (Rabbi Asher ben Yechiel) and Rabbi Avraham ben Ismael, a student of the Rashbam.

Rabbeinu Yerucham composed two halachic works, *Sefer Meisharim*, dealing with civil law, and *Toldot Adam V'Chava*, tracing Jewish law and custom throughout man's lifecycle. Many of the laws and customs quoted by Rabbeinu Yerucham reflect the practices of Provence and other Jewish communities of France and are unknown from other sources.

Rabbi Yosef Caro was greatly influenced by the work of Rabbeinu Yerucham, and quoted him extensively in the *Beit Yosef* (Caro's commentary to the *Tur*) and in the *Shulchan Aruch*.

Radbaz – Rabbi David ben Shlomo ibn Abi Zimra; Talmudic scholar, halachic authority, community leader (Spain, Israel, Egypt, 1479–1573).

The Radbaz was born in Spain to wealthy parents, but, at the age of thirteen, was forced into exile as a result of the Alhambra Decree (the expulsion of the

Jews from Spain in 1492). Together with his family he emigrated to Tzfat, Israel, where he studied under Joseph Sargossi. Moving for a short time to Jerusalem, the Radbaz ultimately emigrated to Egypt, where he remained for forty years, first in Alexandria and then in Cairo. After the conquest of Egypt by the Turks in 1517, the Radbaz became the head of the Egyptian Jewish community, serving in numerous capacities, including *dayan* (judge), head of a yeshiva and administrator of charitable collections. These offices were honorary in nature, as the Radbaz was independently wealthy. Revered beyond the borders of Egypt for his vast knowledge, personal integrity, rigorous scholarship and deep humanity, the Radbaz regularly responded to legal and religious questions sent to him from other communities. Although a kabbalist, the Radbaz introduced Kabbala into his halachic decisions only when there was no contraindicating Talmudic position.

Shortly before 1553, the Radbaz resigned his position as chief rabbi of the Egyptian Jewish community and traveled back to Israel, settling for a short time in Jerusalem and then returning to Tzfat, where he remained until his death.

Ralbag – Rabbi Levi ben Gershon; Talmudic scholar, commentator, philosopher, mathematician, astronomer/astrologer (France, 1288–1344).

Little is known about the life of this revolutionary Jewish philosopher who authored works ranging from biblical commentary to acclaimed philosophical and mathematical treatises. His major philosophical text, *Sefer Milchamot Hashem* (The Wars of the Lord), was composed over a twelve-year period and earned the Ralbag renown well beyond the Jewish community.

In opposition to the generally accepted position of classical Judaism, the Ralbag maintained that God deliberately limits his own omniscience with regard to his foreknowledge of human acts. By stating that God knows the choices available to us but consciously chooses not to know the specific decisions that we will make, the Ralbag addressed the age-old dilemma of how man's free will can exist in the face of God's omniscience.

Rambam – Rabbi Moshe ben Maimon, also known as Maimonides; widely recognized as the greatest post-Talmudic authority on Jewish law and thought (Spain, Morocco, Egypt, 1135–1204).

The Rambam's works include *The Guide to the Perplexed*, a philosophical work on Jewish theology; *Sefer Hamitzvot*, a compendium of the 613 commandments of the Torah; a commentary on the Mishna; and his magnum opus, the *Mishneh Torah*, a masterful, comprehensive code of Jewish law. In his commentary on the Mishna, the Rambam delineated thirteen principles still considered to be the cornerstones of Jewish belief. His *Mishneh Torah* launched the course for halachic codification across the ages and served as the forerunner of other essential texts such as the *Arba Turim* and the *Shulchan Aruch*.

A royal physician and world-class philosopher, the Rambam made a monumental impact upon the development of Jewish tradition and law, reflected in the well-known dictum inscribed on his tomb: "From Moshe (Moses) to Moshe (Rambam) no one arose like Moshe."

Ramban – Rabbi Moshe ben Nachman, also known as Nachmanides; biblical and Talmudic commentator, scholar, physician (Spain, Israel, 1194–1270).

The Ramban's commentary on the Torah combines *pshat*, Midrash and kabbalistic insights. A towering figure in the history of Jewish scholarship, the Ramban authored numerous works on the Talmud as well as Jewish law and thought. His vigorous defense of Judaism in the face of Christian attack culminated in a public disputation with the Jewish apostate Pablo Christiano, in the presence of King James of Spain in 1263.

The Ramban's deep love for the Land of Israel is manifest in his writings and in his philosophy of Jewish law. In 1267, at the age of seventy-two, the Ramban settled in the Land of Israel and worked vigorously to rebuild Jerusalem's Jewish community.

Ran – Rabbi Nissim ben Reuven; Talmudic scholar, rabbi, halachist, philosopher, physician (Spain, 1290–1380).

Widely recognized as the greatest rabbinic authority of his time, the Ran served as rabbi of Barcelona and responded to thousands of halachic inquiries from across the Jewish diaspora. The Ran is best known for his practical commentary on the halachic work of Rabbi Yitzchak ben Yaakov Alfasi (the Rif). Through this commentary, the Ran achieved a revered position in the world of Talmudic scholarship. The Ran's compendium of sermons, *Drashot HaRan*, provides insight into many of the basic tenets of Jewish faith.

Rashbam – Rabbi Shmuel ben Meir; biblical commentator, Talmudic scholar (France, 1080–1158).

The Rashbam, Rashi's grandson, was a leading member of the Tosafists (a large group of medieval rabbis whose critical and explanatory glosses are basic to the study of the Talmud). The Rashbam's commentary on the Torah is remarkable for its bold adherence to *pashut pshat* even when the *pshat* leads to controversial conclusions. The Rashbam took issue with his renowned grandfather's periodic Midrashic interpretation of the text and, in fact, claimed, "I debated with him [Rashi] and he admitted to me that, if he had the time, he would be obligated to author other commentaries based upon the straightforward explanations of the text…."

So great was the storm concerning some of the Rashbam's views that his commentary on the first chapters of Bereishit was omitted in many earlier editions of the Bible.

Rashi – Rabbi Shlomo Yitzchaki; arguably the greatest of all biblical and Talmudic commentators (France, 1040–1105).

Rashi's commentary on the Torah, considered an essential companion to the study of the text, combines *pshat* with the periodic referencing of Midrash (when he feels such referencing is necessary for textual comprehension).

In addition to commentaries on the Prophets and Writings, Rashi also authored an indispensable running commentary on the Talmud, known for its brevity and clarity.

No course of study in the Torah or Talmud is considered complete without the accompanying study of Rashi's commentary.

Ravad – Rabbi Avraham ben David; Talmudic scholar and commentator, halachist, philosopher, commentator on the *Mishneh Torah* of the Rambam and other halachic works (Provence, 1125–1198).

The center of the Ravad's activities was Posquières, a small city near Nîmes, where he established a yeshiva to which advanced students from all parts of Europe flocked. A man of great wealth, the Ravad provided for all the needs of indigent students out of his own pocket.

Greatly respected by scholars throughout Europe, North Africa and the Middle East, the Ravad gained a reputation for his incisive, penetrating and analytic approach to the Talmud and other halachic texts. His varied and extensive works included responsa, homiletic discourses and commentaries on the Talmud and other codes of law. He also asserted formative influence on the study of Kabbala.

The Ravad is perhaps best known for his *hasagot*, critical annotations on the Rambam's *Mishneh Torah* and on other halachic works. Combining commentary and criticism, these annotations clearly display the Ravad's great analytical powers.

In general, the Ravad opposed any attempt, such as that of the Rambam in the *Mishneh Torah*, to codify Jewish law in cut-and-dry fashion without explanations or references.

Rema – Rabbi Moshe Isserles; Talmudic scholar, *dayan*, rosh yeshiva, preeminent halachic authority for Ashkenazic Jewry (Poland, 1520–1572).

Born in Cracow, Poland, the Rema studied in Lublin where he married the daughter of Rabbi Shalom Shachna, the rosh yeshiva. Upon his wife's untimely death at the age of twenty, the Rema honored her memory with the building of a synagogue which stands in Cracow to this day. The Rema's second wife also came from a scholarly family.

The Rema distinguished himself as an outstanding scholar at an early age and by 1550 was a member of the Cracow Beit Din (religious court). He established a yeshiva in Cracow, supported its students through his own resources and earned a worldwide reputation as a brilliant and effective *posek* (halachic arbiter). Humble and self-effacing, the Rema was, nonetheless, so confident and incisive in his halachic positions that he became known to his contemporaries as the "Maimonides of Polish Jewry." Like Maimonides, the Rema also pursued secular knowledge through the study of history, astronomy and philosophy.

While the Rema authored many works, he is best known for his *Mapa* (Tablecloth), a series of annotations inserted into the body of Rabbi Yosef Caro's halachic compendium, the *Shulchan Aruch* (Set table). These glosses append the legal positions and customs of Ashkenazic Jewry to Caro's Sephardic-oriented work, thus transforming the *Shulchan Aruch* into the primary universal code of law for the entire Jewish nation.

Saadia Gaon – Talmudic scholar, philosopher, halachist (Egypt, Babylonia, 882–942).

Arguably the greatest scholar of the Geonic period (late sixth–eleventh centuries), Saadia Gaon is also considered by many to be the "father of Jewish philosophy." Sensing the twin dangers posed to rabbinic Judaism by Karaism (a movement that accepted the Written but not the Oral Law) and rationalistic thought, Saadia developed a systematic philosophy of Judaism which examined its truths and teachings in the light of reason.

Saadia played a major role in a calendar controversy between the Jerusalem and the Babylonian scholarly communities which threatened to create a dangerous schism concerning the fixing of festival dates. At the request of the Babylonian scholars, Saadia effectively refuted the position of Aharon ben Meir, the head of the Jerusalem Academy, and solidified the supremacy of the Babylonian scholars. Both as a result of this effort and in the merit of his extraordinary abilities, Saadia was appointed head of the famed Babylonian Academy of Sura in 928, at the age of forty-six.

So important were Saadia's contributions to Jewish thought that, centuries later, the Rambam proclaimed in his *Iggeret Teiman*: "Were it not for Saadia, the Torah would almost have disappeared from among Israel."

Sefer Hachinuch – Systematic analysis of the 613 commandments of the Torah, published anonymously in thirteenth-century Spain.

Following the order of the Torah text, the Ba'al Hachinuch (as the anonymous author of the *Sefer Hachinuch* is called) links each mitzva to the parsha in which it is found and discusses both the philosophical underpinnings and halachic parameters of that mitzva.

Sforno – Rabbi Ovadia Sforno; biblical commentator, Talmudic scholar, philosopher, physician (Italy, 1470–1550).

The Sforno's broad-based education earned him recognition in many fields including law, philosophy, mathematics, medicine, Hebrew language and Hebrew literature. When the famous German humanist Johan Reuchlin desired to perfect his knowledge of Hebrew literature, Cardinal Domenico Grimani advised him to approach the Sforno. A prolific writer, the Sforno is best known for his clear commentary on the Torah and many books of Tanach. These works reflect great respect for the *pshat* of the text and are written in a beautiful, almost lyrical style.

Shach – Rabbi Shabbetai ben Meir Hacohen; Talmudic scholar, *dayan*, halachic authority and commentator (Poland, Lithuania, 1621–1662).

Born in Amstivov, Lithuania, Shabbetai moved to Poland, studying in Tykocin, Krakow and Lublin. While still young, he returned to Vilna, where he married a woman from a wealthy family, descended from the Rema (Rabbi Moshe Isserles). Financially supported by his father-in-law, the Shach was able to devote his time solely to study.

After serving for a period of time in the *beit din* (rabbinical court) in Vilna, Shabbetai returned to Krakow where, in 1646, he published his classic work, the *Siftei Kohen*, a commentary on the Yoreh Deah section of the *Shulchan Aruch* (thus he became known by the title the Shach, comprised of the initials of the title of this work). Towards the end of his life, Shabbetai expanded his commentary to include the Choshen Mishpat section of the *Shulchan Aruch*, as well. The *Siftei Kohen* revealed Shabbetai's towering intellect, incisive mind and mastery of Jewish law and is widely accepted as an authoritative source for halachic decisions.

Shabbetai was forced to flee repeatedly in order to escape the religious persecution and slaughter of Polish Jewry during his lifetime. In 1651, he published *Megilat Eifa*, which portrays the suffering of the Jewish community at the hands of Chmielnicki and his followers.

Siddur – The Jewish prayer book.

The Siddur mirrors the historical journey of the Jewish people. While the earliest prayers were primarily spontaneous, prayer services became codified over time, stemming from various sources.

Biblically mandated prayers include the Shma Yisrael, the Birkat Kohanim (priestly blessing) and the Birkat Hamazon (grace after meals). The central prayer of the Jewish liturgy, known as the Amida (the standing [prayer]), was edited by Rabbi Gamliel and his colleagues in Yavne, after the destruction of the Second Temple.

The earliest true Siddur was drawn up in the ninth century by Rav Amram Gaon, at the request of the Jewish community of Spain. One hundred years later, Rav Saadia Gaon compiled a Siddur, as well. Critical to the development of the Jewish prayer book was the Machzor Vitri, edited in the eleventh century by Simcha ben Shmuel, a student of Rashi. The Machzor Vitri contained all the regular prayers according to the custom of northern France.

The Siddur continues to evolve to this day, as evidenced by prayers included in many contemporary prayer books relating to the welfare of the State of Israel and its armed forces.

Soloveitchik, Yosef Dov – The Rav; rabbi, pioneering spiritual leader of the Modern Orthodox movement in America and throughout the Jewish world (Lithuania, America, 1903–1993).

Scion of a two-hundred-year-old rabbinic dynasty, the Rav arrived in America in 1932 armed with an education that combined traditional Lithuanian Talmudic studies and a PhD in philosophy from the University of Berlin. He assumed a rabbinic position in Boston where he established the Maimonides School and played a major role in many facets of the community's development. In 1941, he succeeded his father, Rabbi Moshe Soloveitchik, as the head of the Rabbi Isaac Elchanan Theological Seminary rabbinic school of Yeshiva University. For decades thereafter he commuted weekly between Boston and New York.

The Rav combined vast Torah and secular knowledge, a deeply analytical mind, powerful teaching ability and majestic oratorical skill with a magnetic leadership personality. Through his classes, widely attended public lectures, writings and policy decisions he furthered the philosophy of encounter between the highest form of Torah knowledge and the best secular scholarship of Western civilization. Adviser and teacher to tens of thousands, the Rav shaped the course of Modern Orthodox philosophy through the twentieth century and beyond.

Talmud Bavli – Babylonian Talmud; foundational compilation of the halachic (legal) and aggadic (ethical-homiletical) discussions of the sages of the Babylonian academies from the second through the fifth centuries CE.

The scholars of the Talmud, known as the Amoraim, expound at great length upon the concise teachings of the Mishna, often digressing to discuss loosely related issues and ideas. Structurally, the style of the Talmud Bavli can best be described as "conversation in suspended animation," reflecting the origin of its subject matter, which was memorized and transmitted orally for centuries before its eventual written recordation.

Together with the Mishna, the Talmud Bavli serves as the basic source for the continually developing Oral Law.

Talmud Yerushalmi – Jerusalem Talmud; collection of the teachings of the sages of the Israeli academies from 200 to 350 CE.

Like the Talmud Bavli, the Talmud Yerushalmi centers on the discussions of the Amoraim (Talmudic scholars) concerning the Mishna. The Talmud Yerushalmi, however, is smaller in scope, more fragmented, and more difficult to study than its Babylonian counterpart; consequently, over the centuries, the Yerushalmi has exerted less influence upon the development of Jewish law. The return to the land of Israel in recent years has given birth to a renewed interest in the Talmud Yerushalmi and the laws it contains pertaining to the land.

Targum Yonatan – Interpretive Aramaic translation of the Torah commonly attributed to Yonatan ben Uziel. The correct name of this translation, according to most biblical scholars, is Targum Yerushalmi (Jerusalem Targum [translation]). Probably due to a printer's error (in Hebrew, as in English, the first letters of Targum Yerushalmi and Targum Yonatan are the same), the work was mistakenly labeled Targum Yonatan and attributed erroneously to Yonatan ben Uziel, an outstanding pupil of the renowned Mishnaic sage Hillel. Yonatan ben Uziel did produce a famous translation of the Books of the Prophets which, according to the Talmud, reflects the interpretation of the prophets Chagai, Zacharia and Malachi. The Talmud makes no mention, however, of a Targum on the Torah produced by this sage. The erroneous attribution is perpetuated in many current Chumashim. To address the issue, scholars refer to this biblical translation as the Targum Pseudo-Yonatan.

The Targum Pseudo-Yonatan contains much aggadic material from various sources and is both translation and commentary. The actual date of its composition remains a matter of dispute.

Yalkut Shimoni – An important, comprehensive Midrashic anthology compiled in the twelfth or thirteenth century.

The *Yalkut Shimoni* contains over ten thousand aggadic and halachic observations on the entire Torah text. Both the authorship and the exact date of the *Yalkut*'s publication are the subject of dispute.

Zohar – Central work in the literature of Kabbala (Jewish mysticism).

The Zohar is essentially a collection of several sections containing Midrashim and discussions on a wide array of topics.

The Zohar's main section is arranged according to the parshiot of the Torah text, although the latter part of the book of Bamidbar and the book of Devarim are not completely covered. Other portions of the work include the teachings and experiences of the second-century Tanna Rabbi Shimon bar Yochai; mystical studies on specific sections of the Torah and other books of Tanach; and discourses on a variety of topics including the nature of God, the origin and structure of the universe, good and evil, man's relationship to God, etc.

While the authorship of the Zohar is subject to dispute, many traditionalists have, for centuries, traced its origins to Rabbi Shimon bar Yochai.

Index

A
Abba bar Kahana, R., 232
Abravanel
    connecting laws in Parshat Naso, 32
    and counting of the Israelites, 9, 12
    and God's intervention to prevent Bilam from cursing, 230
    and punishment fitting the crime, 195–196
    and purpose of wilderness travelogue, 320
    and the reward of Pinchas, 260, 262
    and rules of Birkat Kohanim, 58, 63
Achiya the Shilonite, 246
Adam, 57, 224, 229
adultery. *See* Sota, regulations governing a
aguna, plight of the, 284–289
Aharon
    and counting of the Israelites, 9
    death of, 203, 319
    descendents of, 19–24, 26–27
    as Kohen Gadol, 175–177
    as leader, 176
    as Moshe's partner, 22
    as Pinchas's grandfather, 259–263
    and punishment fitting the crime, 194–196, 199–202
    and the rebellion of Korach, 145–148, 152, 156–158, 164, 167, 169–173, 176
    and rules of Birkat Kohanim, 55
    and the sin of the spies, 119, 130
Akeidat Yitzchak
    and counting of the Israelites, 13
    and punishment fitting the crime, 200n18
Akiva, R.
    and the mitzva of *succa*, 86–87
    and rules of Birkat Kohanim, 56
Albo, R. Joseph, 200
Alshich, R. Moshe
    connecting laws in Parshat Naso, 32
    and rules of Birkat Kohanim, 58–59, 63
Amalek, 119, 292–294, 299–301
American Grace (Putnam and Campbell), 87–88
Amram, 20
anger as a sin, 198
animals, Bilam talking to, 234–243
Arama, R. Isaac
    and the laws of the red heifer, 184
    and rules of Birkat Kohanim, 55
    and the sin of the spies, 120
Avihu, 19, 21–23
Aviram, 145–146, 148–149, 155–156, 160, 169–170, 172–173
Avraham
    and asking God for forgiveness, 127
    brother of, 23
    as patriarch, 228, 238n14
    powers of, 223–224, 229
    and the rebellion of Korach, 156
    and rules of Birkat Kohanim, 57
Aza and Azael, 225

B

Ba'al Akeida
  and the mitzva of *tzitzit*, 139
  and purpose of wilderness travelogue, 321
Ba'al Hachinuch
  and the mitzva of *tzitzit*, 137
  and rules of Birkat Kohanim, 60–61
Ba'al Haturim
  and descendents at Sinai, 21
  and the nature of natural events, 205
Ba'al Pe'or, 225, 230, 250–251, 255, 258–263, 290, 302
Babad, R. Yosef, 300
Bachya, Rabbenu
  and descendents of Aharon, 22
  and structure of encampment, 11
Balak
  and Bilam talking to animals, 234–237, 239–241
  and Bilam's change in attitude, 245–247
  and the connection between Bilam and Ba'al Pe'or, 250–251
  and God's intervention to prevent Bilam from cursing, 228–232
  and the prophetic powers of Bilam, 219–224
Bar Kochba revolt, 303
Be'or, 222–223
Berlin, R. Zvi Yehuda. *See* Netziv
Bilam
  and the battle against Midian, 290
  change in attitude of, 244–249
  and the connection to Ba'al Pe'or, 250–251
  God's intervention to prevent cursing of, 228–233
  prophetic powers of, 219–227
  talking to animals, 234–243
Birkat Kohanim, rules of, 31–34, 55–64
blessings, man's power to give, 56–57, 63–64
Burke, Edmund, 173

C

Calev
  and division of Canaan among tribes, 266n3
  and falling short of the Promised Land, 309–310
  and the sin of the spies, 121, 125
calf, sin of the golden
  Aharon's involvement in, 195
  and asking God for forgiveness, 126
  Bilam at the site of, 246
  and counting of the Israelites, 9
  Moshe's defense of, 104
  punishment of firstborns involved in the, 146, 313
  red heifer laws as atonement for, 185
  Yom Kippur a punishment for, 130–132, 134
Campbell, David, 87
Canaan
  and the battle against Midian, 293–294
  and the connection between Moshe's death and *korbanot*, 271
  division of among tribes, 264–268
  failure to enter, 148, 194–197
  and falling short of the Promised Land, 305–306, 308–311, 314–315, 317
  laws applying to the land of, 149
  and purpose of wilderness travelogue, 323

and the sin of the spies, 119, 121–122, 130, 141, 191–192, 196
Chafetz, R. Moshe, 43
Chama bar Chanina, R., 16–18
Chana bar Bizna, R., 167
Chananel, Rabbeinu
   and punishment fitting the crime, 199, 200n18
   and the rebellion of Korach, 170
Chanina, R., 210
Chasida, Shimon, 167
Chatam Sofer
   and descendents of Aharon, 23
   and descendents of Moshe, 26–27
   and laws of a Nazir, 52
   and the rebellion of Korach, 147–148
Chiya, R.
   and descendents of Aharon, 23
   and rebellion of Israelites, 101
Chizkiyahu, King, 204
Chizkuni
   and descendents of Aharon, 23
   and the nature of natural events, 205
   and the rebellion of Korach, 156
   and regulations governing a Sota, 40
   and time jumps in the Torah, 191
chochma vs. *da'at* in mitzva performance, 150–153
chukim, purpose of, 166–167, 181–189, 278
Clouds of Glory, 82–87, 89–90
commandments
   Bamidbar limited to temporal, 5–6, 36
   not logical. *See chukim*, purpose of
   obligation vs. opportunity, 317–318
   transmitted in the wilderness, 5

conversion, discouragement of, 72–74
counting of the Israelites, 7–9, 12–13
covenantal Jewish history, 17–18

D

da'at vs. *chochma* in mitzva performance, 150–153
Da'at Zekeinim Miba'alei Hatosafot
   counting of the Kohanim and Levi'im, 20
   and descendents at Sinai, 21
   and purpose of wilderness travelogue, 321
Dan
   as a gathering tribe, 16
   as a leading tribe, 7, 11–12
Datan, 145–146, 148–149, 155–156, 160, 169–170, 172–173
death, purification after contact with, 181–189
descendents, disappearing, 19–27
diversity, national, 14–15
Divine Providence, 207–209, 211–215, 242

E

Elazar, 19–20, 22–23
Elazar ben R. Shimon, R., 138
Elazar ben Shammua, R., 47–48
Eldad, 109–111
elders, seventy, 103–104, 109–111, 113
Eliav, 155
Eliezer, 24–26
Eliezer, R., 86–87, 89
encampment, travel, 82–84
Ephraim
   as descendent of Yosef, 146
   as a leading tribe, 7, 11

Esav, 23, 225, 244
exile of individuals with *tuma*, 31, 34
extremes vs. equilibrium in life, 50, 54, 139, 186

F
facts vs. opinions, 124
fast days, origins of the major, 129–134
Feinstein, R. Moshe, 286
forgiveness, God's offers of, 125–128, 130, 132–134
forty, significance of the number, 191–192
free will, 124, 238
Fried, Stephen, 88

G
Gad, 305–315, 317–318
Gamliel, 11
gematria, 138
Gentile prophecy, place in Judaism, 226–227
Gershom, 24–26
Gershom, Rabbeinu
  and the laws of *nedarim*, 285
  and regulations governing a Sota, 39

H
HaCohen, R. Meir Simcha
  and God's intervention to prevent Bilam from cursing, 231
  and laws of a Nazir, 50–51
Hadarshan, R. Moshe, 320–321
hagbala, occurring at Sinai, 10
Hakapar, R. Elazar, 47–48
Hanasi, R. Yehuda, 100, 102
Har Nevo, 195
Haran, 23
heifer, laws of the red, 181–189

hester panim, 213
Hillel, 147
Hirsch, R. Shimshon Raphael
  and Bilam talking to animals, 239
  and Bilam's change in attitude, 246
  comparison between Sinai and the Sanctuary, 11
  and counting of the Israelites, 13–14
  and God's intervention to prevent Bilam from cursing, 231
  and the laws of *nedarim*, 281–282
  and the laws of the red heifer, 186–187
  and the nature of natural events, 205–206
  and the reward of Pinchas, 261
  and rules of Birkat Kohanim, 59–60
history
  Bamidbar limited to events in, 5–6
  Exodus as dawn of Jewish, 15
  Exodus as paradigm of Jewish, 12–13, 17–18, 84–85
Hitler, Adolf, 301
Holocaust, 173–174, 213
Hoshaya, R., 16–18

I
Ibn Ezra
  connecting laws in Parshat Naso, 32
  and the connection between Moshe's death and *korbanot*, 270
  and counting of the Israelites, 12
  and descendents of Aharon, 22
  and God's intervention to prevent Bilam from cursing, 230
  and the nature of natural events, 204
  and punishment fitting the crime, 200

and purpose of wilderness travelogue, 319–320
and the rebellion of Korach, 145–148
and the reward of Pinchas, 262
idolatry vs. paganism, 105–107
incense used in test of Korach, 164–168
inheritance, laws of, 79
interruptions in Torah narrative, 99–102
interventions of God, 228–233
Israel, State of
 aliya to the, 85
 battlefield conduct of, 303–304
 Biblical sites in, 195
 lack of idealism regarding, 315–317
 rallies for, 97
 religious harmony in, 14–15, 54
Isserles, R. Moshe. *See* Rema
Itamar, 19–20, 22–23

J
Jacob, Benno, 11
"jihad," Jewish, 290–304

K
Kadesh, 190
Kanatopsky, R. Harold, 200–201
Kant, Immanuel, 317
karet, 76
Kehat, 155
Kivrot Hata'ava, 104–106, 108–110, 112, 146
Kli Yakar
 and Bilam talking to animals, 239
 and laws of a Nazir, 52
 and the laws of the red heifer, 185
 and the rebellion of Korach, 170
 and structure of encampment, 12

Kodesh Kadashim, 165
Kohanim
 Aharon's sons as, 19–20, 22–23, 26
 and laws of a Nazir, 48–49
 and the laws of the red heifer, 187
 legal rights of, 31–33
 Levi'im's feelings of subordination to, 146
 Pinchas as, 259–263
 and regulations governing a Sota, 35, 43
 and rules of Birkat Kohanim, 55–64
 separation of, 21
 and the use of incense, 165
 use of the Urim and Tumim, 271
Korach, rebellion of, 145–174, 176–177, 190, 200n18, 241
Korban Pesach, rituals of the, 71–72, 74–78, 80
korbanot, connection between Moshe's death and, 269–273
korbanot nesi'im, 65
Ktav Sofer, 263

L
Lavan, 222n20, 225
law, taking into one's own hands, 255–258
laws, connecting in Parshat Naso, 31–34
leader, succeeding as a Jewish, 108
Leibowitz, Nehama
 and Bilam talking to animals, 238
 and falling short of the Promised Land, 308–309
 and the prophetic powers of Bilam, 221–222
 and the rebellion of Korach, 167
 and rules of Birkat Kohanim, 59
 and the sin of the spies, 121

Levi Yitzchak of Berdichev, R., 184
Levi'im
   Aharon as leader of the, 175
   excluded from census, 7
   Korach as descendent of, 155
   ritual privileges transferred from firstborns to, 146–147, 312–313
   in separate census, 19–20
   separation of, 21
Lichtenstein, R. Aharon, 317–318
Lot, 156
love, blessings with, 61–62
Luzatto, R. Shmuel David, 240–241

M

Maharal of Prague, 24
Maharam, 205
Malbim
   and the connection between Moshe's death and *korbanot*, 270
   and purpose of wilderness travelogue, 322–323
   and the rebellion of Korach, 147–148
marriage, different laws for men and women regarding, 38–39
mazal, role of in Judaism, 209–210
Medad, 109–111
Mei Meriva, 194–196, 198–202
Meir ben Baruch of Rothenberg, R. *See* Maharam
Menashe, 305–306, 312
Menashe [Moshe], 25
Meshech Chochma, 239–240
Messiah, introduction of, 18, 98
Micha, 249
Midrash, understanding a, 65–67
miracles, God's performance of, 175–178, 197–198, 200, 204–206, 242–243, 322

Miriam
   death of, 190, 194
   well of, 241
Mishkan. *See* Sanctuary
misunderstanding, Korach's rebellion as a, 169–174
mitzvot. *See* commandments
Mizrachi, R. Eliyahu, 156
Moshe
   asking God for forgiveness, 125–127, 134
   and the battle against Midian, 290, 295–296, 302
   and the burning bush, 22
   commandments transmitted through, 190, 255, 262, 280
   connection between death of and *korbanot*, 269–273
   conversation with Yitro within text, 99
   counting the Israelites, 7, 9
   descendents of, 19–21, 24–27
   and division of Canaan among tribes, 264
   and falling short of the Promised Land, 305–314
   forty days spent at Sinai, 191–192
   God performing miracles through, 175
   and God's intervention to prevent Bilam from cursing, 231
   initial meeting with God, 245
   and laws of inheritance, 79–80
   and laws of *nedarim*, 277
   as leader, 176
   and the nature of natural events, 203–205, 210–211
   as prophet, 221–223
   and punishment fitting the crime, 194–202

and purpose of wilderness
 travelogue, 319–320
and rebellion of Israelites, 103–
 104, 106–108
and the rebellion of Korach,
 145–152, 156–158, 160–163,
 164–165, 167, 169–173, 176
and rituals of the Korban Pesach,
 71, 77–78, 80
and rules of Birkat Kohanim, 55
and sharing leadership, 109–111,
 113
and the silver trumpets, 91, 95
and the sin of the golden calf,
 130–131
and the sin of the spies, 119–120,
 141
staff of, 241
Torah of, 242
viewing Canaan from afar, 195

N
Nadav, 19, 21–23
natural events, nature of, 203–215
Nazir, laws of a, 31–34, 46–54
nedarim, laws of, 277–289
Netanel, 11
Netziv
 and laws of a Nazir, 51
 and the reward of Pinchas, 260–261
The New Rabbi (Fried), 88
Noach, 57, 192, 224, 229
Noachide laws, 295

O
obligations, denial of financial, 31, 34
offerings, sin, 46–47, 50, 185
offerings, tribal, 65
Ohr Hachaim
 and Bilam talking to animals,
  236–237
 and the connection between
  Moshe's death and *korbanot*, 270
 and laws of a Nazir, 52
On, 145–146, 155–156, 160
Onkelos
 and Bilam's change in attitude, 246
 and nature of prophecy, 113, 115
 and the rebellion of Korach, 155
opinions vs. facts, 124

P
paganism vs. idolatry, 105–107
Pagiel, 11
peace
 covenant of, 259–261, 263
 offering before battle, 293–295
Pelet, 155
Pesach Sheini, 71–72, 74–78, 80
Pharaoh, 225
physicality vs. Spirituality in this
 world, 48, 50–51, 53–54, 141
Pinchas [ben Elazar]
 and the battle against Midian, 290
 reward of, 259–263
 zealotry of, 255–258, 263
Plotski, R. Meir Dan, 258
power of words, 229
prayer, God's response to, 204
prophecy, transient or permanent,
 113–115
prophetic powers of Bilam, 219–227
punishment fitting the crime, 194–202
purification after contact with death,
 181–189
Putnam, Robert, 87

R
Ra'avad
 and the battle against Midian,
  293–294
 and rituals of the Korban Pesach,
  76

Radbaz, 297, 299
Ralbag
   connecting laws in Parshat Naso, 34n6
   and the connection between Moshe's death and *korbanot*, 270
Rambam
   and the battle against Midian, 294–301
   and Bilam talking to animals, 240, 242
   and creating individuality from ritual, 66
   historical context as basis for textual approaches, 279
   and laws of a Nazir, 48–50
   and the laws of *nedarim*, 280, 286
   and the laws of the red heifer, 185–186
   and the mitzva of the shofar, 95
   and the mitzva of *tzitzit*, 141
   and the nature of natural events, 211–212
   and punishment fitting the crime, 198–199
   and purpose of wilderness travelogue, 320–322
   and regulations governing a Sota, 40, 42–43
   and rituals of the Korban Pesach, 75–78
   and the use of incense, 166
Ramban
   and the battle against Midian, 294
   and Bilam talking to animals, 237, 242
   and Bilam's change in attitude, 245–246
   and the connection between Moshe's death and *korbanot*, 271
   and counting of the Israelites, 9
   counting of the Kohanim and Levi'im, 20
   and descendents at Sinai, 21
   historical context as basis for textual approaches, 279
   and laws of a Nazir, 49–50
   and the mitzva of *tzitzit*, 138
   and the nature of natural events, 205, 211
   and the prophetic powers of Bilam, 222–223, 227
   and punishment fitting the crime, 199–200
   and purpose of wilderness travelogue, 320
   and the rebellion of Korach, 146–148, 156, 170–172
   and regulations governing a Sota, 42
   and the reward of Pinchas, 262
   and the sin of the spies, 119
   and structure of encampment, 10, 12
   and the travel encampment, 83–84
   and uniqueness of Bamidbar, 5
Rashbam
   and Bilam's change in attitude, 245
   and counting of the Israelites, 8–9, 12
   counting of the Kohanim and Levi'im, 20
   and descendents at Sinai, 21
   and division of Canaan among tribes, 266n3
   and laws of a Nazir, 46n1
   and the mitzva of *tzitzit*, 136
   and the prophetic powers of Bilam, 223
   and punishment fitting the crime, 197, 201
   and the rebellion of Korach, 156, 161

and rules of Birkat Kohanim, 57, 63
Rashi
   and the battle against Midian, 293
   and Bilam talking to animals, 238
   and Bilam's change in attitude, 246, 248
   and the connection between Moshe's death and *korbanot*, 269–270
   and descendents of Aharon, 23
   and descendents of Moshe, 24
   and falling short of the Promised Land, 308
   and laws of a Nazir, 46n1
   and laws of inheritance, 79
   and the mitzva of *succa*, 86
   and the mitzva of *tzitzit*, 136, 138–139
   and punishment fitting the crime, 196–199, 201
   and purpose of wilderness travelogue, 320
   and rebellion of Israelites, 105n9, 106
   and the rebellion of Korach, 155–156, 161, 170–172
   and the reward of Pinchas, 260, 262
   and rituals of the Korban Pesach, 78
   and rules of Birkat Kohanim, 56
   and the sin of the spies, 121n8
   and structure of encampment, 13–14
   and the travel encampment, 82
Rava, 209
realities, differences in personal, 158–159
rebellion
   of Israelites upon receiving the Torah, 4–5, 101–102
   and Kivrot Hata'ava, 104–106
   of Korach, 145–174, 176–177, 190, 200n18, 241
   preventing further, 175
   and the sin of the golden calf. *See* calf, sin of the golden
   and the sin of the spies. *See* spies, sin of the
   of Taveira, 100, 146
red heifer, laws of the, 181–189
Refidim, 197, 201–202
relationships, man-God
   changing from *yira* to *ahava*, 177–178, 201–202
   as equal, 157, 212–213
   within marriage, 45
   in the wilderness, 6
Rema, 50
Reuven
   Datan and Aviram as descendents of, 155
   as descendent of Yaakov, 146
   and falling short of the Promised Land, 305–315, 317–318
   as a leading tribe, 7, 11
Revelation
   comparison to conversion, 74
   encampment as recreation of, 10
   generation as slaves, 201
   generation disappearing, 177
   God's presence during, 11
   impact on Israelites, 3–5
   Kohanim's appointment at, 21
   leaving the site of, 8
   length of, 191
   merit of the, 230
   Moshe's teachings as essential to, 24
   rebellion right after, 101–102, 122, 130
   unity as prerequisite of, 13–14, 247

reward of Pinchas, 259–263
ritual, creating individuality from, 66–67
Rosh Hashana, 93–95, 97–98

S
Saadia Gaon, 161
Sancheriv, King, 297–301
Sanctuary
    assembling elders outside, 109–111
    being away from at time of Korban Pesach, 72, 75–78
    and the Clouds of Glory, 82
    comparison to Sinai, 10–11, 13
    departure from, 26
    descendents of Aharon before erection of, 21
    encampment around the, 16, 247
    God's presence at the, 194
    importance of the, 91
    and the laws of the red heifer, 185–186
    and regulations governing a Sota, 35, 43
    and the role of *mazal* in Judaism, 210
    and rules of Birkat Kohanim, 59
    sanctification of the, 65
    staffs in the, 175, 177
    and the use of incense, 165–166
Sanhedrin, 109–111, 113–115, 293
Sara, 23
Sarai [Sara], 156
second chance for a mitzva, 71–81
serpent, significance of copper, 203–206
Sforno
    and Bilam talking to animals, 239
    and Bilam's change in attitude, 246
    and descendents of Aharon, 22
    and the laws of the red heifer, 186

    and the mitzva of *tzitzit*, 137
    and the nature of natural events, 205
    and punishment fitting the crime, 197–198
    and purpose of wilderness travelogue, 321
    and the rebellion of Korach, 149
    and the reward of Pinchas, 260
    and the sin of the spies, 121n8
    and the travel encampment, 83
Shadal, 240–241
shalom bayit, 44–45
Shammai, 147
Shaul, King, 292
Shavuot, timing of reading of Bamidbar and, 3–5
Shevuel, 25
Shimon, R., 111
Shimon ben Elazar, R., 265, 266n3
Shimon ben Gamliel, R., 99–102
Shlomo, 49
Shlumiel, 11
shofar, connection between the trumpet and the, 93–98
Sifrei
    and the battle against Midian, 295–296
    and nature of prophecy, 113–114
    and the prophetic powers of Bilam, 221, 227
    and regulations governing a Sota, 39
silver trumpets, 91–93, 95–98
sin of the golden calf. *See* calf, sin of the golden
sin of the spies. *See* spies, sin of the
sin offerings, 46–47, 50, 185
Sinai
    arrival to, 3, 13, 74
    becoming a nation at, 267

INDEX 359

and the burning bush, 22
comparison to the Sanctuary, 10–11, 13
departure from, 3–6, 8–9, 14, 17, 26, 31, 33, 82, 84–85, 91–92, 95–97, 99–103, 247, 312
descendents at, 19–21
and descendents of Moshe, 25
forty days spent at, 191–192
law originating at, 114, 146, 152, 165, 203, 255
merit of Revelation, 230
Moshe's teachings as essential to Revelation at, 24
overpowering experience of, 13, 177
rebellion of Israelites upon receiving Torah, 106
rebellion right after, 122–123, 130–131, 167
Revelation at, 245
shofar sound at, 98
and the sin of the golden calf, 104, 126, 132
tablets created during Creation, 241
timeline of references to, 21
Solomon, King, 182, 241
Soloveitchik, R. Joseph
and the battle against Midian, 300–301
and covenantal Jewish history, 17
and the mitzva of *tzitzit*, 139–140
and the nature of natural events, 212–213
and rebellion of Israelites, 105, 107
and the rebellion of Korach, 150–151
Sota, regulations governing a, 31–32, 34–45

spies, sin of the
and asking God for forgiveness, 127
and falling short of the Promised Land, 305, 309–310
and the mitzva of *tzitzit*, 136, 141
Moshe's defense of, 104
and purpose of wilderness travelogue, 320
rebellion culminating in, 4
and rebellion of Israelites, 101
and the rebellion of Korach, 146, 148, 177
Tisha B'Av a punishment for, 130–131, 133–134
and unfair blame, 119–125
spirituality vs. physicality in this world, 48, 50–51, 53–54, 141
structure of encampment, 7–8, 10–13
succa, mitzva of, 86–90
"superfluous" words in the Torah, 125–126

T

Targum Onkelos. *See* Onkelos
Taveira, rebellion of, 100, 146
techeilet, significance of, 135–136, 138–140, 149
temporal commandments, Bamidbar limited to, 5–6, 36
Terach, 23
theft, laws concerning, 31, 34
time
Bamidbar as blueprint for journey across, 6
jump in the Torah, 190–193
power of, 192–193
Tisha B'Av, origin of, 129–131, 133–134
tolerance in Orthodoxy, 188–189

Tosafot. *See* Da'at Zekeinim Miba'alei Hatosafot
traveling formation of the Israelites, 16–18
travelogue, purpose of wilderness, 319–323
trumpets, silver, 91–93, 95–98
trust, cultivation of, 44
tuma
   exile of individuals with, 31, 34
   and the laws of the red heifer, 181–189
   and second chances in halacha, 71–72, 75–78
Tur, the, 86
Tzelafchad, 79–80
Tzin, 190–191
tzitzit, mitzva of, 135–141, 149
tzniut, importance of, 248–249
Tzvi Elimelech of Dinov, R., 185

U
Urim and Tumim, 271

V
violence, God-ordained, 290–304

W
women, inequality among laws of men and, 277–289
word of God, traveling at the, 83–85

Y
Yaakov, 23, 146, 222n20, 225, 245
Yaakov [Yisrael], 127
Yehonatan, 25–26
Yehoshua, 109, 125, 146, 266n3, 269–271, 294, 309–310
Yehuda, 7, 11–12
Yehuda ben Pazi, 256
Yishmael, 225
Yishmael, R., 56
Yisrael [Yaakov], 127
Yitro, 99
Yitzchak, 127
Yitzchak, R., 23
Yitzhar, 155
Yochanan, R.
   and God's intervention to prevent Bilam from cursing, 232
   and the role of *mazal* in Judaism, 210
Yochanan ben Zakai, R., 182, 184
Yom Kippur
   and the laws of the red heifer, 186
   origin of, 129–134
   and the use of incense, 165
Yona, 222
Yonatan, R., 265
Yonatan, Targum, 225
Yosef, 146
Yoshea, R., 265

Z
zealotry, legal allowance for, 255–259
Zimri, 256, 260, 262
Zionism, 315–317

Praise for *Unlocking the Torah Text*

"Rabbi Goldin's superb collection of essays in *Unlocking the Torah Text* illuminates basic themes in Vayikra. Through careful reading of the Torah text, especially through the prism of Chazal, he interprets what to some might seem philosophically remote. His scholarship and pedagogy make the Torah text…easily accessible and alive. It is a wonderful and inspiring read."

– **Rabbi Menachem Genack**
General Editor, OU Press

"I have found in Rabbi Goldin's volumes a fascinating mix: his thoughts are refreshingly original, while being well grounded in the classic commentaries; his conclusions are profoundly relevant to the contemporary scene, while remaining true to our age-old traditions."

– **Rabbi Dovid Miller**
Rosh Yeshiva and Associate Director
Yeshiva University's Joseph S. and Caroline Gruss Institute, Jerusalem

"Rabbi Goldin performs his task with consummate skill and in a style of writing that will appeal both to the scholar and to the ordinary reader interested in gaining an insight into the Torah text. The result is a grand tapestry of *pshat* and *drash*, classic exegesis and original thought, biblical narrative and issues facing our own society today."

– **Moshe Aumann**
Former Israeli Consul General to the United States
Counselor for Relations with the Christian Churches, *Jewish Press*

"[A] challenge to the reader, a challenge well worth taking. Rabbi Goldin is both a skillful teacher and writer…. [T]he book will serve as a valued resource in better understanding all the events of the Exodus, Matan Torah (Giving of the Torah) and the Mishkan's construction, as well as the incident of the Golden Calf."

– **Alan Jay Gerber**
"Kosher Bookworm," *Jewish Star*

"Rabbi Shmuel Goldin demonstrates in his volumes of *Unlocking the Torah Text* a remarkable knack for identifying [compelling] topics. He surveys the classic approaches to the issues addressed and then adds a new and often surprising layer of interpretation that addresses contemporary concerns and sensibilities. Many of Rabbi Goldin's novel insights serve as a springboard to vigorous classroom discussion and debate. The combination of the old and the new provides for an enriching and vigorous learning experience for a wide range of audiences.... [A] major contribution to serious study of Chumash in our day."

– **Rabbi Chaim (Howard) Jachter**
Rebbe, Torah Academy of Bergen County
Co-rabbi, Shaarei Orah, the Sephardic Congregation of Teaneck
Dayan, Beth Din of Elizabeth; author, three volumes of *Gray Matter*

"Rare is a study of the weekly parsha which speaks to all the generations. Rabbi Goldin's *Unlocking the Torah Text* breaks new ground not only in its clear, fascinating insights into the Torah text but in its compelling appeal to young and old alike. Many of our school's parents use Rabbi Goldin's books as the basis of their Shabbat dinner Torah discussions and have shared with me how much their children look forward each week to the challenging and dramatically presented questions which Rabbi Goldin explores. For any parent and Jewish educator seeking to inspire their children with the love of Torah, *Unlocking the Torah Text* is essential."

– **Dr. Elliot Prager**
Principal, The Moriah School, Englewood, NJ

והאמרי והפרזי והחוי והיבוסי אל ארץ זבת
חלב ודבש ושמעו לקלך ובאת אתה וזקני
ישראל אל מלך מצרים ואמרתם אליו יהוה
אלהי העבריים נקרה עלינו ועתה נלכה נא
דרך שלשת ימים במדבר ונזבחה ליהוה